ADOLESCENT IDENTITIES

A Collection of Readings

Edited by

Deborah L. Browning

 The Analytic Press
Taylor & Francis Group

New York   London

Hans Reichel. Composition, 1921, #28. Location:Private Collection, New York. Copyright Estate of Jean G. Schimek. Photo by Deborah Browning.

The Analytic Press
Taylor & Francis Group
270 Madison Avenue
New York, NY 10016

The Analytic Press
Taylor & Francis Group
27 Church Road
Hove, East Sussex BN3 2FA

© 2008 by Taylor & Francis Group, LLC

Printed in the United States of America on acid-free paper
10 9 8 7 6 5 4 3 2 1

International Standard Book Number-13: 978-0-88163-461-7 (Hardcover)

Library of Congress Cataloging-in-Publication Data

Adolescent identities : a collection of readings / editor, Deborah L. Browning.
    p. cm. -- (Relational perspectives book series ; v. 37)
    Includes bibliographical references and index.
    ISBN-13: 978-0-88163-461-7 (alk. paper)
    ISBN-10: 0-88163-461-1 (alk. paper)
    1. Identity (Psychology) in adolescence. I. Browning, Deborah L. II. Series.

BF724.3.13A27 2008
155.5'182--dc22   2007012574

Visit the Taylor & Francis Web site at
http://www.taylorandfrancis.com

and The Analytic Press Web site at
http://www.analyticpress.com

To the memory

of

Jean Georges Schimek

Contents

Preface

The modal age of the female suicide bomber is 20 (Zedalis, 2004, pp. 3–5). Of the 27 male Palestinian suicide bombers from the two years, 2003–2005, whose age is known, the modal age is 19 (Hafez, 206, pp. 79–86). Is this an accident? Should we consider them late adolescents? Might we ask if they are struggling, among other significant things, with issues of identity, autonomy, and intimacy? Are they, as Erikson (1962) warned, so in search of causes and adults to satisfy their need for loyalty and fidelity, that they will allow themselves to be inspired to martyrdom?

In a recent analysis, *Manufacturing Human Bombs* (2006), Mohammed Hafez implies that may be so. He identifies potential organizational, societal and individual motives with regard to the use of suicide bombers, and he suggests that "militant groups frame suicide attacks as acts of unparalleled heroism, as a means to religious and national salvation, and as opportunities for empowerment and vengeance, and in doing so they foster the myth of the 'heroic martyr'" (pp. 6–7).

And if one considers the case of Darine Abu Ayshe (age 21), the second female Palestinian suicide bomber, who blew herself up at an Israeli checkpoint rather than accept a forced marriage, one sees the additional role of gender in the convergence of issues that motivate adolescents in their search for commitment to a viable future. In an interview with Barbara Victor (2003) only months after Abu Ayshe's death, her closest friend Nano explained, "Of course it was because of the occupation, but it was also because her parents were putting a lot of pressure on her to be an obedient, full-time childbearing and child-rearing spouse in a family where the husband was all-powerful and had absolute authority. Darine [a student of English literature at Al-Najah University] resisted that. She told me she would rather die" (p. 105).

Adolescence and adolescents — each term only vaguely and ambiguously definable — nevertheless represent a time in life and a collection of people that require serious recognition. There are those (Ariès, 1963) who scoff at the notion of adolescence, declaring it to be an invention of modern industrial society. And there are others who question the existence of self, the subject, and most certainly identity. And if this is not problematic enough, others challenge the very categories of gender, ethnicity, religion, and race because of the delimiting, confining (and I would add, potentially prejudicial), aspects of labeling an individual according to a single categorical identity.

The image of war-time German documents identifying a 14-year-old boy as a Jew by inserting the name Israel (not his), after his given name of Hans, casts a warning shadow. There are risks in all considerations and research studying race, ethnicity, or religion. So too are there risks in the phenomenon of what is termed "Identity Politics" — advocacy by specific groups — Black pride — Woman's liberation — although crucial for social awareness and change, and providing potential healing through assertive self-declaration.

These are some of the problems that inhere in any project concerning the study of adolescence and adolescent identity. I have taught a graduate course on adolescent psychology at New York University for the last 10 years, and, during that time, I have revised and re-revised the syllabus, finding, time and again, that Erikson's concept of identity "worked" as an organizing feature. Teaching in New York City affords one a multicultural classroom, and, soon after the start of a new semester, students readily offer examples from their lives — in several cases, of how they used one language at home, their best American-English in the classroom, and their particular slang with their friends — and how they pulled all this together into a comfortable (or sometimes painfully disjointed) sense of self.

Adolescence is examined in this volume through the various lenses of history, anthropology, sociology, psychology, and psychoanalysis, each frame of reference shifting the focus, but enlarging the view. I want, particularly, however, to draw readers' attention toward an *interior* view of the adolescent — to invite you to try to understand the adolescent's personal experience. Focusing on the inner world of the adolescent, one becomes quickly aware of the variety of possible inner worlds that may exist. There is no single normal adolescent, nor singular adolescent experience. Rather, in the course of development, each individual must somehow integrate one's unique biologically-given constitution and temperament, one's personal life history, and the influences of the social and cultural milieu — that milieu which is interpreted initially through one's family and then experienced more fully through school and community and now, increasingly, the media.

This point of view reflects the thinking of Erik Erikson, his elaborations and explorations of the life-span concept of identity formation, and his assertion of the crucial salience of identity processes during adolescence. At its simplest, Erikson's concept of identity can be understood as the experience "of a persistent sameness within oneself (self-sameness) and a persistent sharing of some kind of essential character with others" (1956, p. 57). "Its most obvious concomitants are a feeling of being at home in one's body, a sense of 'knowing where one is going,' and an inner assuredness of anticipated recognition from those who count" (p. 75). These statements indicate the constant interplay of the self and its experience of the other person, and also the interweaving of biological processes, social and cultural influences, with the personal, psychological meaning that the individual makes of these experiences.

The papers in this volume can be viewed as a whole through their relationship to Erikson's thinking about identity formation and adolescent development. Each of the papers was selected for its ability to convey a unique or important set of ideas or observations that can be helpful in understanding the psychology of the individual adolescent. Very few refer to quantitative research; there are no charts or tables. Consistent with the basic premise of this collection — that of diversity within normality — no one observation will apply to all adolescents, even if the author may imply this. Each selection contributes to an overview of the various kinds of tasks inherent in the ongoing process of adolescent identity formation.

The volume is divided into six sections. Following Erikson's contention that even the most interior and unconscious aspects of identity are profoundly influenced by one's social milieu and time in history, I have arranged the papers according to concentric circles of influence, from the most exterior, identifiable, and potentially overt and conscious — social and cultural identity issues — to the most internal, private, and potentially unconscious concerns. In section I, "Identifying Adolescence" — the papers are drawn from sociology (Jensen), European history (Hanawalt), and cross-cultural anthropology (Schlegel) and address the question of whether and how adolescence can be considered a stage in development. The second section — "Identity, Diversity in the Cultural Milieu" — looks at how visible or potentially knowable minority statuses — based on race (Gibbs), ethnicity (Phinney) same-sex attractions (Savin-Williams), teen pregnancy (Schultz) are experienced with respect to the majority culture's response — and how these interact with individual identity processes. Moving closer into the adolescent's interpersonal world, section III — "Adolescent Identity Formation and the Relational World" — provides papers about the more intimate relationships (family and friends) of adolescent girls (Gilligan) and boys (Chu), and about the conscious preoccupations of adolescents when they are alone (Flum). In addition, Inhelder and Piaget's (1963) consideration of the relationship between the development and utilization of formal operation thinking and the adolescent's interaction within their social world is included here.

Section IV — "Erik Erikson and Psychosocial Identity" — provides extensive excerpts of the two most important contributions of Erikson on identity formation and adolescence — including his considerations of fidelity and loyalty referred at the beginning of this preface. Section V — "Adolescent

Identity Formation and the Internal World" — includes papers dealing with the most internal, private, and potentially unconscious conflicts that pose significant challenges to identity consolidation — for adolescent girls with respect to their mothers (Horney); boys and their fathers (Blos); and idealization, de-idealization, shame, and rage (Lampl-de Groot).

The final section — "Challenges to Identity Coherence and Maintenance" — includes papers on a selection of adolescent problems, each of which may reflect an attempted "solution" to escape identity dissolution — running away and homelessness (Hyde), drug abuse and other self-destructive behaviors (Noshpitz), eating disorders (Gordon), and suicide (King).

My goal in drawing together this set of papers is to offer mental health practitioners, teachers of adolescents, and graduate students in both these fields a variety of points of view on the internal experience of adolescents. Alerted to an awareness of this diversity of formulations and observations, we are, I hope, in a better position, when we listen to and interact with our students and patients, to hear and recognize the unique and individual stories with which they entrust us.

References

Ariès, P. (1960). *Centuries of childhood: A social history of the family* (R. Baldick, Trans.). New York: Vintage Books, 1962.

Erikson, E. (1956). The problem of ego identity. *Journal of the American Psychoanalytic Association, 4*, 56–121.

Erikson, E. (1962). Youth: Fidelity and diversity. *Daedalus, 91*: 5–27.

Hafez, M. (2006). *Manufacturing human bombs. The making of Palestinian suicide bombers.* Washington, DC: United States Institute for Peace Press.

Victor, B. (2003). *Army of roses. Inside the world of Palestinian women suicide bombers.* Emmanus, PA: Rodale Press.

Zedalis, D. (2004). *Female suicide bombers.* Carlisle, PA: Strategic Studies Institute Press.

Acknowledgments

First, I want to thank Lew Aron and Adrienne Harris, co-editors of the Relational Perspectives Book Series for their encouragement and support of this project. I thank Paul Stepansky, managing director of the The Analytic Press when this project was first begun, for his wise advise on the planning and organization of the volume. Kristopher Spring, with his combination of good humor and diplomacy, helped me with the practicalities of the publishing process from beginning to end. I want to thank Leo and Nancy Goldberger who had many helpful suggestions in the beginning stages of the work. I also thank Barry Cohen and Sergej Zoubok from New York University's Department of Psychology. Marsha Levy-Warren has shown interest and offered advice along the way, which I greatly appreciate.

The Library of the Austen Riggs Center in Stockbridge, Massachusetts, was both an impressive and indispensible resourse and also a friendly and welcoming place for me, as I studied the hundreds of papers, from which the 20 that follow were selected.

And special thanks go to those authors, journals, and publishers who either waived or significantly reduced their permission fees: Judy Chu, Kai Erikson, Hanoch Flum and Michal Lavi-Yudelevich, Carol Gilligan, Lene Jensen, Robert King, Jean Phinney, Katherine Schultz, the American Psychological Association, Cambridge University Press, Harvard University Press, *Journal of the American Psychoanalytic Association*, *Journal of Orthopsychiatry*, Lawrence Erlbaum Associates, W. W. Norton, New York University Press, and Sage Publications, Ltd. This book could not have been produced without their generosity.

Although most crucially salient at adolescence, identity processes begin with the earliest awareness of the other and continue throughout life, reconfiguring the self with each major life change. Paul Seton played the essential roles of ally and witness for me during my early middle-age identity research. His contribution to my development has been invaluable and long-lasting. His successor, unnamed, but not anonymous, accompanies me with respect, wisdom, and warmth on yet one more search.

Diane and Alan Sholomskas, Richard Bock, Victoria Mills, Michael, Barbara, and Beth Lebo, and Kristin White have offered much inspiration, kindness, and support over the years, particularly in the aftermath of the death of my husband, Jean Schimek. To them I am extremely grateful.

Most of all I want to write of Jean. Throughout the nearly 30 years that our lives intersected, he enriched mine in innumerable ways, always challenging me to work at my best, always offering enthusiasm and encouragement for all my endeavors. The role of editor requires among other things, oppressive obsessiveness. Jean's sense of humor was the counter-balance that helped me persevere. His critical thinking and skeptical questioning challenged me to clarify my own thinking about all matters intellectual. His commitment to the life of the mind and to the importance of understanding how the individual interprets his world and assigns meaning to events has not only provided an example for me to follow but has also influenced those people who have studied with him, learned from him. It is to him that I dedicate this volume.

About the Editor

Deborah L. Browning, Ph.D. is an adjunct associate professor in New York University's Department of Psychology, Graduate School of Arts and Sciences, where she teaches courses on adolescence, developmental psychopathology, and psychoanalysis. In addition to her research and publications on adolescence and life-span development, her interest in art and music history has lead her to her current work on the psycho-biography of the modern European painter and violinist, Hans Reichel. Dr. Browning maintains a private psychotherapy practice in New York City.

Part I

Identifying Adolescence

1

Coming of Age in a Multicultural World
Globalization and Adolescent Cultural Identity Formation

LENE ARNETT JENSEN

Contemporary adolescents are coming of age in a world that is considerably more multicultural than the world in which their parents and grandparents grew up. Due to the processes of globalization, adolescents increasingly have knowledge of and interactions with people from diverse cultures. The flow across cultures of ideas, goods, and people is not new, but the current extent and speed of globalization are unprecedented. With increasing migrations, worldwide media disseminations, multinational corporations, tourism travel, and so forth, diverse peoples interact with one another more than ever (Friedman, 2000; Giddens, 2000; Hermans & Kempen, 1998; Sassen, 1998).

My aim in this chapter is to explore implications of globalization for adolescent cultural identity formation. I will argue that developing a cultural identity in the course of adolescence has become more complex. Adolescents seldom grow up knowing of only one culture but increasingly have interactions with people from diverse cultures, either first-hand or indirectly through different media. Increasingly, then, adolescents forge multicultural identities.

There are many issues to address on the topic of globalization and adolescent identity formation. My aim here is to draw attention to some of the emerging issues. Writings that specifically address adolescent psychology in light of globalization are still few (e.g., Arnett, 2002; Larson, 2002). I will draw on writings on globalization as well as writings from related areas on ethnic and immigrant identity formation (e.g., Berry, 1997; Phinney, 1990; for other specific issues on ethnic identity formation see Spencer, Fegley, & Harpalani, 2003).

In the following, I will start by defining the term *cultural identity* and discuss why globalization may be particularly salient for adolescent cultural

From: *Applied Developmental Science*. Vol 7(3), 2003, pp. 189–196. Copyright © Lawrence Erlbaum Associates. Reprinted with permission.

identity formation. Then, I will provide a few examples illustrating how adolescents increasingly grow up in a multicultural world and form multicultural identities. Next, I will discuss three issues pertaining to adolescent multicultural identity formation that would seem to be fruitful and timely areas for research:

1. The issue of the extent to which it is important whether a multicultural identity is based on first-hand versus indirect (media-based) interactions with diverse peoples.
2. The issue of how cultural identity formation may take diverse developmental paths depending on the particular cultures involved.
3. The issue of gains and losses that occur when a person forms a multicultural identity rather than an identity based primarily on one cultural tradition.

Finally, I will end on a brief methodological note, raising the issue of using culturally sensitive and valid methods when studying cultural identity formation.

A Definition of Cultural Identity

What is a cultural identity? Forming a cultural identity involves taking on worldview beliefs and engaging in behavioral practices that unite people within a community (Shweder, Goodnow, Hatano, LeVine, Markus, & Miller, 1999). Typically, a worldview provides answers to four questions: Who am I? Where am I? Why do people suffer? What is the remedy for suffering? (Walsh & Middleton, 1984). Thus, worldview beliefs often pertain to conceptions of human nature, the relation of the individual to others in society, and moral and religious ideals.

Worldview beliefs find expression in and are passed on from generation to generation through a variety of everyday practices (such as behaviors pertaining to eating, dressing, sleeping, work, and recreation) as well as practices marking life course transitions (such as graduating from school, marriage, and having children). One's cultural identity, then, subsumes a broad range of beliefs and behaviors that one shares with members of one's community.

Cultural identity formation also, in some respects, intersects with the formation of identity in spheres such as religion and morality. Often religious beliefs and behaviors as well as moral beliefs and behaviors are crucial elements in peoples' understanding of their cultural identity. For example, the extent to which one values autonomy and independence, or familial duties and obligations, or adherence to spiritual precepts and practices constitute important elements in one's understanding of one's cultural identity. In fact, the globalization ethos, in many ways a Western and even American ethos, often emphasizes individual autonomy and secular values, and quite frequently these values are not easily reconciled with those of more traditional cultures emphasizing community cohesion and religious devotion. Thus challenges involved in forming an adolescent cultural identity in the face of globalization extend to aspects of one's identity formation centering specifically on moral and religious issues. (For articles on emerging issues in moral and religious identity formation, see Benson, Roehlkepartain, & Rude, 2003; Damon, Menon, & Bronk, 2003; King, 2003; Nasir, 2003; Reimer, 2003).

One's cultural identity, then, encompasses a broad set of worldview beliefs and behavioral practices.

Half a century ago, anthropologists (Whiting & Child, 1953) described the relation between these cultural beliefs and practices as a "custom complex" consisting of "customary practice and of the beliefs, values, sanctions, rules, motives and satisfactions associated with it" (quoted in Shweder et al., 1998, p. 872). Given the broadness of beliefs and practices that a cultural identity subsumes, it in many ways includes the key areas that Erikson (1968) emphasized as central to the formation of an adolescent's identity as a whole. These key areas pertain to ideology (beliefs and values), love (personal relationships), and work. However, Erikson's focus was on how adolescents make choices about ideology, love, and work in order to arrive at an independent and unique sense of self *within* the cultural context in which they live (Erikson, 1950, 1968). Forming a cultural identity, however, involves making choices about the cultural contexts that one identifies with in the first place. Put another way, the Eriksonian identity formation task centers on deciding what distinguishes you as an individual among the members of your cultural community, whereas forming a cultural identity involves deciding on the cultural communities to which you will belong — a task that has become more complex as more and more people have exposure to multiple cultural communities with their diverse and divergent custom complexes. In fact, forming a cultural identity becomes mainly a conscious process and decision when you have exposure to more than one culture.

Researchers conducting work on ethnic identity formation in many ways address issues similar to those involved in cultural identity formation. As Phinney (1990) pointed out, there are widely discrepant definitions of ethnic identity. However, a central focus of research on ethnic identity formation is how members of ethnic and racial minority groups negotiate their identifications with their own group in the context of living among other ethnic and racial groups. One difference between research on ethnic identity formation and cultural identity formation as described here is that the former focuses on minority groups. However, cultural identity formation in the context of globalization also pertains to people who form part of a majority culture but who still have exposure to other cultures as well. For example, an Indian adolescent living in India but with exposure to the global economy and media will likely negotiate culturally diverse custom complexes in forming a cultural identity.

One important similarity between ethnic and cultural identity formation pertains to the issue of power and dominance. As diverse ethnic, racial, and cultural groups come into contact with one another there are invariably differences in power and status among those groups. This is clearly the case with respect to processes pertaining to globalization. Later in this article, I will discuss some problems and losses that arise in forming a multicultural identity in the context of globalization.

One last issue is worth mentioning with respect to defining the concept of cultural identity. Although one's cultural identity subsumes a broad range of beliefs and behaviors that one shares with members of one's community or communities, this does not entail that all members of a cultural community hold uniform beliefs and engage in identical practices. There is invariably variation within communities based on factors such a generation, gender, individual differences, religious affiliation, and social class (e.g., Jensen, 1997, 2003; Turiel & Wainryb, 2000).

Adolescence and the Saliency of Global Identity

The influence of globalization on cultural identity formation may be particularly salient in adolescence. Some have argued that adolescents are at the forefront of globalization (Dasen, 2000; Schlegel, 2001). Popular and media culture (television, movies, music, and the Internet) contribute to the rapid and extensive spread of ideas across cultures, and adolescents have more of an interest in popular and media culture than children or adults.

Adolescence may also be a time of life with a more pronounced openness to diverse cultural beliefs and behaviors. Adolescents have developed enough maturity to think in more complex ways about that which is new and different, and often there are many areas of life in which they have not yet settled on particular beliefs and behaviors (Arnett, 2002). Some research with immigrants to the United States indeed shows that sometimes adolescents change their beliefs and values more than adults. Nguyen and Williams (1989) in a study with Vietnamese immigrants found that adolescents' values varied with length of time in the United States whereas parents' values did not. Also, Phinney, Ong, and Madden (2000) found greater value discrepancies between adolescents and parents who had lived in the United States for a longer time, than between adolescents and parents who had immigrated more recently. Phinney et al. (2000) found this pattern for Vietnamese and Armenian immigrants. This phenomenon is also known as dissonant acculturation (Portes, 1997), when exposure to a new culture leads to more rapid change among adolescents than among adults. The research results with immigrants to the United States suggest that adolescents may be more receptive to new and foreign cultural values and beliefs as compared to adults. Thus processes of globalization may particularly influence adolescents in their cultural identity formation.

It Is a Multicultural World

The title for this chapter, "Coming of Age in a Multicultural World," was inspired by Margaret Mead's (1928/1961) title for her well-known book, *Coming of Age in Samoa*. The focus of Mead's work on the socialization of adolescents and ways that culture influences socialization remains important. Yet, descriptions such as Mead's of adolescents coming of age within one cultural tradition are becoming a rarity. Mead spoke of "one [Samoan] girl's life [being] so much like another's, in an uncomplex, uniform culture like Samoa" (p. 11). What is striking about much contemporary anthropological and cross-cultural work from all over the world is the way it describes the many changes that traditional societies undergo due to globalization "the ways that many societies have ceased to be uncomplex and uniform" (e.g., Brown, Larson, & Saraswathi, 2002; Burbank, 1988; Condon, 1988; Liechty, 1995; Naito & Gielen, 2002). In the following, I will discuss a few examples from ethnographic and psychological work of the ways that globalization is changing traditional cultural beliefs, everyday practices, and life-course transitions. The intent of these examples is to provide specific qualitative illustrations of changes that occur in adolescents' custom complexes as they are exposed to diverse cultures.

The Inuit of the Canadian Arctic

The anthropologist Richard Condon (1988) provided a fascinating ethnographic description of dramatic cultural changes occurring in a relatively short period of time among the Inuit of the Canadian arctic. Just a generation ago, the Inuit were nomadic. Family groups followed the movements of fish and game. Children and adolescents assisted their parents and elders with work necessary for daily survival, and they grew up under the close protection and supervision of their families. There were few influences from the outside.

Today's Inuit children and adolescents, however, live very different lives. They reside in fixed settlements established by the Canadian government. The traditional nomadic work of ice fishing and hunting has become recreational, and Inuit children and adolescents now attend school in pursuit of skills required in a changed world. Unlike before, Inuit children and adolescents now spend much time outside of the socialization environment of the family both in school and in peer groups.

Inuit adolescents have also gained access to Western media, especially television. According to Condon (1988), the influences of television on Inuit adolescents have been striking. He had a rare opportunity to observe a variety of clear effects of the introduction of television because he studied the Inuit both before and after the introduction of television. Adolescent boys and young men avidly took up the game of hockey after being exposed to pro hockey games on TV. During the long summer nights, they play hockey for hours on end. Along with playing the sport has come a new ethos. Traditional Inuit culture discourages calling attention to individual skills and accomplishments. From watching pro hockey players, however, adolescent boys learned to be competitive and even to brag about their sports abilities. TV also seems to have brought along a new ethos for dating and relationships between girls and boys. Previously very reserved about their romantic relationships, after the introduction of TV young couples became publicly affectionate. When Condon queried adolescents about this change, they attributed it to watching the show *Happy Days*.

Today, then, Inuit adolescents no longer form a cultural identity solely based on their traditional culture. Their worldview and everyday behaviors (such as dating, sports participation, and school work) reflect and express values that derive from multiple cultures. From their traditional Inuit culture, adolescents still take collectivist values. Condon (1988) wrote that young people grow up with a "pronounced sense of belonging, of being integrated into a social network" (p. 92). From Canadian culture and Western culture more generally, Inuit adolescents also take new values and identity ideals centering on individual expressiveness and accomplishment.

Condon's ethnography reflected how Inuit adolescents form multicultural identities that incorporate diverse beliefs and practices. This is a complex task as some beliefs from the different cultures can be integrated with ease, but others are more difficult to reconcile — a point that I will elaborate on later.

An Example from India

As described earlier, cultural identity formation occurs in the context of everyday cultural practices. It also occurs in the context of practices marking life course transitions. One example of how globalization has influenced life course transitions comes from research in India, where marriage (a highly significant life course transition often culturally marking the transition into adulthood) appears to have become subject to diverse cultural interpretations. In an in-depth interview study in which Indian young and midlife adults where asked to describe a personal moral experience (i.e., a time in their life when they had faced an important decision pertaining to right and wrong), almost 50% chose to discuss the issue of whether to have a traditional arranged marriage, that is, a marriage where a person's parents and family decide who they will marry, or whether to have what Indians call a "love marriage," that is, a marriage where persons decide for themselves whom to marry (Jensen, 1998).

These two types of marriages reflect very different conceptions of individual choice, family obligations, and the purpose of marriage. Arranged marriages seem perfectly sensible within a traditional Indian worldview that emphasizes duty to family, respect for elders, and behaving according to one's station in life rather than according to individual preferences. Love marriages fit much better with the values of globalization and the West that emphasize freedom of choice and individual rights, as well as a media culture saturated with images of romance and interpersonal attraction. In the interviews, one young woman discussed her unwillingness to have an arranged marriage in the context of a changing Indian society. She said:

> I've always insisted that I've got to have the right man and I won't just be able to adjust to anyone. There have been pressures, if I can call them that, from family, but I've not given in to it. I won't do that ever because I know the situation now. From the very beginning, things foreign and imported were very glamorous to me. From those days onward [when I became familiar with things foreign], I was against having an [arranged] marriage — Arranged marriages in India are becoming obsolete, I think. Because even now in [arranged marriages], girls and boys they talk to each other. They come to know each other. Perhaps the decision may not be theirs, because in some traditional households it's not theirs. But they get to know each other. But as for me, I should [decide] and know him.

Although arranged marriages are still by far more common than love marriages in India, the research finding reflects how Indian adolescents and adults now are aware of and at times contend with values and identity conceptions that are different from the traditional Indian conceptions with respect to a life course transition as crucial as marriage (for more on globalization in India, see Verma & Saraswathi, 2002).

The findings from India and the Inuit are by no means unique or unusual. What is striking about much contemporary ethnographic and cross-cultural work is the way it describes the many changes that traditional societies undergo due to globalization. Descriptions of adolescents coming of age within one cultural tradition are becoming less and less common. Adolescents increasingly come of age in a multicultural world and they face the task of forming their identities in the context of multiple traditions. Robertson (1992) phrased it very well when writing that today's children and adolescents develop "the intensification of consciousness of the world as a whole" (p. 8).

Three Emerging Research Issues

With contemporary adolescents growing up in a multicultural world, many complexities of adolescent identity formation arise that merit further research. In the following, I will discuss three such issues.

First-Hand Reality Versus Virtual Reality

One issue pertains to the agents of cultural socialization: To what extent is it important whether adolescent cultural identity formation is based on the first-hand reality of interactions with diverse peoples or based on indirect exposure to diverse cultural traditions through the virtual reality of media? Or to use Robertson's (1992) language, does it matter if an adolescent's consciousness of the world as a whole derives primarily from first-hand interactions with diverse people or from media exposure?

The classical definition of acculturation by Redfield, Linton, and Herskovitz (1936) assumed direct interactions; "acculturation comprehends those phenomena which result when groups of individuals having different cultures come into *continuous first-hand contact* [italics added] with subsequent changes in the original culture patterns of either or both groups" (p. 149). Increasing numbers of adolescents indeed do experience first-hand contact with people from different cultures as a consequence of migrations and tourism. However, for many adolescents much of their exposure to cultures other than their traditional one occurs indirectly through media. Thus in a world of fast-paced and abundant media transmissions and interactions, Redfield et al.'s definitions of acculturation might fruitfully be expanded to encompass more indirect interactions occurring in virtual reality.

Arnett (2002) proposed that many adolescents in today's world of globalization develop a "local identity" based on their indigenous tradition, as well as a "global identity" based on their exposure to a global (often Western) culture conveyed through media. Television, in particular, provides exposure to new ideas, events, and people. For example, the number of televisions per 1,000 persons rose from 5 in 1970 to 255 in 1995 in East Asia, and from 70 in 1970 to 220 in 1995 in Latin America and the Pacific. The comparable figures were from 280 in 1970 to 525 in 1995 for Western industrialized countries (United Nations Development Programme, 1998). As described previously for the Inuit, television exposure can influence adolescent identity formation in important ways. (The Internet may at some point rival or even surpass TV in providing adolescents with global access.) Friedman (2000) described how companies cater in global media to a new market of "global teens" because urban adolescents from all over the world follow similar consumption patterns. To conceptualize adolescent development that entails both a local and a global identity, Arnett suggested a need to expand the traditional use of the concept of bicultural identity. In this expanded use, the term *bicultural identity* would refer not only to acculturative processes occurring with first-hand exposure to different cultures (as for immigrants, minority groups, or workers who come in frequent contact with foreigners) but also to acculturative processes occurring with exposure to different cultures through media.

It may make a difference in identity formation whether contact occurs first-hand or through media. One possibility is that identity formation on the basis of media exposure is more *subjectivized* or *individualized*. Sociologists of religion have used these two concepts fruitfully to refer to the ways that people increasingly construct individual and idiosyncratic religious or spiritual belief systems, as the establishment of a religious identity less frequently occurs in the context of shared practices with a community of fellow believers and more frequently as an individual process of exploration (Arnett & Jensen, 2002; Berger, 1967; Luckman, 1963).

Media, more so than first-hand interactions with others, allow the adolescent to choose what to see and hear. Also, media usage would seem to allow for more individual interpretations than first-hand interactions in which other people are more likely to co-construct experiences. Media messages are not interpreted within an immediate group context (unless, e.g., a group of adolescents watch a TV program together and talk about it). Thus when Inuit or Indian adolescents watch an American TV show or a music video, the messages they come away with may vary substantially from individual to individual. Adolescent cultural identity formation on the basis of media exposure, then, may be more subjectivized or individualized than cultural identity formation on the basis of first-hand interactions.

Clearly adolescent identity formation in the face of globalization encompasses the classic form of acculturation based on first-hand interactions as well as a more recent form of acculturation based on media exposure. The extent to which a person's cultural identity is influenced in different ways by these two types of acculturation merits further attention.

Not One, but Multiple Developmental Paths

A second research issue meriting attention pertains to the extent to which adolescent cultural identity formation may take diverse developmental paths depending on the particular cultures to which they have exposure. In a very interesting study by Phinney, Kim, Acer, and Vilhjalmsdottir (2002), they asked 240 adolescents to reason about vignettes describing adolescents and parents disagreeing about a variety of everyday and major issues. The vignettes pertained to issues such as doing household chores, everyone gathering for family dinner, and dating.

The research included four different ethnic groups residing in the United States and showed interesting interactions between culture and development. European American adolescents moved from assertions of autonomy in mid-adolescence (ages 14 and 17) to increased consideration of the views and feeling of their parents in late adolescence (ages 18 to 22). This pattern fits well with what some psychologists have described as a movement from unilaterality to mutuality in young persons' relationships with parents (Youniss & Smollar, 1985). Armenian American and Mexican American adolescents, however, moved from consideration of parents in midadolescence to self-assertion in late adolescence. Finally, Korean American adolescents maintained a high degree of consideration for parents' point of view at all ages.

As discussed earlier, conceptions of individual autonomy and family obligations are typically important aspects of people's cultural identities. Phinney et al.'s (2002) research indicated that during adolescence these conceptions appear to develop in different ways and in varying orders across cultural traditions. Thus cultural identity formation becomes more complex as adolescents have exposure to more cultures. They have to form identities in the face of cultural traditions that may hold out different end goals (such as differing emphases on the assertion of autonomy from parents and the fulfillment of responsibilities to parents) and different pathways to those end goals (such as acceptance of assertions of autonomy in midadolescence but not in late adolescence or acceptance of assertions of autonomy in late adolescence but not in midadolescence). This suggests, then, that we cannot assume a universal developmental pathway to adolescent cultural identity formation in a world of globalization.

Gains and Losses

A third research question that arises is what gains and losses occur when an adolescent forms a multicultural identity rather than an identity based primarily upon one cultural tradition. Based on a review of the immigration literature, Berry (1997) suggested that the psychological adjustments and problems accompanying acculturation can be divided into three levels, moving from minor to severe adjustment issues. These levels are helpful in thinking about adolescent multicultural identity formation. At one level, acculturation may involve "culture shedding" in which an adolescent has to leave behind or unlearn aspects of their parents' culture. Such culture shedding may entail some sense of loss, as well as some positive sense of leaving behind undesirable beliefs and practices. At a second level, acculturation may involve more serious psychological adjustment in which an adolescent experiences "culture shock" or "acculturative stress." In other words, the adolescent has difficulty forming a coherent identity in the face of culturally distinct worldviews that are difficult to reconcile. Finally, at a third level, acculturation may lead to major difficulties in the form of psychopathology.

Many factors will influence the kind of psychological adjustment experienced by adolescents who are forming multicultural identities. One notable factor that may influence the balance between gains and losses is the degree of cultural distance between the cultures to which an adolescent has exposure. Here the immigration literature suggested that the greater the cultural distance in beliefs and behaviors between cultures, the greater the psychological and social problems (Berry, 1997). Returning to the Inuit, Condon's (1988) work showed how Inuit adolescents attend school in sporadic ways because they find it boring and alienating. Perhaps the distance between the traditional Inuit nomadic ways of life and the sedentary school culture introduced by the Canadian government is too great to be smoothly bridged. In fact, Condon suggested that boredom and alienation are among the factors contributing to adolescent risk behavior, such as shoplifting and alcohol use, in contemporary Inuit society.

Arnett (2002) suggested that recent increases in adolescent problem behaviors such as substance use, prostitution, armed aggression, and suicide that have occurred in a variety of traditional cultures may in part result from processes linked to globalization and attendant identity confusion and sense of marginalization in the face of diverse cultural values that are difficult to reconcile.

Forming a multicultural identity clearly presents adolescents with psychological challenges that may be difficult to meet in a positive way. Yet, it may be worthwhile to keep in mind potential positive outcomes. Berry (1997) pointed out that with respect to immigrants (with most of the research focusing on immigrants in North America), the assumption among scholars used to be that acculturation inevitably brings social and psychological stress and problems. However, this view has changed as research has indicated that the gains and losses of immigrant acculturation are varied and complex (varying by factors such as age, gender, level of education, degree of social support, intergroup attitudes, and discrimination). Also, research indicates that children and adolescents who are first and second generation immigrants to the United States tend to do very well with respect to grades in school, physical and mental health, and avoidance of risk behavior (Fuligni, 1998).

Multicultural identity formation in adolescence, then, is likely to involve gains and losses, sometimes mostly losses, sometimes mostly gains, and sometimes both. The factors that influence the outcomes are likely to be varied and complex. Also, assessment of what constitutes gains and losses may at times be complex. Whereas some outcomes seem clearly to be either a gain or a loss, other times perceptions of what is a gain or loss may be dissonant. For example, adolescents may see shedding some parts of their parents' cultural traditions as a positive (e.g., getting rid of an outdated custom), whereas the parents and other adults of the community experience this as a loss of a valuable tradition. Clearly, we have to carry out research on psychological gains and losses entailed by adolescents forming multicultural identities in a world of globalization. This is a vast area requiring research on many factors influencing acculturation, and the research must be carried out in a way that is sensitive to divergent conceptions of what constitutes gains and losses.

Methodological Multiplicity

Earlier in this chapter I discussed several issues that seem to me to merit further attention. The nature of these issues and the nature of the topic of globalization more generally point to the need for the use of research methods that are culturally appropriate. I will end by briefly discussing a few methodological points. In recent years, cultural psychologists have called for the need to reassess more common and standard methodologies when working with participants from different cultures (e.g., Shweder et al., 1998; Stigler, Shweder, & Herdt, 1990). Their advice would seem particularly apt as more and more cultures come into contact due to the processes of globalization.

In studying adolescent cultural identity formation in which different socialization agents, different cultures, different pathways to identity formation, and different conceptions of the best end goals are in play, methodological multiplicity would seem to be helpful. By this, I mean two things. First, by using more than one method we might better capture different cultural concepts, and capture these concepts as they are understood within their respective cultures. Of course in deciding on more than one method, it helps to use those that maximize cultural sensitivity and ecological validity (Briggs, 1986). Second, methodological multiplicity also entails understanding globalization from different perspectives. As mentioned previously, adolescents and parents may not view the gains and losses of multicultural identity formation in the same ways. In fact, adolescents themselves may at times view the same outcome as both a gain and a loss. Hermans and Kempen (1998) pointed out that in the face of globalization, "self or identity can be conceived of as a dynamic multiplicity of different and even contrasting positions or voices that allow mutual dialogical relationships" (p. 1118). Thus using methodologies that allow room for different perspectives or voices (Gilgun, 1992; Gilligan, 1982), would be helpful.

Conclusions

Contemporary adolescents are coming of age in a multicultural world where creating a cultural identity has become complex. Often, they face the task of integrating diverse cultural beliefs and behaviors conveyed them by multiple agents of socialization — socialization agents that at times are at odds with one another, e.g., parents and TV). The task of forming a coherent cultural identity that allows adolescents to become contributing members of society presents challenges that may be stressful or even considerably more problematic. However, adolescent cultural identity formation also presents challenges that may be met by developing new skills, the kinds of skills necessary for a multicultural world, that allow adolescents to function well psychologically and to contribute to society.

REFERENCES

Arnett, J. J. (2002). The psychology of globalization. *American Psychologist, 57,* 774–783.

Arnett, J. J. & Jensen, L. A. (2002). A congregation of one: Individualized religious beliefs among emerging adults. *Journal of Adolescent Research, 17,* 454–67.

Benson, P. L., Roehlkepartain, E. C., & Rude, S. P. (2003). Spiritual development in childhood and adolescence: Toward a field of inquiry. *Applied Developmental Science, 7,* 205–213.

Berger, P. L. (1967). *The sacred canopy: Elements of a sociological theory of religion.* New York: Anchor.

Berry, J. W. (1997). Immigration, acculturation, and adaptation. *International Journal of Applied Psychology, 46,* 5–34.

Briggs, C. L. (1986). *Learning how to ask: A sociolinguistic appraisal of the role of the interview in social science research.* Cambridge, UK: Cambridge University Press.

Brown, B. B., Larson, R., & Saraswathi, T. S. (2002). *The world's youth: Adolescence in eight regions of the globe.* New York: Cambridge University Press.

Burbank, V. (1988), *Aboriginal adolescence.* New Brunswick, NJ: Rutgers University Press.

Condon, R. G. (1988). *Inuit youth: Growth and change in the Canadian Arctic.* New Brunswick, NJ: Rutgers University Press.

Damon, W., Menon, J., & Bronk, K. (2003). The development of purpose during adolescence. *Applied Developmental Science, 7,* 119–127.

Dasen, P. (2000). Rapid social change and the turmoil of adolescence: A cross-cultural perspective. *International Journal of Group Tensions, 29,* 17–49.

Erikson, E. H. (1950). *Childhood and society.* New York: Norton.

Erikson, E. H. (1968). *Identity: Youth and crisis.* New York: Norton.

Friedman, T. L. (2000). *The Lexus and the olive tree: Understanding globalization.* New York: Anchor.

Fuligni, A. J. (1998). The adjustment of children from immigrant families. *Current Directions in Psychological Science, 7,* 99–103.

Giddens, A. (2000). *The consequences of modernity.* Cambridge: Polity Press.

Gilgun, J. F. (1992). Definitions, methodologies, and methods in qualitative family research. In J. F. Gilgun, K. Daly, & G. Handel (Eds.), *Qualitative methods in family research* (pp. 22–39). Newbury Park, CA: Sage.

Gilligan, C. F. (1982). *In a different voice: Psychological theory and women's development.* Cambridge, MA: Harvard University Press.

Hermans, H. J. M. & Kempen, H. J. G. (1998). Moving cultures: The perilous problems of cultural dichotomies in a globalizing society. *American Psychologist, 53,* 1111–1120.

Jensen, L. J. (1997). Different worldviews, different morals: America's culture war divide. *Human Development, 40,* 325–344.

Jensen, L. J. (1998). Moral divisions within countries between orthodoxy and progressivism: India and the United States. *Journal for the Scientific Study of Religion, 37,* 90–107.

Jensen, J. L. (2003). A cultural-developmental approach to moral development. Unpublished manuscript. Catholic University of America, Washington, DC.

King, P. E. (2003). Religion and identity: The role of ideological, social, and spiritual contexts. *Applied Developmental Science, 7,* 196–203.

Larson, R. (2002). Globalization, societal change, and new technologies: What they mean for the future of adolescence. *Journal of Research on Adolescence, 12,* 1–30.

Liechty, M. (1995). Media, markets, and modernization: Youth identities and the experience of modernity in Katmandu, Nepal. In V. Amit-Talai & H. Wulff (Eds.), *Youth cultures: A cross-cultural perspective* (pp. 166–201). New York: Routledge.

Luckman, T. (1963). *The invisible religion.* New York: Macmillan.

Mead, M. (1928/1961). *Coming of age in Samoa.* New York: Morrow Quill Paperbacks.

Naito, T. & Gielen, U. P. (2002). The changing Japanese family: A psychological portrait. In J. L. Roopmarine & U. P. Gielen (Eds.), *Families in global perspective.* Boston: Allyn & Bacon.

Nasir, N. & Kirshner, B. (2003). The cultural construction of moral and civic identities. *Journal of Applied Developmental Science, 7,* 138–147.

Nguyen, N. & Williams, H. (1989). Transitions from east to west: Vietnamese adolescents and their parents. *Journal of the American Academy of Child and Adolescent Psychiatry, 28,* 505–515.

Phinney, J. (1990). Ethnic identity in adolescents and adults: A review of research. *Psychological Bulletin, 108,* 499–514.

Phinney, J., Kim, T., Osorno, S., & Vilhjalmsdottir, P. (2002). Self- and other-orientation in the resolutions of adolescent-parent disagreements: Cultural and developmental differences. Unpublished manuscript. California State University, Los Angeles.

Phinney, J., Ong, A., & Madden, T. (2000). Cultural values and intergenerational values discrepancies in immigrant and non-immigrant families. *Child Development, 71,* 528–539.

Portes, A. (1997). Immigration theory for a new century: Some problems and opportunities. *International Migrant Review, 31,* 799–825.

Redfield, R., Linton, R., & Herskovitz, M. (1936). Memorandum on the study of acculturation. *American Anthropologist, 38,* 499–514.

Reimer, K. (2003). Committed to caring: Transformation in adolescent moral identity. *Applied Developmental Science, 7,* 129-137.

Robertson, R. (1992). *Globalization: Social theory and global culture.* Chicago: University of Chicago Press.

Sassen, S. (1998). *Globalization and its discontents: Essays on the mobility of people and money.* New York: New Press.

Schlegel, A. (2001). The global spread of adolescent culture. In L. J. Crockett & R. K. Silbereisen (Eds.), *Negotiating adolescence in times of social change.* New York: Cambridge University Press.

Shweder, R. A., Goodnow, J., Hatano, G., LeVine, H., Markus, H., & Miller, P. (1998). The cultural psychology of development: One mind, many mentalities. In W. Damon (Ed.), *Handbook of child development* (pp. 865–937). New York: Wiley.

Spencer, M., Fegley, S., & Harpalani, V. (2003). A theoretical and empirical examination of identity as coping: Linking coping resources to the self processes of African American Youth. *Applied Developmental Science, 7,* 181–188.

Stigler, J. W., Shweder, R. A., & Herdt, G. (1990). *Cultural psychology: Essays on comparative human development.* New York: Cambridge University Press.

Turiel, E. & Wainryb, C. (2000). Social life in cultures: Judgments, conflict, and subversion. *Child Development, 71,* 250–256.

United Nations Development Programme. (1998). *Human development report.* New York: Oxford University Press.

Verma, S. & Saraswathi, T. S. (2002). Adolescents in India: Street urchins or Silicon Valley millionaires? In B. B. Brown, R. Larson, & T. S. Saraswathi (Eds.), *The world's youth: Adolescence in eight regions of the globe* (pp. 105–140). New York: Cambridge University Press.

Walsh, B. J. & Middleton, J. R. (1984). *The transforming vision: Shaping a Christian worldview.* Downers Grove, IL: Varsity.

Whiting, J. & Child, I. (1953). *Child training and personality.* New Haven, CT: Yale University Press.

Youniss, J. & Smollar, L. (1985). *Adolescent relations with mothers, fathers, and friends.* Chicago: University of Chicago Press.

2

Historical Descriptions and Prescriptions for Adolescence

BARBARA HANAWALT

No other stage in the life cycle has engaged historians in so much debate as that period between childhood and adulthood. One hesitates to even put a label on this life stage because the very names for the period are in hot dispute. Some historians, for instance, argue that if society did not have a word for it, it could not exist. Others have argued that biology is a strong determinant and that puberty is too basic a physiological and psychological phenomenon to ignore. With or without names, crude biology intrudes. That fact has not stopped some historians from arguing that puberty can be culturally suppressed or at least well camouflaged, even from those experiencing it. Because in defining stages in the life cycle we like to ascribe a term of years or the ages to which the experiences might apply, many have tried to establish an explicit time frame. But the range is vast. Some argue that it lasted anywhere from zero to 20 years and could start either not at all or at 7, at 12, at 14, at 16, at 18, or at 20 and end anywhere from 7, 12, 14, and so on. Clearly, the period between childhood and adulthood, should it exist, is a subject that lends itself well to historical examination, particularly that of *le long durée* since we are investigating arguments about nurture versus nature, changing cultural perceptions, and major societal accommodations to economic, demographic, and cultural changes. The essays in this volume [*Journal of Family History*, 1992, vol. 17] will go far to clarify the definitions and treatment of this interesting life stage because they span the time period between the thirteenth through the twentieth centuries.

For medievalists the question of naming has always had a special fascination. The nominalist controversy, which so disturbed Abelard's Europe, seems to live on with a surprising vividness in late twentieth-century family history. Does giving the life stage a name — "adolescence" — make it real and therefore a phenomenon that is historical and can be dealt with, or should we

From: *Journal of Family History*, *17*(4), 1992, pp. 341–351. Copyright © Sage Publications. Reprinted with permission.

assume that because it had no medieval name it was not real, because to have no name means it has no existence? Is the current meaning of "adolescence" so specific to the twentieth century that to use it for earlier periods is to distort? Those wishing to reserve the word for the modern period should consider that medieval society also did not have a word for family and yet had nuclear, extended, and stem families.

Scholastic arguments such as these have tended to more modern generations to appear of little consequence, so it is with some puzzlement that medieval social historians have watched modern social historians avidly consume Philippe Ariès' syllogisms about naming. He maintained that medieval "children were mixed with adults as soon as they were considered capable of doing without their mothers or nannies." By the age of seven, he concluded, they entered directly into the "great community of men." He argued that people in the Middle Ages did not reserve a particular term for the period, thereby indicating that it did not enjoy a separate identity (Ariès, 1960/1962, p. 411). Readers of Augustine of Hippo (who used the term *adolescentia)* and commentators on the "ages of man" know that medieval society recognized a distinct period of adolescence. In the medical literature, adolescence was classified as hot and dry as summer is and as fire is; its humor was red choler. In poetic versions of the ages of man the period was dominated by the planet Venus and characterized by love and lust (Burrow, 1988, pp. 12–37). The European medieval world certainly recognized and defined adolescence. It also had a number of formal and informal mechanisms, such as apprenticeship or squirehood, for noting its existence as a life phase. But to say that it was a recognized social construct is not to say that it was the same as the nineteenth- or twentieth-century concept of adolescence.

Preoccupation with nominalist arguments is not limited to medievalists. Robert Wegs's [1992] essay points out that historians of modern adolescence, notably John Gillis [1981], Joseph Kett [1977], and Harry Hendrick [1990] argue about who introduced the term and when. Did the new disciplines of social science invent current usage or did the upper middle class bring the term into popularity?

Modern Western Europe did not invent adolescence, but it did alter its definition. One of the advantages of this collection of essays is that it permits scholars to move beyond Ariès's simplistic and inaccurate pronouncement that adolescence did not exist in the Middle Ages. The issue is not a nominalist one of existence or non-existence in one historical period or another, but rather it is how Europe changed its cultural definitions and perceptions of adolescence. Working with the basic biological realities of puberty, European society manipulated the cultural attributes that surrounded it.

Social scientists in their relatively short existence in our intellectual history have contributed much to our ability to analyze the life stage. Medieval and early modern historians have found the work of the early twentieth-century anthropologist, Arnold van Gennep, particularly helpful. In *Les Rites de Passage* (1908/1960) he distinguished between "physical puberty" and "social puberty." He saw the two processes as very distinct and not necessarily coinciding. Societies did not make their initiation rites coincident with the appearance of adult sexual attributes. They could make the passage from one life stage to another either earlier or later than the onset of puberty. He, therefore, urged that the term "puberty rites" not be used. In his analysis, he wished to place the emphasis on the cultural or social aspects of adolescent initiation (pp. 65–77). More recently, Victor Turner, another anthropologist, contributed the idea of the passage from one life stage to another as being in a liminal state; that is, on the threshold of leaving one stage and entering another (Turner, 1969, pp. 94–103). The adolescent period is the liminal stage between childhood and adulthood. As such, adolescence carries with it a sense of becoming rather than a sense of full participation. The adolescent has absence of status versus status of the adult, absence of property versus property, silence as opposed to speech, sexual continence in contrast with sexuality, and so on in binary categories that show the incomplete state of the liminal (Turner, 1969, pp. 106–107).

Concepts that distinguish between cultural and biological definitions of puberty and describe the characteristics of liminality for the group are most helpful, but defining the parameters of the life stage presents further complications. The sociologist Glen Elder, Jr. has offered a very useful framework for making cross-time and cross-cultural comparisons among adolescent experiences. The definition of the life stage varies with the historical period under investigation, with the urban and rural setting, and with the social and economic status of the individuals labeled adolescent. In order to understand or define the period, reference must be made to the adjacent life stages, that of the child and the adult. Boundaries of entry into the period are, on the whole, more difficult to establish than the transition out of it. For the latter, for instance, one might cite concrete examples of the assumption of adult roles such as marriage or economic independence, but does entry into adolescence begin with biological puberty, a first job, removal from natal dwelling to that of a master, beginning of education, and so on (Elder, 1974, pp. 1–3)?

Since culture plays such a large role in shaping the adolescent experience, some basic areas of inquiry concerning the relationship between society and adolescents arise. A natural tension exists between the aspirations of youths and adults. The adult population wants to establish a transition to adult behavior and consequently seeks to direct, train, and control adolescent behavior. The adolescent, on the other hand, seeks to establish a personal identity and independence. In the socialization process of youth the question arises of whether the family, an adult-based surrogate for family, or peers will be most influential as socializers. As Elder (1974) observes, the process may also be reciprocal, with youth to some extent educating adults. It is perhaps this last category, as we shall see, that is crucial in distinguishing adolescence then and now. The institutions and informal mechanisms for segregating the male from the female adolescent experience and the adolescent from the world of the child and the adult are also of importance (pp. 9–15).

In the essays in this issue, Elder's observations help one to distinguish between what is constant in the interaction between youth and society and what is different over a long historical time frame. A perennial issue is, indeed, the struggle between youth and adults for the control and definition of adolescence. But closely related are the expectations that youth have of family and state and vice versa. Societies have internal conceptions of youth which are not always explicit in the literature; gender and class were among the most important. Youth also created their own internal conceptions that influenced their attitudes toward both children and adults.

For all periods covered in these essays, the most consistent issue is the struggle between adults and youth; it cuts across national, class, gender, and time lines. The basic issue was whether adults or youth controlled entrance to or exit from the liminal stage. As long as adults could manipulate access to the economic advantages of the adult world, they had a powerful tool for social definition of adolescence as a life period. The essays demonstrate that the greatest shift in the definition of adolescence came when adults were not the only conduit to economic independence.

In the "traditional" society of medieval and early modern Europe, parents or parental surrogates stood at the thresholds of entry and exit from adolescence regardless of gender or social class. When entry meant controlled access to training for the adult world, the age at which social puberty began was in the hands of adults. The exit thresholds of marriage (particularly for women), completion of apprenticeship and establishment of a trade or business, inheritance, graduation from school and entrance into a profession, a position in government or the army, and so on were also in the control of adults.

Kathryn Reyerson's [1992] essay provides an excellent discussion of how adults manipulated entrance and exit from adolescence. Apprenticeship contracts are the quintessential example of a threshold device that shifted the child from parental control to that of a master thus moving it into an adolescent position. In order to enter into an apprenticeship, a young person needed adult sponsors, usually family as Reyerson shows, and money to pay the master for training. The terms of the contract were set so that the age of exit was contractual as well. Rights of disciplining as well as training were transferred to the master. Marriage, an all consuming youth culture, independent wages, and living arrangements were all denied to the apprentice. Punishment for failing to keep the terms of the contract was denial of the economic benefits that went with its successful completion.

The age at which training began and ended was altered to suit adults. In London, for instance, young men began their apprenticeships at age 14 prior to the Black Death in 1349, but increasingly in the fifteenth century the age of entry was raised to 16 and then to 18 so that the age of exit from adolescence became much later. Furthermore, the terms were increased from seven to ten years. Social puberty was thus extended from age 18 to 28 by the sixteenth century. The reason for the later and longer apprenticeship was that with a depleted population of young people, the parents kept their sons laboring in the country longer before releasing them to apprenticeship, and the urban masters wanted skilled workers for longer terms once they could get an apprentice (Rappaport, 1989, pp. 295–298).

The apprenticeship arrangement was typical for the urban population of Europe until the beginning of the twentieth century. Kathleen Alaimo [1992] and W. Scott Haine [1992] both mention the rapid decline of apprenticeship in France. By the middle of the nineteenth century it had dropped considerably, and by the end of the century it was almost non-existent. The loss of control over adolescents that apprenticeship provided accounts for some of the measures that society took by way of substitute.

In patrician Venice, parents and adults controlled access to marriage, as well as entry into business and government. Because dowry was so important in the marriage market of Italy, control over access to it meant control over who would marry and at what age. As Stanley Chojnacki [1992] has shown, a girl with sufficient dowry would be married very close to biological puberty (12 to 14) to a husband of her parents' choosing. Those without adequate funds were put into a nunnery. The girls were not consulted about their preferences, although Chojnacki finds evidence that mothers, at least, increasingly tried to provide some choice or delay in marriage. Because of early marriage, girls moved rapidly into adult status. Young men, on the other hand, spent many years in preparation for adult roles. Their careers had to be well established before they were ready for marriage at 30 or older. Eighteen to 20-year-olds became state-appointed crossbowmen, traveling with the Venetian fleets as part of their social puberty until they could move into business. Those with rather more lavish fortunes became members of the *compagnie della calza,* dining clubs requiring lavish costume and celebrations, particularly at the marriage of a member. They moved up gradually through the patrician-controlled ranks of government until they reached an adult status.

Patrician and bourgeois control over their offspring continued through the nineteenth century. Delayed inheritances, arranged marriages, and increasing emphasis on education armed the upper class adults with traditional controls, but they faced frustration in trying to control working class youth. As Wegs (1992) points out, in Germany and Austria separate words developed for upper class youth (*Jungling*) and working class youth (*Jugendliche*). These words were not neutral: the first was a romantic concept about upper class youth and the latter was almost always tied to a derogatory modifier.

The control that characterized urban and patrician parent child relations in traditional Europe was also true for the peasantry. The presumption was that children would aid in the family economy by working the land and producing supplemental economic items such as thread, bread, beer, and wine. When they reached marriageable age the parents would endeavor to arrange the best marriage possible. Peasants were ingenious in their economic strategies for marrying off their children. They rented or purchased pieces of land, gave children land use for set terms of years and then provided that it pass on to a younger sibling, married sons to heiresses, and arranged for their children to take on retirement contracts of elderly villagers in return for becoming their heirs. However they arranged these marriages they controlled whom the young people married and when they married. A young male or female, who wanted part of the family wealth would be constrained to go along with the plans. Only the very poor or the very foolish fell outside the adult-arranged track to exit from adolescence (Hanawalt, 1986, pp. 188–204).

The real revolution for defining adolescence came as parents and adults in general no longer controlled access to economic independence and all that went with it. In the century following the fourteenth-century plagues, when population was low, wages rose to an adequate level to support a young person who wanted to escape from his or her village and seek an independent life. But this new freedom lasted only about a century and it was not until the nineteenth century and the Industrial Revolution that working-class children could earn wages that cut them loose from their elders.

Haine's essay explores this transition. Workshops, guilds, and workers' companies had become so oppressive that even in Paris, which was not an industrial city, youth preferred the freedom of service sector jobs to the control that apprenticeship implied. The *gamin,* a youth from late childhood to under 21 who earned a living by finding jobs outside the apprenticeship or formal work structure, typified these independent youths. The *gamin* coexisted with working-class families that followed traditional patterns of parental control over adolescents. But by the end of the nineteenth century and especially after 1900 all Europe experienced the growing numbers of independent, working-class adolescents. Wages freed them from the economic domination of parents or some parental surrogate. Youth in Austria started to work at the age of 14, which was the legal school-leaving age, or even earlier.

The new freedom that wages gave to adolescents left modern Western Europe's newly disempowered adults struggling to define and control what they perceived as an unfortunate transformation in the behavior of youth. The areas of leisure pursuits, sexual activity, and juvenile violence all drew their attention. Most alarming was that peers rather than adults now determined entrance and exit from adolescence and the socialization within the teenage years.

If we look at changes from "old European adolescence" to the Industrial Revolution, perhaps one of the most disconcerting aspects for adults and their children was that working-class youth set their own agendas for rites of passage about sex, marriage, and wage labor. These rites were more individual rather than societal: getting drunk for the first time or loss of virginity or any other ritual that the peer group defined as passage. In the rituals of "old Europe" the adults controlled the really important rites of passage and paid for the appropriate celebrations: entry into apprenticeship; marriage; establishing a trade, profession, knighthood, or government service; and inheritance. The modern working-class youth might enter adolescence at confirmation or after compulsory schooling, but the real determinant of entry and exit was the peer group, not parents.

Adolescent leisure in traditional Europe was also regulated. The "boy bishops" and the "world turned topsy turvy" could be tolerated on an annual festive basis or in the occasional apprentice or student riot, but these were dim shadows of the youth culture that working-class adolescents would develop with their wages in the twentieth century. The dramatic content of early modern carnivalesque rituals such as charivari (Davis, 1971) or ritual rape (Roussiaud, 1976) have led historians to regard these relatively rare events as having more significance in defining adolescent culture than they actually had. We know about most of these events because adults punished the culprits. In fact, much of youthful exuberance was channeled, as in Venice, into military purposes or brotherhoods, or occurred within parameters that adults set (Darnton, 1984, p. 88).

The leisure that Haine chronicles in late nineteenth- and twentieth-century Paris in the cafes, night clubs, and streets is youth-created and dominated. Moving from the *gamin,* or poor street urchin type, youth formed a leisure culture that was based on such internal identifying features as a modish, young style of dressing, dancing the can can or the waltz that emphasized contact of couples rather than group dancing, a distinctive slang, gang violence, and an ethos that emphasized spending wages on leisure and its accoutrements. *Apache* was the loose label that summed up this youth culture, although it took on a more specific, gang-oriented meaning. The advent of cinema and proletarian sports such as foot and bicycle racing increased the participation and appeal of the youth culture.

To some, mostly early writers such as Victor Hugo, who placed the *gamin* on the barricades of Paris during revolutions (as many were) and later bohemian artists and poets who shared café life with the *apache,* the way of life was romantic. Social reformers and moralists of all religions, all political persuasions, and all branches of the new social sciences looked with alarm at the youth culture. The bourgeoisie saw threats to the old order, the socialist, working-class leaders saw an unacceptable morality for the future domination they projected for their class. Government bureaucrats of the new nation states wanted an orderly life that satisfied established adult interests, minimized the possibility of revolt, and reflected the very modern and up-to-date views of the latest social theories. It is to these concerns that the articles on modern Europe direct our attention and ask us to look at the attempts to define adolescence in its new and threatening guise.

If criminology with its series of "experts" stretching back into the nineteenth century has come up with any lasting medium-range theory, it is that being young and male has a high correlation with crime and violence. Traditional Europe made only a rough distinction. Before the age of 12 a child did not know the difference between right and wrong and so should not be punished. The crimes that teenagers committed were not legally distinct from those that adults committed. Part of the reason for a lack of legal distinction was the presumption that adult males were responsible for their households so that women, children, servants, and dependents under their roof were their responsibility and should be under their control, including their corporeal punishment. Increasingly when adolescents and servants escaped the control of *pater familias* in the late nineteenth and twentieth centuries, state and local authorities became the responsible parties. In England, Austria, France, and the other countries in Europe reformers, social scientists, and finally politicians and bureaucrats became increasingly alarmed about "juvenile" crime.

An obvious solution was incarceration. The observation of an increase in youth on the street and, therefore, an increase in youth crime, prostitution, pimping, disorderly conduct, and so on suggested special labels for this behavior and special penal institutions. Obviously, these youths were not hardened criminals and should not be locked up with them, but they were disruptive and needed discipline.

Turn-of-the-century moralists were fond of the truism that a healthy mind existed in a sound body. Late nights at cafes, masturbation, early sex, excessive drink, and lack of a solid work ethic would certainly promote the very worst qualities in youth by undermining their health and therefore their minds. For some, the solution was to sponsor sporting events that would increase the healthy body in the hopes that sound minds would follow. Haine [1992] points to the development of bourgeois sponsored foot and cycle racing and, after some delay, better facilities for working-class sports in public parks.

Following agendas that would restore adult control to adolescence, various groups advocated a range of plans. In a true conservative lament for the "good old days," one finds among Haine's examples a man advocating a return to the apprenticeship system. But a more obvious approach was to extend required schooling longer into the teenage years, an expedient that Wegs shows was used in Austria and Alaimo in France. The hope was that schools could become *in loco parentis* and instill values that parents no longer did. Even this experiment did not work since technical schools remained the preserve of artisans and bourgeoisie.

One of the great marriages of convenience in the twentieth century, to which historians have become accomplices, is that between the new social science disciplines and the new adolescent culture. Alaimo's essay demonstrates the lengths to which early twentieth-century psychologists and bureaucrats went to try to recapture adult control over youth (their imposed definition was those between 13 and 18). In a period which saw an alarming decline in this age group in France because of World War I and the very low birth rate both before and after the War, French social scientists, do-gooders, and government bureaucrats rushed to study and cultivate the age group.

Realizing that biology was not all, as van Gennep (1908) was stating from an anthropological viewpoint, psychologists sought ways to channel the mental anarchy that accompanied puberty into adult-approved and controlled objectives. A flurry of adult-sponsored clubs, discussion groups, evening schools, and so on were aimed at instilling adult values into youth. The efforts came from all segments of society. Governments, church groups, rightists, socialists, and communities all tried to attract youth to their vision of values that led to useful, happy adult life. Alaimo [1992] questions how many poor young people actually were involved in these activities and how effective they were. But the moralizing and outreach programs certainly influenced some young people. Haine tells of a poor youth who in addressing a socialist crowd, says he was never an *apache* and if he had been he would not expect them to listen to him.

In some respects, our discussion has taken us too far from the biology of puberty. Only the early marriage of Venetian patrician girls has raised the subject of rites of passage, as has the delayed marriages of their brothers. In the female case marriage was so close to the onset of puberty that adults began to be concerned that they were moving too swiftly. The young men created different problems. Forced to delay marriage for such a long period, some developed lasting homo- or heterosexual unions outside marriage while others became accustomed to bachelorhood. Official houses of prostitution were one solution that city fathers offered to their sons to avoid some of the problems created by delayed marriage.

M. J. Maynes' [1992] article on adolescent sexuality and social identity in French and German lower class autobiography provides both information on sexuality and the only view of adolescence from the inside. Most sources for studying adolescence are formal contracts, court cases, wills, governmental surveys, speculations, and measurements of the new social scientists, and observations by either participating or disapproving adult commentators. Maynes and Wegs both speak of the middle-class observation that the working class entered into sex casually and at relatively young ages. But the autobiographies that relate "success" stories among the lower classes speak of sexual abstinence and care in not forming inappropriate alliances. Some lower class women and a few men spoke of sexual harassment at the hands of employers or co-workers. Like the young socialist who disclaimed any ties to the *apaches*, the socialist autobiographers tended to emphasize sexual restraint as a desirable social goal for adolescents. As Maynes points out, autobiographies seek to place sex within a life trajectory. While they are revealing of sexual experiences, they may be more revealing of later, adult attitudes toward youthful experiences of sex. An autobiographer usually is not an ordinary person, even if coming from the working class.

Discussions of adolescence, whether they are medieval or modern, tend to generalize from the male experience. For historians, the obvious problem is that sources bias discussion to the male milieu, because it is a public one. Women's experiences are centered in private space where female culture is preserved by word of mouth rather than by public recording either in official documents or by literate recorders. But the problem is one that goes deeper than recording. Historians and social scientists tend to look at the adolescent experience as uniform for men and women rather than seeing the differences. Van Gennep, Turner, and Elder, who have guided much of our theoretical discussion heretofore, seem less relevant when one looks at the gender of the adolescent. Biological puberty, for instance, plays a much greater role in determining an adolescent female's life than it does the equivalent male's. A nubile female's sexuality was, and is, a matter of engrossing concern for parents, moralists, unscrupulous exploiters, and ardent young men (and sometimes young women). The female's pubescent body can be dealt with as in Venice by rushing them either into marriage or a nunnery. As Chojnacki points out, the problems of marking both the entrance and exit from adolescence and adulthood are thus obscured for women. These women emerge as adult when they place their children in marriages or government, but what marks the transition for them? For nineteenth-century lower class women, Maynes points to two generations of females who suffered from sexual exploitation or indiscretions that produced illegitimate daughters. Some responded to this early biological initiation by abusing the daughter who reminded them of their own transformed and segregated state. But was this an entrance or an exit from adolescence? The markers that we have evolved serve us imperfectly or very poorly in our discussion of the female adolescent experience. While the flapper of Haine's essay tells us that a female culture of dress, sport, and leisure activity developed, how distinct was this from the male image and male control?

We conclude both with puzzles left unsolved and definitions better drawn. The long historical perspective of this collection of essays on European adolescence gives a more complete picture of the adolescent years than has been brought together previously. A brief summary helps to show both the road traveled and the unexplored terrain. To the debated question of using the term "adolescence" for any historical period other than our own, the answer must be that if the researcher and analyst of historical material is so engrossed with presentist meanings that he or she cannot use the term as a hypothetical statement of what one might look for, then it is best to avoid it. But since anthropologists have been able to use the term in looking at primitive and pre-colonial societies, it seems that historians of the pre-twentieth-century can also find it valuable. The advantage of using it in historical perspective is that it permits us to see changes that are both dramatic and nuanced. For instance, the essays clearly indicate that the age of entry and exit from adolescence, at least for males, was a subject of much manipulation. The control over females is also very obvious, but how ultimately this defines their stages of life is less apparent. That adults in any period want to be the manipulators is completely clear. Be they parents, moralists (secular and religious), social scientists, or government bureaucrats the desire is to define the period and behavior of adolescence and to guard the threshold that permits these designated people to enter into the world of adulthood. When most successful, the adult world keeps the door closed until the age of 30. Graduate schools are, in the long run, one of the most successful of door keepers. The dramatic change has been the development that youth culture has seen in the twentieth century. Peers now exert a great influence over the socialization of adolescents and our American/European society has even moved on to one of Elder's observations that youth can now socialize adults. That our society has reached this exalted recognition of adolescent power is seen in autobiographies of people under 30; for them the glory years have ended; whereas for their medieval counterparts they would just be beginning.

REFERENCES

Alaimo, K. (1992). Shaping adolescence in the popular milieu: Social policy, reformers, and French youth, 1870–1920. *Journal of Family History, 17,* 419–438.

Ariès, P. (1960/1962). *Centuries of childhood: A social history of the family,* trans. R. Baldick. New York: Vintage Books.

Burrow, J. (1988). *The ages of man: A study in medieval writing and thought.* Oxford: Clarendon Press.

Chojnacki, S. (1992). Measuring adulthood: Adolescence and gender in Renaissance Venice. *Journal of Family History, 17,* 371–395.

Darnton, R. (1984). *The great cat massacre and other episodes in French cultural history.* New York: Basic Books.

Davis, N. (1971). The reasons of misrule: Youth groups and charivaris in sixteenth-century France. *Past and Present, 50,* 41–75.

Elder, Jr., G. (1974). Adolescence in the life cycle: An introduction. In S. Dragastin & G. Elder (Eds.), *Adolescence in the life cycle* (pp. 1–22). New York: Wiley.

Gillis, J. (1981). *Youth and history: Tradition and change in European relations, 1770–present.* New York: Academic Press.

Haine, W. (1992). The development of leisure and the transformation of working-class adolescence, Paris 1830–1940. *Journal of Family History, 17,* 352–376.

Hanawalt, B. A. (1986). *The ties that bound: Peasant families in medieval England.* New York: Oxford University Press.

Hendrick, H. (1990). *Images of youth: Age, class, and the male youth problem, 1880–1920.* Oxford, UK: Clarendon.

Kett, J. (1977). *Rites of passage: Adolescence in America 1790 to the present.* New York: Basic Books.

Maynes, M. (1992). Adolescent sexuality and social identity in French and German lower-class autobiography. *Journal of Family History, 17,* 397–418.

Rappaport, S. (1989). *Worlds within worlds: Structures of life in sixteenth-century London.* Cambridge, UK: Cambridge University Press.

Reyerson, K. (1992). The adolescent apprentice/worker in medieval Montpellier. *Journal of Family History, 17*(4), 353–370.

Roussiaud, J. (1976). Prostitution, jeunesse, et société dans le villes du Sud-est au XIVe siécle. *Annales: Economie, Sociétés, Civilisations, 31,* 289–325.

Turner, V. (1969). *The ritual process: Structure and anti-structure.* New York: Aldine De Gruyter.

van Gennep, A. (1908/1960). *The rites of passage,* trans. M. Vizedom & G. Caffee. Chicago: Chicago University Press.

Wegs, J. (1992). Working-class "adolescence" in Austria, 1890-1930. *Journal of Family History, 17,* 439–450.

3

A Cross-Cultural Approach to Adolescence

ALICE SCHLEGEL

It is commonly assumed that adolescence is the creation of industrial society, with its need for occupational training that cannot be well accommodated during childhood. This assumption seems natural, since adolescence in industrial societies is generally viewed as the period of training for specialized manual and cognitive skills. Even Erik Erikson (1950), who was aware of cross-cultural variation and wrote about childhood in American Indian societies, assumed that the psychological task of adolescents is to define themselves according to their adult occupations. He gave a new, psychological twist to the medieval concept of life as a series of steps, upward from the cradle to middle adulthood and from then on downward to the grave, by calling the fifth "stage of man," the one introduced by puberty, the stage of "identity versus role diffusion." Adolescents are uncertain as to who they are, and "it is primarily the inability to settle on an occupational identity which disturbs young people" (p. 228).

Such a concept of adolescence, grounded in the view that production is the engine driving social organization, is not helpful in understanding adolescence in pre-industrial societies. In places where productive tasks are learned during childhood or boys continue to work alongside their fathers even after they marry and bring wives into the home, boys should have no need for social adolescence. Even less should girls need such a stage, for by puberty almost everywhere most girls have mastered the skills they will require as wives and mothers. Nevertheless, anthropologists such as Mead (1928) and Elwin (1947) found adolescence in such places as Samoa or the hill country of central India.

The argument in this article is that adolescence as a social stage is a response to the growth of reproductive capacity. Where further training is required before the individual can assume adult social or occupational responsibilities, training can be accommodated during this period; but adolescence was not created to meet the need of complex economic systems. The orientation here is away from the focus on cognitive and affective reorganization (common to psychologists) and the focus on role learning of sociologists (Bush & Simmons, 1981) toward a biosocial theory.

It derives from the observation that the human life cycle includes a period between childhood and adulthood during which its participants behave and are treated differently than either their seniors or their juniors. A similar social stage has also been observed for sexually mature but unmated males among primates such as baboons and macaques (Walters, 1987). During this stage, young males are extruded from the company of females and adult males and tend to be spatially and socially placed at the peripheries of these social groupings. In some cases, peer groups of adolescent males have been observed.

If a distinctive social stage is present across species, then adolescence is not a product of culture, although many of its features in humans are. The disjuncture between the physical readiness to engage in sexual activity and the social permission to reproduce implies that adolescence is a time of preparation for adult reproductive life. Social adolescents of all primate species, including humans, engage in sexual activity, but the birth of offspring is a rare occurrence. Older animals tend not to find the younger ones attractive: newly mature males and females tend to be selected as mates less than fully mature ones. A similar attraction pattern holds for humans, as only rarely is the accepted heterosexual partner for a social adolescent anyone other than another adolescent. Since human reproduction is embedded in kinship and marriage, and full social adulthood is almost everywhere associated with the married state, social adolescence across cultures can best be viewed as a time of preparation for marriage.

Adolescence as a Social Universal

The ubiquity of social adolescence was revealed in a cross cultural study of tribal and traditional societies (Schlegel & Barry, 1991) using data from the 186 cases in the Standard Cross-Cultural Sample. For every society for which there is information (173), boys go through a social adolescence. Girls do as well, with one possible exception (175 societies).

In some instances, adolescence is socially marked and even institutionalized. The Navajo and the Melanesian Trobriand Islanders, among others, have special terms for the person between puberty and marriage comparable to our term *adolescent*. The Mehinaku and other tribes of tropical Brazil, and some peoples elsewhere, seclude their postpubertal children for several years, seeing this as necessary for proper growth.

Boys' adolescence is generally longer than girls', as girls in many places are deemed ready for serious courtship or marriage proposals right after menarche.[1] Boys, on the other hand need more time, for reasons that have more to do with social relationships than with occupational or role training.

In the eyes of those who have daughters to bestow, the boy just past puberty does not cut a very striking figure. The child may be the father of the man, but the older, adolescent boy is a better predictor of the man he will be. While it is true that bride-bestowers are interested in the kin of the future groom, they are also interested in acquiring the best son-in-law they can. They need time to look over candidates and to assess the value of any particular one. Adolescence gives them this needed period of assessment. The fact that age of marriage for boys is likely to be younger in matrilocal societies than in ones with other residence patterns may well be a consequence of this: it is easier to get rid of a disappointing son-in-law by sending him away than by bringing back a daughter. The extreme youth at marriage of heirs to thrones or high titles of nobility is made understandable by this explanation, for the social position of kings and high nobles supersedes their personal qualifications in the eyes of their in-laws.

When social adulthood is delayed beyond the late teens, there is generally a social stage that intervenes between adolescence and adulthood, a time when young people gain more privileges than adolescents without reaching those of adults. It is useful to distinguish this as a separate stage, youth, rather than to consider it a continuation of adolescence. The 18-to-20-year-old may not be socially mature, but he or she is very different from the 14- or 15-year-old. The line between adolescents and youths may be blurred, as when the unmarried young males between about 14 and the mid-20s constitute a single, often-named social category with specified duties to the community. Two examples are the *moran,* the warrior grade of the African Maasai (Llewelyn-Davies, 1981), and the class of bachelors in preindustrial European villages and towns. Nevertheless, it is usually possible to distinguish differences in behavior, as juniors defer to seniors, and the older "boys" may be engaging in serious courtship, of which the younger ones are still only dreaming.

The discussion in the following pages will address some of the issues of adolescence that have caught the attention not only of scholars but also of those who deal with adolescents, that is to say, a broad spectrum of parents and concerned adults. The findings of cross-cultural research can be applied to topics of current interest such as gender differences and their origins, the management of adolescent sexuality, competitiveness and aggressiveness among adolescents, adolescent activities outside the home with peers and in the community, and the generation gap. Comparative research illuminates the breakdown of adult authority and the lowering of restraints on adolescent sexual activity and self-centered behavior, resulting in an explosion of teenage pregnancies and delinquency in many parts of the world.

The Social Settings of Boys and Girls

Adolescents are not in school in the large majority of societies in the sample. Where schools exist, they are part-time (such as the Aztec Telpochcalli or the mosque schools of Turkish villages), or short-term (such as the African "bush schools"), or only for elite boys (such as the schools of early modern Europe). Boys and girls in these preindustrial societies spend most of their time with adults. Except for the boys in pastoral societies who herd animals away from the village, or forager boys who are not skilled enough to be taken on serious hunting expeditions, boys work alongside their fathers or other kin. Girls everywhere work with their mothers. While the cross-cultural study did not assess hours of leisure (Schlegel & Barry, 1991), there is considerable evidence that boys, like men, have more leisure time than girls and women.

There is a very widespread, possibly universal, pattern of social organization by age and sex. Girls and women aggregate, so that much of the association that girls have with other girls is when they are in a multi-age female assemblage. Boys associate with their fathers when they are working together, but when the tasks are done the boys do not join groups of men. They aggregate either at some distance from the adult men or at the periphery of the cluster of men. They are not incorporated physically or socially in the men's group, as girls are in the women's group. (There are similarities in human age-sex grouping to what primatologists call the "female assemblies," "male cohorts," and "bachelor bands" of terrestrial primates.)

With few exceptions, boys spend more time in the company of age-mates than girls do. Even when girls assemble away from women, their groups are smaller and less formally organized than are boys' groups. Girls together are likely to be engaged in conversation and unstructured play rather than in the goal-oriented activities with which boys' peer groups are frequently occupied. The settings in which adolescent girls spend their days are hierarchical by age, girls deferring to women (see also Gilligan et al., 1988). Hierarchy inhibits competition for status, as there would be no point for girls to attempt to compete for leadership with adult women. It also promotes adherence to social norms, since the only way that junior participants will earn the respect and favorable attention of seniors is by conforming to their expectations. Consequently, girls learn an interactional style that emphasizes achieving their ends through such social skills as agreeableness and self-effacement.

Boys not only spend more time than girls do with age-mates, they also have more involvement with their peers. The peer group is egalitarian: even where the society is stratified or ranked (such as the Maori of Polynesia), leadership in boys' peer groups is achieved rather than ascribed.[2] The egalitarian nature of a boys' peer group promotes competition among its members for leadership. Although boys almost everywhere show more competitive behavior than girls, their greater involvement in goal-oriented activities means that boys have to learn to cooperate at the same time that they are competing. Whereas competitiveness and cooperation are inversely related for girls, there is no correlation between these traits for boys.

The gender difference noted across cultures — that boys are more competitive, aggressive, and self-reliant than girls — may be partially due to the settings of adolescence. Boys learn a more aggressive style than girls, who attempt more to influence than to coerce. Girls are socialized for greater compliance than are boys, which is reflected in the much lower incidence of girls' than boys' antisocial behavior reported in the ethnographies. (This difference is unlikely to be an artifact of reportage, as it holds true regardless of the amount of information on adolescence.)

Sex separation characterizes most of the interactions of younger children as well as of adolescents (Whiting & Edwards, 1988). It is my view that this separation begins in infancy and is due, in part, to the differential treatment of girl and boy infants by the mother. Mothers bind daughters to them more closely than sons and encourage sons to be more independent, a process that I call extrusion (see also Chodorow, 1978).[3] This is not rejection, but a subtle process in which infant and juvenile boys may cooperate by turning more than girls to the exploration of the surrounding environment. Extrusion can take a more direct form when the child is discouraged from remaining in the proximity of his mother and other women: "run along now" is more often said to little boys than to little girls. This kind of extrusion of small boys from multi-age assemblies of females is not unusual in human societies — I have witnessed it among Hopi Indian women — and a similar extrusion of juvenile males is common among troup-dwelling primates. Sex separation becomes accentuated after young people enter social adolescence. This is true even in those societies in which adolescent boys and girls meet publicly for specified social occasions like dances or clandestinely for sexual encounters. In some places, boys' and girls' peer groups may cooperate in organizing activities, as they do in Transylvanian villages. Institutionalized nonsexual friendships between adolescent girls and boys, such as the *nwa ulo* relationship of the Afikpo Ibo of Nigeria (Ottenberg, 1989), are very rare. It is only in the few places that have adolescent houses, where girls and boys relax and engage in sexual relations in the evenings, that there is much sustained interaction between the sexes.

The Cultural Management of Adolescent Sexuality

Adolescent girls and boys are sexually active in the majority of societies in the sample. In spite of this, pregnancy out of marriage is rare. This has been widely attributed to adolescent subfecundity, in that females are rarely fully fertile for a year or two after menarche (see Whiting et al., 1986). When marriage occurs within a couple of years after menarche, by about age 16 or 17, the likelihood of premarital pregnancy is low.

Nevertheless, some societies, even those in which girls marry shortly after puberty, do prohibit sexual intercourse for adolescent girls. If girls are not permitted to engage in sexual relations, it is not expected that adolescent boys will either; in other words, there is only rarely a sexual double standard for adolescents. A double standard exists only where there are sexually available females: adolescent boys may be allowed to have heterosexual relations with prostitutes (although most will lack the goods to pay them); in some stratified societies, elite boys may not be severely sanctioned for seducing girls of lower classes or ranks. If there were a double standard in egalitarian societies without prostitutes, boys who could not approach girls sexually would turn to the wives of adult men — something these men are unlikely to encourage!

There are three factors that appear to underlie the attitude toward premarital sexual intercourse for girls (in other words, the value placed on virginity). The first is the length of adolescence, discussed above, as Whiting et al. (1986) have demonstrated.

The second factor is the economic or social value of children. Where children are an unqualified asset, they are likely to be welcome regardless of their legitimacy. Variations in the value of children as social or economic assets occur within as well as among societies. This can help to account for the high rates of bastardy in some periods and at some times in European history, in spite of the general Christian value on virginity.

The third factor underlying the value on virginity is the exchange of goods that accompany the marriage. Goody pointed out the association between dowry and virginity, but his explanation for this was inadequate: he said that the loss of virginity may "diminish a girls honor and reduce her marriage chances" (1973, p. 14). Such an explanation presupposes that virginity has some inherent value, which is improbable when more than half of the societies in the standard sample do not value it.

The results of a study of the value on virginity (Schlegel, 1991) show that dowry-giving societies value virginity, but so do those practicing indirect dowry and gift exchange. Contrary to the belief of many that in bridewealth-giving societies men seek to "buy" virgins, in almost two-thirds of such cases in the standard sample, nobody cares whether the bride is a virgin or not.

The value on virginity in societies that give dowries or indirect dowries or exchange gifts can be understood as a mechanism for forestalling any paternity claims on a daughter's child. These claims are most likely to be made when property or a title accompanies the girl into her marriage. The upward mobility of a man through marriage is a possibility in rank or class societies; the seduction of a girl with property or from a high-ranking family is a temptation to the boy or man who would improve his position in life. Parental and fraternal surveillance of a girl's behavior, and the socialization for guilt or shame at premarital sex, are widely effective methods for preventing a mésalliance through seduction. (For a fuller development of the argument, see Schlegel, 1991.)

Although most ethnographers do not report on homosexual activities among adolescents, enough do to permit some tentative generalizations. Among those societies for which there was information (24 societies with information on both sexes, 13 with information only on boys), homosexual activity is more often permitted than prohibited, even when it is prohibited for adults. In a few societies in Melanesia, homosexual acts are institutionalized for all adolescent boys because the ingestion of semen is believed to be necessary for proper growth; there is no evidence that this practice leads to a preference for homosexual activity in adulthood or even that most men engage in it.

There is very little detailed information on girls' homosexual activity. One of the few reports available is by Gay (1986) on friendship relationships among older and younger Basotho girls of Lesotho, which sometimes include sexual stimulation. It is not improbable that casual sexual play is widespread among girls in societies that do not expressly prohibit it or that turn a blind eye to discrete erotic caresses.

In general, homosexual activity appears to be viewed as a substitute for relations with the opposite sex or just a natural feature of social immaturity that is set aside when adolescents become adults and can freely engage in sex with spouses and other opposite-sex partners. Homosexual play is reported even for societies that tolerate heterosexual adolescent relationships, such as the Nyakyusa of Tanzania (boys) and Basotho (girls). While opposite-sex partners may be available in theory, they are not always so in practice, or the shyness of young adolescents may inhibit them from approaching potential partners. In such cases, children may turn to others of their own sex.

The sexual activities of adolescents are tolerated or prohibited depending on the consequences of these activities for the adults who are responsible for them. But it is not only adults who monitor the sexual behavior of adolescents — peers also do it. Where young girls and boys are allowed a great deal of freedom, the group often pressures them to spread their favors. In the adolescent houses of the Muria, a hill tribe of India, the head girl and boy make sure that sleeping partners are rotated. Even where sexual play without penetration is permitted, such as the interfemoral intercourse practiced by the Kikuyu and other African peoples, participants are expected to change partners, and it would be selfish and unsociable to restrict one's attention to a special friend. The peer group protects itself against exclusive attachments to lovers, which would weaken the bonds of peers.

The Development of the Self

When Erikson called adolescence the "stage of identity," he was echoing a widespread sentiment that adolescence is a time when young people set the patterns for their future lives. While the ethnographic literature does not lend itself to studying the process of personality development, it does give us a window onto the behavioral traits that adolescents exhibit and the kinds of relations they have with others.

It is clear that adolescence is a testing period for both sexes. Adolescents are newly arrived players, standing in the wings of the adult stage on which the dramas of kinship and marriage are played. They are on trial for the roles they will assume as spouses and affines. Memories are long in small communities, and one rarely has the opportunity to start over somewhere else. Present and future resources are finite in closed societies; adolescence must be a time of growing awareness of life's limitations.

Two behavioral traits that have long captured the attention of psychological anthropologists and social psychologists are competitiveness and physical aggressiveness. These traits, among others, were rated along an 11-point scale, separately for girls and boys, and the sample was divided into societies above and below the means for testing (Schlegel & Barry, 1991). Tests showed that their cross-cultural variation is associated with variations in the settings of adolescent life. These are the only two behavioral traits for which the means for girls and boys differed markedly.

This article has already discussed the differential setting of girls and boys and suggested that the hierarchical setting of the multi-age female assemblage leads to a generally lower level of competitiveness among girls (boys' mean = 4.8, girls' mean = 3.2). In no society was the boys' score lower than the girls'. Aggressiveness shows a similar sex difference (boys' mean = 4.9, girls' mean = 3.4).

Both competitiveness and aggressiveness are related to what happens in the peer group and the household, the two social structures within which (unschooled) adolescents operate most of the time. Table 1 [omitted] indicates that the size of the peer group is linked to competitiveness of boys. It also shows that the structure of the household is an associated factor, the stem-family household depressing competitiveness and the nuclear-family household stimulating it.

Table 2 [omitted] shows that the amount of peer contact is related to aggressiveness for boys but not girls; as discussed above, much of the contact girls have with one another is in the multi-age female assemblage. Aggressiveness is associated with a higher degree of peer competitiveness for both sexes. The stem family household reduces aggressiveness in boys, while the nuclear-family household raises it in girls.

The common factor in these various associations is the degree of involvement adolescents have with adults and with one another. While the peer-variable correlations are self-evident, the associations with household structure can be interpreted in light of the adult-to-child ratio.

The nuclear or two-generation family contains two core adults, the parents, although other adults such as widowed grandparents, unmarried aunts and uncles, servants, and boarders may also live in the household, usually as temporary members. Given four living children, the adult-to-child ratio is minimally 1:2. In the three-generation, stem-family household, there are four adults, the senior couple (grandparents), and the junior couple (parents). Unmarried adult children of the senior couple (aunts and uncles) are also (often permanent) members of the household. Given four living children of the younger couple, the adult-to child ratio is at a minimum 1:1. Competitiveness and aggressiveness show no significant association with the extended-family household, comprising several married couples and their unmarried children. This category contains several forms, so that there is no clear adult to child ratio for the extended family as a structural type.

While adult-to-child ratio is only a proxy measure for the amount of contact and the degree of involvement of adult and child family members, the two family forms do result in quite different household settings. Boys are responsive to both stem- and nuclear-family household structures, but girls' competitiveness and aggressiveness are associated only with the nuclear-family form. The nuclear-family household appears to be the form least conducive to an easy mother-daughter relationship. In the stem- or extended-family household, the daughter is in almost continual contact with her mother and the other adult women members of the family, each household forming a small female assemblage. In the nuclear-family household, the mother is the only permanent adult female member. Even when there are adult servants, they are subordinates, closer in status to daughters than to the mother. The nuclear-family household lacks a true female assemblage. In addition, when the mother is the only adult female in the household, or the one solely responsible for directing the female activities, she has less leisure time and is tempted to fob off much of the drudgery onto her adolescent daughter. This can lead to resentment on the daughter's part.

Participation in Community Life

While younger children may be highly visible in the community as they play or run errands, they rarely contribute to community well-being. In a large number of societies, adolescents do. Peer groups of girls and boys may be expected to decorate neighborhoods at festival times, as they were in the traditional towns of Malaysia (Khadijah Muhamed, personal communication, 1982), or to organize dances and other festivities as in the preindustrial European village or town. They are also expected to do community labor, like the Micronesian teenagers of Palau. It is probably easier to mobilize the labor of adolescents when they are organized into formal age-sets; but even when they are not, they may do community work under the direction of adults or an appointed leader from their midst. The Muria adolescents mentioned above, who spend their nights relaxing in tile adolescent houses, also work hard as peer groups for the public good, doing much of the drudgery connected with road repair or in preparation for weddings and funerals.

Adolescents may be called on to provide another kind of community service, the social "dirty work" that is beneath the dignity of adults. Under the tolerant eyes of their elders, adolescent boys in such far-flung places as the Ituri Forest of Zaire, the villages of early modern Europe, and contemporary American Chinatowns have been allowed to behave in ways that would be considered antisocial if they were not directed at social deviants or persons identified as community enemies. Their action is usually restricted to mockery, but it can go so far as the destruction of property or physical assault. Are the destructive youths of the modern world who burn crosses on the lawns of Black householders in the United States, or destroy immigrant hostels in Germany, acting out the will of that segment of the community of which they are a part?

Whether or not adolescents take charge of specific activities for community welfare, almost everywhere they add to community life through the enjoyment they provide by their team sports and dances. While they display their strength and beauty to hoped-for boyfriends and girlfriends and try to impress important adults, they put on a show that entertains their audience of neighbors and kin.

Relations Between Generations

The cross-cultural data do not indicate much sustained conflict between adolescents and older family members or other adults. There are several possible reasons for this apparent harmony.

One reason is that under circumstances in which conflict is likely to occur, there is some avoidance between adults and children. For example, there may be great potential for conflict in societies in which older men monopolize young women, marrying brides still in their physical adolescence and leaving adolescent boys with the knowledge that they will not find wives until they are well into their twenties. One would expect the older boys and youths to challenge their elders; one example of just this is the Australian Tiwi, whose young bachelors surreptitiously meet the young wives in the bush. When such affairs come to light, the senior male age cohort draws together and supports the aggrieved husband in his (mild) punishment of the offending junior. Youths and socially mature men among the Tiwi seem not to interact very much.

Even less do age cohorts of males interact in the age-graded societies of Africa, in which seniors also marry the girls of the junior's generation. One stimulus to the formation of age-grades may be marriage across age cohorts, that is, when 12 to 15 years or more is the normal age difference between spouses. Age-sets serve to institutionalize the differences between age-cohorts in ways that promote social separation of them and to draw the lines that emphasize the power of the elders and the submission of the juniors. Females, on the other hand, are seldom organized into age grades. Even in those societies that recognize female age-grades, these are but pale reflections of the age-grades of boys and men. Girls, who marry young in almost all societies, do not have marital interests that compete with those of older women.

If one reason for a low level of conflict between adults and adolescents is institutionalized separation of boys and men, another is adolescents' understanding that they have no recourse to the authority of their families. Hopi girls, for example, may become so resentful of their mothers' authority that they run away, usually to the home of a paternal aunt. Nevertheless, they return when tempers have cooled, for they have no alternative (Schlegel, 1973). In small and stable communities, where children are known to all adults, there is little that the child can do that will not be reported at home. The community reinforces the authority of the family.

While avoidance and suppression may account for some of the low level of overt conflict, it is probable that conflict simply does not arise much. It is not in the interest of children in most places to challenge the authority of their adult kin, for it is these kin who will give them the material and social support they need to move into adulthood. Deference and compliance attract the favorable attention of adults; rudeness or rebelliousness would get adolescents nowhere.

The Changing Picture

The preindustrial world has practically disappeared, and with it have gone the earlier patterns of adolescent life. As nation-states expand their hegemony over formerly tribal peoples, they impose the changes that redirect the gender- and age-related behaviors of former times.

For adolescents, the most far-reaching change is the introduction of full-time schooling. For many adolescents in the advanced industrial nations, the teenage years have become a kind of "time-out." Children are allowed this period of self-absorption, freed somewhat from parental surveillance and yet not given the responsibilities of adulthood. But misuse of this freedom extracts a heavy toll; Willis (1977) has shown how one variant of English working-class youth culture, which denigrates learning and rewards toughness in aggressive and sexual encounters, traps boys into a future of meaningless and ill-paid labor. Once they leave school and enter the workplace, the door snaps shut on these young men and their opportunities for more interesting and better-paid work have vanished. The adolescents who succeed in school are those who, like adolescents in preindustrial societies, have learned how to comply with the order imposed by adults.

Schooling for all will have different meanings to adolescents and their families in modernizing populations. Conditions are so variable that it is impossible to generalize: children whose grandparents were foragers, such as Inuit (Condon, 1995) or Australian Aborigines (Burbank, 1995), are likely to have very different perceptions from children who are the heirs of a long literate tradition, such as Moroccan town-dwellers (Davis, 1995).

The one common factor is the shift in orientation from adults to peers. Schools put adolescents in a peer context for most of their days, reducing the amount of time they spend with adults and increasing the salience of their involvement with age-mates. What we learn about situated behavior from studies of unschooled societies raises questions about the effects, often unintended or unforeseen, of the transition to schooling.

Conclusion

This article has argued that the social function of adolescence across cultures is to prepare children for their adult reproductive careers; in this, the social adolescence of humans is similar to social adolescence among the higher primates. For humans, adolescence can also be a time of further preparation for adult occupational careers in those societies in which training beyond childhood is necessary.

As industrialization and the cognitive demands of a modern economy expand worldwide, the secondary function of adolescence takes on greater importance for boys, and, increasingly, for girls as well. Adolescence for girls has been extended well beyond the age range found in most preindustrial societies. Societies that had no youth stage for boys now consider a period of further education, military service, or occupational testing a normal stage in the life cycle; in many cases, such a stage is coming to be considered normal or desirable for girls as well.

Erikson's (1950) concern with occupational identity as a feature of adolescent development is increasingly applicable to peoples who identify social status and style of life with the individual's occupation. It is a great historical misfortune that conception of the self should change in this direction at a time when there are too many adolescents worldwide to fill existing occupational niches. The result of population explosions is that poor and developing countries have more young people than can be accommodated by their economic systems. For many, perhaps most, young people in such countries, the cards are stacked against their reaching a satisfactory occupational identity, as they find themselves torn between the possibilities held before their eyes and the reality of few good jobs and poor preparation for those that do exist. Occupational identity cannot develop if there is no attainable occupation with which to identify.

Boys are unlikely to be recognized as adults in their reproductive lives, that is, to become socially recognized fathers responsible for the well-being of their children and accountable for them, unless they can help support children and their mothers. Girls, on the other hand, can claim reproductive adulthood by bearing and caring for children, regardless of where their support comes from. While it is impossible to determine exact chronological age of marriage when people do not keep account of dates, 15 to 17 seems to have been a common age in traditional societies outside of preindustrial Europe and Southeast Asia, where it was later. Thus, first pregnancy at age 17 to 19 is not unusual and may in fact be biologically desirable (Konner & Shostak, 1986). Teenage pregnancy is a worldwide norm, even though most such pregnancies have occurred within marriage. It is predictable that girls will begin their reproductive careers during their teen years when conditions permit. Such conditions include the toleration of sexual activity, the assurance of support for the child by the family or state welfare, and the absence of any well-defined occupational career plans that would be endangered by childbearing. (Burbank's study of Australian Aborigines (1995), illustrates such conditions.)

It is difficult to see any improvement in the prospects for adolescents in poor countries, or among the badly educated populations of the developed nations, without serious efforts to improve the education of girls and boys and at the same time make reproductive control available and attractive. Adolescents may be experiencing a time out, but it is time that can easily be lost unless they have a clear sense of direction and the help of adults to clarify and achieve realistic goals. These are issues of great importance to all nations, as their future depends on the success of today's adolescents in successfully reaching adulthood.

Notes

1. Marriage, that is, the wedding that seals the social contract may occur before menarche, but in almost every case of which I am aware, girls do not engage in full sexual intercourse with their husbands until after their first menstruation. The presexual period of marriage could be considered social adolescence or a continuation of it.
2. In early modern Europe, peer groups in cities and towns seem to have been segregated by class, nobles and apprentices and other status categories all forming their separate groups.
3. This does not imply that mothers and adolescent daughters are always in harmony in preindustrial societies. For a discussion of the sometimes troubled mother-daughter relationships of the Hopi, see Schlegel, 1973 and 1975.

REFERENCES

Burbank, V. (1995). Gender hierarchy and adolescent sexuality. *Ethos*, 23, 33–46.

Bush, D. & Simmons R. (1981), Socialization processes over the life course. In M. Rosenberg & R. Turner (Eds.), *Social psychology: Sociological perspectives* (pp. 33–64). New York: Basic Books.

Chodorow, N. (1978). *The reproduction of mothering: Psychoanalysis and the sociology of gender.* Berkeley: University of California Press.

Condon, R. (1995). Modernizing the sexes: Changing gender relations in a Moroccan town. *Ethos, 23,* 47–68.

Davis, D. (1995). The rise of the leisure class. *Ethos, 23,* 69–78.

Elwin, V. (1947). *The Muria and their Ghotul.* Bombay: Oxford University Press.

Erikson, E. (1950). *Childhood and society.* New York: Norton.

Gay, J. (1986). "Mummies and Babies" and friends and lovers in Lesotho. In E. Blackwood (Ed.), *Anthropology and homosexual behavior* (pp. 97–116). New York: Haworth Press.

Gilligan, C., Ward, J., Taylor, J., & Bardige, B. (Eds.). (1988). *Mapping the moral domain: A contribution of women's thinking to psychological theory and education.* Cambridge, MA: Harvard University Press.

Goody, J. (1973). Bridewealth and dowry in Africa and Eurasia. In J. Goody & S. Tambiah (Eds.), *Bridewealth and dowry* (pp. 1–58). Cambridge: Cambridge University Press.

Konner, M. & Shostak, M. (1986). Adolescent pregnancy and childbearing: An anthropological perspective. In J. Lancaster & B. Hamburg (Eds.), *School-age pregnancy and parenthood: Biosocial dimensions* (pp. 325–346). New York: Aldine De Gruyter.

Llewelyn-Davies, M. (1981). Women, warriors, and patriarchs. In S. Ortner & H. Whitehead (Eds.), *Sexual Meanings: The cultural construction of gender and sexuality* (pp. 330–358). Cambridge: Cambridge University Press.

Mead, M. (1928). *Coming of age in Samoa.* Ann Arbor, MI: Morrow.

Ottenberg, S. (1989). *Boyhood rituals in an African society: An interpretation.* Seattle: University of Washington Press.

Schlegel, A. (1973). The adolescent socialization of the Hopi girl. *Ethnology, 4,* 449-462.

Schlegel, A. (1975). Situational stress: A Hopi example. In N. Datan & L. Ginsberg (Eds.), *Life span developmental psychology: Normative life crises* (pp. 209–216). New York: Academic Press.

Schlegel, A. (1991). Status, property, and the value on virginity. *American Ethnologist, 18,* 719-734.

Schlegel, A., & Barry, H. (1991). *Adolescence: An anthropological inquiry.* New York: Free Press.

Walters, J. (1987). Transition to adulthood. In B. Smuts, D. Cheney, R. Seyfurth, R. Wrangham, & T. Struhsaker (Eds.), *Primate societies* (pp. 358–369). Chicago: University of Chicago Press.

Whiting, B. & Edwards, C. (1988). *Children of different worlds.* Cambridge, MA: Harvard University Press.

Whiting, J., Burbank, V., & Ratner, M. (1986), The duration of maidenhood across cultures. In J. Lancaster, & B. Hamburg (Eds.), *School-age pregnancy and parenthood: Biosocial dimensions* (pp. 273–302). New York: Aldine De Gruyter.

Willis, P. (1977). *Learning to labor.* Farnborough: Saxon House.

Part II

Identity and Diversity in the Cultural Milieu

4

Ethnic Identity Exploration in Emerging Adulthood

JEAN S. PHINNEY

The concept of emerging adulthood refers to a period when young people are legally adult but do not yet see themselves as fully adult and have not taken on the range of responsibilities that are characteristic of adulthood in developed societies (Arnett, 2000). The challenges of this period have been defined largely in individualistic terms, such as forming a personal identity, attaining independence from one's parents, and assuming financial responsibility for oneself.

For members of ethnic minority groups in a society such as the United States, the criteria for reaching adulthood may be different for both demographic and cultural reasons. Specific experiences can either shorten or extend the period of emerging adulthood. Many factors, both individual and contextual, determine whether and to what extent young people experience a period when they are no longer adolescents but not yet adults. Young people from American ethnic minority backgrounds deal with many of the same issues as do their White peers, but they may have additional challenges and strengths that influence the point at which they attain adulthood (Arnett, 1998, 2003; Arnett & Galambos, 2003). Many minority youth are expected to take on adult responsibilities earlier than their peers from the mainstream culture (Cauce, Stewart, Roderguez, Cochran, & Ginzler, 2003). Minority young people, as part of their cultural heritage, typically value close and interdependent relationships with their family more strongly than do European American youth (Fuligni, Tseng, & Lam, 1999; Phinney, Ong, & Madden, 2000); as a result, they may feel obliged to assist the family with chores and to contribute financially

From: Arnett, Jeffrey Jensen, & Tanner, Jennifer Lynn (Eds.). (2006). *Emerging adults in America: Coming of age in the 21st century* (pp. 117–134). Copyright © American Psychological Association. Reprinted with permission.

to the family. For example, with socioeconomic status controlled, significantly more minority college students than European American students report that an important reason for attending college is to be able to help their family financially (Phinney, Dennis, & Osorio, in press). Young people from minority and immigrant backgrounds often provide support for their family when they are able (Fuligni & Witkow, 2004).

Because of their sense of interdependence and of responsibility to their families, minority young people may consider themselves as adults at an earlier age. Research with Canadian aboriginal college students has shown that they believe that they reach adulthood at a younger age than their European origin peers (Cheah & Nelson, 2004). Youth from some minority cultures also experience pressure to marry and have children at an early age (Phinney, 1999); if they become parents, these young people are likely to consider themselves adults. Although marriage is not always an indicator of adulthood in the majority culture (Arnett, 1998), it is seen as an important marker in many cultural contexts. Thus young people from minority and immigrant backgrounds may reach at least some of the markers of adulthood earlier than do their peers from the dominant culture and experience a shorter period of emerging adulthood.

However, in other respects, emerging adulthood may be extended for members of ethnic minority groups. Identity exploration in the areas of love, work, and worldviews has been cited as one of the defining characteristics of emerging adulthood (Arnett, 2000). In addition to identity exploration in those areas, ethnic group members must deal with identity issues in relation to their ethnic and racial heritage. These identity domains are far more central for minorities than for majority group members (Phinney & Alipuria, 1990). Their sense of membership in an ethnic, racial, or cultural group is an underlying issue that pervades and influences progress toward adulthood (Phinney, 1990). The need to explore the implications of their group membership may extend the identity exploration period throughout the 20s and often beyond. Minority young people may therefore experience a longer period of the fluidity that characterizes emerging adulthood. In fact, evidence of ethnic identity exploration well beyond adolescence provides the strongest argument for a distinct period of emerging adulthood for these young people. Fluidity in identity for minority persons may relate to the conflicting images of their ethnic group in American culture and the difficulty of finding a satisfactory identity option available to them. For European Americans, even if they do not buy into the stereotypical White image, the White image is generally positive and does not entail the more limited range of possibilities with which minority persons may be confronted. The goals of this chapter are to examine the exploration of ethnic and racial identity issues beyond adolescence among minority group members. There is wide variation in the extent of ethnic identity exploration during the transition to adulthood, depending on aspects of both the individual and the context. Within the American context, ethnic identity exploration differs with individual characteristics such as ethnic background, racial heritage or phenotype, and generation of immigration, as well as with family and community context, socioeconomic status, and educational experience. There is even greater variability in ethnic identity meanings and processes across countries and cultures, but that topic is beyond the scope of the present chapter. Thus, this chapter focuses on ethnic identity exploration in the American context and specifically on ethnic and racial minorities within that context. I consider individual processes and characteristics that influence ethnic identity exploration and the contextual factors that shape the course of such exploration during emerging adulthood.

For convenience, I use the term ethnic identity to encompass three aspects of group identity processes: ethnic heritage, racial phenotype, and cultural background. Although these three aspects of group identity can be distinguished conceptually and have different implications for the individual (Alipuria, 2002), they often overlap as individuals strive to construct a coherent sense of self as group members. However, I use separate terms when discussing research that explicitly focuses on one or another aspect.

I begin with a summary of the development of ethnic identity before and during adolescence and then examine this process following adolescence in a variety of contexts and for individuals with a range of group identity challenges, such as being bicultural or being biracial.

Early Development of Ethnic Identity

Socialization within the family provides the initial foundation for ethnic identity (Bernal, Knight, Ocampo, Garza, & Cota, 1993). Children learn about their culture within the family, through daily activities, language, and traditions. For young children, whose family and community constitute their world, the customs and values in which they are immersed are seen as the way things are, the norm, rather than as group characteristics. Ethnic identity development begins with the awareness of distinctive characteristics that differentiate oneself from some people but that are shared with others. Children growing up in a modern society soon become aware of people who act and think differently, who may look different from them, and who differ in visibility and status in society.

The ways in which these differences are viewed vary with the context. Depending on the messages that children receive, differences may be seen as reflecting something bad or inferior; conversely, they may be seen as something to be valued and emulated. The task of ethnic identity formation involves sorting out and resolving positive and negative feelings and attitudes about one's own group and about other groups and identifying one's place in relation to both. One of the challenges for members of nondominant groups is that they must understand those of higher status. In contrast, dominant group members in the United States can live and work largely without having to understand other groups. Thus ethnic identity is far less salient for European Americans than it is for ethnic minority group members (Phinney, 1989).

The task of making sense of differences based on ethnicity and race begins in childhood and is highly salient during adolescence. It depends in part on developmental capacities. A cognitive-developmental perspective on awareness of ethnicity and ethnic differences has been described by Quintana and colleagues (Quintana, 1994; Quintana, Castaneda-English, & Ybarra, 1999). Ethnic differences are first understood by young children in concrete, physical terms, such as clothing and skin color, followed by literal features such as language and food preferences, and later by a nonliteral, social perspective of ethnicity, including an awareness of the social implications of ethnicity, such as prejudice. By adolescence, young people have the ability to understand an ethnic group as a communal whole, with a shared perspective; they can develop an ethnic group consciousness and explore the implications of their own ethnicity.

Quintana's model is consistent with research that has shown adolescence to be a critical period for ethnic identity development (Phinney, 1989, 1990). Before adolescence, children from minority backgrounds are aware of their group membership but they have little understanding of its meaning and implications for their lives. Adolescents move into a wider range of contexts, including ethnically diverse high schools and part-time jobs. Increased contact with people from backgrounds other than their own leads to greater awareness of differences and more questions about their own group membership. During the high school years, many young people explore their ethnicity through talking to people, reading, and learning about the history and customs of their group, thus laying the foundations for a secure ethnic identity. This exploration is assumed to lead eventually to a resolution in the form of a secure and stable sense of self as an ethnic group member.

However, the process of attaining a secure identity is not completed during adolescence. Phinney (1989) found that only about one-quarter of 10th graders from ethnic minority backgrounds had explored and resolved ethnic identity issues and could be considered to have an achieved ethnic identity. This fact may be related in part to differing degrees of exposure to other groups. Research examining contextual effects on ethnic identity development (Umana-Taylor, 2003) showed that Latino adolescents in a high school that was predominantly non-Latino reported higher levels of ethnic identity than did those in schools with a larger proportion of Latinos. As a result of changing residential patterns, minority adolescents are increasingly likely to attend schools that are homogeneous rather than ethnically diverse. Many adolescents from ethnic minority backgrounds may thus have relatively little exposure to other ethnic groups during high school. Even in ethnically diverse high schools, there is considerable evidence of ethnic and racial self-segregation. Although adolescents may interact with students from a range of backgrounds in structured activities, they are likely to spend leisure time with same-group peers (Tatum, 1997). Research showing that three quarters of the high school students either had not examined ethnic issues at all or had explored but not resolved them (Phinney, 1989) suggests that ethnic identity formation often continues beyond adolescence.

Ethnic Identity Development Beyond Adolescence

Emerging adulthood implies a period during which identity issues continue to be explored and are not yet satisfactorily resolved. The years beyond high school lead to a variety of experiences that can enhance or reduce identity exploration. When young people leave high school, their pathways diverge, depending in part on the extent to which they pursue further education. Young people may attend any one of a range of institutions of higher learning, including elite research universities or private colleges, less selective public universities, community colleges, and trade schools, or they may not attend college but rather work, take time off, or stay at home to raise children. Ethnic identity in emerging adulthood cannot be considered apart from the contexts in which young people are living, studying, and working. The contexts they experience provide important settings for the exploration of ethnic identity. In addition to their immediate home and work contexts, they may be influenced by broader exposure, such as the media and national political movements.

If young people move directly from high school into stable jobs within their community, and also marry and settle down in the same setting, there may be no further pressure to examine their ethnicity. They can be considered identity foreclosed; they attain the markers of adulthood with little evidence of an extended exploration, and hence cannot be said to experience emerging adulthood.

However, with the transition into the wider world beyond high school, many emerging adults face situations in which their race, ethnicity, or culture is made salient. Research with adolescents has shown that issues of ethnic and racial identity are most salient in culturally diverse settings (Ogbu, 1987; Oyserman, Gant, & Ager, 1995; Phinney, 1989; Phinney & Rosenthal, 1992). Contrasts between their own background and those of others whom they encounter highlight cultural or ethnic differences and raise identity issues.

Even if a secure identity has been achieved during adolescence, it is likely to be reexamined as a result of changing contexts. Research on ego identity has established that individuals often reexamine identity issues after the initial resolution of the identity crisis (Stephen, Fraser, & Marcia, 1992) With regard to racial identity, Parham (1989) has similarly suggested that people return to racial identity issues as new situations arise. When lives are characterized by changing circumstances and new experiences, exploration is likely to continue.

Furthermore, developmental changes make ethnic identity increasingly important beyond adolescence. Increasing cognitive abilities can raise awareness of the implications of one's ethnic group membership. Quintana's (1994) model describes further progress beyond adolescence in the understanding of ethnicity. In their 20s, young people become capable of seeing ethnicity in a wider context. They can take the perspectives of other ethnic or racial minority groups and of the dominant ethnic group. They can thus develop a multicultural viewpoint that includes an increased understanding of both intergroup conflict and the possibility of intergroup acceptance and positive interaction. Furthermore, they have a greater awareness of the diversity within their own group and other groups that can lead to an increased appreciation for the complexity of experiences related to ethnicity. These broader perspectives are likely to contribute to continued exploration of the implications of ethnicity.

Ethnic Identity Development During the College Years

Most of the research on ethnic identity beyond adolescence has been with college students. College has been seen in the identity literature as a moratorium, a period when young people are allowed the opportunity to explore options before making commitments that will provide the basis for decisions regarding important identity domains.

Studies on ethnic and racial identity with college students have been carried out primarily at the prestigious universities where most researchers work. Research with students who attend major research universities has focused largely on discrimination and threats to one's ethnic identity that these students, typically a small minority of the student body, experience on predominantly White campuses (e.g., Mendoza-Denton, Downey, Purdie, Davis, & Pietrzak, 2002). As college students attempt to understand and negotiate being a minority in a setting dominated by members of another group, ethnic identity is highly salient. Two pathways have been identified among minority students at largely White institutions (Ethier & Deaux, 1994); students with initially strong ethnic identities become more involved in cultural activities, which thus strengthens the identity, whereas those with a weaker initial ethnic identity perceive more threat and experience a further weakening of the identity. In either case, ethnicity is an issue that must be dealt with.

A narrative account by Ruben Navarrette, Jr. (1993) of his experience as a minority student at an elite university provides a particularly vivid description of an extended ethnic identity exploration. Navarrette grew up in a small farming community in California and became one of the few Latino students at Harvard University. After arriving at Harvard, he became keenly aware of being different from the majority of students. Being Latino, which had not been salient in his hometown, became a focus of attention. He became deeply involved in programs and activities aimed at supporting Latino students and promoting ethnic awareness generally, but this did not resolve the conflicts he felt. He referred to himself and other members of the ethnic club that he was involved in the following:

> We were consumed with simply finding a precarious place to perch between two opposing worlds....These were people poised to conquer the future, but who had not yet reconciled themselves with their past. We were torn, divided, conflicted. I loved and respected my parents and yet I wanted nothing as much as to live a life that was different, better, than theirs. I had avoided being part of a sorrowful statistic [of those who drop out of high school]...and yet instead of feeling lucky, I felt guilty, illegitimate, embarrassed. (pp. 135-136)

Navarrette (1993) described alternative ways of handling the feelings of difference. Some Latino students avoided involvement with ethnic activities and took an assimilationist position, attempting to become part of the larger campus community. However, they faced disapproval from the majority of Latinos for not being part of the Latino student groups. Usually they also lacked acceptance among students from the dominant White majority. Not only ethnic and cultural differences set Latino students apart: Skin color differences and the privilege that accompanied light skin were an ever-present aspect of the college experience of Navarrette and his Latino peers. An awareness of difference kept ethnic identity at the forefront of their developing sense of self. In accord with Quintana's model, Navarrette also became more aware of the experience of other minority groups on campus and developed a sense of solidarity with them. Eventually, over time, Navarrette also came to know and understand many White students and to develop a more nuanced appreciation of the diversity in their attitudes and experiences.

Although Navarrette's account provides a clear example of ethnic identity exploration, relatively few minority college students attend elite, selective institutions such as Harvard. Many more attend urban commuter universities in which a larger proportion of students are minorities and issues of discrimination are less salient. College freshman at an urban university in which 80 percent of the student body was from non-European backgrounds rated perceived discrimination very low, with a mean between never and rarely on a 5-point scale (Phinney & Tomiki, 2002). In such a setting, in which most other students were from similar backgrounds, there may be little pressure to examine ethnicity per se. A study of ethnic identity at the same institution (Romero, 2001) showed no change in ethnic identity exploration during the first 3 years in college. It seems likely, however, that once they leave the relatively homogeneous college atmosphere, they will face situations that provoke exploration.

Even if ethnic identity is not being actively explored, it remains an important concern. College students may study their ethnic language or take ethnic studies classes that allow them to learn more about the history and culture of their group. A study comparing the importance of five identity domains in college students from four ethnic groups attending the same urban university (Phinney & Alipuria, 1990) found that although occupation was rated as the most important identity issue for all ethnic groups, ethnic identity remained a significantly more important identity issue for ethnic minorities than for European American students. For the minority students, ethnic identity was rated equal in importance to two other identity domains, sex role and religious identity; for the European Americans, ethnic identity was rated as the least important domain. Continued uncertainty about ethnic identity is revealed in a statement by a 19-year-old Latino college student: "I consider myself Hispanic, but I'm not sure what ethnicity means" (Phinney, 2004). As long as underlying identity concerns about ethnicity remain unresolved, these students could be considered emerging adults.

Ethnic Identity Development Outside Educational Settings

Although college has been described as a moratorium period that allows young people time to resolve identity issues, not all emerging adults attend 4-year colleges. There is little or no research on ethnic identity among minority youth who do not go to college. However, their experience outside educational settings may reflect to some extent that of their peers who attended college and are now working. A basic premise of identity theory is that new experiences can trigger identity exploration. The period of emerging adulthood is marked by a widening exposure to new situations, ideas, responsibilities, and persons. Whether they have attended college or not, emerging adults must make decisions about the kind of occupation to commit to, where to live, and the people they choose to associate with. They must also deal with the attitudes they encounter from others. In particular, as they enter the workplace and become more involved in the wider society, they are likely to face new challenges regarding the meaning and implications of their ethnicity. Such challenges typically provoke ethnic exploration.

Throughout development, but perhaps increasingly with age, as one has more contact with strangers, one's appearance provides others with the first evidence as to one's background. Being classified on the basis of appearance and treated differently, and negatively, because of it is a central issue of racial identity (Helms, 1990). For Black Americans especially, appearance, or pheno-type, clearly identifies one's African origins. Asian Americans also are easily identifiable and often assumed to be immigrants or foreigners; for example, they report frequent comments such as how well they speak English. Latinos and members of other non-European groups are less easily identified by appearance alone, but they nevertheless are typically seen as non-White. The way in which one is seen by others is an important part of one's identity. A 26-year-old man with a Black father and a White mother stated that he calls himself African American: "That's what everyone sees when they look at me, so that's what I am" (Phinney, 2004). A Mexican American emerging adult expressed a similar idea when she said, "I think it is ridiculous to say I am American when people see a Mexican looking girl" (Phinney, 2004).

Although race has no biological reality, it is real in the way it is socially constructed and in the impact it has through racism. The pejorative implications resulting from society's need to classify people as us or them can result in internalized racism among minorities, leading to negative views of themselves. The task for visible minorities is to overcome such internalized negative images (Helms, 1990). The experience of being initially identified and categorized on the basis of appearance is universal, but there is wide variation in how individuals respond to the ways in which they are perceived. As an identity issue, responses to others' perceptions are as important as the perceptions themselves. An aspect of ethnic identity formation involves coming to understand others' perceptions but not allowing oneself to be defined by them.

A case study of an Asian American woman (Ho, 2004) illustrates the changes in the way the young woman's experience with racial categorization led to exploration. She reported experiencing hostility and feelings of noninclusion at her job and in the media, because of her Asian features. "I was raised American like everyone else, but I wasn't allowed to be American. And the media images! It was all White, sexy females, and that wasn't me." These feelings can result in internalized racism and self-hatred, as has been described in research with adolescents generally (Phinney, 1989) and with African Americans in particular (Cross & Fhagen-Smith, 2001). The Asian woman reported, "It got to a point where I hated myself because I was Asian.... My bad driving habits at that time were indicative of my self-hatred. If I was killed in an accident I wouldn't have to deal with being Asian." With support of her family and friends, this young woman engaged in a period of exploration or immersion (Cross & Fhagen-Smith, 2001), including the study of Asian culture, and was able to reclaim her Asian heritage. She stated, "I finally realized that it was all right for me to be an Asian American...I am what I am." This woman's story provides a clear depiction of the resolution of an identity crisis, in which the process of exploration leads to a clear, secure sense of self in terms of one's race, that is, an achieved racial identity.

A study of Hispanics working in a European American business (Ferdman & Cortes, 1992) highlights the ways in which ethnic identity exploration may continue even with familiar colleagues in a work setting. Although it is not clear whether the participants in this study could be considered emerging adults on the basis of age, the experiences described are as likely to occur for employees in their 20s as for older ones. As minorities within the company, the Hispanic employees were aware of both differential treatment and cultural differences between themselves and their European American colleagues. To deal with these experiences, some employees Anglicized their names. Some tried to counteract stereotypes: "Too many people have a stereotypical view of what Hispanics are, and I, just through normal day-to-day activity. . . . give them visible proof that. . . . it's not necessarily true" (p. 269). Hispanic employees reported that their coworkers showed varying degree of awareness of their ethnic background, but most Hispanics felt that they were seen as being different. One stated, "Even though you consider yourself one of the guys, American, and a professional . . . people have subtle ways of letting you know that when they look at you they see . . . a Hispanic first" (p. 272).

These examples provide evidence about ethnic identity processes in emerging adulthood. Being seen as a minority and as different from the dominant group is a constant throughout life for many Americans from non-European backgrounds. What is important developmentally is the extent to which individuals have developed a confident sense of their own ethnicity. An achieved identity contributes to a positive sense of self and provides protection against those who are dismissive or demeaning toward one's group or see only a stereotype rather than the person (Phinney, Cantu, & Kurtz, 1997). One measure of reaching adulthood, in terms of ethnicity, might be the point at which individuals who have wrestled with negative feelings about their group membership no longer experience doubt or self-hatred based on their race or ethnicity. A 21-year-old Mexican American demonstrated his secure identity in stating "Even though a person may be racist — I don't think that's good obviously — but I'm not going to tell myself I shouldn't like myself because I'm Mexican" (Phinney, 2004).

Bicultural and Multicultural Identity

Any individuals living in settings that are different from their culture of origin are faced with questions regarding their bicultural or multicultural identity. They must determine how and to what extent to identify with the cultures they are exposed to: their native or parental cultural, the culture of the larger society in which they reside (LaFromboise, Coleman, & Gerton, 1993), and perhaps also other cultures with which they come in contact (Phinney & Alipuria, in press). Much of the research on this topic has been carried out with adolescents (Phinney, 2003). Ethnic minority adolescents in the United States are involved in exploring the meaning of being American as well as ethnic (Phinney & Devich-Navarro, 1997). They develop different approaches to this issue, such as keeping the ethnic and national identities separate, combining them in some way, or rejecting one of them.

Beyond high school, issues of bicultural and multicultural identity are likely to become more important as young people move away from their families and neighborhoods into the broader worlds of higher education and work. The widening experience of emerging adults from minority backgrounds can lead to a questioning of the traditional cultural values of their ethnic group. The mainstream cultural values of independence and self-assertion contrast with the family's expectations for family closeness and interdependence (Phinney et al., 2000). Young people who live at home are expected to show deference to parents and to respond to the needs of the family find themselves in educational or work settings in which individual achievement is more valued and they are expected to be autonomous and assertive. Latino young people report family pressures to stay close to home that may restrict their options for job promotions that involve a move or graduate school in a distant city (Phinney, 2004).

The need for young Americans from non-European cultural backgrounds to make choices between contrasting values can result in the kind of identity crisis described by Erikson (1968). The crisis is assumed to provoke an exploration of the meaning of being members of both an ethnic group and the larger society. In interviews with college students regarding cultural identity issues (Phinney, 2004), an Asian American student stated, "I am attracted to the values of independence and doing my own thing, but it is also important for me to be close to my parents; it is sometimes hard to do both" (p. 11).

The differences in cultural values that are experienced by ethnic minorities can become sources of stress when young people are expected to put the needs of their family before their own needs. Tseng (2004) demonstrated the impact of cultural values and practices on academic achievement in a diverse sample of college students from immigrant backgrounds. A stronger endorsement of the cultural values of family interdependence was related to greater academic achievement. However, demands by the family for behavioral assistance, such as doing chores, detracted from academic achievement. In an interview, an Asian American college student reported that she had to "work to share the rent with my parents. Sometimes I am bothered because my parents ask me to help them out while I am studying" (Phinney, 2004, p. 12). Emerging adulthood for these young people includes efforts to understand and find a balance between the competing demands of their two cultural contexts.

Bicultural identity issues are framed in terms of the ways in which a person considers himself or herself to be both ethnic and part of the larger (e.g., American) society. A Latino college student identified differing sources of ethnic and American identity; she saw herself Latino on the basis of "the color of my skin, my language, the food, my place of birth." However, regarding her American identity, she stated, "the values and beliefs I hold come from American culture." A 21-year-old technical school graduate likewise endorsed

American values of equality in a marriage, in contrast to what he saw as a Mexican tradition of men controlling their wives; but he also stated, "That doesn't mean that I'm going to close the door on Mexico and its traditions" (Phinney, 2004, p. 14).

Exploration of cultural identity issues is evident as well in a 24-year-old American from a Russian background, who reported learning about his culture of origin from stories by his grandfather. However, he also emphasized the importance of exploring other cultures. "To be a true American...you have to immerse yourself in the diversity that is around you" (Phinney, 2004, p. 16). The achievement of a secure ethnic identity requires coming to an understanding of oneself as part of an ethnic group and also of a larger, diverse national entity.

Biracial and Multiracial Identity

Young people who have parents from two or more different ethnic or racial backgrounds face particularly complex identity issues. Even the best way to describe these people is unclear; various terms are used, including biracial, multiracial, and multi-ethnic. The term multiracial is used here to encompass all those whose ancestors are from two or more ethnic or racial groups. These people must deal with the basic issues faced by all minorities, of developing a secure sense of who they are in ethnic terms. However, they develop their identity in the context of two (or more) families or groups, each of which they are part of to some extent but not exclusively (Phinney & Alipuria, in press). They must deal with, and explore, issues about both their racial identity, related to their appearance, and their ethnic identity, regarding a sense of group belonging. Because their appearance is often ambiguous, people cannot easily identify how to categorize them ethnically. They are therefore often faced with the question "What are you?" Depending on the background of their parents, the challenge of being biracial may overlap with that of being bicultural, that is, having different cultural traditions to choose from. In addition to having ties to at least two ethnic groups, they must also consider a third membership group, the larger society and the related national identity.

Because of the complexity of forming an identity as a multiracial person, the process appears to begin earlier and continue longer than for a mono-racial person. Multiracial children are typically aware at an early age that they are different from each of their parents (Kich, 1992). Depending on socialization within their family and contact with their parents' families of origin, they learn not only that they belong in some ways to both parental ethnic groups but also that they do not belong exclusively to either. From their awareness of difference, they struggle for acceptance as being biracial. In most cases they lack an existing biracial group with which to identify; identification with the group of one parent implies rejection of the other parent. Furthermore, they are unlikely to have peer groups of multiracial individuals to identify with. Kich (1992) suggested that self-acceptance of themselves as biracial, that is, an achieved biracial identity, is likely to occur during or after college or in the workplace; thus it extends into emerging adulthood.

A recent qualitative study of multiracial people in their 20s and early 30s from East Indian and European American backgrounds (Alipuria, 2002) provides strong evidence of continuing exploration of identity in these emerging adults. Virtually all areas of their lives are affected by their multiracial status as they seek to establish relationships and find communities that support their efforts to understand who they are. Perhaps no other group of young people is as strongly influenced by their context as are multiracial people. Because of their dual heritage, multiracial young people face continual challenges to find a place where they fit in. A 25-year-old graduate student in anthropology stated, "I have never had a comfort group. There just isn't one. Period....I'm always a different person among different contexts" (Alipuria, 2002, p. 112). Another woman, at 31, continued to feel ambivalent about her dual heritage,

> My emotions are really mixed...I sense on the one hand happiness that I...have seen so much of the world that I can appreciate....and feel like I am part of. But at the same time, I also have a sadness because I think it's harder, much harder, to grow up as a bicultural or multicultural person....I never felt like I fit in totally in one place. (Alipuria, 2002, p. 133)

The feeling of not fitting in may be due in part to cultural differences, but it is perhaps more strongly influenced by phenotypic ambiguity. The graduate student previously quoted looked somewhat Indian but reported often being taken for Middle Eastern.

> A large part of any sort of awareness of identity would be how others treat you....I haven't formed my identity in a vacuum, thinking 'what do I want, what do I like?' I mean, that's been part of it, but it is also what others impose on you, for better or worse. (Alipuria, 2002, p. 109)

She noted, as well, that people who have not been challenged or stereotyped because of their appearance have no idea of the problems faced by those who have dealt with these experiences.

> I've had to have [racial consciousness]....I have people constantly telling me, 'What's the big deal? Get over it.' Which is why I like to hang out with Black people. Because they never say, 'What's the big deal?' They know what the big deal is and talk about it explicitly. (Alipuria, 2002, p. 119)

For multiracial emerging adults, the search for supportive people to associate with is an important aspect of their identity exploration. The awareness of being different no doubt continues to some extent throughout life. However, many multiracial people reach a resolution of their status that leads to identity achievement. One woman in her early 30s reported feeling like "a social misfit" (Alipuria, 2002, p. 137) when she was growing up. Eventually she found a group of racially mixed friends with whom she could discuss the reactions they got from other people. She stated, "I've gotten a lot better as I've gotten older at not always wondering how people are perceiving me" (p. 139). Another biracial woman in her early 30s, working in a nonprofit organization dealing with immigrants' rights, appeared to have achieved a secure sense of her dual heritage as East Indian and European American. She stated,

> When I was younger I felt I didn't belong anywhere. But now I've just come to the conclusion that...that's just the way I am,...and my home is inside myself....I no longer feel the compulsion to fit in 'cause if you're just trying to fit in you never do. (Alipuria, 2002, p. 143)

Other research suggests various ways in which multiracial people resolve their ethnic identity (Root, 1996). Four alternatives have been described: One can identify with just one of one's heritage groups; identify with both and switch between them; claim membership in a new category as mixed; or choose not to identify ethnically or racially but rather think of oneself in other terms (Renn, 2000; Rockquemore & Brunsma, 2002). The setting is often a critical factor in the type of resolution chosen. In a study of multiracial university students on three different campuses, Renn (2000) found that the campus climate was a strong influence on identity processes. One campus, with a large group of multiracial students, provided a community in which being multiracial was accepted. In contrast, on a campus that had organized groups only for specific ethnic groups, multiracial students were less accepted. Experiences such as these can advance or delay the resolution of identity issues in multiracial emerging adults.

Clearly, exploration of ethnic identity continues for multiracial people throughout and beyond college and is common for people in their 20s and early 30s. Multiracial emerging adults who have attained many markers of adulthood, such as being settled into a career and fully responsible for themselves financially, may still be wrestling with fundamental identity questions. In that sense, they retain aspects of emerging adulthood.

Conclusions

It is evident that for members of ethnic minority groups within the United States, formation of a group identity relative to one's ethnic, racial, or cultural heritage is a salient, important, and extended process. Exploration and questioning about one's heritage and its implications continue well beyond adolescence, although the process varies widely across individuals and groups. Identity exploration has been seen as a characteristic of emerging adulthood (Arnett, 2000). Emerging adulthood is a period in which the identity issues encountered in adolescence are tested for fit with new experiences. New issues arise because of the unique experiences that may be encountered after schooling, involving financial responsibilities and decisions about life commitments in establishing a career and a home. However, several unresolved questions limit any conclusions about whether ethnic identity exploration is a defining characteristic of a distinct developmental period between adolescence and adulthood.

First, the environment is a critical determinant of the timing, duration, and nature of ethnic identity exploration, and the environments to which ethnic group members are exposed vary widely within the United States. Thus, there is necessarily variation in the identity formation process across groups and individuals. In largely homogeneous settings, ethnic exploration may be deferred indefinitely; it may occur in middle or later adulthood, or never take place. Individuals who have not explored but who have a committed sense of their ethnicity, that is, who have a foreclosed ethnic identity, can be fully functioning adults, comfortable with their ethnicity within their environment. From adolescence on, they have a clear and workable understanding of who they are, ethnically or racially, based on their early socialization in the family and community. If there are no striking changes in their environment, they may never initiate an exploration. For them, the concept of emerging adulthood in the domain of ethnicity does not seem to apply, although they may be exploring in other important domains, such as occupation and personal relationships.

For other individuals, typically those who live in a diverse setting or change their place of residence, ethnicity and the questions it raises are likely to be salient throughout life. Because members of ethnic and racial minority groups are frequently faced with discriminatory attitudes and evidence of their lower status and power in society, they may continually be negotiating their sense of self in relation to other groups; that is, they experience an extended moratorium in this domain. When this process of negotiation continues into the 30s, 40s, and beyond, it can hardly define emerging adulthood.

The concept of emerging adulthood is most relevant to those who, in whatever context, engage in exploration in their teens and 20s and then reach a relatively comfortable, stable understanding of their ethnicity that serves as a basis for dealing with ethnic and racial issues; that is, they have achieved an identity. The Asian American woman developing a confident sense of herself as Asian is a good example of this process.

However, context alone does not determine the extent or quality of exploration. Even within the same environment, individuals have varying degrees of need to confront and deal with ethnic issues. For example, the Asian woman described earlier developed self-hatred whereas other members of her family did not. One factor underlying individual differences in exploration stems from personality characteristics; some people may be more temperamentally inclined to explore. With regard to ethnic identity, some people feel a strong need to belong to a group; they may seek out people who share their ethnic background and obtain information about their ethnic heritage as a way of developing a place to belong. Others feel less need to belong or else fulfill the need within a different context, such as family or friends.

There are differences, as well in sensitivity to discrimination. A study of perceived discrimination among a diverse group of adolescents attending ethnically mixed high schools (Phinney, Madden, & Santos, 1998) showed that some people were more likely to perceive discrimination than others; furthermore, individual differences in depression were a positive predictor, and intergroup competence a negative predictor, of perceived discrimination. People who perceive more discrimination are likely to engage in more exploration.

Another individual factor influencing exploration is phenotype. People whose appearance identifies them as members of a particular group are likely to be treated as members of that group. However, people whose appearance is ambiguous and does not allow easy categorization may be frequently asked to identify themselves ethnically. Experiences of being treated stereotypically or discriminated against, or being asked to label oneself ethnically, can be strong motivators of exploration, regardless of the larger context.

In addition to individual differences, group differences influence the extent of exploration. Both racism and cultural values may influence the course of exploration in emerging adults. In the United States, African Americans have experienced far more discrimination than have other groups. They consistently report stronger ethnic identity than do other groups (Phinney, 1992; Phinney et al., 1997) and may well face a more extended exploration period. The identity issues faced by other groups, such as Asians and Latinos, may focus more on cultural differences and stereotypes, although discrimination may also be involved. As discussed earlier, persons who have more than one cultural or ethnic heritage face other identity questions that influence their exploration. In addition, even for monoethnic members of the dominant culture, the exposure to a mix of cultural values and practices that results from the nation's growing diversity is likely to lead to exploration about how other cultures can impact one's own identity, even for the dominant group.

Level of education is also likely to influence ethnic identity exploration. Because of the lack of research with emerging adults who do not have a college education, there is little information about differences in exploration based on level of education. In addition to ethnic minorities, European Americans from noncollege backgrounds have been studied very little in terms of group identity formation. Although they typically face less discrimination, they have more limited options than do their peers with a college degree and may face ethnic identity issues related to being White but not fitting the images they see of prosperous Whites. There is clearly need for more research on the impact of education on emerging adulthood.

Because both environmental and individual characteristics influence exploration, conceptualization about a period of emerging adulthood needs to recognize the complexity of the topic. Researchers should consider and incorporate current views from developmental psychology regarding the interaction of the person and the environment. Depending on the interaction of both personal and contextual factors related to race and ethnicity, some people in some environments experience a distinct period of exploration between adolescence and adulthood, whereas others do not explore at all, or continue exploring throughout life. Little is known about factors that influence the initiation and duration of ethnic identity exploration. A task for future research is to identify more precisely which people in which circumstances are most likely to engage in, and complete, a period of exploration between adolescence and adulthood and thus fit the label of emerging adults.

An additional question is the importance of ethnic exploration as a marker of emerging adulthood. Cross and Fhagen-Smith (2001) suggested that for Black Americans the end product of racial identity exploration is a reference group orientation that, along with other key psychological characteristics, "undergirds the psychological platform upon which will be transacted certain adult challenges, tasks, and opportunities" (p. 258) that are encountered in the varied contexts of work, education, relationships, and family. From this perspective, resolving the question of who one is in ethnic or racial terms is critical to decisions in other areas of one's life. However, as has been noted, this identity domain is more important for some people than for others. For those who define themselves by their occupations or other salient identifications, ethnicity may never be a salient issue and hence have little or no role in defining emerging adulthood. Research on ethnic identity needs to take into account individual differences in both the extent of exploration and the importance of this group identity. Among those for whom ethnicity is highly important, an extended exploration beyond adolescence is most likely to indicate emerging adulthood, but not everyone has this experience. A more nuanced view of emerging adulthood should therefore include recognition that even among people from the same background in the same environment, there is wide variation in whether the concept of emerging adulthood applies.

In sum, a secure sense of oneself as a member of an ethnic or racial group is a defining attainment of adulthood for most people from minority backgrounds and is becoming important for nonminorities in many contexts. However, the completion of identity exploration and the achievement of a group identity cannot clearly be assigned to any given age range. Studying the interaction of personal and environmental factors that influence this process across a range of ethnic groups and contexts remains an important challenge for developmental researchers concerned with identity processes in emerging adulthood.

References

Alipuria, L. (2002). Ethnic, racial, and cultural identity/self: An integrated theory of identity/self in relation to large scale social cleavages. (Doctoral dissertation, UMI No. 3039092). *Dissertation Abstracts International, 63B*, 583.

Arnett, J. (1998). Learning to stand alone: The contemporary American transition to adulthood in cultural and historical context. *Human Development, 41*, 295–315.

Arnett, J. (2000). Emerging adulthood: A theory of development from late teens through the twenties. *American Psychologist, 55*, 469–480.

Arnett, J. (2003). Conceptions of the transition of adulthood among emerging adults in American ethnic groups. In J. Arnett & N. Galambos (Eds.), *Exploring cultural conceptions of the transition to adulthood* (pp. 63–75). San Francisco: Jossey-Bass.

Arnett, J. & Galambos, N. (2003). Culture and conceptions of adulthood. In J. Arnett & N. Galambos (Eds.), *Exploring cultural conceptions of the transition to adulthood* (pp. 91–98). San Francisco: Jossey-Bass.

Bernal, M., Knight, G., Ocampo, K., Garza, C., & Cota, M. (1993). Development of Mexican American identity. In M. Bernal & G. Knight (Eds.), *Ethnic identity: Formation and transmission among Hispanics and other minorities* (pp. 31–46). Albany: State University of New York Press.

Cauce, A., Stewart, A., Roderguez, M., Cochran, B., & Ginzler, J. (2003). Overcoming the odds? Adolescent development in the context of urban poverty. In S. Luthar (Ed.), *Resilience and vulnerability: Adaptation in the context of childhood adversities* (pp. 343–363). New York: Cambridge University Press.

Cheah, C. S. L. & Nelson, L. J. (2004). The role of acculturation in the emerging adulthood of aboriginal college students. *International Journal of Behavioral Development, 28*, 495–507.

Cross, W. & Fhagen-Smith, P. (2001). Patterns of African American identity development: A life span perspective. In C. Wijeyesinghe & B. Jackson III (Eds.), *New perspectives on racial identity development: A theoretical and practical anthology* (pp. 243–270). New York: New York University Press.

Erikson, E. (1968). *Identity: Youth and crisis*. New York: Norton.

Ethier, K. & Deaux, K. (1994). Negotiating social identity when contexts change: Maintaining and responding to threat. *Journal of Personality and Social Psychology, 67*, 243–251.

Ferdman, B., & Cortes, A. (1992). Culture and identity among Hispanic managers in an Anglo business. In S. Knouse, P. Rosenfield, & A. Culbertson (Eds.), *Hispanics in the workplace* (pp. 246–277). Thousand Oaks, CA: Sage.

Fuligni, A., Tseng, V., & Lam, M. (1999). Attitudes toward family obligations among American adolescents with Asian, Latin American, and European backgrounds. *Child Development, 70*, 1030–1044.

Fuligni, A. & Witkow, M. (2004). The postsecondary educational progress of youth from immigrant families. *Journal of Research on Adolescence, 14*, 159–183.

Helms, J. (1990). *Black and White racial identity: Theory, research, and practice*. New York: Greenwood Press.

Ho, M. (2004). "I am what I am": A case study of ethnic identity development. Unpublished manuscript, California State University, Los Angeles.

Kich, G. (1992). The developmental process of asserting a biracial, bicultural identity. In M. Root (Ed.), *Racially mixed people in America* (pp. 304–320). Newbury Park, CA: Sage.

LaFromboise, T., Coleman, H., & Gerton, J. (1993). Psychological impact of biculturalism: Evidence and theory. *Psychological Bulletin, 114*, 395–412.

Mendoza-Denton, R., Downey, G., Purdie, V., Davis, A., & Pietrzak, J. (2002). Sensitivity to status-based rejection: Implications for African American students' college experience. *Journal of Personality and Social Psychology, 83*, 896–918.

Navarrette, R., Jr. (1993). *A darker shade of crimson: Odyssey of a Harvard Chicano.* New York: Bantam Books.

Ogbu, J. (1987). Opportunity structure, cultural boundaries, and literacy. In J. Langer (Ed.), *Language, literacy, and culture: Issues of society and schooling* (pp. 149–177). Norwood, NJ: Ablex.

Oyserman, D., Gant, L., & Ager, J. (1995). A socially contextualized model of African American identity: Possible selves and school persistence. *Journal of Personality and Social Psychology, 69*, 1216–1232.

Parham, T. (1989). Cycles of psychological nigrescence. *The Counseling Psychologist, 17*, 187–226.

Phinney, J. (1989). Stages of ethnic identity development in minority group adolescents. *Journal of Early Adolescence, 9*, 34–49.

Phinney, J. (1990). Ethnic identity in adolescents and adults: A review of research. *Psychological Bulletin, 108*, 499–514.

Phinney, J. (1992). The Multigroup Ethnic Identity Measure: A new scale for use with diverse groups. *Journal of Adolescent Research, 7*, 156–176.

Phinney, J. (1999, May). Symposium. Ethnic families in Southern California: Change and stability in multicultural settings, ch. J. Phinney. Western Psychological Association Annual Convention, Irvine, CA.

Phinney, J. (2003). Ethnic identity and acculturation. In K. Chun, P. Organista, & G. Marin (Eds.), *Acculturation: Advances in theory, measurement, and applied research* (pp. 63–81). Washington, DC: American Psychological Association.

Phinney, J. (2004). Cultural identity in college students. Unpublished manuscript, California State University, Los Angeles.

Phinney, J. & Alipuria, L. (1990). Ethnic identity in college students from four ethnic groups. *Journal of Adolescence, 13,* 171–184.

Phinney, J. & Alipuria, L. (in press). Multiple social categorization and identity among multiracial, multiethnic, and multicultural individuals: Processes and implications. In R. Crisp & M.Hewstone (Eds.), *Multiple social categorization: Processes, models, and applications.* Hove, Sussex, England: Psychology Press.

Phinney, J., Cantu, C., & Kurtz, D. (1997). Ethnic and American identity as predictors of self-esteem among African American, Latino, and White adolescents. *Journal of Youth and Adolescence, 26*, 165–185.

Phinney, J., Dennis, J., & Osorio, S. (in press). Motivations to attend college among college students from diverse ethnic and social class backgrounds. *Cultural Diversity and Ethnic Minority Psychology.*

Phinney, J. & Devich-Navarro, M. (1997). Variations in bicultural identification among African American and Mexican American adolescents. *Journal of Research on Adolescence, 7*, 3–32.

Phinney, J., Madden, T., & Santos, L. (1998). Psychological variables as predictors of perceived discrimination among minority and immigrant adolescents. *Journal of Applied Social Psychology, 28*, 937–993.

Phinney, J., Ong, A., & Madden, T. (2000). Cultural values and intergenerational value discrepancies in immigrant and non-immigrant families. *Child Development, 71*, 528–539.

Phinney, J. & Rosenthal, D. (1992). Ethnic identity formation in adolescence: Process, context, and outcome. In G. Adams, T. Gulotta, & R. Montemayor (Eds.), *Identity formation during adolescence* (pp. 145–172). Newbury Park, CA: Sage.

Phinney, J. & Tomiki, K. (2002). Perceived discrimination among minority students at a predominantly minority institution. Unpublished manuscript, California State University, Los Angeles.

Quintana, S. (1994). A model of ethnic perspective-taking ability applied to Mexican-American children and youth, *International Journal of Intercultural Relations, 18*, 419–118.

Quintana, S., Castaneda-English, P., & Ybarra, V. (1999), Role of perspective-taking abilities and ethnic socialization in development of adolescent ethnic identity. *Journal of Research on Adolescence, 9*, 161–184.

Renn, K. (2000). Patterns of situational identity among biracial and multiracial college students. *The Review of Higher Education, 23*, 399–420.

Rockquemore, K., & Brunsma, D. (2002). *Beyond Black: Biracial identity in America.* Thousand Oaks, CA: Sage.

Romero, I. (2001). A longitudinal study of ethnic identity among college students. Unpublished master's thesis, California State University, Los Angeles.

Root, M. (1996). The mulitracial experience: Racial borders as a significant frontier in race relations. In M. Root (Ed.), *The mulitracial experience: Racial borders as the new frontier* (pp. xiii–xxviii). Thousand Oaks, CA: Sage.

Stephen, J., Fraser, E., & Marcia, J. (1992). Moratorium-achievement (MAMA) cycles in lifespan identity development: Value orientations and reasoning system correlates. *Journal of Adolescence, 15*, 283–300.

Tatum, B. (1997). *"Why are all the Black kids sitting together in the cafeteria?" and other conversations about race.* New York: Basic Books.

Tseng, V. (2004). Family interdependence and academic adjustment in college: Youths from immigrant and US-born families. *Child Development, 75*, 966–983.

Umana-Taylor, A. (2003). Ethnic identity and self-esteem: Examining the role of social context. *Journal of Adolescence, 27*, 139–146.

5

Refusing and Resisting Sexual Identity Labels

RITCH SAVIN-WILLIAMS

For an issue in early 2004, the *Gay and Lesbian Review*, a scholarly journal, asked several senior gay statesmen to reflect on developments during the previous decade. Most sound unhappy with how things are going. Historian Martin Duberman feels compelled to castigate modern gay men and lesbians as wanting to be "just folks," to simply fit in. Rather, writes Duberman (2004), they should be demanding a radical analysis of contemporary culture. "Where is the Gay Liberation Front of 1970 now that we need it?" he asked (p. 22). Similarly, novelist Sarah Schulman (2004), a founder of the Lesbian Avengers, bemoans the lack of an activist movement among young people. Youth, she says, are being duped into conformity because they believe the media's representation of their lives.

But what if no duping has occurred and it's real? What if young people with same-sex desires are basically content with modern culture and don't desire a critical analysis? What if the media is reflecting, rather than manipulating, the reality of contemporary teens' lives? Maybe real changes in society's politics, laws, and consciousness toward gay people have raised the possibility that sexual orientation is or will soon be irrelevant in all important respects. Writer Michael Hattersley (2004) poses these possibilities, and others:

> What would it mean to be gay in a world in which the fact that a friend, sibling, aunt, or uncle was gay was about as relevant as her hair color? What are the implications of a world in which GLBT people have become familiar features in the family, the media, literature, and the political scene? Such a scenario would pose a serious challenge to the perpetuation of "gay politics," to say the least; less clear is what would happen to gay and lesbian literature, art, and popular culture. (p. 33)

This is what really frightens the gay movement's senior statesmen. The potential of leading a normal life is not what they want. Their romantic ideal is being transgressive, being the rebel. Hattersley wonders if this attitude is more self-destructive than noble.

> It can reflect self-hatred, legal difficulties, mental illness, suicide, family rejection, and thwarted love... Who can blame a persecuted and threatened people if they live for the day and seek immediate gratification, or burn to make something new, to survive, to thrive on being different? How would we define ourselves if that were no longer necessary? (p. 34)

In the same special edition, novelist Andrew Holleran (2004) also expresses doubts about the overriding significance of being gay. At a dinner with Harvard University students, he wondered, "What was our bond, after all?" Was it appropriate to be segregated at the "gay table?"

> Wasn't it better when a student belongs to the common culture? Could identity politics be a mistake? Just what is there in the space between two gay people who meet today? The same old same old, or something new? So why — the question I asked ten years ago — *did* we make so much of our homosexuality? (p. 12)

Today, fewer young people are making so much of their gayness, which is, according to Holleran, "virtually unrecognizable — evaporated, almost, into assimilation and cyberspace" (p. 12). This he finds to be not a source of celebration, but of resignation. But isn't this what gay activists have been supposedly working for during the past four decades — to be treated as equals, as individuals, to have our humanity rather than our sexuality valued? If the analysis in the *Gay and Lesbian Review* is true, we've been successful beyond our wildest dreams!

The Cultural Landscape

Debates about whether and how gay people are similar to or different from heterosexuals have gone on for decades (D'Emilio, 1983). If gay people are different, then is it a good different or a bad different? Are they creative, witty, and intelligent or promiscuous, immoral, and mentally ill? Should they identify loud and proud or blend in? Should they fight for political rights or seek social acceptance? It has long been argued whether gay people may, on the one hand, have a distinctive life course that reflects a deep sense of their "queerness," their sense of difference; or, on the other, whether they are basically similar to straight people — that is, whether they look and act like heterosexuals, value marriage and family like heterosexuals, have the same career aspirations, and hold the same mainstream values (D'Emilio, 1983; Savin-Williams

& Diamond, 1997, pp. 218–219). A differential developmental trajectories perspective allows that *both* notions are true *and* that remarkable diversity characterizes individuals with same-sex desire. They seek to adapt to mainstream culture even as they demand acceptance of their sexuality as normative and as they appreciate the increasingly gay quality of the culture.

This real-world complexity is muted among older commentators. The most vociferous among them take extreme positions. One prime example is the writer and activist Larry Kramer (1997), who rants against accommodating gays who he says are losing themselves in the massive, vanilla-heterosexual culture. In a *Rolling Stone* article, he argues that a concern about the fate of one's people should stand at the very center of a gay person's being. "We are a body of people, a nation of gays, a huge political group capable of exercising power!...We are the straight white man's slaves" (p. 70).

As a college student at Yale University, Larry Kramer (1997) recalls that he was "a pretty lonely young gay man...It has always been my dream that I'd leave what I could to insure that gay kids at Yale today would have a better time than I did." Naively buying into reports of high gay youth suicide, he reasons that through portrayals of the unique developmental experiences endured by gay youth, their suffering can be alleviated. Gay writers should write about gay people's lives, and universities should teach gay history. The goal? The development of a new gay culture. This, Kramer believes, is the way to "begin to escape this plague [suicide] that continues to kill off our children one by one" (pp. 67, 70).

Several other older gay writers agree with Kramer. Michelangelo Signorile (1999) rails against gay people who embrace political and social conservatism, and he is contemptuous of the "ex-gay," "too gay," and "postgay" movements that have "slithered onto the scene." Those who reject a gay identity are, according to Signorile, conforming to the dominant heterosexual culture in thought, values, looks, lifestyle, and political complacency (pp. 73, 75). Similarly, social critics Michael Bronski (1998) and Jeffrey Weeks (1995) warn about the perils of blending. Gay sex, they say, is central to being gay, to being different from straights, to forging gay identities.

Nothing could be more foreign to young people today than these senior perspectives. The vast majority of same-sex-attracted teens dismiss these extreme stands. Rather, they simultaneously highlight their commonalities with humanity while challenging, according to D'Emilio (1999), "the dehumanizing stereotypes that weigh heavily on our lives and target us for oppression" (p. 48). The culture of contemporary teenagers easily incorporates its homoerotic members. It's more than being gay-friendly. It's being gay-blind.

James Getzlaff, star of the 2003 television reality show Boy Meets Boy, reacts negatively to being tricked by the show's producers, who secretly included straight men pretending to be gay among the mix of fifteen men from whom he could choose a date. He says, "The last thing we need is to have anyone think of us as a joke or to make fun of us just for entertainment. We try so hard to put out a positive image as just normal people, looking for the same stuff everyone else is, and that's what I was hoping for" (quoted in Champagne, 2003).

Those responsible for the show contend that they support accommodation goals. Douglas Ross, the executive producer and co-director of *Boy Meets Boy*, says that he wants his "truly groundbreaking television" show to appeal to a broad audience. We anticipate a lot of both gay and straight viewers will have their assumptions challenged about what it means to be gay and what it means to be straight" (Reuters News Service, 2003) By exploring the sociology of male stereotypes, Ross says, the show promotes accommodation:

> [W]hat are we to make of these straight men who were willing to pretend they were gay and were comfortable enough with themselves to admit that they don't embody the perfect macho image of "straight"? It certainly suggests an evolution in the consciousness of some straight men; and it seems to me that the program did have the effect of shattering stereotypes for both gay and straight viewers. (quoted in Cohen, 2003)

So, too, other recent television shows with a youthful audience ease the separation between gay and straight. Some examples:

Queer Eye for the Straight Guy, according to reviewer Art Cohen (2003), is "about straight men seeking the advice of gay men, laughing with them, and wanting to be more like them" (p. 50).

The L Word presents women-loving women as totally enviable. The lesbians portrayed on this show tend to be beautiful, ambitious, modern women who have no work problems, zero percent body fat, blindingly white teeth, and constant sex, living in a glowing and delectable world (D'Erasmo, 2004).

In a recent episode of *South Park*, Butters confesses, "Now you know my terrible secret!" Stan reassures him, "You're gay? I don't mind you're gay. That's okay with me."

On the television show *Oliver Beene*, actor Taylor Emerson portrays Michael, an 11-year-old whose interests and mannerisms quite clearly characterize him as a future gay man (confirmed by a flash forward) (Goodridge, 2003).

MTV's Chicago edition of *Real World* features Aneesa and Chris, two attractive participants who are not straight (Epstein, 2002a).

On *Boston Public*, bisexual high school senior Jeremy Peters is reported to have had anal sex with another guy (Epstein, 2002b).

This perspective is readily apparent in many other aspects of young people's lives, all of which tell of a dramatic cultural shift. In sports, high school

honor student and varsity athlete Jason Fasi asks his teammates for signa-
tures in support of forming a Gay-Straight Alliance group at Mission Viejo,
California. They sign. No one beats him up, no one shies away from dressing
next to him, and no one heckles him (Shaikin, 2000). Two Ohio high school
heterosexual runners wear flashy rainbow socks, symbolic of gay pride, during a state track meet to show support for their two gay teammates (Shaikin,
2000).

In the movies, two "straight but spunky" girls decide to make their friendship more complete by testing out a lesbian relationship in *Kissing Jessica
Stein* (Stukin, 2002). Young *Harry Potter* actor Sean Biggerstaff receives a ton
of fan mail, not all from girls (Lynch, 2002).

A Kaiser Family Foundation and *Seventeen* magazine poll finds that the
proportion of 13- to 19-year-olds who "don't have any problem" with homosexuality more than triples, to 54%, during the 1990s (Shaikin, 2000). Two
Illinois girls are voted the school's "cutest couple" by their fellow high school
seniors (Irvine, 2002). Lesbian 19-year-old twin sisters, Tegan and Sara Quin,
tour North America performing songs from their new musical CD that promote tolerance and acceptance (Gdula, 2000).

Perhaps young people didn't notice that the newest version of the popular
computer game "The Sims" has gay characters (Dukowitz, 2003). Or that the
first baby born in the nation's capital in 2003 has two mothers, Helen Rubin
and Joanna Bare (Whoriskey, 2003). This younger generation is amused by the
invention of the "metrosexual," but they're surprised that a straight urban male
with enough feminine affinities and ambiguity in his sexuality to make him
attractive to both sexes creates such a stir (Flocker, 2003).

This shift is reflected in two articles in *Rolling Stone* magazine. Several
years ago a feature article, "To Be Young and Gay," recounted the growing
number of teenagers who were coming out of the closet and were finding peer
and family acceptance. The author, David Lipsky (1998), concludes that gay
adolescence is being redefined as a time of angst and struggle and is, a time
of pleasure, acceptance, and limitless possibilities. Three years later in the
same magazine, author Jay Dixit (2001) reports further refinement. Same-sex-
attracted students at Kramer's university no longer feel that "being gay" is a
primary aspect of their identity. Gayness has been "backgrounded," as indicated by the following quotes from Yale students Dixit (2001) talked with:

> A lot of people don't feel the need to foreground that part of their iden-
> tity. Most gay people spend the majority of their time outside of strictly gay
> situations.
>   There's a prevailing attitude of, because I'm gay, it doesn't mean that's
> my life. I'm not a "gay person," I'm a person who happens to be gay.
>   It makes it possible to just go about your daily life, rather than having
> to sit around reminding yourself that you're gay all the time, fighting for all
> these causes.

Rather than obsessing over their sexuality, these young adults are occupied with typical college pursuits, including sports, fraternities, and careers. One student observes that the "new gay Yalie dresses, talks, and acts no differently than his straight peers." The sex scene is similar to that of straights, with lots of hookups and few long-term romantic relationships. Few assert a gay identity or define themselves in relation to straight culture:

> No one really cares or objects to you if you're gay. In fact, making a big deal about being gay is seen as distasteful. The unwritten rule is, you can do whatever you want as long as you don't act like you're part of an embittered minority.
>
> It's sort of avoiding the "I'm here, I'm queer, and I'm pissed off" attitude, because that just turns everybody else off, especially because it's so unnecessary...many gay students actually shun activism.
>
> This is going to sound really terrible, but in order to improve their sex lives on campus, people actually try to avoid being labeled as activists. People who are out on the front lines are almost viewed as unpopular in a certain way. I'm not going to use the word stigma, because that's too harsh—but there is a sense of that. (Dixit, 2001)

Perhaps these "new gay" or "postgay" students would agree with novelist Armistead Maupin, author of the *Tales of the City* series, who believes that "the only way to lift the stigma of homosexuality is to be matter-of-fact about it." His stories are for everyone and about everyone, regardless of sexual status. Some characters are gay and others aren't. The goal is to normalize the existence of same-sex-attracted people. When asked why he writes about heterosexuals in San Francisco, Maupin refutes the notion that he is "shunning my identity. I want to be myself in the world at large, and that's a far more radical act than confining yourself to a single audience." He claims not to be a gay writer, but a writer who is gay (quoted in Minzesheimer, 2000, p. 2D).

Contemporary same-sex-attracted teens essentially agree with the Yalies and Maupin, and not with Kramer and Signorile. Writer bell hooks reminds us, however, of the difficulties faced by marginalized group members if they disagree with the "official position" of their group, such as Kramer and Signorile represent. Is there room for dissent? Although older gay adults may feel pressure to conform to group norms, and this may result in self-censorship and fear that their "minority dissent" will undermine group solidarity, younger people shrug off such pressure. Let the old, professional gays be eccentric, outrageous, and radical, think these members of the younger generation. The oldsters have already lost. Young people have little interest in subverting American civilization. It's the humanity of individuals with same-sex attractions that has won the hearts and minds of middle America (Bawer, 1993) Besides, young people never joined up to be members of a marginalized gay group in the first place.

Why Haven't Teens Signed Up?

What has caused this radical generational shift from "gay and proud" to "adolescent and proud"? How prevalent is the transformation? What is the difference between same-sex-oriented adolescents who question and identify from those who don't — or between heterosexual adolescents who question and identify as straight from those who don't? What are the factors that determine this? Is it personal experiences? Strength of libido? Does gender matter? How about cohort? How may we best understand the extent to which this indifference to being gay is a healthy outcome? Should teens be encouraged to identify as gay?

I'd like to answer these questions, but I can't. From the information we do have, the information presented in this book, I do know several things. First, adolescents, regardless of sexual orientation, vary in the degree to which sexuality is a core component of their identity. But what makes an individual's sexuality more or less central is baffling. Perhaps it is the degree to which an adolescent feels sexually distinct from the mainstream. A butch girl might centralize a sexual identity because she has encountered unbearable teasing for her supposed lesbianism. Or perhaps the strength of an adolescent's sex drive determines the significance of sexuality for personal identity. An early or particularly significant erotic experience or infatuation might influence the potency of sexual identity. Perhaps it depends on whether the adolescent lives in a home or a community or a time in which sexuality is robust and omnipresent. Maybe the young person has a lesbian aunt or a gay uncle, or other siblings have identified as gay, or friends have come out, and that has influenced the person's degree of gay identity.

Second, adolescents with same-sex desire are not the only ones to question their sexuality, to explore what their sexuality means for their identity. Nor do all adolescents question their sexuality or seek to establish a sexual identity. Sexual orientation per se is not a factor, except to the degree that the individual and the society at large choose to make it one — and this has often been the case, for obvious reasons, given the assumption of universal heterosexuality. Moreover, when we talk only with those for whom sexuality is an important and influential aspect of who they are, those who are doing least well with their sexuality, we won't wind up with an accurate picture. Of course these individuals would make much of their sexual identity.

Third, though it is true that an individual's "unorthodox" sexuality may, for reasons alluded to above, result in that person's focusing more on sexual identity than a heterosexual person might, it does not necessarily follow that the full extent of a person's behaviors, perceptions, cognitions, and social interactions is influenced by that sexuality. Maybe young gay men as a group are more drawn than straight men to occupations such as interior decorator and flight attendant and are less interested in occupations, such as auto mechanics and athletics. Maybe young gay women are more drawn to carpentry and auto mechanics and are less interested in becoming a beauty consultant or fashion model than their straight sisters. The fact is, relatively few same-sex-attracted adolescents actually pursue (or avoid) these occupations (Lippa, 2000). Sexuality can be an important factor in determining career choice, but only for a few. Physical and mental assets, personality, family pressure, and social opportunities are of far greater significance in career choice — for adolescents of all sexual persuasions.

Fourth, despite the speculations of some clinicians, the idea that it is healthy for an adolescent to identify with a sexuality has not been proved. Clinicians are fond of assuming that not adopting a label is unhealthy, that it may be an indication of possible psychological problems (Fergusson, Horwood, & Beautrais, 1999; Meyer, 2003). An individual's reluctance to embrace a sexual identity, they say, suggests that the person is in denial, afraid to confront his or her sexual reality. Yet how do we square this view with the overwhelming evidence — produced by these same clinicians — of alarmingly high levels of depression, substance abuse, dangerous sexual activities, and suicidality among those young people who self-identify as gay (Savin-Williams, 1994)? Is it possible that self-identifying gay youth are more unhealthy than non-identified same-sex-attracted young adults?

I believe this is entirely possible. Some gay teens come out "loud and proud" as an act of self-affirmation, and some non-identified same-sex-attracted young people are in hiding for self-destructive reasons. But it is also true that some declare their sexuality as a cry for help from horrific circumstances and that others are psychologically healthy because they have bases for self-definition other than sexuality that are more developmentally appropriate.

Is it possible that our advice to same-sex-attracted young people has been wrong, and that perhaps we should be encouraging them not to identify as gay? Right-wing politicians and ministers advocate this position — but they want more. They want adolescents to give up their same-sex sexuality. In this they are naive, because giving up ones sexuality is impossible to do.

As millions of teens are demonstrating, it's possible not to identify oneself sexually and still embrace one's sexuality. The inclination to shun "being gay" can be an adaptive strategy for emotional survival during hostile times and in dangerous environments. Or not identifying can be indicative of a self-loving and wise adolescent. Or perhaps the motivation to self-identify or not has little to do with one's mental health. Gay identity can be indicative of both good and bad mental health.

In these matters, teens with same-sex desire might well mimic heterosexual teens. The fact is, it's a completely individual matter. For Alex, it's his core; sexual identity defines his personal identity. Alex lives in Chicago's

Boys Town, is majoring in gay studies with the intent of becoming an attorney who adjudicates same-sex discrimination cases, and writes angry letters to the national gay magazine *The Advocate* because their cover features hot *straight* actors. By attending the Chicago-based youth group Horizons, Alex discovered as a 15-year-old "what I needed for myself, that there were other gay people and that gay was not just a phase and that there were older role models." Gay Pride marches, radio interviews, statements to the press — Alex describes himself as a "professional faggot. I'm as queer as they get and proud of it." (Savin-Williams, unpublished interview).

In contrast to Alex, Jen tells me that her sexual identity is simply one facet of her core identity and that it has little to do with other aspects of her life. She occasionally attends a meeting of her high school's Gay-Straight Alliance to demonstrate her support for sexual diversity. Only within the last year has she revisited her sexuality.

> Just recently I've put some attention to it. Haven't before because school was occupying my time. Just not enough time because I have a boyfriend. This past summer he was out of the country and I had lots of time and one day I noticed I had undiagnosed strong feelings — I was crying all the time.
>
> This hasn't been easy because I was the first person lots of people told. As a straight ally, I went to Pride Festivals several times, wore supportive ally buttons, but did not attribute anything to myself (Savin-Williams, in preparation)

Jen is considering double-dating Lisa with two gay male friends at her high school prom. She prefers not to be so out, however, if it would injure her college applications.

Thomas's sexual identity went unrecognized until he was in college. Then he developed a chaotic, passionate relationship with his roommate.

> I wanted desperately to be straight, and the label implied some level of commitment. I dated females and realized that I was attracted to females and so I thought of myself as straight. I sort of let all of this go for awhile and then in the early months of my sophomore year I realized that my feelings for guys must mean something, and it must mean that I'm bisexual. Or maybe what I was, was just sexual.
>
> I've lived with it as if it were a part of me but not that it was real important...I don't want to go out and just have sex, but I want to find emotional attractiveness with males like I have with females. Now I know that I prefer males, though I'm probably more bi than most gays. (Savin-Williams, 1998a, p. 135)

At the time of the interview, Thomas told me he is engaged and that he plans to marry a woman because it offers what he most wants — an emotional, intimate relationship.

For Sheena, sexual identity is not what she's into — although she loves questioning and thinking about her sexual attractions. When asked she'll say, "I guess I'm heterosexual with lesbian tendencies!" She continues,

> If given the right situation and if given a chance, I'd definitely try it, the physical part that is. Friendships with women are so intense, co-dependent-like. I recognized this last week. Always before I had looked the other way, but now I'm willing to consider.
>
> This year has really opened me up, sexually speaking. My best friend came out to me as heterosexual with lesbian tendencies. We were at a party and wasted and she wanted me to French kiss her on the mouth so I did and it was so soft. Sober she'd never do it, but I would. I definitely need my quality girl-time!
>
> So what does this mean? I'm equally attracted to males and females. If, like, I come into a room, I see both the beautiful guys and girls. So I guess I'm 50/50. I see particular qualities in women and this attracts me. I'd love to spend the rest of my life with my best friend. I look at girls the way I look at boys. It's not fair that I can't find boys like her! (Savin-Williams, in preparation)

Sheena admits that these issues are interesting, but she finds that they usually fade to insignificance next to more relevant concerns in her life.

Any idea that adolescent same-sex sexuality is all the same, or that it has predetermined developmental trajectories and consequences, is belied by the life narratives of contemporary teenagers. Their sexuality is but one facet of an interactive system that makes up their lives (Steinberg, 1995). Any presumption that teens have identical developmental pathways because they share a same sex sexuality or that their sexuality is equally important to various teens' sense of self is not only implausible, it is a gross misrepresentation of their lives. The notion of there being a single gay identity or lifestyle is, in short, absurd, especially to adolescents.

To overcome our prevailing misperceptions, we must demystify sexuality and see it as a valid developmental topic, not a clinical risk factor. Sexual development should be seen as a legitimate, growth-promoting, and core aspect of what it means to be an adolescent (Savin-Williams & Diamond, 2004). At the same time, we must understand that the extent to which sexuality defines identity spans from all-important (it is what I am) to a mere biological fact.

Refusing a Label

A recent survey of a Massachusetts high school revealed that over 11% of the students ascribed to themselves at least one aspect of homoeroticism. Seldom, however, did they report having sex with someone of the same gender or identifying as gay. Fewer than 3% were willing to assume a gay or bisexual label (Orenstein, 2001). In a California high school, 6% reported that they "know that I am homosexual or bisexual" and an additional 13% said that they frequently or sometimes wonder if they are homosexual (Lock & Steiner, 1999).

Naming sexuality as a means to stamp a personal and positive understanding to a life narrative is a relatively recent development. Identifying as gay first became prevalent among those who came of age in the 1970s and 1980s (Chauncey, 1994) As Gil Herdt and Andy Boxer (1993) put it, people who gave themselves such an identification signified "living with their desires, not in hiding and alienation, but out in the public, in the light of social day — leading to adaptation and greater creative fulfillment than they could have imagined at the beginning of the process" (p. 202).

Although some young people today might also get these advantages from identifying as gay, perhaps especially if they live in secluded, conservative regions of the country, many others object to self-labeling. Some find their sexuality to be more fluid than that permitted by constructed models of sexual identity. Some have notions of what a gay person looks like, acts like, and believes — and it's not them. They cannot or do not want to attribute these features to themselves. Some are philosophically opposed to the idea of placing their sexuality into "identity boxes." To them, the mere creation of sexual categories reifies the labels across time and place and exaggerates differences that don't exist (Muehlenhard, 2000). Some young people give themselves an uncommon or unrecognized label (e.g., two-spirit) or one that encompasses multiple identities (e.g., bi-lesbian). Many simply find the labels an annoyance. One young woman told me:

> I felt there just was no need for labels, so I didn't tell anyone. But when I was in tenth [grade] I got interested in this other girl and we were in a romantic relationship. Then I began to define myself differently, more definitely, that it was more real. I just thought labeling was silly, but then people began to ask me for a label. To calm them I said bisexual.
>
> I had wanted to be friends with this girl and then I became more and more interested and then a crush developed. This did not change my self-concept... What I wanted to say was that I simply was just in a relationship with a woman. People asked because most of my friends were involved in the gay community and most of my friends were lesbian or gay. (Savin-Williams, in preparation)

In her work with young people, Beatrice Green (1998) observes adolescents who engage in same-sex behavior and yet "refuse the politics of sexual identity, arguing that these are the issues of the older generation. They claim the right to love and have sex with whomever and in any way they want." She refers to them as the "new Act Up generation" and speculates that although they might threaten both the gay and the straight establishment, "they may be the future in a post-identity politics society" (p. 91). I agree.

These young people are repudiating the appropriateness and artificiality of dichotomous definitions of sexual identity as they challenge cultural definitions of gay lives. Gay and straight categories may have been fine for their parents, but not for them. Youth culture is permeated by nuance, especially with regard to sexuality. Sexual behavior and sexual orientation flow within various gender expressions and changing definitions of what is gay, bisexual, and straight. If pushed, they might agree to vague terms such as "queer" or "not straight." Their preference is to not call themselves, or their futures, anything at all. They refuse to label themselves because they wish to separate sexual desire from the friction of politics. One person who was interviewed for a popular article on the "polymorphous normal" asserted that sexuality is not about politics but about pleasure and happiness. Another eschewed identity categories because "my experience is continuous. It's not compartmentalized into poetry and sexuality and rational thought. We confuse the map with the territory" (D'Erasmo, 2001, p.106).

Some of these young people have been called "queer," defined by anthropologist Melinda Kanner (2003) as individuals intent on "destabilizing conventional categories, subverting the identities derived from and normalized by heteropatriarchy. Queerness defies binary and fixed categories such as homo-/heterosexual, female/male, even lesbian/gay. Queerness, in both social performance and in lived identities, interrupts both convention and expectations" (p. 34). Most teens, however, do not think of themselves as queer or appreciate the word. They simply reject the potentially life-altering repercussions of such a label.

Their rejection of label designations is motivated by many things — for philosophical reasons, because the labels seem irrelevant and uncharacteristic, in an attempt to avoid homophobia, or because the label is simply felt to be inaccurate. Some may believe that their current attraction or relationship is a "special" one, an aberration that implies little about them or their sexuality. Others fear the consequences of being gay and so remain unlabeled and closeted, perhaps coming out later in their lives. We know little about these non-identified teens, but we know they exist.

In a 2001 interview, actor and filmmaker Jason Gould was asked about being gay, coming out, and disclosing his sexuality to his famous parents, Barbra Streisand and Elliott Gould. Jason, who recalled having his first "gay impulse" at age eight, says that he has not come out as gay because he has never said to himself, "Oh, I'm gay." He denies living a closeted life or being ashamed of who he is. "I'm pretty comfortable with my sexuality," he says, adding,

> You know, the more I understand my own sexuality the more I...I mean I don't mind being called gay, because I'm certainly attracted to men. But I also think that it's limiting. I think that within the gay community — and as a member of the gay community — it's limiting for us to stereotype ourselves. Attraction is more complex than the terms gay, straight, and bisexual. And I hope that eventually people will evolve into accepting a broader understanding of attraction. (Bahr, 2001, pp. 74, 70, 72)

Gould's refusal to declare a sexual identity is apparently not a function of internalized homophobia or self-hatred or fear. He has declared his sexuality — he is attracted to men; he simply finds the term "gay" an inadequate descriptor of his sexuality.

Jason Gould is not alone. Comedian Rosie O'Donnell doesn't appreciate the adjective "gay" permanently attached to her name. Being attracted to other women, she says, was never a "big deal for me" (Bauder, 2002, p. 42). Sophia of MTV's *Road Rules* downplays her sexuality: "It's not a big deal to me because I don't make it a big deal...It's just part of who I am" (Champagne, 2001).

The balkanization of sexuality, according to one writer, is especially prevalent among artists, students, cultural explorers, and young women. They prefer an alternative, self-generated identity label or no label at all rather than those typically offered in research investigations (Hillier et al., 1998, p. 26; D'Erasmo, 2001, pp. 104, 106.) Two of these groups, young women and cultural explorers, in particular have not been well served by standard sexual taxonomies (D'Erasmo, 2001.)

Young Women and Fluidity

Inflexible, distinct boundaries rarely apply to young women's sexuality (Rodriguez Rust, 2001, 2002; Rothblum, 2000). A young woman's most enjoyable sexual fantasies might be of other women while her most enjoyable sex is with men — or vice versa. Young women are more likely than young men to incorporate partners of both sexes in their behavior and fantasies. When shown explicit sex films, lesbians and heterosexual women do not differ in their subjective and genital arousal to either male-female or female-female sex scenes (Laan, Sonderman, & Janssen, 1996), and the highest arousal for both groups of women is to heterosexual sex scenes. In their research, Meredith Chivers and her colleagues suggest that women, regardless of sexual orientation, have a "nonspecific" pattern of sexual arousal (Chivers, Rieger, Latty, & Bailey, 2004). That is, although heterosexual college women might say that they prefer heterosexual over female-female and male-male erotica, their actual genital arousal to sex scenes indicates no significant preference of male-female over female-female scenes. They prefer and become more aroused by female-female than male-male sex scenes. By contrast, gay and heterosexual men show a strong preferred-sex ("categorical") pattern. Gay men are more aroused by male–male than male–female scenes, and heterosexual men are more aroused by male-female scenes, although heterosexual men react most strongly to female-female erotica. Perhaps as a result, women are less apt to be stigmatized for engaging in same-sex behavior (Pattatucci & Hamer, 1995; Rodriguez Rust, 2000, 2001; Rothblum, 2000; Schneider, 2001; Weinberg, Williams, & Pryor, 1994).

In eighth grade Stephanie and Lolita were best friends. Stephanie recalled that

> Lolita would sleep over a lot and one night she was talking about her boy-friend Juan and talking about sex. I was pretending to know more than I did. We had been very affectionate, like most girlfriends. I asked her how he kissed her, and so she kissed me like her Juan did. This was quite a shocker. From then on we kissed a lot when we got together, and began touching and caressing. To make it "okay," one of us would be the boy. Was penetration with our fingers but never oral sex. She's straight as far as I know.
>   Never talked about it. I can't tell what Lolita is, but I was the only girl she did anything with. We never said we were lesbians. I kind of knew that it was not right, but it felt okay. Mom caught us in bed and this was a big uproar. We had gotten together every day after school for six to seven months but Mom made that more difficult.

Stephanie's attitude was that her experience with her friend was just a kid experience. Lots of peers were having sex, only with guys, so having sex was not unusual (Savin-Williams, in preparation).

Once a young woman recognizes that she's not totally straight, there is lit-tle guarantee that she'll declare herself to be lesbian or bisexual. In an attempt to identify "authentic" lesbians, researchers have traditionally relied on what they believe has worked for identifying gay young men: the achievement of developmental milestones. But, as we have seen, such models won't distin-guish lesbians who maintain their lesbian identity over time from those who don't. It is more informative to examine patterns of attraction and behavior (Diamond, 2003, p. 360).

Over the course of 8 years, nearly two-thirds of the young women Lisa Diamond interviewed changed identity labels at least once, often because "sexual identity categories failed to represent the vast diversity of sexual and romantic feelings they were capable of experiencing for female and male part-ners under different circumstances" (Tolman & Diamond, 2001, p. 61). Some of these women expressed their ambivalence by viewing their sexuality as fluid. Love depends on the person, they told her, not the gender of the person.

Those women Diamond studied who relinquished their lesbian or bisexual identity for a heterosexual or an unlabeled status had similar developmental his-tories. What differed was their interpretation of their sexual experiences. The women who would not be labeled described their sexuality as fluid and expressed uncertainty about their future sex lives. Those who changed to a heterosexual label had lower levels of same-sex attractions and behavior throughout the study than did the other women. A heterosexual identification was, for them, a viable solution to the "problem" of their nonexclusive attractions and behavior.

Relinquishing a sexual identity label, however, did not mean that these women relinquished their same-sex sexuality. Their same-sex attractions and behavior were real, not a phase. All maintained that they might identify as lesbian or bisexual in the future. Diamond (2003a) noted that

> [t]hese findings are consistent with the notion that identity relinquishment does not represent a fundamental change in sexual orientation itself, but rather a change in how women interpret and act upon their sexual orientation....Nonexclusivity and plasticity in women's attractions and behaviors potentiate multiple transitions in identification and behavior over the life course. (pp. 361–362)

In short, attempts to fit an adolescent girl's "complex, highly contextualized experiences of same-sex and other-sex sexuality into cookie-cutter molds of 'gay,' 'straight,' and (only recently) 'bisexual'" are doomed to failure (Tolman & Diamond, 2001, p. 61.) The exception of these young women to follow sexual identity models of identity progression simply reflects the complexity of their lives.

Cultural Explorers and Alien Notions

A similar disconnect between orthodoxy and life histories is evident for young people in non-U.S. cultures and subcultures within the United States. In reviewing the cross-cultural evidence, Fernando Luiz Cardoso and Dennis Werner (2004) conclude, "People vary tremendously in their same-sex behaviors, in their sexual desires, and in the ways they define themselves. Cultures also differ widely in the ways they define and treat these relationships and the people who engage in them" (p. 204) Western definitions of sexuality are viewed as exceedingly rigid. For example, as one writer notes, in some communities "same-sex relationships are defined between individuals and may involve sexuality, eroticism, and very intensive friendships and emotions. Men can therefore hold hands in public or sleep naked in the same bed together." One Iranian remarks that in his culture labels for sexuality are relatively rare (Scalia, 2003, p. 204).

It is not difficult to find cross-cultural examples of a homoerotic life that are not identified as such. One has been referred to as "Mediterranean homosexuality." In a culture with this type of sexuality, according to Inaki Tofino (2003), a gay activist in Catalonia, there is a "large zone of liberty for homoerotic activity between males, but no such thing as a 'homosexual identity' as such." The sexes are often separated during adolescence and young adulthood; homoerotic friendships, alliances, and physical contact are not uncommon. A person's identity (for both men and women) is not usually defined by what one does sexually or who one falls in love with. To do so would be to deny the more legitimate cultural prescriptions for identification based on religion, region, or ethnicity. To "come out as gay" makes little sense in such a culture. To attach a gay persona "in every situation is an alien notion" and can often be problematic when sex is not part of the public discourse (p. 18).

Tofino argues that Western notions of a public or private gay identity that one carries from one situation to the next are not necessary for large-scale cultural changes to take place. For example, in Spain few identify as gay; yet sexual orientation is a category that enjoys broad protections in that country's Penal Code, which acknowledges same-sex couples and provides gays with protection against hate crimes.

An example within the United States of how a gay identity has been subverted is described in a recent New York Times Magazine article. Author Benoit Denizet-Lewis (2003) explores the world of African American young adult men who have sex and romantic relationships with men and who are forging an "exuberant new identity" based not on their sexuality but their skin color and culture.

> Rejecting a gay culture they perceive as white and effeminate, many black men have settled on a new identity, with its own vocabulary and customs and its own name: Down Low . . . [T]he creation of an organized, underground subculture largely made up of black men who otherwise live straight lives is a phenomenon of the last decade. . . . Most DL men identify themselves not as gay or bisexual but first and foremost as black. To them, as to many blacks, that equates to being inherently masculine. (p. 30)

A DL identity signifies a virulent rejection of a gay identity associated with "drag queens or sissies." One 18-year-old whom Denizet-Lewis spoke with clearly wants this separation. "Gays are the faggots who dress, talk and act like girls," he said. "That's not me." These men acknowledge the sexuality in their lives, but being DL is not perceived as merely another sexual identity label. It is about "being who you are, but keeping your business to yourself" (p. 31). It is a selection of ethnic affinity over sexuality and masculinity over femininity.

The majority of young people of both sexes with same-sex desire resist and refuse to identify as gay. We know little about them because they usually opt out of research, educational programs, and support groups. Their desire is not to stand out "like a semen stain on a blue dress," but to be as boring as the next person, to buy an SUV and to fade into the fabric of American life (Bergman, 2004, p. 17).

Ordinary Jane, Ordinary Joe

In the previous chapter [of Savin-Williams, 2005], I discussed the nascent movement underway to change our preoccupation with deficit models to one that acknowledges the resiliency of gay teens. Although I generally applaud this change — a resiliency script is certainly preferable to a suicidal one — I believe it too is ultimately flawed, for it simply substitutes one universal, over-wrought characterization for another. The reality is that both at-risk and resil-ient gay teens are minor players among the symphony of the same-sex attracted. Most are no more or less resilient or healthy than their straight friends. Most remain, well, ordinary as they negotiate routine and uneventful lives.

An alternative perspective, one I believe is closer to the truth, is to rec-ognize not only the positive features of being "different from the norm" but also the ordinariness of most young people with same-sex desire. Resistance to this notion is stiff, perhaps less from popular culture than from the world of scholarship and academia, which is blinded to the existence of the ordinary because of the biases inherent in typical survey questions. As the previous chapters have made clear, not all adolescents who experience same-sex desire identify as gay or engage in same-sex activities. Not all adolescents who iden-tify as gay have a same-sex orientation or engage in same-sex behavior. Not all adolescents who have sex with their own gender identify as gay or have same-sex attractions. Scholarship that neglects these facts seldom finds "hid-den" populations who have one or two of these features but not all three. Or who have all three, but to varying degrees.

If the "nongay majority with homosexual feelings" group of adolescents could be found (McConaghy, 1999, p. 296), what might be discovered is not their exceptionality but their normal adolescent concerns. Lisa Diamond (2003) notes that adolescents with same-sex desires ruminate far more about "love and romance than about suicide, hate crimes, or homelessness, and they currently have nowhere to turn with their concerns" (p. 86). Love does not dis-criminate based on sexual orientation or the object of ones infatuation. Con-sider the following quotes — first, from Catherine Deneuve:

> But to be in love with a man or a woman, it's the same thing; it has to do with giving and listening and being very open to someone, so it does not make much difference. (Duralde, 2002b, p. 53)

And next, from Dennis Quaid:

> We're attracted to whomever we're attracted to. We can't help loving the people we love, and we can't help being attracted to what we're attracted to. (Duralde, 2002a, p. 44)

One needn't identify as gay or engage in same-sex behavior to fall in love with another girl or boy. Indeed, most same-sex lovers do not claim a gay identity. The most accurate, albeit not breathtaking, conclusion is that sexual orientation dictates some of the essence of what it means to be alive, but not everything.

Thus, to understand same-sex-oriented teens we must first understand adolescence in general. Too frequently our investigations ignore the vast theoretical and empirical literature on adolescence in favor of methodologically flawed gay research. Conversely, rarely is it suggested that scholarship on gay youth can add to a general understanding of adolescent development.

Consider John Gottman and his colleagues' (2003a, 2003b) recent research on same-sex relationships. Placing their investigation within the larger context of research on couples generally, the team found the following:

1. Similar to heterosexual couples, same-sex couples' expressions of contempt, disgust, and defensiveness are associated with a decrease in relationship satisfaction; humor and affection, to high relationship satisfaction.
2. In situations of conflict, same-sex couples are less belligerent, domineering, and tense and display greater concern with equity, humor, affection, and joy than heterosexual couples. Whereas heterosexual couples often display detachment in times of conflict, same-sex couples become more emotionally and mentally involved and engaged.
3. Within the relationship, lesbians are more likely than gay males to overtly display their affection for each other (emotional expressiveness); gay males are more likely to verbally validate each other. These differences are consistent with sex differences among heterosexuals.

In speculating about these differences, Gottman and his team (2003b) note that same-sex couples are more likely to value equality and to be more positive toward each other. The inherent status differential between men and women in heterosexual relationships, which "breeds hostility, particularly from women, who tend to have less power than men, and who also typically bring up most of the relationship issues," is largely absent in same-sex couples. According to the authors, "Because there are fewer barriers to leaving homosexual compared to heterosexual relationships, homosexual couples may be more careful in the way they accept influence from one another. Thus, we suggest that the process variables by which they resolve conflicts may be the very glue that keeps these relationships stable" (p. 88). In other words, same-sex couples have something to teach heterosexual couples about respect, equity, and stability.

These dual responsibilities of research on same-sex-attracted young people — rooting research hypotheses and interpretations within the larger context of adolescent development and translating results in terms of how they extend knowledge about adolescence in general — are routinely ignored. It is as if no one has ever conducted research on school achievement, peer harassment, self-esteem, romantic relationships, or family relations prior to our particular investigation of these issues with gay youth.

Given these shortcomings, there should be little wonder that gay teens are believed to experience meaningfully different life trajectories from heterosexual teens. To Middle America, gay teens are arrogant aliens from another culture, at the margins of society with multiple body piercings, purple hair, and pointedly non-Abercrombie and Fitch clothing; to gay adults, they are supposed to be the next generation of political activists who will fight for gay rights and against heterosexism, racism, sexism, and classism.

These young people, however, are neither our enlightened heirs nor our prodigal descendants. Sexual diversity is becoming normalized, and the gay–straight divide is becoming blurred. Straight teens are acting, looking, and becoming gayish, and an expansive array of non-straight teens is becoming visible. These young people are more apt to say things like "Why won't my parents let me go to the concert?" and "If I take chemistry, how will that affect my grade point average?" than "I'm gay, I'm gay, oh my, what am I going to do?"

This is not to deny that some are ridiculed because of their gender expression. Or that they cannot openly date those they love most because same-sex dating in high school is still difficult for most. Or that they feel they must keep something of themselves secret from their parents and friends. But same-sex-attracted teenagers are not the only young people facing these kinds of problems. Disabled kids, above- and below-average-intelligence kids, unattractive kids, overweight kids, and ethnic-minority kids are also ridiculed. Many teens from these groups do not date the person they desire because they feel that the desired person is "unreachable." Many have profound secrets they do not tell their parents or friends, such as those relating to pregnancy, substance use, nontraditional sexual longings, and psychic beliefs. So why should the life experiences of same-sex-attracted teens only be of such singular significance that they are seen as being unable to cope with their problems and incapable of leading happy, productive lives?

We see gay *adults* as being able to lead happy, healthy, and productive lives; they are said not to differ from heterosexuals in psychological adjustment (DiPlacido, 1998, pp. 139, 148; see also Meyer, 2003; Sandfort, 1997). We could also see young people this way. Same-sex-attracted young people want to join and become involved in the heterosexual world of their fellow teenagers. A previous generation established "gay proms" — first in Detroit and later in Los Angeles — as a means to build support, pride, and social change. Nowadays, the inclination is to have same-sex couples attend regular high school proms. This is the far greater revolution. It normalizes same-sex sexuality in a way that was not possible when only separate gay proms welcomed same-sex couples (Levey, 2002).

Nothing I have stated in this book justifies neglect of gay young people who suffer and entertain thoughts of suicide because of their sexuality. I am willing to believe that this reality *might* have been more characteristic of earlier generations than it is today But whatever motivation might prompt us to sensationalize the fate of gay teens or represent them as heroic survivors, it's not scientifically valid now, and it was not scientifically valid in years past.

Both the national and the gay press misrepresent most gay teens and deliver a risky message to those wondering if they might be gay. Consider the following headlines from various publications over the past several years:

Dying to Be a Boy Scout? (*The Advocate*, June 19, 2001, p. 15)
Suicidal Tendencies: Is Anguish over Sexual Orientation Causing Gay and Lesbian Teens to Kill Themselves? (*The Advocate*, April 5, 1994, p. 35)
Gay Youths' Deadly Despair (*Washington Post*, October, 24, 1988, p. A1)
Robbie's Story: How a Fragile 14-Year-Old Boy Was Crushed in His Struggle to Accept Being Gay (*Cleveland Plain Dealer*, April 6, 1997)
"I Couldn't Have Saved Him the Rest of His Life" (*Texas Triangle*, July 21, 1993)
Bad Days for Gay Teenagers (*Raleigh News and Observer*, June 30, 2000, p. 1)
The Hidden Plague (*Out*, July 2001).

Scholarship must rise above such "doom and gloom" caricature, and present the larger context of teenagers' lives.

Why is there such profound resistance to the normalization of same-sex-attracted young people? Why is the focus on the outliers rather than the majority? Here are four (bad) reasons:

1. Because the positive and healthy lives of typical contemporary gay teenagers contradict the tumultuous and painful adolescence of gay scholars and policy makers.
2. Because well-adjusted gay teens present problems for those applying for problem-focused research grants and for the need, as one critic put it, to "manufacture victims for the psychology industry" (Dineen, 1996).
3. Because otherwise today's teens would not fully appreciate what researchers, educators, mental health professionals, and activists did for them to allow them to live their lives without fear. How can this "gift" be thrown away so cavalierly?
4. Because today's young people are harbingers of a time in which sexual identity will have no importance, thus thrusting past research into the garbage heap of antiquated science, making it nothing more than a curiosity for historians and anthropologists.

New gay teenagers disdain sexual categories, and they believe, as Michael Bronski (1998) writes, "that some of 'us' have more in common with some of 'them' than we have with each other.... Within all of these identities are some who are as mainstream as can be, and some who march to their own drummer" (pp. 48–49). It might be wise to listen to their voices and appreciate the reasons they reject the notion of being identified by their sexuality. Led by contemporary young women who are trading in the labels "lesbian" and "bisexual" for descriptors that better reflect their reality, new gay teens are simply trying to live within the flux of adolescence (Tolman & Diamond, 2001, p. 61). Their lives, as Jeffrey Weeks (1995) observes, provide "continuous possibilities for invention and reinvention, open processes through which change can happen" (p. 44). Some assimilate, and some accommodate. Some embrace gayness, and some refuse it. It's just that the old categories of gay and lesbian don't fit anymore (Alexander, 1999, p. 289).

Banality

The fact is, the lives of most same-sex-attracted teenagers are not exceptional either in their pathology or their resiliency. Rather, they are ordinary. Gay adolescents have the same developmental concerns, assets, and liabilities as heterosexual adolescents. This unnoteworthy banality might well be their greatest asset. It suggests that they are in the forefront of what can be called a postgay era, in which same-sex-attracted individuals can pursue diverse personal and political goals, whether they be a desire to blend into mainstream society or a fight to radically restructure modern discourse about sexuality.

It is my fervent hope that what is being achieved in the real world can be achieved in scholarship. I hope to see the elimination of same-sex sexuality as *a* defining characteristic of adolescents in my lifetime. If it can be relegated to insignificance, the lives of millions of teens will be dramatically improved.

I give the final word to "Andrew James," (1999) a college student who concluded his essay "In Search of Ordinary Joes" with a simple goal: "Raising the profile of banal homosexuals... It's not going to be fabulous, it's not going to be cutting edge, but I think its got to be the next wave of the gay movement."

References

Alexander, J. (1999). Introduction to the special issue: Queer values, beyond identity. *Journal of Gay, Lesbian, and Bisexual Identity, 4*, 287–292.

Bahr, D. (2001, January 16). This boy's life. *The Advocate*, 68–75.

Bauder, D. (2002, March 27). Rosie O'Donnell says being gay was "never a big deal for me." *Newsweekly*, 11/31, 42.

Bawer, B. (1993). *A place at the table: The gay individual in American society*. New York: Poseidon Press.

Bergman, D. (2004). Please pass the pepper. *The Gay and Lesbian Review, 11*, 17–19.

Bronski, M. (1998). *The pleasure principle: Sex, backlash, and the struggle for gay freedom*. New York: St. Martin's Press.

Cardoso, F L. & Werner, D. (2004), Homosexuality. In C. R. Ember & M. Ember (Eds.), *Encyclopedia of sex and gender: Men and women in the world's cultures, Vol. 1* (pp. 204–215), New York: Kluwer Academic/ Plenum.

Champagne, C. (2001, August). On the road. *Out*, 30.

Champagne, C. (2003, September 4). "Gaywatch: The dish from James of "Boy Meets Boy." Retrieved from www.planetout.com/entertainment/news/splash.

Chauncey, G. (1994). *Gay New York: Gender, urban culture, and the making of the gay male world, 1890–1940.* New York: Basic Books.

Chivers, M. L., Rieger, G., Latty, E., & Bailey, J. M. (2004). A sex difference in the specificity of sexual arousal. *Psychological Science, 15*, 736–744.

Cohen, A. (2003). Eyes on the guys: Gay men's turn on TV. *Gay and Lesbian Review, 10*, 50.

D'Emilio, J. (1983). *Sexual politics, sexual communities: The making of a homosexual minority in the United States, 1940–1970.* Chicago: University of Chicago Press.

D'Emilio, J. (1999). The gaying of America. *Harvard Gay and Lesbian Review, 6,* 48–49.

Denizet-Lewis, B. (2003, August 3). Double lives on the down low. *New York Times Magazine,* 28–33, 48, 52–53.

D'Erasmo, S. (2001, October 14). Polymorphous normal: Has sexual identity — gay, straight or bi — outlived its usefulness? *New York Times Magazine,* 104–107.

D'Erasmo, S. (2004, January 11). Lesbians on TV: It's not easy being seen. *New York Times,* Arts & Leisure, p. 1.

Diamond, L. M. (2003). Was it a phase? Young women's relinquishment of lesbian/ bisexual identities over a five-year period. *Journal of Personality and Social Psychology, 84*, 352–364.

Dineen, T. (1996). *Manufacturing victims: What the psychology industry is doing to people.* Montreal: Robert Davies.

DiPlacido, J. (1998). Minority stress among lesbians, gay men, and bisexuals: A consequence of heterosexism, homophobia, and stigmatization. In G. M. Herek (Ed.), *Psychological perspectives on lesbian and gay issues: Vol. 4. Stigma and sexual orientation: Understanding prejudice against lesbians, gay men, and bisexuals* (pp. 138–159), Thousand Oaks, CA: Sage.

Dixit, J. (2001, October 11). To be gay at Yale. *Rolling Stone.* Retrieved from www. rollingstone.com/features/college/article.asp?id=7.

Duberman, M. (2004). The unmaking of a movement. *Gay and Lesbian Review, 11,* 22–23.

Dukowitz, G. (2003, February 4., Virtually gay. *The Advocate*, 21.

Duralde, A. (2002a, October 29). A man's man. *The Advocate*, 44–48.

Duralde, A. (2002b, October 29). Belle toujours. *The Advocate*, 53–54.

Epstein, J. (2002a, January). Sensitive souls. *Out*, 38–44.

Epstein, J. (2002b, May). Boston Public sex. *Out*, pp. 30–32.

Fergusson, D. M., Horwood, L. J., & Beautrais, A. L. (1999). Is sexual orientation related to mental health problems and suicidality in young people? *Archives of General Psychiatry, 56*, 876–880.

Flocker, M. (2003). *The metrosexual guide to style: A handbook for the modern man.* Cambridge, MA: DaCapo Press.

Gdula, S. (2000, November 21). Double the power. *The Advocate*, 80.

Goodridge, M. (2003, April 1). Pre-Stonewall preteen. *The Advocate*, 52.

Gottman, J. M., Levenson, R. W., Gross, J., Frederickson, B. L., McCoy, K., Rosenthal, L., Ruef, A., &. Yoshimoto, D. (2003a). Observing gay, lesbian and heterosexual couples' relationships: Mathematical modeling of conflict interaction. *Journal of Homosexuality*, *45*, 23–43.

Gottman, J. M., Levenson, R. W., Swanson, C., Swanson, K., Tyson, R., & Yoshimoto, D. (2003b). Observing gay, lesbian and heterosexual couples' relationships: Mathematical modeling of conflict interaction. *Journal of Homosexuality*, *45*, 65–91.

Green, B. C. (1998), Thinking about students who do not identify as gay, lesbian, or bisexual, but...*Journal of American College Health*, *47*, 89–91.

Hattersley, M. (2004, January–February). Will success spoil gay culture? *Gay and Lesbian Review*, *11*, 33–34.

Herdt, G., & Boxer, A. M. (1993). Children of Horizons: *How gay and lesbian teens are leading a new way out of the closet.* Boston: Beacon Press.

Hillier, L., Dempsey, D., Harrison, L., Beale, L. Matthews, L., & Rosenthal, D.(1998). *Writing themselves in: A national report on the sexuality, health and well-being of same-sex attracted young people. Monograph series 7.* Australian Research Centre in Sex, Health and Society, National Centre in HIV Social Research, La Trobe University, Carlton, Australia.

Holleran, A. (2004, January-February). The day after. *Gay and Lesbian Review*, *11*, 12–16.

Irvine, M. (2002, December 16). Two Illinois girls voted high school's "cutest couple." *Ithaca Journal*, 9.

James, A. (1999). In search of ordinary Joes. *McGill News*, 52.

Kanner, M. (2003). Can Will & Grace be "queered"? *Gay and Lesbian Review*, *10*, 34–35.

Kramer, L. (1997, May 27), Sex and sensibility. *The Advocate*, *59*, 64–65, 67–70.

Laan, E., Sonderman, M., & Janssen, E. (1996). Straight and lesbian women's sexual responses to straight and lesbian erotica: No sexual orientation effects. Paper presented at the annual meeting of the International Academy of Sex Research, Rotterdam, The Netherlands, June.

Levey, B. (2002, June 14). Gays at the prom: Less of an issue than ever. *Washington Post*, Cll.

Lippa, R. A. (2000). Gender-related traits in gay men, lesbian women, and heterosexual men and women: The virtual identity of homosexual–heterosexual diagnosticity and gender diagnosticity. *Journal of Personality*, *68*, 899–926.

Lipsky, D. (1998, August 6). To be young and gay. *Rolling Stone*, 55–65, 80, 82–85.

Lock, J., & Steiner, H. (1999). Gay, lesbian, and bisexual youth risks for emotional, physical, and social problems: Results from a community-based survey. *Journal of the American Academy of Child and Adolescent Psychiatry*, *38*, 297–304.

Lynch, L. (2002, February 15–17). Questions. *USA Weekend*, 2.

McConaghy, N. (1999). Unresolved issues in scientific sexology. *Archives of Sexual Behavior*, *28*, 285–318.

Meyer, I. H. (2003). Prejudice, social stress, and mental health in lesbian, gay, and bisexual populations: Conceptual issues and research evidence. *Psychological Bulletin*, *129*, 674–697.

Minzesheimer, B. (2000, September 14). "Listener" tells tales from Maupin's life. *USA Today*, 1D–2D.

Muehlenhard, C. L. (2000). Categories and sexuality. *Journal of Sex Research*, *37*,101–107.

Orenstein, A. (2001). Substance use among gay and lesbian adolescents. *Journal of Homosexuality*, *41*, 1–15.

Pattatucci, A. M. L. & Hamer, D. H. (1995), Development and familiality of sexual orientation in females. *Behavior Genetics*, *25*, 407–420.

Reuters News Service (2003, May 27). Bravo to keep gay reality date. Retrieved from www.reuters.com.

Rodriguez Rust, P. C. R. (2000). *Bisexuality in the United States: A social science reader.* New York: Columbia University Press.

Rodriguez Rust, P. C. (2001). Two many and not enough: The meanings of bi-sexual identities. *Journal of Bisexuality*, *1*, 31–68.

Rodriguez Rust, P. C. R. (2002). Bisexuality: The state of the union. *Annual Review of Sex Research*, *13*, 180–240.

Rothblum, E. D. (2000), Sexual orientation and sex in women's lives: Conceptual and methodological issues. *Journal of Social Issues*, *56*, 193–204.

Sandfort, T. G. M. (1997). Sampling male homosexuality. In J. Bancroft (Ed.), *Researching sexual behavior: Methodological issues* (pp. 261–275), Bloomington: Indiana University Press.

Savin-Williams, R. C. (1994). Verbal and physical abuse as stressors in the lives of sexual minority youth: Associations with school problems, running away, substance abuse, prostitution, and suicide. *Journal of Consulting and Clinical Psychology*, *62*, 261–269.

Savin-Williams, R. C. (1998). "…and then I became gay": Young men's stories. New York: Routledge.

Savin-Williams, R. C. (in preparation). "…and then I kissed her": Young women's stories.

Savin-Williams, R. C. & Diamond, L. M. (1997). Sexual orientation as a developmental context for lesbians, gays, and bisexuals: Biological perspectives. In N. L. Segal, G. E. Weisfeld, & C. Weisfeld (Eds.), *Uniting psychology and biology: Integrative perspectives on human development* (pp. 217–238), Washington, DC: American Psychological Association.

Savin-Williams, R. C. & Diamond, L. M. (2004). Sex. In R. M. Lerner & L. Steinberg (Eds.), *Handbook of adolescent psychology* (2nd ed.) (pp. 189–231), New York: Wiley.

Scalia, R. (2003, September 27). When roots, sexuality clash. *Montreal Gazette*, E1–E3.

Schneider, M. S. (2001). Toward a reconceptualization of the coming-out process for adolescent females. In A. R. D'Augelli & C. J. Patterson (Eds.), *Lesbian, gay, and bisexual identities and youth: Psychological perspectives* (pp. 71–96), New York: Oxford University Press.

Schulman, S. (2004). What became of "freedom summer"? *Gay and Lesbian Review*, *11*, 20–21.

Shaikin, B. (2000, September 18). Coming out to face the team. *Los Angeles Times*. Retrieved from www.newsdesk@channelq.com.

Signorile, M. (1999, January 19). Ex-gay Too gay Postgay What happened to gay? *The Advocate*, 71, 73, 75, 77, 81.

Steinberg, L. (1995). Commentary: On developmental pathways and social contexts in adolescence. In L. J. Crockett & A. C. Crouter (Eds.), *Pathways through adolescence: Individual development in relation to social contexts* (pp. 245–253). Mahwah, NJ: Erlbaum.

Stukin, S. (2002, March 19). How the other half laughs. *The Advocate*, 52–53.

Tofino, I. (2003, May–June), Spain and the Mediterranean model." *Gay and Lesbian Review, 10*, 17–18.

Tolman, D. L. & Diamond, L. M. (2001). Desegregating sexuality research: Cultural and biological perspectives on gender and desire. *Annual Review of Sex Research, 12*, 33–74.

Weeks, J. (1995). History, desire, and identities. In R. Parker & J. H. Gagnon (Eds.), *Conceiving sexuality: Approaches to sex research in a postmodern world* (pp. 33–50). London: Routledge.

Weinberg, M. S., Williams, C. J., & Pryor, D. W. (1994), Dual attraction: Understanding bisexuality. New York: Oxford University Press.

Whoriskey, P. (2003, January 2), First D.C. baby of '03 has two moms. *Washington Post*, 10.

6

Identity and Marginality
Issues in the Treatment of Biracial Adolescents

JEWELLE TAYLOR GIBBS

Since the early 1960s there has been a steady increase in the number of inter-racial marriages and relationships, probably due to a combination of several significant social forces — including the civil rights movement, the counter-culture movement, and the women's movement — which resulted in more liberal social attitudes toward race relations, sexual mores, and the status of women. While the proportion of interracial marriages between blacks and whites is still quite small, the actual number of such unions has increased from 65,000 in 1970 to 164,000 in 1983, an increase of 150% (National, 1985). For over two decades these marriages have produced biracial children, many of whom are now adolescents and young adults, located primarily in urban areas in the East, the Midwest, and the West Coast (Childrens, 1984).

It has been estimated that there are approximately one million interra-cial children in the U.S. While the number of offspring of black-white mar-riages is not known, it can be safely stated that they represent a fairly recent phenomenon in American society, i.e., a group of mixed-race young people who resist simple racial classification and who have legitimate claims to both majority and minority social castes (*Newsweek*, 1984). Their dual racial iden-tity can pose dilemmas for these adolescents in developing a cohesive, well-integrated self-concept (Childrens, 1984; *Children's Advocate*, 1986). Biracial adolescents are still not highly visible in the society and there is not a large body of literature about them. Most of the relevant theoretical, empirical, and clinical studies can be briefly summarized.

Erikson (1950/1963) proposed that the central task of adolescence is to form a stable identity, which he described as "a sense of personal sameness and historical continuity." Along with other ego-psychologists, he delineated a series of developmental tasks to be negotiated in the development of a healthy

From: *American Journal of Orthopsychiatry*, 57, 1987, pp. 265–278. Copy-right © American Psychological Association. Reprinted with permission.

and positive identity. These tasks include the development of a personal identity (sense of uniqueness and self-esteem), the establishment of a sense of autonomy and independence from parents, the ability to relate to same-sex and opposite-sex peers, and the commitment to a vocational choice (Marcia, 1980).

Several authors have pointed out that identity formation for black adolescents may be a more difficult and problematic task, particularly in view of the messages they receive from the dominant society that they are members of a disadvantaged and devalued minority group (Erikson, 1959; Gibbs, 1974; Jenkins, 1982; Pierce, 1968). Chestang (1984) noted that blacks must integrate a "personal" and a "racial" identity in order to form a cohesive total identity.

If identity formation is more problematic for black than for white adolescents, then one can hypothesize that it would be even more difficult for adolescents with a biracial background. Several authors have pointed out the issues inherent in a dual racial or cultural identity (Ladner, 1977; Lyles, Yancey, Grace, & Carter, 1985; Sebring, 1985; Sommers, 1964; Teicher, 1968).

Hauser (1972), in his study of identity development among black and white male adolescents, used empirical measures to identify five distinctive patterns of identity formation: progressive identity development, identity diffusion, identity foreclosure, negative identity, and psychosocial moratorium. Although the sample was small (22) and nonrandom, he found that the black and white boys had different patterns of development, with blacks more likely than whites to demonstrate "identity foreclosure" and "negative identity."

Few empirical studies of biracial adolescents in community settings have been published, but there is some evidence that this group faces a particularly difficult task in developing positive identities in terms of their racial identification. In an ethnographic study of mixed-race families in London, Benson (1981) found that nearly all the children and adolescents ($N = 27$, ages 3 to 16) rejected their black identity verbally, behaviorally, or through social identification with white peers.

In a related area, empirical studies of biracial children indicate that their racial attitudes and self-concepts develop differently from those of either black or white children (Gunthorpe, 1978; Payne, 1977). One study found that accurate perception and acceptance of biracial status decreased as skin color darkened, suggesting a relationship to a more negative self-concept among the darker children. However, other studies have found that biracial children had equivalent or higher levels of self-esteem as compared to their non-mixed peers (Chang, 1974; Jacobs, 1978).

In a clinical study of biracial children begun in the late 1960s at Los Angeles County Hospital, Teicher (1968) proposed a series of hypotheses about this population: 1. children would identify with the parent perceived as less socially depreciated; 2. problems of sexual identity would occur with greater frequency among children whose same-sexed parent is markedly different from them in racial characteristics; 3. problems of sexual identity would also occur with greater frequency among children who themselves depreciate the racial characteristics of the same-sexed parent or who perceive that the opposite-sexed parent depreciates the child's or the spouse's racial characteristics; 4. the greater the child's problem of racial identification, the greater the problem of sexual identification; 5. biracial children have fewer problems of racial identity if they live in a community of mixed marriages than if they live in a predominantly white or black community.

In my own 1986 survey of 50 social service, mental health, special education, and probation agencies located in the San Francisco Bay Area, a preliminary analysis of the results indicates that, of the 31 responding agencies, 71% served minority youth and their families and that in the past 10 years referrals of biracial adolescents had increased. Sixty percent (22) of these agencies reported that this latter group was over-represented among their adolescent client population.

These biracial teens must integrate identifications with parents from two racial backgrounds while simultaneously negotiating their own social status in their peer group, learning how to deal with their sexuality, and making a commitment to school or work. If they have supportive families and supportive social networks, then they will probably master these tasks successfully, though more slowly than adolescents of either race (Childrens, 1984; *Children's Advocate*, 1986).

Conversely, those teens who have difficulty in negotiating this identity process are likely to be seen in child welfare, mental health, and juvenile probation settings as they exhibit psychological and behavioral problems associated with severe identity crises. Three sources of clinical information suggest that this group may have unique problems and needs. First, a study of high-risk youth and parents conducted by a San Francisco youth advocacy agency found that 24.9% of the youths were interracial and that this group reported higher rates of victimization than all other ethnic groups (Window, 1983).

Second, several studies of small samples of biracial youth and their families in agency and community settings point out the salience of identity conflicts for the adolescents and their parents, who themselves are often in conflict about these issues and give mixed messages to their children (Faulkner, 1985; Faulkner & Kich, 1983; Lyles et al., 1985; McRoy, Zurcher, Landerdale, & Anderson, 1982). The third and final source of clinical data is from my own professional experience as a clinician, teacher, and supervisor. In these multiple roles I have noted a steady increase over the past 15 years in the number of referrals of biracial children and adolescents for psychological evaluation and treatment from public and private agencies, in the number of case presentations by social work graduate students, and in the number of case consultations requested by youth-serving agencies, all resulting from emotional and behavioral problems in this particular group.

Finally, articles in the mass media have portrayed these families as socially marginal and discussed the implications of marginality on the children's identity (*Detroit*, 1985; *Newsweek*, 1984). These articles often point out that interracial families tend to seek out communities which are more tolerant of diversity and to develop social networks with other interracial families in an effort to erect a protective barrier against potential negative responses and rejection by both ethnic groups.

In spite of the problematic findings from clinical samples of biracial adolescents, other data based on surveys of well-functioning biracial young adults and personal accounts of biracial adults suggest that many make a positive adjustment and are successful in achieving their goals (Childrens, 1984; *Children's Advocate*, 1986; Houstin-Hamilton, personal communication, 1986; Poussaint, 1984). For example, Poussaint's study of a small nonrandom sample of biracial Harvard University students found that, as a group, they were psychologically well-adjusted, very competent, and very comfortable with their biracial identity.

Thus, it seems appropriate to take a closer look at this unique population of adolescents in an effort to increase our understanding of their needs more effectively. It is important to remember, however, that this paper specifically addresses the issues of biracial adolescents who have been referred to social service and mental health agencies, so the sample is not drawn from a "normative" population, nor from a single community. Implications for clinical treatment of these adolescents will be discussed at the conclusion of the paper.

This paper has four goals: 1) to identify the major conflicts and coping mechanisms in the maturation of biracial adolescents; 2) to analyze the relationship between these conflicts and the developmental tasks of adolescence in an ego-psychology theoretical framework; 3) to delineate clinical and sociocultural issues in the assessment and diagnosis of this group; and 4) to propose specific treatment techniques that have proven effective with these adolescents.

The data and conclusions presented here are based on the author's 15 years of clinical experience with biracial (black and white) adolescents and college students in a variety of mental health settings in the San Francisco Bay Area, including two college mental health clinics, private practice, supervision, and consultation. The clinical material is drawn from intensive case studies of 12 biracial youth, eight females and four males, ranging in age from 13 to 19, and in educational level from eighth grade to the second year of college. Case examples will be used to illustrate the issues in assessment, and the themes and techniques in treatment.

The clinical material has been supplemented by the author's empirical studies of normal and delinquent female adolescents, some of whom were of mixed racial backgrounds (Gibbs, 1974, 1982, 1984). The findings from the empirical studies have also contributed to a broader base for the conceptual scheme of adolescent developmental tasks and a deeper understanding of the various forms of adaptive and maladaptive coping behavior and defensive strategies utilized by adolescents in their attempts to master these tasks.

Conflicts

During their treatment, these biracial adolescents were found to be in conflict about their dual racial and sociocultural heritage, their social marginality, their sexuality and choice of sexual partners, their autonomy and dependency on their parents, and their educational and career aspirations. The nature of these conflicts, the behavioral symptoms associated with them, and the defensive strategies and coping mechanisms employed to deal with them are described below.

Racial Identity

This is the core conflict for these adolescents who describe themselves variously as "half and half," "Heinz's 57 varieties," and "Oreos." The basic question in this area is: "Who am I?" In these cases there has been a partial or complete failure to integrate both racial heritages into a cohesive sense of racial identity. The more frequent tendency is to overidentify with the parent who is perceived as the most similar in terms of physical features, particularly in terms of skin color; the adolescent prefers that parent's racial group and incorporates the perceived attributes of that group. There are also cases where the teenager identifies with the white parent as the symbol of the dominant majority, rejecting the black parent even if there is a closer physical resemblance. Many of these adolescents express ambivalent feelings toward the racial backgrounds of both parents, alternately denigrating and praising the perceived attributes of both races. There are also sex differences in patterns of adjustment, but they are not always consistent or predictable, as hypothesized by Teicher (1968).

Some of the teenagers, particularly the girls, feel ashamed of their black physical features such as dark skin, curly hair, or broad facial features. They reject identification with black culture as it is expressed in the music, dance, and dress style of black teenagers in their schools and neighborhoods. They have incorporated negative attitudes and stereotypes about blacks and try to distance themselves from them in school and social situations.

In cases where teens have overidentified with the black parent, the similar phenomenon of rejecting white culture and white people is played out. This overidentification may take the form of adopting attitudes, behavior, and styles of dress associated with lower-class black culture rather than those associated with a middle-class black life-style. Since many of the biracial adolescents seen in treatment are from middle-class families, such behavior is not only quite dissonant with the family life-style but also tends to result in a negative identity formation, particularly among boys. That is, the negative identity is associated with the dissonant and devalued social status of lower class black culture, which is neither reflective of nor congruent with the reality of these teens' social status and life experiences. This phenomenon supports Hauser's (1972) findings on negative identity development among black male adolescents.

Case 1

Thirteen-year-old Marcia, born out of wedlock to a white mother and black father, was referred by her white adoptive parents because of rebellious behavior, truancy, and stealing from family members. The parents also suspected she was sexually active and using drugs. In individual sessions, Marcia, who had very light skin but negroid facial features and hair, spoke of always feeling inferior to her younger sister (also adopted) who was part Asian and who, Marcia said, had always been favored by the adoptive parents. Her behavioral problems surfaced when she entered junior high school and felt she didn't belong with any of the cliques, was rejected by former white neighborhood friends, and drifted into a group of "dopers" who were alienated from school and society. In family sessions it was clear that Marcia had assumed the role of the "bad child," identifying with the negative stories she had been told about her black father who had been imprisoned for drugs and burglary, and playing out an unspoken script to fulfill the negative expectations communicated to her by her parents. Marcia tried to resolve her racial identity conflict through assuming a negative identity and seeking out deviant peers whose antisocial behavior reinforced that identity. By "acting just like my Dad," Marcia was identifying with her natural black parent while also punishing her adoptive white parents for their ambivalence toward her "blackness."

Social Marginality

Although this conflict is inextricably related to the core identity conflict, it can be assessed as a separate problem. The basic question in this area for all of these biracial teens is: "Where do I fit?" This question is especially salient as they enter early adolescence and begin to participate in heterosexual social and extracurricular activities. During this phase of development, when peer groups begin to assume a much greater significance in shaping attitudes and behavior, teens are particularly vulnerable to anxieties about social acceptance (Coleman, 1980).

Biracial children who may have had a closely knit peer group and satisfying social relationships in elementary school, often experience social problems on entering junior high or high school. Typically, girls seem to experience more anxiety about social acceptance, based on the realistic perception that they begin to be excluded from same-sex slumber parties, ski trips, and boy–girl parties which begin in seventh or eighth grade. They also report that they are often excluded from the high-status social cliques and from sororities, and are not selected for cheerleading squads or other socially prestigious, extracurricular school activities. As these girls enter high school, their fears of social rejection increase as they realize that the white boys who are often perceived as the most attractive and desirable are not usually interested in dating them because of the powerful proscriptions against interracial dating in most communities. Thus, the earlier security of childhood social life is progressively threatened until, by midadolescence, the children realize the need to redefine their social status and renegotiate their social relationships.

This process of redefinition and renegotiation can be both painful and challenging. The task is to identify peers who accept one's uniqueness as a person, who validate one's personal identity, who are not uncomfortable with or fascinated by one's biracial identity, and who are supportive in interpersonal and social situations.

In a phase of life where conformity is expected and valued, these teens are often rejected by both majority and minority groups because they fit neither in terms of physical appearance, family background, and loyalty to a specific teen subculture.

Case 2

Jill, a 19-year-old daughter of a white mother and black father, was from a well-to-do Eastern family. After growing up in a white neighborhood and attending an exclusive prep school, she enrolled in a West Coast university for a "change of scenery." Her first year was difficult because she preferred to socialize with the white students from similar backgrounds and felt that the black students were very hostile to her. After an unsuccessful affair with an older white male who physically abused her, she became very depressed and stopped going to classes. She was brought into the student mental health clinic by her roommate after she took an overdose of sleeping pills. While she was hospitalized for several days, Jill confided to the therapist that she felt as if she had a foot in two worlds but couldn't stand on both feet in either one. She was very angry with her parents "for treating me like I was white and not preparing me for the real world as a black person."

Sexuality

This conflict emerges in tandem with the conflicts of racial identity and social marginality. The basic question in this area is: "What is my sexual role?" This conflict finds expression in several ways, i.e., in issues of sexual orientation, gender identity, choice of sexual partners, and patterns of sexual activity.

The general identity confusion of biracial adolescents seems to extend to ambiguities about gender identity or sexual orientation in some of these clients. Thus, females may exhibit very masculine mannerisms in speech, dress, and behavior long beyond the normal "tomboy" stage, or males may be quite effeminate and engage in activities such as shopping with their mothers and gossiping with female friends. These blurred gender roles are usually more exaggerated than the androgynous identity assumed by many counter-culture youth and often result in social exclusion from same-sex peers.

Sexual orientation is also an issue with some of these teens, perhaps as a result of their failure to make appropriate sex-role identifications during the oedipal phase of development. Sexual orientation seemed to be more conflictual in cases where the adolescent felt very negative toward the parent of the same sex who was also the minority parent, as Teicher (1968) predicted. Thus, boys with black fathers and girls with black mothers with whom their relationships were predominantly hostile were more likely to report confusion or conflicts in the areas of sexual identity and sexual orientation than were teens with black parents of the opposite sex.

Choice of sexual partners and patterns of sexual activity are also highly charged issues for these teens. As a consequence of their social marginality, many of them, especially the females, perceive their dating options to be limited to other minority adolescents, a group toward when they are often ambivalent and from which they frequently feel alienated. Biracial females tend to experience greater anxiety in this area because they feel unable to take the initiative in the dating situation, while the boys perceive that they have a wider selection of girls from a variety of racial backgrounds.

Patterns of sexual activity also tend to be an "all or none" situation. Those biracial teens who have assumed a militant black identity report higher levels of sexual activity and occasional promiscuity, as if they were fulfilling a stereotyped role of the earthy, sensual black female or macho, exploitative black male. Alternatively, those teens who have overidentified with their white heritage are less likely to be sexually active, and more likely to describe sex as "repulsive or disgusting," and be highly invested in a puritanical moral code, as if they were reacting against those same stereotypes of black sexuality.

Case 3

Laura, a 15-year-old born to a black mother and white father, was reared for 7 years by her maternal grandmother after her parents divorced when she was 6 years old. She reported that she had been "treated like a stepchild" and sexually assaulted by two maternal uncles, and that her maternal aunts were very ambivalent toward her, often teasing her about her light skin. At age 13 she was reunited with her mother and black stepfather because her grandmother couldn't manage her any longer.

After arriving in San Francisco, she became friendly with a group of "punkers," cut and dyed her hair in rainbow colors, and ran away from home on several occasions. She was referred by a school counselor who was concerned about her increasing truancy, drug use, and masculinized appearance. In treatment she expressed negative feelings toward her mother "for marrying a black man," bragged about looking "like a Latino," and complained that she couldn't get along with "these stupid black kids." In discussing her sexual activities, she said she really didn't like boys because they only wanted to get girls pregnant, but sometimes she felt strongly attracted to girls and couldn't handle the thought of being a lesbian. Laura's aversion to males apparently stemmed from the sexual victimization she had experienced in relationships with her uncles (and her stepfather), all of whom were black. Thus, for Laura, heterosexual activity was negatively associated with black males while the relatively happy recent period in her life involved supportive and exciting relationships with white females. Her basic failure to make a positive identification with any of the black females in her family contributed to a confused sexual identity, making it difficult for her to commit herself fully to either a heterosexual or homosexual orientation.

Autonomy

This conflict is an exaggerated version of the normative adolescent separation-individuation conflict over the balance between autonomy and dependency in parent-teen relationships. The basic question in this area is: "Who is in charge of my life?"

These teenagers seem particularly vulnerable to external assaults on their self-esteem, so their parents often have a tendency to be overprotective and to try to shelter their teenagers from the pain and prejudice which they anticipate for them. The teenagers respond either by becoming overly dependent on their parents and using home as a haven of refuge and security against the mixed signals of society, or by rebelling against parental protection and seeking premature freedom from all parental control.

These contrasting responses are expressed in a variety of ways. Those adolescents who prolong their dependency are usually also more immature physically and socially. They are more obedient, more conforming, and more passive in their relationships with adults and peers. On the other hand, they appear clinically to be more depressed or emotionally constricted and do not seem to be handling the task of separation very effectively, apparently accepting the parental message that they need protection from a potentially hostile society.

Among those adolescents testing the limits of autonomy, there is an overt posture of pseudo-sophistication and maturity. Their behavior at home and in other situations is more assertive, more confrontational, and more risk-oriented. They engage more frequently in delinquent behavior, report more problems in school and more conflicts with parents, siblings, and peers. They appear to be challenging society to acknowledge and validate them, refusing to accept parental discipline or protection.

Case 4

Maria, an 18-year-old daughter of a black mother and white father lived with both parents until she graduated from high school. She had been a "model child," a very good student, had a very close supportive relationship with her mother, but thought her father was hypercritical. She began to have problems soon after she went away to college, where she felt lonely and socially isolated. She had always been slightly overweight, so she began to diet and exercise vigorously hoping that it would make her more attractive and self-confident. She was referred to the college mental health clinic by her dormitory resident who suspected she had an eating disorder. Maria was very depressed, felt she couldn't handle all the demands of the college environment, and asked for a medical leave to drop out of school. When she was encouraged to talk about her feelings, she explained that she had felt "special" at home and didn't have much social life outside her family, so she was unprepared for the freedom of college and couldn't seem to fit in with either the whites or the blacks. She said, "When I'm with the white students, I think like a black person and when I'm with the black students, I think like a white person."

Aspirations

This conflict stems from ambivalence about achievement and upward mobility felt by many of these adolescents. The basic question in this area is: "Where am I going?" Those biracial teens who have overidentified with their version of black ghetto culture adopt a casual attitude toward their studies, express anti-achievement values, and fear rejection by their black peers if they are perceived as "bookworms" or "nerds." Some become involved in truancy, deliberately fail their courses, and express consistently negative attitudes toward school. For those teens who identify with the white middle-class culture, educational achievement is consistent with their peers, including an emphasis on academic competition and aspirations for a college education. In fact, academic achievement may be one area in which they excel in order to prove that they are as smart as their white peers. In the clinical setting, the more typical pattern is nonachievement, negative attitudes toward school, and unclear or unrealistic career aspirations.

In several cases, teens who have very poor records in school announce plans to attend highly competitive colleges and do not seem to see the connection between their current behavior and future options. In still other cases, mostly male, they express cynicism about college education and the possibil-itity of ever obtaining a high status job in the future, even if their fathers have such positions. The majority of these teens seem to be well aware of racial prejudice and barriers to mobility and shape their current academic behavior and future aspirations accordingly.

Case 5

David, a 17-year-old-high school senior, was the son of a German American woman and a black soldier. He had grown up on Army bases in Europe until he moved to the States to complete high school. David had attended base schools with children from many nationalities and he thought of himself as a "military brat." While he was a good student, he particularly enjoyed athletics and tried out for several teams in his U.S. high school. His teammates were friendly at school, but rarely included him when they went out on weekends after games. White girls rejected his overtures to date and he gradually withdrew and lost interest in school. His parents encouraged him to apply to college, but he said he couldn't make up his mind about what he wanted to study. When his coun-selor referred him for treatment, he was apathetic and refused to talk. After a few sessions, he confided that he always felt more "white than black" because he spoke German and had very light skin. He said he didn't like living in the United States because "you have to choose to be something you would rather not be." He didn't want to go to college at this point because "most black people don't go to college and, anyway, nobody expects me to set the world on fire." While David's uprooting in high school may have been dis-tressing to him, he seemed more disturbed by having to conform to the role of a "black teenager" in his new milieu. Since his father and uncles were not college graduates, David could identify with their working-class orientation while simultaneously responding to the subtle messages of his high school counselor that college was an unrealistic goal for him. This strategy also per-mitted him to rationalize his academic underachievement and to substitute activities that made him feel more comfortable with his non-college-bound black classmates.

Case 6

Greg, a 16-year-old, was the only child of a black mother and white father who separated soon after his birth. Greg had a very unstable childhood, moving constantly with his mother who was an alcoholic and a borderline personality. He was finally placed in foster care and lived in a series of foster homes for four years. He was referred for psychological evaluation after a period of low school achievement, frequent psychsomatic complaints, difficulties in relating to his peers, and feelings of depression. Greg was initially resistant, but gradu-ally revealed that he didn't like himself very much, didn't care about school, and didn't care about the future. He expressed the feeling that he would never find a niche in society because "blacks think I'm too white and whites think that I'm too black." He felt he was going to grow up to be a "basket case" just like his mother or a "drifter" like his father, so he didn't see any reason to go to school or "to play by society's rules."

Defenses and Coping Strategies

The preceding case presentations have described the focal conflict presented by these biracial adolescents as the primary issue for treatment. It is important to emphasize that all these clients reported conflicts in several of the dimensions of identity development, but one area was usually more painful or more immediately accessible to insight than others.

The defense mechanisms and coping strategies employed by these adolescents to deal with their multiple conflicts may be maladaptive or adaptive, depending on their context and the function they serve in the adolescent's overall psychological adjustment. Many of the behavioral strategies are aimed at protecting their feelings of low self-esteem and warding off the anxiety associated with their feelings of identity diffusion. Thus, in order to cope with their conflicts over racial identity and social marginality, they use defense mechanisms of denial (e.g., "I am not black, I'm mixed"), reaction formation (e.g., "I don't like to hang around with the black kids at school because they always segregate themselves"), and overidentification with the idealized racial group (e.g., "I prefer to go to white parties"). In some cases, what may appear to be a defense mechanism is in fact a realistic response to an ambiguous or difficult social situation, for example, when biracial teens feel that they are more comfortable with others who have similar mixed backgrounds or when they prefer to resist peer pressure and associate with a group with similar interests regardless of racial divisions in their school or neighborhood. It is the function and flexibility of the behavior rather than its manifest content that is crucial in determining its adaptive significance.

Their fears of social rejection may result in social withdrawal as "loners" or in overconformity to group norms. In their attempts to be accepted by a group, they are especially vulnerable to peer pressure in the areas of drugs and delinquent behavior, which they may subconsciously perceive as the price they must pay for group membership and social acceptance.

In order to cope with their sexual identity conflicts, they tend to employ two contrasting sets of defense mechanisms and behavior. On the one hand, some use either a pattern of repression (e.g., asceticism and lack of any interest in sexual activity) or sublimation (e.g., excessive involvement in sports or extracurricular activities); others act out their sexual impulses with promiscuous relationships and, in a few instances, experimentation with homosexuality, bisexuality, or prostitution.

In order to cope with their conflicts between autonomy and dependency, they also exhibit contrasting defenses. Some of these teens use reversal or regression to deal with their anxieties about separation from their parents. In the former instance, they behave in a pseudomature manner, adopting a stance of precocious independence from parental supervision and reversing the parent-child roles in many areas (e.g., verbally abusing parents and rejecting parental rules and values). This mode seems to occur more frequently in single-parent homes and adoptive homes where the teenager is defending against fears of abandonment in a problematic or unstable family situation.

For those teens who employ regression as a defense, excessive dependency emerges, and they appear to be extending childhood behavior and attitudes (e.g., allowing parents to select clothes and friends). In families where parents have been extremely overprotective of their children in order to shield them from negative social responses, teens may want to prolong the resulting feeling of security by delaying their psychological and social separation from their parents.

Finally, these biracial teens use rationalization and projection or intellectualization and identification with the aggressor to cope with their conflicts over educational and career goals. Those teens who use rationalization (e.g., "I'm not going to waste my time studying because I probably won't be able to get a good job anyway") or projection (e.g., "None of the teachers like me because I'm different") are more likely to be underachievers. They are also more likely to be negatively invested in their "black" identity, to have problematic relationships with their teachers, to blame their erratic academic record on external causes, to have a record of truancy or acting-out in school, to express low aspirations for college, and to have no clearly articulated career goals.

Intellectualization (e.g., "If you're smart, people don't care about your color") and identification with the aggressor (e.g., "White people run the country because they are smarter than blacks") are more frequently used as defenses by those teens who demonstrated a pattern of compensatory overachievement. These youngsters are more likely to be positively invested in their white identity, to feel personally responsible for their academic performance, to be "superstudents" in their school conduct and relationships with teachers, to be very involved in extracurricular activities, and to express high aspirations for college and future career plans.

In evaluating this spectrum of defense mechanisms and coping strategies, three trends emerge. First, those teens who assume a negative identity tend to exhibit more primitive defense mechanisms (e.g., denial, acting out) and their coping strategies are more maladaptive and socially dysfunctional (e.g., sexual promiscuity, low school achievement). Second, those who do develop a negative self-concept usually identify with the most devalued and deviant stereotypes of their black racial heritage and then, having patterned their behavior accordingly, fulfill their own negative prophecy. Third, those teens who identify with their white racial heritage tend to maintain an overt façade of adaptation to the majority culture but experience some degree of identity confusion which exacts a high psychic cost. Thus, they are more likely to be sexually and emotionally inhibited, overenmeshed in their families, and overachieving in school and community contexts. However, it is more difficult to predict the defensive strategies of biracial teens who were adopted or were in out-of-home placements, since they must cope as well with the issues of parental rejection or neglect, further complicating their identity development.

Issues of Assessment

In the assessment of biracial adolescents, there are four areas of special importance: 1. age-appropriate developmental behavior and concerns; 2. identity development and issues; 3. parental and family attitudes toward their biracial identity; and 4. peer relationships. It is essential to view all these issues in the broader context of normative adolescent development since this is generally a phase of experimentation, mood variations, and limit testing. However, clinical and empirical studies of biracial adolescents strongly suggest that a mixed ethnic heritage serves to exacerbate the normal process of identity development by creating ambiguity and uncertainty in individual identification with parents, group identification with peers, and social identification with a specific ethnic or racial group.

Age-appropriate behavior

In early adolescence teenagers are concerned primarily about same-sex peer group acceptance and body image (Coleman, 1980). In midadolescence these concerns shift more to involvement in heterosexual activities, school achievement, and increasing independence from parents. In late adolescence, concerns focus on separation from parents, career planning, and consolidation of identity (Marcia, 1980). These concerns are normative and may induce periods of transitory anxiety or depression, minor rebelliousness in the family, and some fluctuations in school performance, peer relationships, and community activities. Such symptoms and mood shifts occur frequently among "normal adolescents" and are not indicative of severe pathology or maladjustment (Offer, 1969).

Identity development and issues

These should not be confused with age-appropriate developmental behavior and concerns. The process of identity formation should be evaluated for evidence of successful identity integration versus identity foreclosure, identity diffusion, or negative identity. As described earlier, the latter three outcomes tend to be expressed in exaggerated, deviant, or self-destructive behavior in the areas of personality functioning, family and peer relationships, school achievement, and antisocial activities.

These adolescents often call attention to themselves because they are oversocialized (overachieving, constricted, and overconforming) or undersocialized (impulsive, antisocial, and alienated). Even if they are superficially adapted, they may be paying a high psychological price for their external conformity. Alternately, their behavior may be dysfunctional and maladaptive to the environment in which they are living.

Parental and family attitudes

Biracial adolescents often receive conflicting messages about their identity from parents and family members on both sides. White parents may not be able to accept the fact that society will not define their children as "white" and may give them mixed messages about their skin color and nonwhite appearance (Benson, 1981; *Children's Advocate*, 1986; Ladner, 1977; Lyles et al., 1985). Some parents may handle their child's biracial identity through denial, simply refusing to discuss it or deal with it until a crisis occurs. Others assume a Pollyanna-like attitude, behaving as if the society were truly color-blind and minimizing problems experienced by the child and the family in interracial encounters.

Grandparents, aunts, uncles, and cousins may not accept the children as relatives at all or may treat them in an ambivalent, demeaning, or rejecting manner. They may also tease the children or make racist statements about either parent's racial background.

Assessment of parental attitudes is especially important in family treatment. Parents should be encouraged to confront and clarify their own racial attitudes so that they can provide clear, consistent, and positive feedback to their children about both sides of their racial heritage (Faulkner, 1985; Lyles et al., 1985).

A particularly difficult situation is faced by the child who, as a result of parental divorce, is rejected by one of his parents. This outcome is more frequently reported by adolescents whose white mothers express negative feelings toward them and view the children as causes of their devalued social status as well as daily reminders of their failed marriages.

In cases where these adolescents are in out-of-home placements, it is sometimes difficult to tease out the psychological effects of parental rejection or neglect from the effects of biracial identity. However, since the issues of identity development for all adolescents in this society are presumably quite similar and the patterns of adaptation to a biracial heritage develop within those finite parameters, a careful assessment of preadolescent adjustment and current environmental stressors should enable the clinician to determine the relative contribution of each factor to the adolescent's current adjustment.

It is important to make a differential assessment of the effects of biracial status vs. the effects of an inappropriate or abusive living situation on the teenager's behavior.

Peer Relationships

This is a critical area for all teenagers and especially for biracial teens who are concerned about social acceptance. It is important to evaluate not only the size and cohesiveness of the current social networks, but also the dynamics of the interpersonal relationships to determine whether the adolescent is playing an unhealthy role or being scapegoated in order to be accepted by the group. The adolescent's self-perception in relation to peer groups in the neighborhood and school should be assessed. Opportunities for alternative peer groups should be evaluated if the current relationships do not seem to be contributing to a happy social experience and a healthy self-concept. Finally, when these youth are referred the clinician should not assume that biracial identity *per se*, is the only or primary cause of problem behavior. A thorough evaluation of other developmental, environmental, and social factors which might have caused or contributed to the problem is mandatory.

Implications for Treatment

The major task for these adolescents is to integrate the dual racial identifications into a single identity that affirms the positive aspects of each heritage, acknowledges the reality of societal ambivalence, and rejects the self-limitations of racial stereotypes or behavior on the process of self-actualization.

To facilitate these goals, the therapist must first develop a working relationship with the teenagers, following the general principles of short-term, ego-oriented adolescent treatment (Faulkner, 1985; Gibbs, 1974; Lyles et al., 1985; Sebring, 1985). In addition, the therapist must be particularly sensitive to the possibility of mistrust and hostility based on racial factors in the therapeutic relationship.

Second, the therapist must permit the teenagers to ventilate feelings about their biracial identity and its meaning in our society and must be able to provide confirmation and assurance that those feelings are not irrational or paranoid. In these sessions the therapist must demonstrate cognizance of the social realities and must be aware of his or her own attitudes and feelings about majority–minority race relations.

Third, the therapist should help these teenagers to build up their self-esteem as unique individuals by identifying and supporting their positive coping mechanisms, their abilities, and those of their interests that are independent of their racial heritage. In this process, the therapist will have to help these youngsters distinguish between their own personal interests and abilities and those they have adopted out of a stereotyped notion of their racial identity. This is particularly important for those teens who exhibit signs of identity diffusion.

Fourth, the therapist must help these teenagers to see the link between their confusion over their racial identity and their confusion in other areas of behavior or developmental tasks. It is important to challenge those with foreclosed or negative identities so as to unlock their potential for growth in a positive direction. They should be encouraged to explore alternatives to current behavior and to project reasonable options for their future; they should also be confronted with the realistic fact that continued dysfunctional or antisocial activities will result in a self-fulfilling prophecy for their "negative" or foreclosed identities.

Fifth, the therapist should encourage the teenagers to explore both sides of their racial heritage in order to form a positive sense of identification with their ethnic and cultural roots. They can be assigned "homework" to read and report on heroes and achievements of both groups for school essays; assisted in drawing up a family tree to illustrate the various facets of their heritage; encouraged to put together scrapbooks about their family, friends, and neighbors to illustrate the cultural diversity in their lives; and urged to participate in holiday celebrations, parades, and other activities which recognize the contributions of both of their racial groups (e.g., Black History Month, St. Patrick's Day, Cinco de Mayo).

Finally, parents and siblings should be involved in treatment if at all possible, particularly so that one child can avoid being stigmatized as the family problem. The teenager who is seriously confused about racial identity has probably received mixed signals from the immediate family. By exploring the parental attitudes toward race in general and the teenager in particular, the therapist can attempt to clarify and modify attitudes so that a more supportive family environment may be developed (Faulkner, 1985).

In addition, the therapist can involve the entire family in activities which will promote individual self-esteem and family pride; e.g., recreational and cultural activities involving ethnic themes, church-based interracial activities, and political activities to enhance the status of the black minority group.

Some other strategies that are effective in working with these teenagers to help them consolidate their identities and to improve their self-esteem include: role playing, keeping diaries to record feelings and concerns, expressing conflictual feelings in creative writing or other forms of creative endeavor, story-telling about the past, and fantasizing about the future. More traditional psychodynamic techniques can also be supplemented by behavioral techniques such as contracting for short-term behavioral goals, giving "homework" assignments for specific behavioral change, and self-monitoring of negative attitudes and feelings.

Demographic trends suggest that rates of interracial marriages between blacks and whites will increase as the two groups come into closer contact and as social attitudes continue to become more cosmopolitan. Intermarriage between whites and other nonwhite groups will also increase as the proportion of nonwhites increases in the population due to immigration, high birth rates, and lower mortality rates (National, 1985). Thus, the proportion of biracial children in general will continue to rise, and as they enter adolescence, they may prove to be particularly vulnerable to the vicissitudes of this developmental stage. This paper has attempted to offer a conceptual framework for the understanding of the special issues these teenagers face, as well as a set of therapeutic goals and techniques for their effective treatment. As these biracial children increase in the population, many will manage to achieve truly integrated identities; chronic identity conflicts, however, will continue to plague many. This latter group will pose a growing challenge to mental health practitioners in the twenty-first century.

References

Benson, S. (1981). *Ambiguous ethnicity*. London: Cambridge University Press.

Chang, T. (1974). The self-concept of children of ethnically different marriages. *California Journal of Educational Research, 25*, 245–253.

Chestang, L. (1984). Racial and personal identity in the black experience. In B. White (Ed.), *Color in a white society*. Silver Spring, MD: National Association of Social Workers.

Children of interracial families. (1984). *Interracial books for children,* Bulletin: *15.*

Children's Advocate. (1986 May/June), p. 95.

Coleman, J. (1980). Friendship and peer group in adolescence. In J. Adelson (Ed.), *Handbook of adolescent psychology*. New York: Wiley.

Detroit Free Press (1985, Dec. 31), p. C-1.

Erikson, E. (1950/1963). *Childhood and society* (rev). New York: Norton.

Erikson, E. (1959). *Identity and the life cycle*. New York: International Universities Press.

Faulkner, J. (1985). Women in interracial relationships. In J. Robbins & R. Siegel (Eds.), *Women changing therapy*. New York: Harrington Park Press.

Faulkner, J. & Kich, G. (1983). Assessment and engagement stages in therapy with the interracial family. *Family Therapy Collections, 6*, 78–90.

Gibbs, J. (1974). Patterns of adaptation of black students at a predominantly white university: selected case studies. *American Journal of Orthopsychiatry, 44*, 728–740.

Gibbs, J. (1982). Personality patterns of delinquent females: ethnic and sociocultural variations. *Journal of Clinical Psychology, 38*, 198–206.

Gibbs (1985). City girls: Psychosocial adjustment of urban black adolescent females. *Sage: Scholarly Journal of Black Women, 2*, 28–36.

Gunthorpe, W. (1978). Skin color recognition, preference and identification in interracial children: a comparative study. *Dissertation Abstracts International, 38*(10-B), 3468.

Hauser, S. (1972). Black and white identity development: aspects and perspectives. *Journal of Youth and Adolescence, 1,* 113–130.

Jacobs, J. (1978). Black/white interracial families: marital process and identity development in young children. *Dissertation Abstracts International, 38*(10-B), 5023.

Jenkins, A. (1982). *The psychology of the Afro-American.* New York: Pergamon Press.

Ladner, J. (1977). *Mixed families.* New York: Anchor Press/Doubleday.

Lyles, M., Yancey, A., Grace, C., & Carter, J. (1985). Racial identity and self-esteem: Problems peculiar to biracial children. *Journal of the American Academy of Child Psychiatry, 24,* 150–153.

Marcia, J. (1980). Identity in adolescence. In J. Adelson (Ed.), *Handbook of adolescent psychology.* New York: Wiley.

McRoy, R., Zurcher, L. Landerdale, M., & Anderson, R. (1982). Self-esteem and racial identity in transracial and interracial adoptees. *Social Work, 27,* 522–526.

National Data Book and Guide to Sources. (1985), Statistical Abstract of the United States (105th Ed.), Washington, DC: US Bureau of the Census.

Newsweek. (1984. Nov. 19), p. 120.

Offer, D. (1969). *The psychological world of the teenager.* New York: Basic Books.

Payne, R. (1977). Racial attitude formation in children of mixed black and white heritage: Skin color and racial identity. *Dissertation Abstracts International, 38*(6-B), 2876.

Pierce, C. (1968). Problems of the Negro adolescent in the next decade. In E. Brody (Ed.), *Minority group adolescents in the U.S.* Baltimore: Williams and Wilkins.

Poussaint, A. (1984). Study of interracial children presents positive picture. *Interracial Books for Children Bulletin, 15,* 9–10.

Sebring, D. (1985). Considerations in counseling interracial children. *Journal of Non-White Concerns in Personnel Guidance, 13,* 3–9.

Sommers, V. (1964). The impact of dual cultural membership on identity. *Psychiatry, 27,* 332–344.

Teicher, J. (1968). Some observations on identity problems in children of Negro-white marriages. *Journal of Nervous and Mental Disorders, 146,* 249–256.

Window on the Future: Executive Summary (1983). San Francisco: Coleman Children and Youth Service.

7

Constructing Failure, Narrating Success
Rethinking the "Problem" of Teen Pregnancy

KATHERINE SCHULTZ

At the end of her senior year in high school, Jo wrote the following message in her friend Aster's yearbook.[1] It was a variation of the message that she wrote in the yearbook of nearly every African American female classmate, and it reflected the talk I frequently heard between the Black female students in the urban high school where I conducted research.

> To Aster, We Finally made It out of [high school]. Don't Let Daniel Put Any Kids on you. Alway keep your head up and Dont let anyone Bring you Down. Stay In School. Become a Big Black sucessful Black woman! Much Love, Jo

Two years later Jo had completed the requirements to become a licensed cosmetologist, worked for a year in a hair salon, and begun courses at the local community college in law and criminal justice to become a lawyer. Her first child was born when Jo was not yet 20, during her first semester of community college. Without missing a beat, she decided not to marry the baby's father and to remain in her mother's apartment. Jo's high school friend, Aster, remained at a local state university, with a steady boyfriend, a job in a clothing store, and no children of her own.

In this article, I argue for the importance of including the perspectives of youth such as Jo and Aster in the public dialogue about teaching and learning in high schools. I contrast the discourses of the high school students with those in the media to suggest that we begin to formulate policies and practices that account for youths' complex understandings of the consequences of having a child during their high school years. Many of the youth I spoke with had tentative plans for their future with alternatives in mind in the event they had a child. First, I contrast this perspective with the prevalent assumption that teen

From: *Teachers College Record*, *103*(4), 2001, pp. 582–607. Copyright © Blackwell, Ltd. Reprinted with permission.

pregnancy brings with it the forgone conclusion of dropping out of school, poverty, and failure. Second, I suggest that in contrast to media representations of teen pregnancy as a sign of failure or dysfunction, for some young women, the presence of children in their lives motivates them to stay in school and work toward a career in order to support their children. Finally, I propose that the supposition that school-age youth have babies out of hopelessness and academic failure needs to be seen as only one possibility — these pregnancies are sometimes planned. The "problem" of teen pregnancy can be reinterpreted as a different set of choices that are at variance with the White middle-class norm in terms of timing. In my description of the perspectives of a group of urban high school-age women, I show how children — both their presence and absence, both the reality and the possibility — figure into the future plans of this group of high school students. All too often, rather than accounting for the perspectives brought by youth, discussions with and about teen parents begin with media representations that are punitive and condemning. I suggest that the understandings articulated by youth should be incorporated into discussions in high school classrooms, the preparation of new teachers, the professional development of experienced teachers and the policy-making conversations of educators, researchers, and legislators.

Through a focus on the perspectives and experiences of three high school students in conjunction with those of their peers, I suggest some ways that both the idea and the reality of children and motherhood shaped young women's participation in their senior year at an urban multiracial high school. In this final year of high school, students held on to seemingly contradictory narratives — that parenthood would prevent them from achieving a middle-class lifestyle and that it was desirable to have children at a relatively young age. Once pregnant, young women who had vociferously argued against teen pregnancy changed their narratives to accommodate their new reality. For these young women who had persisted in school until 12th grade, pregnancy and the birth of a child sometimes acted as a motivation to graduate. The presence of children in their lives and the responsibility they felt as new parents gave them new reasons to resist the peer pressure to drop out of school. Too often, pregnancy during high school is a signal for school personnel and families to abandon young women, designating them as school failures. The young women in this study suggest alternative perspectives. Narrow definitions of femininity, restricted notions of the options available to women once they become pregnant, normative views of the "correct timing of parenthood" and the effects of pregnancy on the lives of young women, all serve to limit our visions as educators, policy makers and community members and keep us from observing and noticing the complexity of students' lives. We may be further insuring the failure of many urban youth by silencing conversations and giving up on youth too quickly once they become pregnant rather than providing support for them. I suggest that educators and policy makers use students' understandings of the role that pregnancy and motherhood play in their school careers and futures to rethink the "problem" of teen pregnancy and the opportunity structures for young mothers in high school and beyond.

Research Context

In the fall of 1993, I began a longitudinal, ethnographic research project in an urban high school in Northern California. The project was originally designed to understand the literacies and identities low-income urban adolescent females learned in their homes, communities, schools, and workplaces. Accordingly, I sought to understand these young women's aspirations and notions of success as they spoke and wrote about their identities and their futures. I wanted to add their voices, as poor women of color, to the research literature on school-to-work transitions, a literature that, for the most part, has been focused on the school lives of White males.[2] In order to collect the narratives I describe in this article, I spent 3 to 5 days a week for an entire year in an urban, comprehensive high school. Situated between Black and Latino neighborhoods and surrounded by a high fence with a single gate monitored by a security guard, the school housed a multiracial group of students who were approximately one-third African American, one-third Mexican American or Latino/a, and one-third Asian American. Seventy-nine percent of the students in this school came from families on AFDC (Aid to Families with Dependent Children). Neither the school nor the district maintained accurate dropout and retention statistics, but the population of the school tended to be transient. Students described the auditorium as overflowing when they met as 10th graders in their 1st year of high school. As graduating seniors, they barely filled half the room. Numbers confirm this visual impression: There were 716 students in the 10th grade class and, 2 years later, 354 in the senior class. Thus, the seniors I talked with were the survivors; they were resilient students determined to graduate.[3] During their high school years, I attended two senior government classes and, once a week, an advisory period and English class with many of the same students. After their graduation, I went to their homes, postsecondary schools, and workplaces such as beauty colleges, grocery stores, and data entry offices, to continue systematic observations and interviews.

Data collection included participant observation, the collection of written documents, open-ended and semistructured interviews with most of the females in the two classes, more frequent interviews with about 20 other students and teachers during the 1st year, and regular interviews with 10 focal students over a period of 4 years. The 10 focal students were representative of the females in this class: 2 had become mothers in their junior year of high school and returned to school during summer school to graduate with their class; another 2 became pregnant during their first two years out of high school. The remaining 6 were childless 3 years after their high school graduation.

For this research, I combine macro-level analyses of curriculum and instruction, community and culture, with micro-level investigations of oral and written discourse inside and around an urban high school. In my search for patterns, the thematic prominence of pregnancy and motherhood immediately became apparent. Whereas only four females had children or became pregnant during the time of my study, nearly every young woman talked about pregnancy and motherhood at some point, as either a reality, an event to avoid at all costs, or a future possibility.[4]

I began my research as a participant/observer in the social studies classroom of Andrea O'Neill, a teacher my age who, like me, is a White, middle-class female. Although I had no responsibilities for their instruction, as a former teacher, I fell quickly in to teacher-like patterns of interaction with the students. The students responded by viewing me first as a teacher and later as an interested observer, note-taker and interviewer. They later told me that they had decided to trust me right away because their teacher, whom they both liked and respected, made it clear in her words and actions that I was "okay." In addition, I had not made any mistakes early on. During the second year, when my research led me from the school into their homes and workplaces, some of the students told me that they considered me a friend and mentor; they saw me as someone who was willing and able to help them in a variety of circumstances. Our interviews took place as I transported them to doctors' appointments or to the drugstore to buy diapers and as they practiced for their exams by fixing up my hair or doing my nails. My presence in their lives was one of many factors that affected their daily decisions.

I cannot disentangle whether these young women told me stories about the ways that pregnancy and motherhood — or fears of those conditions — shaped their visions of the future because of who I am or because of our shared standpoints. On some levels, I had little in common with these young women and, at first glance, my White, middle-class life, centered around my family with three young children and my life as a teacher educator and researcher at the university, seemed light-years away from their own. On the other hand, we shared interests and concerns as women and, in some instances, as mothers. As an ethnographer, I worked hard to form relationships during the school year that would continue after their graduation. I had relatively easy access to their lives during the time they attended classes in the high school. Once out of high school, graduates' availability for interviews and meetings was contingent on trust, friendship, and their belief in the research project. The young women in the study allowed me to establish relationships with them in different ways and for a variety of reasons. Some saw me as a resource or source of information and knowledge that they used as they made decisions and looked for schools and jobs. Others enjoyed talking, or more precisely having someone to listen to them. A few valued the connection with someone from the university, whereas most simply thought I seemed trustworthy. More than a handful felt that I might write their stories in a book and that these stories would be useful to teachers and other people whom they saw as powerful or influential. In general, I worried more than they did about the boundaries of race, ethnicity, class, and age that might stand between us (Schultz, 1997).

Dominant Discourses of Pregnancy

Public discussion of teenage pregnancy is a regulated discourse — regulated by the media, by adult professionals, and by young women themselves. There is a narrow range of acceptable ways to talk about issues of teen pregnancy and childbearing in high school classrooms, in teacher education programs, and on the floor of Congress. Public discussion of teen pregnancy began in the 1970s. Before that time the discussion was absent from most public spaces, and pregnant young women, particularly those who were unmarried, were carefully hidden until their children were born. They were rarely talked or written about; the gaze of the media, like that of the public, was averted.

As the discourse of teen pregnancy has entered the public sphere, it has been circumscribed and shaped by the ways in which the media have portrayed and written about youth in poverty and communities of color. This discourse in the media has a regulatory function that is both internalized and contested by the youth themselves (Pillow, 1997). As Walkerdine and Lucey (1989) observe

> The sciences claim to describe a population in order that they can better be governed. The rise of sciences therefore is not simply about academic disciplines, but, as we shall see, it is about the development of specific practices through which families, mothers, children, might be "known" in order to better regulate them.... However, as in all struggles for power, this knowledge is constructed out of an uneasy compromise.... Regulation is not neutral, but is about a knowledge which suppresses and silences other "knowledges" in producing its own vision. (p. 34)

In order to examine the various discourses of teen pregnancy, I introduce three young women and propose we add their experiences and understandings to the dominant and regulated discourses of the media. Although these discourses offer new and different perspectives, the youth's own discourses are regulated by what they hear from the media, their families, communities, teachers, and peers. I offer these perspectives as "knowledge" this group of young women might add to the conventional assumptions about of pregnancy and motherhood. It can be argued that this "knowledge" has been suppressed and controlled to perpetuate limited understandings of the role that pregnancy plays in the lives of school-age youth. A poststructuralist framework allows us to see the ways that individuals are continually shaped by discursive practices even as they remake those practices in their daily lives (Davies, 1993). I argue for the importance of bringing the voices and perspectives of youth into the discussions and decisions about their education. In the narratives that follow, young women assert the salience of decisions about motherhood in their lives as they struggle with and create knowledge about teen pregnancy.

Constructing and Reconstructing Narratives of the Future

The mood of the late 1960s is captured by Campbell's (1968) statement, "When a 16 year old girl has a child...90 percent of her life's script is written for her" (p. 242). That assumption is still prevalent today. In the media and popular press, there tends to be a single message for youth about pregnancy: Don't get pregnant. This message was echoed by the school staff through their words, their texts, and the posters on the walls. Although that is certainly the best single piece of advice, the youth themselves have more complex understandings based on the contingencies of their lives.

A poster designed by the Children's Defense Fund was plastered on the wall in the high school health clinic. The image and the message were simple. Two teenagers were seated in chairs. The teen on the left was visibly pregnant; the teen on the right was not. The caption at the bottom stated, "The student on the right (the one who is not pregnant) will graduate first." Well-intentioned posters such as this one allow school officials and the wider community to give up on young women who have children. The young women I interviewed who had children and made the decision to graduate from high school, and those who had children soon after their graduation, refused to let their families, their peers, and society give up on them. At the same time that this simple poster captures public sentiment, it whites out the particularities of young women's lives.

Although the media tend to portray a single path for youth who become pregnant, the young women I spoke with imagined more possibilities. Young women without children claimed to strive for success by avoiding childbearing in their youth. At the same time, young mothers explained their success or persistence in school as due, in part, to their children. These young women saw children as part of a larger, more complex picture, not the end of a story. At the same time that pregnancy and motherhood shaped who they were, the young women were in the process of defining the ways children would and did have an impact on their lives.

In both my interviews and analyses of their public writing and classroom talk, I discovered frequent references to motherhood as the young women made ambitious plans for their futures and worried about the possibilities of becoming pregnant and bearing children. They wrestled with competing discourses. Students who were not yet pregnant often appeared to be holding their breath, hoping to graduate before they had a child. The most ambitious students frequently asserted that they would never have children, that they could not be both successful and a parent. These were not simple narratives of the future. Rather, the young women I spoke with often held on to several, frequently contradictory, stories.

The case of an African American student, Theresa, provides an illustration of the ways that youth are sometimes able to construct and reconstruct their lives and provides an alternate narrative to the conclusion that there is a single destination for them once they become pregnant. Theresa was an extremely resistant student in danger of failing 11th grade because she avoided many assignments. During more than one semester, she refused to read a single book assigned by her teachers. Her English teacher could not recall a single paper or word that Theresa had been willing to revise. Her family did not have much money and lived in a single-family, two-floor home on a neighborhood street not far from the high school. Theresa described her childhood as "hard." Her father had recently passed away after a long period of instability linked to the time he spent as a soldier in Vietnam. During the time that I spoke with her, Theresa's mother was frequently sick. Her brother had been recently killed in a drug skirmish. Her sister frequently dropped her own child off for her mother, and often Theresa, to care for. In addition, Theresa struggled academically. Her reading skills were weak and she labored both to decode and comprehend the reading required for high school. Her resistant and tough affect seemed to keep teachers and counselors from reaching out to her. She entered the room with an aura of self-confidence that was easily punctured, evoking anger and resistance. She was the kind of student who needed strong and sustained academic support, yet she held herself back from teachers and counselors, maintaining her distance with the illusion of self-sufficiency.

In her senior year, as graduation seemed possible, Theresa became more engaged in school. On a daily basis, she changed her mind about whether she would attend a proprietary school that specialized in business, a local community college, or a state university. She had few models of success or resilience in her life. She simply did not have much information about the realities of a career path that would lead to her goal of a middle-class life. When asked about her future career choices, she replied that she would pursue both medicine and law at the same time. She was quick to explain that this unusual plan was to insure that if she grew bored with one career she could switch to the other. At times, she described her future career as one in which she would practice medicine and law on alternate days.

The school district had recently enacted a rule that students must pass a set of competency exams in order to graduate. Theresa began her senior year with three exams to pass. During the first semester she passed the writing and math exams and failed the reading exam multiple times. By the end of the school year, Theresa was determined to be the first in her family to graduate from high school. After she was accepted at a state university an hour from her home, she had business cards made, purchased a new book bag, and bought professional-looking clothes. She ordered graduation invitations and talked constantly about her plans and her future. Two weeks before the end of her senior year, Theresa was informed that she had failed the reading competency exam for a final time. She was absent from the graduation ceremony.

Although she did not receive a high school diploma, Theresa attended the Summerbridge program, organized to provide support to students considered "at risk," at the state university that had accepted her. After a month, she dropped out to return home to care for her mother. During that summer, she also discovered that she was pregnant with her first child. To many of her teachers, Theresa had seemed an unlikely mother. Although both vocal and adamant in her views against abortion, a belief common among her peers, Theresa frowned upon and censored others during discussions of pregnancy. She frequently made public statements that she might never have a child because it would interfere with her chosen careers. On the other hand, her low academic performance in high school combined with her poverty left her susceptible to becoming a young mother.

Theresa adjusted her life to this new reality. She moved a crib into her bedroom and took on the role of a proud and attentive mother. The baby's father drifted in and out of their lives for a short time and then disappeared. After nearly 2 years spent living with her mother, looking for jobs, working part-time, and caring for her child, together with her best friend Jo, Theresa began to take courses in criminal justice at the local community college. At the time of our most recent interview, she had remained at the community college for 3 consecutive semesters and spoke optimistically about continuing her education and possibly transferring to a 4-year state university. Theresa composed two lists of goals while in high school that capture the inconsistency and contradiction I found in many of the students' narratives. In 11th grade, Theresa wrote the following New Year's resolutions. The resolutions reflect her constant struggle to avoid pregnancy.

January 4, 1992
New Year's resolutions
    The five thinks I would like to accomplish in 1993 is: To finish school; Stay with my boyfriend; Get into a great college; live out "93" to see 94; Without a child

By including the goal that she would remain "without a child," Theresa indicated that she agreed with the dominant narratives of pregnancy and childbearing held by the media, her school, and community. At this time in her life she seemed to believe that children would be a threat to the attainment of her goals.

The following year, when she was closer to graduation, Theresa filled out a more elaborated goal sheet that exemplified the ambiguities and contradictions I found in many narratives of the future. For this worksheet, Theresa's teacher initially asked her to write her fantasies about the future, her long-term goals and, finally, her short-term goals. On her sheet, she listed a house and car as her first fantasy goal. Next, she mentioned children and, finally, a good job. It is notable that in her list of long-term goals, which her teacher emphasized was different from a fantasy, Theresa reversed her priorities and began the list with her professional education. She then suggested a house and a car and, finally, a family that included a husband, though not necessarily children. These "real" goals were practically identical to those on her fantasy list, which suggests the difficulty she may have had in distinguishing between the two categories. She completed the worksheets as follows:

> Goal setting worksheet from advisory, 12/1/93
> Name: [Theresa]
> Gender: female
> Ethnicity: African American
> Fantasies: Well at the age 30 my fantasies is to have a five Bedroom house with my fantasic car (Legend) and two children. And a good working job as a doctor.
> Major Goals: 1. My goals are to get may BA and mast in the medical fields; 2. And return to college to get my degree in law; 3. And have a home and my fantasies car married to a lawyer; 4. or a successful man. Maybe not have a family because my career will be to much to have children.
> Short term goals: Next year: 1. Be Dr. [Theresa Jones]; 2. Going back to college to take up law. 3 years: 1. Still Be a Doctor Just getting tired of it and take in the Criminal Justice to Be a lawyer for to young teen age criminals.
> Immediate goal: One thing I can do is to work harder and get throw school and college. And don't give up.

As a youth struggling with poverty, Theresa's fantasy was a middle-class reality. It is interesting that although children were a definite part of the fantasy plans, they became only a possibility in her more realistic goal list. In her delineation of short-term goals, she wrote that she wanted to become a doctor during the next year, which points to her lack of understanding of the educational path required to reach that goal. Soon after she became a doctor, Theresa's plan was to take up law, all within the next year. Her goal for the next 3 years entailed switching back and forth between law and medicine. These, of course, are wildly unrealistic expectations, especially from a student who was unwilling to read a book in her English class and unable to pass a high school reading competency test. Her timeline emphasizes the impractical nature of these goals. For her immediate goal — to get through school and keep trying — Theresa was more pragmatic; her goal was grounded in a more honest assessment of her circumstances echoing the refrain of her classmates: "Don't give up." Despite these good intentions, there was a gap between words and actions for Theresa and her peers. They knew to say the words; they didn't always know how to perform the actions necessary to live by them.

In a college essay, Theresa wove together her desire to become a doctor and a lawyer with an autobiographical account of her experience of feeling like a mother to her niece at a young age. Theresa's inclusion of this event highlights its importance to her as a defining moment in her schooling and her future. In this essay for college admission, she wrote:

> When I was much younger my mother and grandmother always put me down telling me that I was going to be like the rest of my brothers and sisters how I'll have children and won't finish school due to the crowd I hung around. Now I'm 18 years of age and I have no children and my grades have improved. Preparation for a career is important to myself; but there's more to life, I want to acquire the tools I need to decide what I desire from life. Choosing my career is a crucial decision in my life.
>
> I'm a determined focused individual. I set goals for myself in anything that I do, I pursue and try wholeheartedly in [accomplishing] them. I have dreams about becoming a well responsible college student. Dreams about getting my degree in the medical field and also get a degree in law and graduating from a 5-year institute and dreamed about becoming my best self.
>
> I'm most crecent [recent] goal is to become a doctor and getting my bachelors and master degree in law. When I first became a teen I can remember my sister haven her first child and that was that day I became a mother to that same child as well. I had to do this and that for that baby and not by choice. I had to much responable for my age, thirteen to seventeen years old.... Taken care of my sister three children by the time I reached seventeen she was on her fourth child.

Theresa continued this essay with the description of the hardships she faced as she helped her sister care for her babies. She connected this experience to her future participation in college,

> I bearly had a social life of my own any more due to the responsibibilites I have. But I have less to complain about because the resonsibibites I had to face were preparing me for the real life that I have to face at college and even maybe a family of my own. No, I may not be one of the high income familys; but if there is something I went badly enough I don't mind getting out there working hard for it, becuase it's like my grandmother said "it's not your until you get out there and work for it". My mother always called me selfish; but I look at myself as being aggressive tending to attack and be hastile of my goals.

Theresa concluded her essay,

> There is more to the world than material objects. I want to go beyond that which does not require my thoughts I hope college will train me to make more than career choices I hope it will train me to evaluate choices about how to live my life as a strong minded African American woman.

Theresa summed up her essay by emphasizing her identity as an African American female, restating her independence and her desire to obtain an education to be successful. She knew that her plan, no matter how ambitious it was, would be intimately connected with children in one way or another. In this essay, Theresa asserted her right to be successful despite pressures from her family and society.

Theresa's life events embody the paradox in her narrative. Theresa and her classmates held on to competing visions of their futures; they claimed to want to postpone or avoid having children in order to insure their success, yet when they became pregnant, their children sometimes gave them the motivation to continue with their education. They constructed reasons for having children in their youth, yet they understood and often agreed with the arguments in the media and by their sisters, that parenting at an early age was difficult. Today, as a mother who has returned to a community college, Theresa continues to imagine a future for herself. It could be claimed that Theresa's baby was born out of hopelessness, after she was denied her dream of "walking the stage" with her high school peers because she could not pass the high school competency exam. Yet it must be remembered that she has persisted with her education and in her pursuit of a career, a sign of resilience and proof that she has not given up. Her path is neither linear nor simply explained. As a statistic, Theresa would show up as a high school dropout, an unwed teenage mother, a Black youth living in poverty, and a student who struggled in school. Yet each of these labels would fail to capture her whole story, one that is still unfolding. They also fail to describe the incredible obstacles she faces every day, the alternative routes she has constructed and the sacrifices she must make to even aim for a middle-class lifestyle.

Turning Failure into Success

Current discussions and images in the media often link teenage pregnancy to African American females in the same breath that they link violence and guns to Black males. The African American pregnant teenager, found on covers of Newsweek and Time magazines, has become an icon of the failure of the welfare system and society. Schools, communities, and students themselves often give up when a high school student has a baby. At the same time that young mothers were being pathologized and portrayed as failures in the press, there were young women in this high school who turned the experience of having a child during their high school years into a reason to stay in school.

In the mid-1970s, teen pregnancy suddenly appeared in the news as an epidemic.[5] In the wake of Johnson's War on Poverty, public anxiety over the promise and peril of a relatively new welfare system became focused on teens, particularly poor Black adolescents. It is notable that, as the public concern about teen pregnancy was mounting, the actual number of births to teenagers declined.[6] As Luker (1996, p. 83) points out, "The teenage mother — in particular, the Black teenage mother — came to personify the social, economic, and sexual trends that in one way or another affected almost everyone in America" (see also Rhode & Lawson, 1993; Scott-Jones, 1993).

In the current climate of welfare reform, teen pregnancy has once again been described as an epidemic with a new twist (cf., Vinovskis, 1988). When a study conducted by the Alan Guttmacher Institute (1994) revealed that many of the men fathering the children with teen mothers were older men often over 20 years of age, headlines reframed the women as victims and the men as criminals. A new public outcry ensued. Once again, the voices of the young women themselves were notably absent. Ushering in the new legislation to "reform" welfare, in his 1995 State of the Union address President Clinton called the "epidemic" of teen pregnancies and out-of-wedlock births "our most serious social problem" (Clinton, 1995). At the same time Newt Gingrich ignited controversy when he offered a plan as part of the Personal Responsibility and Work Opportunity Act of 1996 to allow states to abolish aid to children of mothers younger than 21 and use that money to build orphanages. He received both support and criticism for his example of Boys Town orphanage in Nebraska as a model way to care for children born to unmarried teen mothers. Finally, in an effort to revive his political campaign in 1996, Governor Pete Wilson called for Californians to take on the challenge of "recasting and reinvigorating our culture" by reinstating the moral standards needed to curb teen pregnancy. He declared, "All of the problems tearing apart the fabric of our society have deep roots in this exploding epidemic of out-of-wedlock births" (Lesher, 1996, p. A1). Statements such as this blame poor young mothers for the effects of poverty. The language of "epidemics" pathologizes individuals who become pregnant and the communities who support them.

The young parents with whom I spoke — those who were still in their senior year of high school — often remained hopeful. Most held tightly to their plans for their future, although some admitted that children might complicate matters. Lianne's case provides an alternative image to these harsh portraits of young mothers. Her story suggests that rather than failure, a consequence of having children at a young age can lead to new forms of participation in school. Lianne lived with her mother and older sister in a small apartment that was part of a low-rise housing complex. Her house was dark and uncluttered. Large plants straining for light blocked the small windows. The living room was long and narrow with a changing set of furniture purchased by Lianne's sister and mother during their weekly trips to local flea markets. Before her child was born, Lianne was barely engaged in school, passing each year with a minimum number of credits. She described her early years in harrowing terms. Addicted to drugs at an early age, selling drugs to earn enough money for food and clothing, moving from place to place and sometimes ending up without a home due to her mother's own addictions, Lianne had reached a point of stability when I met her.

Lianne retained an optimistic, yet realistic, plan for her future. She was living at home with her baby and working toward finishing school. Her son seemed cheerful most of the time, was interested in books, and was beginning to talk. The father of her child sometimes took him for afternoons or evenings, although his oft-promised money for child support never materialized. He was older than her, out of work and on disability leave, and had abandoned their relationship before their son was born. Lianne was close to her two brothers, and they kept up a correspondence with her while they were in jail, warning her away from their own mistakes.

Lianne matched the portrait most commonly painted of the prototypical teen who becomes pregnant. She drifted through school always on the verge of failure, spent more time selling drugs than studying, all the while living in extreme poverty. However, after the birth of her son during 11th grade, Lianne became engaged in school and, when she was not too tired from sleepless nights caring for her young son, she was a vocal and articulate participant in class discussions. She narrated this story,

> Before [my son] was born...I really didn't think about working or going to school. I used to cut school all of the time and...I didn't care about nothing. But after I got pregnant...I started thinking about what I wanted to do and you know and what I had to do, in order to raise my son and get my act together and start going to school and all that. After I had him, it just seemed like everything changed.... That made me do a lot of thinking about what I wanted to do. (Interview, November 17, 1994)

Lianne's story was typical of that of her peers who remained in school once they had a child. Rather than giving up as a consequence of her pregnancy, Lianne began to imagine a future for herself as a nurse. Unable to count on her son's father, she realized that she had the responsibility not only to care for her son in the present, but also to graduate from high school and attend college to prepare for a career that would enable her to support her child in the future. Through her own determination and with support from a number of teachers and from her mother, sisters, and an extended family network, she managed to accumulate enough credits to graduate from high school. As they recognized her serious approach to school, her teachers paid extra attention to her and began to give her extra work to help her earn enough points in order to pass her courses. During her 1st year out of high school, she drifted between two community colleges and a few minimum-wage jobs, such as working at McDonald's and cleaning houses. The following year Lianne completed a short-term credential program in nursing at an adult school. She was able to find a part-time job as a nurse's assistant at a doctor's office near her home. She made plans to continue with her education while she struggled to keep her job and earn enough money to make ends meet.

Lianne's life is by no means simple. Her compromised choice of a nursing assistant program rather than community college reflects, in part, the added responsibility of a child and her impatience with the time commitment the community college route entailed and the expense of remaining outside of the workforce for that period of time. Staying in her mother's apartment with her son and her grown sister, Lianne is both burdened by the added responsibility of a child and motivated by his presence in her life to complete her education and to work. Lianne's story suggests that having a child as a teenager doesn't always lead to disengagement from school and failure, but in fact motherhood can be a source of motivation. Lianne credits her willingness to stay in school and her subsequent search for a career to her son.

Both the dominant view that pregnancy necessarily leads to poverty and failure and the alternative perspectives suggested by the youth in my study are true and both are incomplete. Youth who have babies are at serious educational and economic risk. Yet they are not without hope or promise (Newman, 1999). Luker (1996) frames the argument this way: Teenage pregnancy doesn't necessarily lead to poverty, although poverty and hopelessness about the future and job prospects often lead to teen pregnancy. The image of hopeless or impoverished teens having babies does not completely capture the lives of the young parents with whom I spoke. Most held tightly to their plans for their future, tending to view children as complications or distractions rather than roadblocks. In fact, the teen parents still in school often had more fully developed plans for their futures than their peers. They had to take life more seriously because they had a child to care for and their future was more clearly drawn. Their difficulty in achieving these goals is attributable to their newborn child and also, in part, to the fact that teachers, counselors, and even, at times, parents often gave up on them and failed to take their plans seriously once they had children. When the world assumed their failure, it was difficult for them to keep reimagining their own success.

A Matter of Timing

In the mid-1980s, Leon Dash (1989) wrote a series of articles for the *Washington Post* that he later turned into a book that many students in this school knew about. Titled *When Children Want Children: An Inside Look at the Crisis of Teenage Parenthood*, this book revealed that the urban teenagers Dash spoke with did not become pregnant out of ignorance; instead they made conscious choices to have babies. The book opens with a conversation between Dash and a teenager who informed him, "Mr. Dash, will you please stop asking me about birth control? Girls out here know all about birth control.... Girls out here get pregnant because they want to have babies!" She continued, giving Dash the explanation that has become a part of the common lore about teen pregnancy, "When girls get pregnant, it's either because they want something to hold on to that they can call their own or because of the circumstances at home. Because their mother doesn't pamper them.... Some of them do it because they resent their parents" (pp. 11–12).

Although they were familiar with this explanation, the older students who were still in high school during their senior year talked to me about children and pregnancy in different terms. They had developed a different set of explanations that had to do with the timing of their careers and the ways they thought about their future. Students saw a child as both a major obstacle to overcome and as a milestone. Some imagined that they could have a child, move past that phase of life and into the next phase that they hoped would include a steady job or a career. Underlying many of the young women's conversations about their future plans was the fear of being derailed by a child. At the same time, the young women I spoke with often wanted to avoid becoming an "old" mother or in a situation in which their children would interfere with their careers. Although pregnancy and childbearing are highly valued in our society, it is the "mis-timing" or "premature" aspect of the event in adolescents' lives that makes it problematic (Scott-Jones, 1993). Today, the accepted wisdom in this country is that early pregnancy leads to hardship and that teens who are considered "children" should be discouraged from having children of their own.

The youth I spoke with defied traditional categorization and cultural stereotypes. They were at once defining themselves against the media representations and their sisters' fates, even as some followed the same patterns. Many had older sisters who were out of work and living impoverished lives with children born during their teen years. These young women who still in high school or just graduated were determined to make different choices than their sisters, and they constructed life trajectories that varied from those around them. Simple explanations of the impact of pregnancy on the lives of youth erase the complex ways youth negotiate and narrate their life decisions. Stereotyped assumptions take away the chance to imagine new possibilities and alternative life paths for poor adolescents that include success rather than failure. Generalizations keep us assuming that youth living in poverty will remain poor, especially once they have a child. The case of Jo provides an alternative set of possibilities.

Jo tended to be goal directed and upbeat. As an African American senior in high school, she divided her life in to neat and compact compartments: a best friend at school from whom she was inseparable and a long-term boyfriend at home; a job where she earned money to buy clothes; and school where she quickly completed her work so it did not interfere with her plans at home. When I asked about her career goals at the beginning of the year, Jo replied that she was going to be either a lawyer or a cosmetologist. She smiled as she explained that everyone always told her she should be a lawyer because she argued so well. On days she stayed home from school, Jo said that she watched and enjoyed Court Television. Later in the year she modified these plans, explaining that initially she would become a cosmetologist and later a lawyer. She elaborated that her decision to become a hairdresser was her backup plan, something she could fall back on if her career as a lawyer did not materialize.

Jo's eye was on the future. Days before she graduated from high school, she had enrolled in a beauty college, a 10-month program to become a licensed cosmetologist. Although her mother, herself a college graduate, encouraged Jo to attend a 4-year college and live in a dormitory, Jo's choice to study cosmetology had a certain appeal because it provided her with a clear path to a job. From the start, Jo was determined to obtain a chair in the salon where she had always gone to get her own hair styled. Her main interest in this field was that she imagined it would provide her with a stable and guaranteed income. It was a familiar path. She had a brother who was a barber and aunts who were hairstylists. As a child, she was always experimenting with her dolls, styling her friends' and even her own hair. And, while she entertained dreams of buying and managing her own shop so that she would not have to work for someone else, using her job as a cosmetologist to pay her way through college, or as a backup plan in case she did not like to practice law, she listed these options in an excited voice at the same time she talked about having a child at 19, the year following her graduation. Her mind was focused on the immediate, not distant, future. Jo graduated from Beauty College in a year, found a job in the shop where she wanted to work, helped her friend Theresa with her baby, and began courses at the community college. Before she had completed a semester of course work, Jo found herself pregnant. The baby's father was thrilled, and Jo acknowledged that this might be the best time to have a child. She immediately enlisted her mother to do the child care, with cousins and a nearby daycare center staffed by relatives as the backup. She made plans to see her regular customers in her mother's apartment and to continue with her studies. The involvement of Jo's mother in her decisions and ability to stay in school and on track cannot be underestimated. To date, Jo has continued studying, styling hair, and caring for her baby. Although her life is far from simple, she is inching along the path she developed in high school.

The following scene from Jo's government class during her senior year captures a discussion among youth regarding the timing of having a child. Although this Social Studies teacher covered traditional topics in her class, she frequently supplemented the curriculum with discussions about relevant events in the students' lives, nearly always tying these discussions into specific policy or government issues. On this particular day, the students read an editorial from *Newsweek* magazine that argued that the rate of teen pregnancy would be reduced if welfare payments were cut off when teens became pregnant or had children — an argument that foreshadowed the debate around welfare reform that followed 2 years later. After reading the editorial aloud, students — both those with and without children of their own — clamored to contribute to the conversation, speaking loudly with passion and conviction. Sofia, an African

American youth who planned to postpone both her college education and children for a few years, stopped the lively conversation with her question.

SOFIA: Why do people have kids anyway when they do not have a career? That's what I want to know.

Her teacher, Andrea, responded with a description of Leon Dash's (1989) study of young mothers. She repeated Dash's argument that some youth don't believe that they can or will have a career. A baby makes them feel as though they have something of their own. Theresa, who frequently spoke adamantly against teen pregnancy while in high school, was quick to respond.

THERESA: You're talking about us teenagers having babies and leaving their careers, weren't you saying that Sofia? Maybe they want to have kids now [as teenagers] so they can get along with their career. And maybe when they get their careers jumping, being the best they can be, they ain't going to have time to have kids.

At this point many students responded at the same time. Theresa kept on talking.

THERESA: Wait a minute. My sister tried to have a child. Okay? And she is 30 years old and she cannot have no kids now, because she didn't have no kids when she was a teenager. But now she can't have no kids. And she tried her hardest. She's 30 years old and her success took over her life. You know, so she can't have kids.

SOFIA: I think it's better to still wait because if you have a college education, you can get a job easier anyway and then you can still hold on to having kids. But if you got a college education even to go back and get a job, you can go on maternity leave. (Audio tape, field notes, Government class, October 7, 1993)

At the conclusion of the discussion, their teacher asked them to write down their opinions about whether or not it was right to cut off welfare for teens. In their writing and conversations, the students repeated the arguments from the media, their friends, and relatives, and added their own experience and understanding to the dialogue. They suggested that young women might have reasons for wanting to have children early, or at least earlier than their middle-class peers. But as a group, they condemned the young girls they knew or those they had seen on TV who had children at 14 and 15. They were unanimous in their desire to stay off of welfare. As one young mother put it, "Males don't get girls pregnant. She has something to do with it." Most refused to accept the assumption that they were victims. As a group, they had complex analyses of the impact that pregnancy and childbearing had on their own lives, which I argue contributes new perspectives to public discussions about teen pregnancy. Often their alternative plans were silenced both implicitly and explicitly by teachers, peers, family, and community members.

Several youth who were either pregnant or parenting explained to me that although they may not have planned to have children at this young age, they wanted to have children before they were too old, which, according to them, was 25 years old. They described their desire to have the same close relationships with their children that they had experienced with their own parents because they were close in age. For the most part, the youth did not describe having children because they needed someone to love. Most claimed to never want to be on welfare and rejected the notion that teens would have babies for that reason. In addition, the students with babies were not always the weakest students or those with single mothers and homes rife with drug and alcohol abuse. These conditions seemed to be present in the lives of youth with and without children. Babies are not always born to teenagers out of hopelessness, nor do they always lead to disastrous consequences.[7] They do shape both the visions and actual plans these young women construct for their futures.

A number of the students I spoke with were fighting to remain childless until they had graduated from high school or reached their goals. An African American student, Tanya, lived in a variety of settings during her adolescence: with her two parents, in foster homes, on the street, and with her sister. When Tanya began her senior year, most of her teachers doubted she would graduate from high school. She had not only failed too many courses during her previous year, she also had a surly and resistant attitude. She constantly challenged her teachers and often leapt into fights with her classmates. During the 1st semester of her senior year, something changed as Tanya realized she might graduate. She began to work hard to pass her classes and achieve good grades. Her academic record improved steadily and by the second semester she had made the honor roll.

Tanya was encouraged by her teachers, counselors, and by the foster parents in her group home to apply to college. In the spring of her senior year, after she was accepted into a state university, she began to doubt herself again. As a result, she began to miss school, get into fights, and put herself at risk for failing. However, her teachers refused to let her fail. When she missed too many days of school, they found her at her older sister's house and gave her another chance. She was both ecstatic and incredulous on the day she graduated. To date, Tanya has remained at a state university as a sociology major. Her goal is to become a social worker so that she can work with troubled youth whose lives are similar to her own. Although Tanya had a tough, nearly impenetrable shell around her, she let a few people help her. Her mentor, a health professional she met during a job-shadowing program set up by the school, was a constant support to her. Abandoned early on by her parents, Tanya has learned to take care of herself and, at the same time, struggle with others. In response to the class discussion about cutting off welfare to teen mothers, she wrote the following entry in her journal.

> 10-7-93
> I think teenagers should be cut off [of welfare] because I feel that it is corrupting our society our Black society rather. Its a copy out for young women, they don't try anymore they rely on welfare and it's really sad.
> The most interesting thing I learned today was that the teen welfare rate is global. It must be in order to make Cover story of *Newsweek*. This is nothing new to me, I see it every day its so common. It doesn't effect me because I'm trying to avoid welfare. I want to be able to say I never applied for welfare and never had it. I want to work for my money and for my children
> I could have been a teen mother twice but I know thats not the life I want for me or my children.

In this essay, Tanya echoed the comments of her classmates that she wanted to avoid welfare and pregnancy. She understood the issue in the larger context of her Black community and also in the context of her own personal battle to get an education. Tanya and her peers perceived having a child as a threat to the fragile path toward success that they had constructed. In their writing and speech they described how they were constantly fighting off this impending danger.

Children were nearly always a subtext of female students' talk and writing about the future. They were a part of a gendered subtext tied to a very particular moment in these young women's lives. In conversations, essays, and college applications, children figured into their self-conceptions and plans for the future. These youth were on the verge of graduating from high school — or so they hoped — and their futures lay in front of them. The potential presence or absence of children in their lives at this moment was particularly significant. Female students from a range of ethnic and racial backgrounds narrated their visions of success as contingent on whether or not they had children. Students with children told stories of success both despite, and in many cases because of, the responsibilities they felt as parents. Public conversations about teen pregnancy and motherhood are often reduced to discussions about poor Black teens defined against their "successful" or "good" White or Black counterparts without children. The narratives of these young women can be read as located in the particularities of their identities and the social, historical, and political contexts of their daily lives. Rather than feeling hopeless when they became pregnant or inferior because they were low-income, as illustrated in the opening note from Aster to Jo, these young women drew pride from their identities as Black women and believed it to be integral to their future success.[8]

Narrating Lives: Some Implications and Conclusions

Annette Lawson (1993) writes about the "gender scripts" or narratives that young mothers follow. She argues that young women are read (or written) as deviant when they have children at a young age and out-of-wedlock because they are constructing a life narrative with a new and threatening chronology. I am left with questions about how I write or tell the gender scripts of the young women who have narrated their stories to me. As someone with a relatively traditional gender script, how am I implicated in my writing of their stories? As a married, White, middle-class woman who waited until I was established in my career to have children, my biography differs sharply from theirs. In schools, alongside the script of the unmarried and childless professional women, my story or gendered script occupies the center stage and is often held up as the unmarked case, as normal. Our task, it seems, is to find ways to de-center this script in our schools and classrooms in order to allow and encourage students to talk and write about their fears and hopes for the future so that their scripts and realities occupy the center stage. Then, we can begin to have honest conversations about the choices, consequences, and opportunities tied to the decisions and events in students' lives. We can only engage students in honest dialogue that respects their perspectives and avoids the trap of always seeing their stories in relation to more "acceptable" ones by de-centering the traditional scripts. Stated in another way, in our classrooms we can help students construct "better" stories, a term Luttrell (1997) has borrowed from Rosenwald (1992). Luttrell (1997) posits that "better" stories make power relations explicit and suggest alternative solutions.

Schools can give young women opportunities to tell their stories without encountering immediate censorship or silencing and to revise them with guidance and mentoring from adults and peers, so that their stories are more realistic, even transformative and are set in the context of power relations and economic realities.

I'm not advocating teen pregnancy. Without a doubt, having a child at a young age, with few economic resources, places a tremendous burden and responsibility on young women's lives. On the other hand, we need to find productive and authentic ways to address issues of motherhood and pregnancy and its relation to schooling and the future with the youth we teach. We need to examine the ways schools and curricula keep young women from imagining futures that take into account their very real circumstances. In addition, we should look at the policies that reify these curricula and reinscribe the status quo. bell hooks (1990) asserts that policy-making debates usually "highlight notions of difference, marginality and otherness in such a way that it further marginalizes actual people of difference and otherness" (p. 125). If we pay attention to the narratives of the youth I interviewed, we have the opportunity to shift these debates.

In the raced, classed, and gendered narratives that were told by the young women in this study, children were an ever-present reality, a fact of life. Most started their high school careers working hard to avoid pregnancy. Some had children before they graduated or soon after graduation. Rather than giving up on this category of teen mothers, educators must find ways to support them when and if their circumstances change. It is clear that we need more effective programs to encourage young poor women to postpone pregnancy, and that we need to work to increase their opportunities for employment and success. At the same time, if as educators and policy makers we recognize that early child-bearing and motherhood can become a motivating factor in young women's lives rather than a source of despair, we can explicitly address the students from this understanding and help them to plan their lives accordingly.

Current policies aimed at preventing or reducing teen pregnancy are generally clustered around abstinence programs and family planning services, coupled with dire warnings issued through the media, billboards, and teen education classes. The data in this study suggest some additional avenues to explore to reduce unintended pregnancies for youth. Educators and policy makers would be wise to listen to and take into account these dialogues in their work with students, preservice and experienced teachers. Rather than relegating conversations about the role of children and the consequences of unintended pregnancies to the ends of periods and the hallways, I suggest that teachers make them more central, incorporating difficult and controversial issues into their curriculum. Explicit instruction in how to do this should begin in teacher education programs. In these conversations with youth, it is critical to pursue, rather than avoid, the complexities. Students need more than information and warnings; they need to participate in the construction of alternate visions.

Yet conversations are not enough. We need to examine schools — their pedagogy and curriculum — to see whether they engage students in learning the literacies and skills that allow them to enact new roles and identities in relation to work and their futures. And, as Natriello, McDill, and Pallas (1990) argue, we must find ways to address these issues with long-term rather than stop gap solutions. We need to ask why students such as Theresa simultaneously gain admission to 4-year colleges and fail high school competency exams at the last minute, leading them to leave high school with vague and unrealistic plans about their futures. In Theresa's case, although there were many teachers who reached out to her, it was not enough. What role might mentoring programs — both in and out of schools — serve for young women such as Theresa? Would the opportunity to talk honestly about options and consequences, and to see how these decisions played out in the lives of others, have helped her to think about her choices differently? We must examine how schools, particularly urban schools, are disrupting the limiting and limited categories and possibilities they offer to female students. And we must take a close and honest look at what is possible in schools and when there is a need to look outside of these institutions.

When students talk about their futures in schools, as educators and policy makers we tend to carve away the complexities. When Jo publicly announced that she wanted to become both a lawyer and a hairdresser, her teacher treated her as a future cosmetologist declaring: "Well, you don't have to read Shakespeare to do hair." Given the current economic climate that has resulted from the dismantling of social service safety nets and increased barriers to postsecondary education, the hurdles faced by these youth have only worsened since their high school years in the early 1990s. Implicit in the note quoted in the opening paragraph of this article is the notion that becoming pregnant would "bring [Jo] down" and keep her from becoming a "big Black successful Black women." The discourses of youth, as well as the narratives of their experiences, raise questions about the automatic link between success and remaining without a child. They encourage us to see the ways that Jo and her peers are struggling to be successful as young mothers. Acknowledging the complex nature of this discourse allows us to imagine new educational practices and policies that will both support youth like Jo to remain childless and support them to continue with their education should they become pregnant. Our task is to adapt our policies and practices, the discourses we use in our teaching and policy making, in order to give students opportunities to translate their experiences, tell their stories, and narrate their lives in order to transform their futures.

Notes

1. See Schultz (1996). For important exceptions, see Katz (1995) and Raissiguier (1994), two studies of vocational students in France. There are a few older studies that focused on White working-class females. One purpose of these early studies was to provide a response to Willis's (1977) study of working-class boys, and to describe the cultures established by females. See, for example, Deem (1980), Griffin (1985), and McRobbie (1978). Other more recent exceptions include, Borman (1991), Holland & Eisenhart (1990), Luttrell (1997), Valli (1986), and Weis (1990).
2. A larger context in which to place this study is a report released by the organization Children Now and described in the *San Francisco Chronicle*, June 22, 1995. The report states that in California in 1993, the 1st year of this study, teen unemployment was the highest in the nation (at 26%), the youth homicide rate was 59% higher than the U.S. average, the teen birth rate was the 7th highest in the nation, and nearly one in three children was living in poverty.
3. For a more detailed description, see Schultz (1996, 1999)
4. See for example, the Allan Guttmacher Institute (1976) report entitled "Eleven Million Teenagers: What Can Be Done About the Epidemic of Adolescent Pregnancies in the United States."

5. While in the mid-1980s these numbers began to climb again (Klerman, 1993), a recent report in the *New York Times* cites evidence of the decline of teen pregnancy perhaps signaling a shift in this trend not yet reflected in a change in public perception (Lacey, 1999).

6. Again, I don't want to minimize the hardship for both the mother and her child of teen pregnancy. See Maynard (1997) for a set of economic analyses that support this point.

7. This pride and frequent assertion of their racial identity provides an interesting contrast to the important work done by Fordham (1988, 1991, 1993) on the relationships between identity and success. See also Schultz (1996, 1999), Steele (1992), and Tatum (1992, 1997).

8. In my work on conversations across race lines, I have called these democratizing conversations (Schultz, Buck, & Niesz, 2000).

References

Allan Guttmacher Institute. (1976). *Eleven million teenagers: What can be done about the epidemic of adolescent pregnancies in the United States.* New York: Planned Parenthood Federation of America.

Allan Guttmacher Institute (1994). *Sex and America's teenagers.* New York: Allan Guttmacher Institute.

Borman, K. M. (1991). *The first "real" job: A study of young workers.* Albany: State University of New York Press.

Campbell, A. (1968). The role of family planning in the reduction of poverty, *Journal of Marriage and the Family, 30*(2), 236–245.

Clark, R. M. (1983). *Family life and school achievement: Why poor black children succeed and fail.* Chicago: University of Chicago Press.

Clinton, W. (1995, January 25). State of the Union address. *Boston Globe*, 8.

Dash, L. (1989). *When children want children: The urban crisis of teenage childbearing.* New York: Morrow.

Davies, B. (1993). *Shards of glass: Children reading and writing beyond gendered identities.* Cresskill, NJ: Hampton Press.

Deem, R. (Ed.). (1980). *Schooling for women's work.* London: Routledge & Kegan Paul.

Fordham, S. (1988). Racelessness as a factor in Black students' school success: Pragmatic strategy or pyrrhic victory? *Harvard Educational Review, 58*(1), 54–84.

Fordham, S. (1991). Peer-proofing academic competition among Black adolescents: "acting white" Black American style. In Christine Sleeter (Ed.), *Empowerment through multicultural education* (pp. 69–93), Albany: State University of New York Press.

Fordham, S. (1993). Those loud Black girls: (Black) women, silence, and gender 'passing' in the Academy. *Anthropology and Education Quarterly, 24*(1), 3–32.

Griffin, C. (1985). *Typical girls?: Young women from schools to the job market.* London: Routledge and Kegan Paul.

Holland, D. C. & Eisenhart, M. A. (1990). *Educated in romance.* Chicago: University of Chicago Press.

hooks, b. (1990). *Yearning.* Boston: South End Press.

Katz, M. (1995). *The education of second generation women of North African descent in France.* Paper presented at the Annual Ethnography in Education Forum, University of Pennsylvania, Philadelphia.

Klerman, L. V. (1993). Adolescent pregnancy and parenting: Controversies of the past and lessons for the future. *Journal of Adolescent Health, 14,* 553–561.

Lacey, M. (1999, October 27). Teen-age birth rate in U.S. falls again. *New York Times,* A 16.

Lawson, A. (1993). Multiple fractures: The cultural construction of teenage sexuality and pregnancy. In A.Lawson & D. L. Rhode (Eds.), *The politics of pregnancy: Adolescent sexuality and public policy* (pp. 101–125). New Haven, CT: Yale University Press.

Lesher, D. (1996, Jan. 9). Wilson makes renewed call for moral values. *Los Angeles Times,* A1.

Luker, K. (1996). *Dubious conceptions: The politics of teenage pregnancy.* Cambridge, MA: Harvard University Press.

Luttrell, W. (1997). *Schoolsmart and motherwise: Working-class women's identity and schooling.* New York: Routledge.

Maynard, R. A. (Ed.), (1997). *Kids having kids: Economic cost and social consequences of teen pregnancy.* Washington, DC: Urban Institute Press.

McRobbie, A. (1978). Working class girls and the culture of femininity. In Women's Study Group (Eds.), *Women take issue: Aspects of women's subordination* (pp. 56–91), London: Hutchinson.

Natriello, G., McDill, E. L., & Pallas, Aaron M. (1990), *Schooling disadvantaged children: Racing against catastrophe.* New York: Teachers College Press.

Newman, K. S. (1999). *No shame in my game: The working poor in the inner city.* New York: Alfred A. Knopf and Russell Sage Foundation.

Pillow, W. (1997). Exposed methodology. The body as deconstructive practice. *Qualitative Studies in Education, 10*(3), 349–363.

Raissiguier, C. (1994). Becoming women/becoming workers: Identity formation in a French vocational school. Albany: State University of New York Press.

Rhode, D. & Lawson, A. (1993). Introduction. In A. Lawson & D. C. Rhode (Eds.), *The politics of pregnancy: Adolescent sexuality and public policy.* New Haven, CT: Yale University Press.

Rosenwald, G. (1992). Conclusion: Reflections on narrative self-understanding. In G. Rosenwald & R. Ochberg (Eds.), *Storied lives: The cultural politics of self-understanding.* New Haven, CT: Yale University Press.

Schultz, K. (1996). Between school and work: The literacies of urban adolescent females, *Anthropology and Education Quarterly, 27*(4), 517–544.

Schultz, K. (1997). Crossing boundaries in research and teacher education: Reflections of a White researcher in urban schools and communities. *Qualitative Inquiry, 3,* 491–512.

Schultz, K. (1999). Identity narratives: Stories from the lives of urban adolescent females, *Urban Review, 31,* 79–106.

Schultz, K., Buck, P., & Niesz, T. (2000). Democratizing conversations: Discourses of "race" in a post-desegregated middle school, *American Education Research Journal, 37*, 33–65.

Scott-Jones, D. (1993). Adolescent childbearing: Whose problem? What can we do? *Phi Delta Kappan*, K1–K12.

Stack, C. (1974). *All our kin.* New York: Harper & Row.

Steele, C. (1992). Race and the schooling of Black Americans. *Atlantic Monthly, 269*, 68–78.

Tatum, B. D. (1992). Talking about race, learning about racism: The application of racial identity development theory in the classroom. *Harvard Educational Review, 62*, 1–24.

Tatum, B. D. (1997). *"Why are all the Black kids sitting together in the cafeteria?" and other conversations about race.* New York: Basic Books.

Valli, L. (1986). *Becoming clerical workers.* Boston: Routledge & Kegan Paul.

Vinovskis, M. A. (1988). *An "epidemic" of adolescent pregnancy?* New York: Oxford University Press.

Walkerdine, V. & Lucey, H. (1989). *Democracy in the kitchen: Regulating mothers and socialising daughters.* London: Virago.

Weis, L. (1990). *Working class without work: High school students in a de-industrializing economy.* New York: Routledge.

Willis, P. (1977). *Learning to labor: How working class kids get working class jobs.* New York: Columbia University Press.

Part III

Adolescent Identity Formation and the Relational World

8

Exit-Voice Dilemmas in Adolescent Development

CAROL GILLIGAN

In *Exit, Voice and Loyalty: Responses to Decline in Firms, Organizations, and States* (1970), Albert Hirschman contrasts two modes of response to decline in social organizations — the options of exit and voice. Exit, central to the operation of the classical market economy, is exemplified by the customer who, dissatisfied with the product of company A, switches to the product of company B. In comparison to this neat and impersonal mechanism that operates "by courtesy of the Invisible Hand," voice — the attempt to change rather than escape from an objectionable situation —is messy, cumbersome, and direct. "Graduated all the way from faint grumbling to violent protest," voice is political action *par excellence*, carrying with it the potential for "heartbreak" by substituting the personal and public articulation of critical opinions for the private, secret vote. Introducing exit and voice as the two principal actors in his drama of societal health, Hirschman puts forth a theory of loyalty to explain the conditions for their optimal collaboration. Loyalty, he maintains, the seemingly irrational commitment of "the member who cares," activates voice by holding exit at bay, while sustaining in the implication of disloyalty the possibility of exit as the option of last resort.

To the economist's view of the individual as motivated by the desire for profit and to the political theorist's view of the individual as seeking power in social organizations, Hirschman adds a new dimension — an image of the individual as motivated by loyalty or attachment to stem decline and promote recuperation. Demonstrating the power of attachment to influence action and shift the parameters of choice, Hirschman illustrates across a wide range of

From: Gilligan, C., Ward, J., Taylor, J., & Bardige, B. (Eds.). (1988). *Mapping the moral domain: A contribution of women's thinking to psychological theory and education* (pp. 141–158). Cambridge, MA: Harvard University Press. Copyright © Carol Gilligan. Reprinted with permission.

situations how the presence of loyalty holds exit and voice in tension and, thus changes the meaning of both leaving and speaking. The psychological acuity of Hirschman's analysis of exit and voice is matched by the transformation implied by bringing the psychology of attachment to the center of the developmental consideration.

In honoring Hirschman's contribution I wish to illuminate the psychological dimensions of this conception by extending it to the seemingly remote domain of adolescent development. Here it is possible to see not only the interplay of exit and voice that Hirschman describes but also the dilemmas posed by loyalty at a time of intense transition in human life. The central themes of Hirschman's work — the importance of values and ideas in the developmental process, the connection between passions and interests, the reflection on historical periods of development — will be addressed here in the context of the life cycle. But following Hirschman's example of trespass, I will suggest that the analysis of loyalty in family relationships speaks across disciplinary boundaries to the problems of interdependence that face contemporary civilization.

Hirschman's focus on loyalty is in part a correction to the more popular view of the exit option as uniquely powerful in effecting change. In challenging this view, he underscores the problems of attachment which arise in modern societies — problems which have taken on an added intensity and urgency in an age of nuclear threat. This threat which signals the possibility for an irredeemable failure of care also calls attention to the limits of exit as a solution to conflicts in social relationships. Yet "the preference for the neatness of exit over the messiness and heartbreak of voice" (p. 107), which Hirschman finds in classical economics as well as in the American tradition, extends through the study of human development, emerging most clearly in the psychology of adolescence. This paradigm of problem solving, based on an assumption of independence and competition, obscures the reality of interdependence and masks the possibilities for cooperation. Thus, the need to reassess the interpretive schemes on which we rely, the need to correct "defensive representation of the real world" (p. 2) in which our actions take place, extends across the realm of economics to the psychological domain, calling attention to shared assumptions about the nature of development and the process of change.

This parallel is forcefully evoked by the easy transfer of the characters from Hirschman's drama to the adolescent scene where puberty signals the decline of the childhood world of relations and exit and voice enter as modes of response and recuperation. The growth to full stature at puberty releases the child from dependence on parents for protection and heightens the possibility of exit as a solution to conflicts in family relationships. At the same time the sexual maturation of puberty — the intensification of sexual feelings and the advent of reproductive capability — impels departure from the family, given the incest taboo. The heightened availability of and impetus toward exit in

adolescence, however, may also stimulate development of voice — a development enhanced by the cognitive changes of puberty, the growth of reflective
thinking, and the discovery of the subjective self. Seeing the possibility of
leaving, the adolescent may become freer in speaking, more willing to assert
perspectives and voice opinions that diverge from accepted family truths.
But if the transformations of puberty heighten the potential for both exit and
voice, the experience of adolescence also changes the meaning of leaving and
speaking by creating dilemmas of loyalty and rendering choice itself more
self-conscious and reflective.

Adolescents, striving to integrate a new image of self and new experiences
of relationship, struggle to span the discontinuity of puberty and renegotiate
a series of social connections. This effort at renegotiation engages the adolescent voice in the process of identity formation and moral growth. But this
development of voice depends on the presence of loyalty for its continuation.
Hirschman (1970), pointing out that the availability of the exit options tends
"to atrophy the development of the art of voice" (p. 43), but also noting that the
threat of exit can strengthen the voice's effective use, observes that the decision
of whether to exit will often be made in light of the prospects for the efficacy
of voice. Development in adolescence, thus, hinges on loyalty between adolescents and adults, and the challenge to society, families, and schools is how to
engage that loyalty and how to educate the voice of the future generation.

In the life cycle the adolescent is the truth teller, like the fool in the Renaissance play,[1] exposing hypocrisy and revealing truths about human relationships. These truths pertain to justice and care, the moral coordinates of human
connection, heightened for adolescents who stand between the innocence of
childhood and the responsibility of adulthood. Looking back on the childhood
experiences of inequality and attachment, feeling again the powerlessness and
vulnerability which these experiences initially evoked, adolescents identify
with the child and construct a world that offers protection. This ideal or uto-
pian vision, laid out along the coordinates of justice and care; depicts a world
where self and other will be treated as of equal worth, where, despite differences in power, things will be fair; a world where everyone will be included,
where no one will be left alone or hurt. In the ability to construct this ideal
moral vision lies the potential for nihilism and despair as well as the possibility for societal renewal which adolescence symbolizes and represents. Given
the engagement of the adolescent's passion for morality and truth with the
realities of social justice and care, adolescents are the group whose problems
of development most closely mirror society's problems with regeneration.

In analyzing these problems I will distinguish two moral voices that
define two intersecting lines of development — one arising from the child's
experience of inequality, one from the child's experience of attachment.
Although the experiences of inequality and attachment initially are concurrent
in the relationship of parent and child, they point to different dimensions of

relationship — the dimension of inequality/equality and of attachment/detachment. The moral visions of justice and care reflect these different dimensions of relationships and the injunctions to which the experiences of inequality and attachment give rise. But these experiences also inform different ways of experiencing and defining self in relation to others and lend different meanings to separation. These different conceptions of self and morality (Gilligan, 1982, chap. 2) have been obscured by current stage theories of psychological development that present a single linear representation, fusing inequality with attachment and linking development to separation. But the problems in this portrayal are clarified by observing how the axis of development shifts when dependence, which connotes the experiences of connection, is contrasted with isolation rather than opposed to independence.

To trace this shift and consider its implications for the understanding of progress and growth, I will begin with theories of identity and moral development that focus on the dimension of inequality/equality, noting that these theories have been derived primarily or exclusively from research on males.[2] Then I will turn to research on females to focus the dimension of attachment/detachment and delineate a different conception of morality and self. Although these two dimensions of relationship may be differentially salient in the thinking of women and men, both inequality and attachment are embedded in the cycle of life, universal in human experience because inherent in the relation of parent and child. By representing both dimensions of relationships, it becomes possible to see how they combine to create dilemmas of loyalty in adolescence and to discern how different conceptions of loyalty give rise to different modalities of exit and voice.

Current Theories of Adolescent Development

The theories that currently provide the conceptual underpinning for the description of adolescent development trace a progression toward equality and autonomy in the conception of morality and self. All of these theories follow William James (1902) in distinguishing the once from the twice-born self and tie that distinction to the contrast between conventional and reflective moral thought. This approach differentiates youth who adopt the conventions of their childhood society as their own, defining themselves more by ascription than choice, from youth who reject societal conventions by questioning the norms and values that provide their justification. The distinction between two roads to maturity and the clear implication that the second leads far beyond the first appears in Erikson's division between the "technocrats" or "compact majority" and the "neo-humanists" (1968, pp. 31–39). The same contrast appears in Kohlberg's division of moral development into preconventional, conventional, and principled thought (Kohlberg, 1981).

This dual or tripartite division of identity formation and moral growth generates a description of adolescent development that centers on two major separations — the first from parental authority and the second from the authority of societal conventions. In this context, loyalty, the virtue of fidelity that Erikson (1964) cites as the strength of adolescence, takes on an ideological cast, denoting a shift in the locus of authority from persons to principles —a move toward abstraction that justifies separation and renders "the self" autonomous. Key to this vision of self as separate and constant is the promise of equality built into the cycle of life, the promise of development that in time the child will become the adult.

Tracing development as a move from inequality to equality, adolescence is marked by a series of power confrontations, by the renegotiation of authority relationships. To emerge victorious the adolescent must overcome the constraint of parental authority through a process of "detachment" described by Freud (1905) as "one of the most significant, but also one of the most painful, psychical accomplishments of the pubertal period," "... a process that alone makes possible the opposition, which is so important for the progress of civilization, between the new generation and the old." This equation of progress with detachment and opposition leads problems in adolescence to be cast as problems of exit or separation. Observing that, as "at every stage in the course of development through which all human beings ought by rights to pass, a certain number are held back; so there are some who have never got over their parents' authority and have withdrawn their affection from them either very incompletely or not at all," Freud concludes that this failure of development in adolescence is one that occurs mostly in girls (all quotations, p. 227).

Thus, exit, in resolving the childhood drama of inequality, symbolized for Freud by the oedipal dilemma, becomes emblematic of adolescent growth. Yet the option of exit, as Hirschman observes, leaves a problem of loyalty in its wake, a problem which if not addressed can lead to the decline of care and commitment in social relationships. In this light, adolescent girls who demonstrate a reluctance to exit may articulate a different voice — a voice which speaks of loyalty to persons and identifies detachment as morally problematic. To represent this perspective on loyalty changes the depiction of adolescent growth by delineating a mode of development that relies not on detachment but on a change in the form of attachment — a change that must be negotiated by voice.

Yet the preference for the neatness of exit over the messiness and heartbreak of voice, the focus on inequality rather than attachment in human relations, and the reliance on male experience in building the model of human growth have combined to silence the female voice. This silence contributes to the problems observed in adolescent girls, particularly if these problems are seen to reflect a failure of engagement rather than a failure of separation. But this silence and the implicit disparagement of female experience also creates problems in the account of human development — a failure to trace the growth of attachment and the capacity for care and loyalty in relationships.

The omission of female experience from the literature on adolescent development was noted by Bruno Bettelheim in 1965, and the significance of this omission was underlined by Joseph Adelson, who edited the *Handbook of Adolescent Psychology,* published in 1980. Adelson had asked a leading scholar to write a chapter for the handbook on female adolescent development, but after surveying the literature she concluded that there was not enough good material to warrant a separate chapter. In their chapter on psychodynamics, Adelson and Doehrman (1980) observe that "to read the psychological literature on adolescence has, until very recently, meant reading about the psychodynamics of the male youngster writ large" (p. 114). They end their chapter by noting that "the inattention to girls and to the processes of feminine development in adolescence has meant undue attention to such problems as impulse control, rebelliousness, superego struggles, ideology and achievement, along with a corresponding neglect of such issues as intimacy, nurturance, and affiliation" (p. 114). They found particularly troubling the fact that current biases in the literature reinforce each other, with the result that "the separate, though interacting emphases on pathology, on the more ideologized, least conformist social strata, and on males has produced a psychodynamic theory of adolescence that is both one-sided and distorted" (p. 115).

In girls' accounts of their experiences in the adolescent years, problems of attachment and detachment emerge as a central concern. Because girls — the group left out in the critical theory-building studies of adolescent psychology — have repeatedly been described as having problems in adolescence with separation, the experience of girls may best inform an expanded theory of adolescent development.

The Missing Line of Adolescent Development

In adolescence the renegotiation of attachment centers on the inclusion of sexuality and inclusion of perspective in relationships — each introducing a new level of complication and depth to human connection. Conflicts of attachment that arise at this time are exemplified by the problems that girls describe when they perceive the inclusion of themselves (their views and their wishes) as hurting their parents, whereas including their parents implies excluding themselves. The revival of the oedipal triangular conflict which psychoanalysts describe demonstrates how such problems tend to be recast by girls as a drama of inclusion and exclusion rather than of dominance and subordination. If the "oedipal wish" is conceived as a desire to be included in the parents' relationship — to be "member of the wedding" in Carson McCullers' phrase — then the oedipal threat in the adolescent years is that of exclusion, experienced as endangering one's connection with others.

But adolescents, gaining the power to form family relationships on their own, confront the implications of excluding their parents as they remember their own experience of having been excluded by them. Construed as an issue of justice, this exclusion seems eminently fair, a matter of simple reciprocity. Construed as an issue of care, it seems, instead, morally problematic, given the association of exclusion with hurt. In resisting detachment and criticizing exclusion, adolescent girls hold to the view that change can be negotiated through voice and that voice is the way to sustain attachment across the leavings of adolescence.

Adolescents, aware of new dimensions of human connection, experiment in a variety of ways as they seek to discover what constitutes attachment and how problems in relationships can be solved. Girls in particular, given their interest in relationships and their attention to the ways in which connection between people can be formed and maintained, observe that relationships in which voice is silenced are not relationships in any meaningful sense. This understanding that voice has to be expressed in relationships to solve rather than escape the dilemmas of adolescence, calls attention not only to the limitations of exit but also to the problems that arise when voice is silenced. In sum, adolescent girls who resist exit may be holding on to the position that solutions to dilemmas of attachment in adolescence must be forged by voice and that exit alone is no solution but an admission of defeat. Thus, their resistance may signify a refusal to leave before they can speak.

Hirschman, describing how the high price of exit and the presence of loyalty in family relationships encourages the option of voice, also indicates that resort to voice will be undertaken in a conflict situation when the outcome is visualized as either possible victory or possible accord. But adolescents in their conflicts with their parents cannot readily visualize victory, nor can they visualize full accord, for given the closeness of the relationships, a meeting of minds may suggest a meeting of bodies which is precluded by the incest taboo. Therefore, exit must be part of the solution, and some accommodation must be found, some mixture of leaving and speaking which typically may occur in different proportions for boys and girls.

The focus on leaving in the psychology of adolescence, manifest by measuring development by signs of separation, may be an accurate rendition of male experience, at least within certain cultures, since the more explosive potential of tensions between adolescent sons and parents highlights the opposition between dependence and independence which renders exit appealing. In contrast, the propensity toward staying, noted as the "problem" in female development, may reflect the different nature of the attachment between daughters and parents and the greater salience for girls of the opposition between dependence and isolation. In this way the two opposites of the word dependence — isolation and independence — catch the shift in the valence of relationships that occurs when connection with others is experienced as an impediment to autonomy and when it is experienced as a protection against isolation. This essential ambivalence of human connection creates an ongoing ethical tension that rises sharply in adolescence and leads to exit-voice problems.

The ways in which adolescents consider decisions about staying and leaving, silence and speaking, illustrate the interplay of exit, voice, and loyalty that Hirschman describes. But the dilemmas of adolescence become more intense when they involve conflicts of loyalty, especially when attachment to persons vies with adherence to principles. Psychological theorists typically have given priority to principles as the anchor of personal integrity and focused their attention on the necessity and the justification for leaving. But in doing so, they have tended to overlook the costs of detachment — its consequences both to personal integrity and to societal functioning. Since adolescent girls tend to resist detachment and highlight its costs to others and themselves, we may learn about ways of solving problems through voice within the context of ongoing relationships by observing the way that they struggle with conflicts of loyalty and exit-voice decisions.

In a series of studies (conducted by the Center for the Study of Gender, Education, and Human Development), concerns about detachment have emerged saliently in girls' and women's moral thinking, pointing to an ethic of care that enjoins responsibility and responsiveness in relationships. In a study of high school girls, these concerns were so insistent and focused so specifically on problems of speaking and listening that it seemed important to inquire directly about situations in which voice failed: we sought to explore empirically the conceptual distinction between problems of inequality and problems of detachment.[3] Thus, two questions were added to the interview schedule in the second year of the study — one pertaining to incidents of unfairness and one to incidents of not listening. Asked to describe a situation in which someone was not being listened to, girls spoke about a wide variety of problems that ranged across the divide between interpersonal and international relations. "The Nicaraguan people," one girl explained, "are not being listened to by President Reagan." Asked how she knew, she said that Mr. Reagan, in explaining his own position, did not respond to the issues raised by the Nicaraguans and, thus, appeared to discount their view of their situation. The absence of response, as it indicated not listening, was acutely observed by girls in a wide range of settings and interpreted as a sign of not caring. The willingness to test the extent of detachment, to ascertain whether not listening signified a transitory distraction or a more deeply rooted indifference, appeared critical to decisions girls made about silence and speaking.

The same moral outrage and passion that infused girls' descriptions of not listening was also apparent in their accounts of unfairness. Yet, over the high school years, concerns about listening tended increasingly to temper judgments about fairness, reflecting a growing awareness of differences in perspective and problems in communication. The amount of energy devoted to solving these problems, the intensity of the search for ways to make connection and achieve understanding, led girls to express immense frustration in situations where voice failed. When others did not listen and seemed not to care, they spoke of "coming up against a wall." This image of wall had as its counterpart the search for an opening through which one could speak. The nature of this search, together with the intensity of its frustration, are conveyed in the following girl's description of an attempt to reestablish communication with her mother without abandoning her own perspective:

> I called my mother up and said, "Why can't I talk to you anymore?" And I ended up crying and hanging up on her because she wouldn't listen to me. She had her own opinion about what was truth and what was reality, and she gave me no opening.... And, you know, I kept saying, "Well, you hurt me." And she said, "No, I didn't." And I said, "Well, why am I hurt?" you know. And she is just denying my feelings as if they didn't exist and as if I had no right to feel them, even though they were.... I guess until she calls me up or writes me a letter saying I want to talk instead of saying, well, this and this happened, and I don't understand what is going on with you, and I don't understand why you are denying the truth... until she says, I want to talk, I can't, I just can't.

Simone Weil (1977), in a beautifully evocative and paradoxical statement, defines morality as the silence in which one can hear the unheard voices (p. 316). This rendering of morality in terms of attention and perception is central to Iris Murdoch's (1970) vision and appears as well in Hannah Arendt's (1972) question as to whether the activity of thinking as such, "the habit of examining whatever happens to come to pass or to attract attention, regardless of results and specific content," can be considered a moral act (p. 5). The visions of these women philosophers illuminate the activities of care that high school girls describe, their equation of care with the willingness "to be there," "to listen," "to talk to," and "to understand." In girls' narratives about conflict and choice, these activities of care take on a moral dimension, and the willingness and the ability to care become a source of empowerment and a standard of self-evaluation.

Detachment, then, signifies not only caring in the sense of choosing to stand apart but also not being able to care, given that in the absence of connection one would not know how to respond. Thus, girls' portrayal of care reveals its cognitive as well as affective dimensions, its foundation in the ability to perceive people in their own terms and to respond to need. As this knowledge generates the power not only to help but also to hurt, the uses of this power become a measure of responsibility in relationships.

In adolescence when both wanting and knowing take on new meanings, given the intensity of sexual feelings and the discovery of subjectivity, conflicts of responsibility assume new dimensions of complexity. The experience of coming into a relationship with oneself and the increasing assumption of responsibility for taking care of oneself are premised in this context not on detachment from others but on a change in the form of connection with others. These changes in the experience of connection, both with others and with oneself set the parameters of the moral conflicts that girls describe when responsibility to themselves conflicts with responsibility to others. Seeking to perceive and respond to their own as well as to others' feelings and thoughts, girls ask if they can be responsive to themselves without losing connection with others and whether they can respond to others without abandoning themselves.

This search for an inclusive solution to dilemmas of conflicting loyalties vies with the tendency toward exclusion expressed in the moral opposition between "selfish" and "selfless" choice — an opposition where selfishness connotes the exclusion of others and selflessness the exclusion of self. This opposition appears repeatedly in the moral judgments of adolescent girls and women, in part because the conventional norms of feminine virtue, which hold up selflessness as a moral ideal, conflict with an understanding of relationships derived from experiences of connection. Since the exclusion of self as well as of others dissolves the fabric of connection, both exclusions create problems in relationships, diminishing the capacity for care and reducing one's efficacy as a moral agent.

The bias toward voice in girls' moral thinking contains this recognition and directs attention toward the ways that attachments can be transformed and sustained. "There is not a wall between us" one adolescent explains in describing her relationship with her parents, "but there is a sort of strain or a sieve." This metaphor of connection continuing through a barrier to complete attachment conveys a solution that avoids detachment while recognizing the need for distance that arises in adolescence. The following examples further illustrate the mixture of exit and voice in adolescent girls' thinking about relationships, indicating the value they place on loyalty or continuing attachment. In addition, these examples suggest how attachments can be sustained across separation and how relationships can expand without detachment.

> I have been very close to my parents mentally. We have a very strong relationship, but yet it is not a physical thing that you can see...In my family we are more independent of each other, but yet we have this strong love.
>
> All the boyfriends that I have ever really cared about, they are still with me...in mind, not in body, because we are separated by miles. But they will always be with me. Any relationship that I have ever had has been important to me. Otherwise I wouldn't have had it.

Such evocations of the mind-body problem of adolescence convey a view of continuing connection as consonant with autonomy and growth. Within this vision, dependence and independence are not opposed but are seen instead to commingle, as exemplified by the following description of a relationship between close friends:

> I would say we depend on each other in a way that we are both independent, and I would say that we are very independent, but as far as our friendship goes, we are dependent on each other because we know that both of us realize that whenever we need something, the other person will always be there.

In this way, the capacity to care for others and to receive care from them becomes a part of rather than antithetical to self-definition.

Defined in this context of relationships, identity is formed through the gaining of voice or perspective, and self is known through the experience of engagement with different voices or points of view. Over the high school years, girls display an increasing recognition that attachment does not imply agreement and that differences constitute the life of relationships rather than a threat to their continuation. The ability to act on this recognition generates a more empirical approach to conflict resolution, an approach which often leads to the discovery of creative solutions to disputes. Hirschman describes how the willingness to trade off the certainty of exit for the uncertainty of improvement via voice can spur the "creativity-requiring course of action" from which people would otherwise recoil. Thus, he explains how loyalty performs "a function similar to the underestimate of the prospective tasks' difficulties" (p. 80). The observation of girls' persistence in seeking solutions to problems of connection, even in the face of seemingly insurmountable obstacles, extends this point and indicates further how attachment to persons rather than adherence to principles may enhance the possibility for arriving at creative forms of conflict resolution.

Yet the vulnerability of voice to exclusion underscores how easily this process can fail when a wish for victory or domination defeats efforts at reaching accord. "If people are thinking on two different planes," one girl explains, then "you can't understand." Asked whether people on different planes can communicate, she describes how voice depends on relationship while exit can be executed in isolation.

> Well, they can try, maybe they can...if they were both trying to communicate. But if one person is trying to block the other out totally, that person is going to win and not hear a thing that the other person is saying. If that is what they are trying to do, then they will accomplish their objective: to totally disregard the other person.

This vulnerability of voice to detachment and indifference becomes a major problem for girls in adolescence, especially when they recognize a difference between their own perspectives and commonly held points of view. Given a relational construction of loyalty, the drama of exit and voice may shift to the tension between silence and speaking, where silence signifies exit and voice implies conflict and change in relationships. Then development hinges on the contrast between loyalty and blind faith, since loyalty implies the willingness to risk disloyalty by including the voice of the self in relationship. This effort to bring the subjectively known self into connection with others signifies an attempt to change the form of connection and relies on a process of communication, not only to discover the truth about others but also to reveal the truth about oneself.

"If I could only let my mother know the list (that I had grown inside me)... of over two hundred things that I had to tell my mother so that she would know the true things about me and to stop the pain in my throat), she — and the world — would become more like me, and I would never be alone again" (Kingston, 1976, pp. 197–198). So the heroine of Maxine Hong Kingston's autobiographical novel, *The Woman Warrior,* defines the parameters of adolescent development in terms of the contrast between silence and voice. The silence that surrounds the discovery of the secret, subjectively-known self protects its integrity in the face of disconfirmation but at the expense of isolation. In contrast, voice — the attempt to change rather than escape from an objectionable situation — contains the potential for transformation by bringing the self into connection with others.

In adolescence, the problem of exclusion hinges on the contrast between selfish and selfless behavior. This is juxtaposed against a wish for inclusion, a wish that depends upon voice. In recent years the exit option has become increasingly popular as a solution to conflicts in human relationships, as the high incidence of divorce attests. The meaning of such leaving, although commonly interpreted as a move toward separation and independence, is, however, more complex. For example, the more unencumbered access to exit from marriage can spur the exercise of voice in marriage, which in turn can lead to the discovery of the truth about attachment. The distinction between true and false connection, between relationships where voice is engaged and relationships where voice is silenced, often becomes critical to exit decisions both for women considering divorce and for adolescent girls. Given the tendency for girls and women to define loyalty as attachment to persons, exit constitutes an alternative to silence in situations where voice has failed. Thus, the recognition of the costs of detachment, not only from others but also from oneself, becomes key to girls' development in adolescence since it encourages voice while sustaining exit as the option of last resort.

The wish to be able to disagree, to be different without losing connection with others, leads outward in girls' experience from family relationships to relationships with the world. The adolescent girl who seeks to affirm the truths about herself by joining these truths with her mother's experiences aspires through this connection to validate her own perceptions, to see herself as part of the world rather than as all alone. But the difficulty for girls in feeling connected both to their mothers and to the world is compounded in a world where "human" often means male.

Consequently, the problem of attachment in adolescent development is inseparable from the problem of interpretation, since the ability to establish connection with others hinges on the ability to render one's story coherent. Given the failure of interpretive schemes to reflect female experience and given the distortion of this experience in common understandings of care and attachment, development for girls in adolescence hinges not only on their willingness to risk disagreement with others but also on the courage to challenge two equations: the equation of human with male and the equation of care with self-sacrifice. Together these equations create a self-perpetuating system that sustains a limited conception of human development and a problematic representation of human relationships.

By attending to female voices and including these voices in the psychological schemes through which we have come to know ourselves, we arrive at a correction of currently defective modes of interpretation. As the understanding of morality expands to include both justice and care, as identity loses its Platonic cast and the experience of attachment to others becomes part of the definition of self, as relationships are imagined not only as hierarchies of inequality but also as webs of protection, the representation of psychological development shifts from a progression toward separation to a chronicle of expanding connection.

Adolescent Development in the Contemporary Context

The student protest movements of the late 1960s focused on the consequences of social inequality and held up against existing unfairness the ideals of justice and rights. But these movements contained as a countercultural theme a challenge to the existing state of relationships, articulated by the generation of "flower children" that included a large female representation. With the disillusionment of the 1970s, these movements for change degenerated into privatism and retreat, as concerns with both justice and care focused increasingly on the self. Yet concomitant changes on the world scene, such as the growing awareness of global pollution and the escalation of the nuclear threat, have underlined the illusory nature of the exit solution and drawn attention to the reality of interdependence. The need to develop the art of voice, then, becomes a pressing agenda for education. The popularity of psychotherapy may reveal the extent to which voice has been neglected in a society that has come increasingly to rely on exit solutions and to prefer neat impersonal often secret forms of communications.

As the youth of both sexes currently oscillate between moral nihilism and moral indignation, given the impending potential for an irretrievable failure of care on the part of the older generation, the relativism that has diluted the engagement between adolescents and adults may give way to a recognition of the moral challenges which they commonly face: the challenges of fairness — that coming generations be allowed their chance to reach maturity; the challenge of care — that the cycle of violence be replaced by an ecology of care[4] that sustains the attachments necessary to life.

When Erikson (1965) pointed to adolescence as the time in the life cycle when the intersection of life history and history becomes most acute, he called attention to the relationship between the problems of society and the crises of youth. In this light the current increase of problems among adolescent girls, including the startling rise of eating disorders among the high school and college population (Crisp, Palmer, & Kalucy, 1976; Bruch, 1978), may reveal a society that is having problems with survival and regeneration. The anorexic girl, described in literature as not wishing to grow up, may more accurately be seen as dramatizing the life-threatening split between female and adult (Steiner-Adair, 1984). This tragic choice dramatizes the extent to which care and dependence have been doubly disparaged by their association with women and children rather than seen as part of the human condition. To heal the division between adult and female, thus, requires a revisioning of both images, and this revision retrieves the line that has been missing from the description of human development.

The unleashed power of the atom, Einstein warned, has changed everything except the way we think, implying that a change in thinking is necessary for survival in a nuclear age. Our indebtedness to Hirschman is that he charts the direction for a change in thinking that also carries with it the implication of a change of heart. By describing modes of conflict resolution that do not entail detachment or exclusion, he aligns the process of change with the presence of loyalty or strong attachment. Thus, he offers an alternative to the either/or, win/lose framework for conflict resolution, which has become, in this nuclear age, a most dangerous game. In this article I have tried to extend the optimism of Hirschman's conception by demonstrating the potential for care and attachment that inheres in the structure of the human life cycle. By describing development around a central and ongoing ethical tension between problems of inequality and problems of detachment, I have called attention to dilemmas of loyalty as moments when attachment is at stake. The importance at present of expanding attachment across the barriers of what Erikson called "sub-speciation" brings problems of loyalty to the center of our public life. As the contemporary reality of global interdependence impels the search for new maps of development, the exploration of attachment may provide the psychological grounding for new visions of progress and growth.

Notes

1. For this analogy I am grateful to Jamie Bidwell, a student at the Harvard Graduate School of Education.
2. Kohlberg's six stages of moral development were defined on the basis of his longitudinal research on 72 White American males, originally aged 10 to 16 (Kohlberg, 1958, 1984). Erikson has drawn almost exclusively on the lives of men in tracing the crisis of identity and the cycle of life (Erikson, 1950, 1958, 1968). Note also Offer (1969) and Offer and Offer (1975).
3. The study was jointly undertaken by the GEHD Study Center and the Emma Willard School for Girls in Troy, New York. The study was designed to address the relationship between girls' development and secondary education.
4. For the phrase "ecology of care," I am grateful to Scott McVay and Valerie Peed of the Geraldine R. Dodge Foundation, Morristown, New Jersey.

References

Adelson, J. (1980). *The handbook of adolescent psychology.* New York: Wiley.
Adelson, J. & Doehrman, M. (1980). The psychodynamic approach to adolescence. In J. Adelson (Ed.), *The handbook of adolescent psychology.* New York: Wiley.
Arendt, H. (1972). *The life of the mind: Thinking.* New York: Harcourt Brace Jovanovich.
Bettelheim, B. (1965). The problems of generations. In E. Erikson (Ed.), *The challenge of youth.* New York: Anchor Books/Doubleday.
Bruch, H. (1978). *The golden cage: The enigma of Anorexia Nervosa.* Cambridge, MA: Harvard University Press.
Crisp, A., Palmer, R., & Kalucy, R. (1976), How common is anorexia nervosa? A prevalence study. *British Journal of Psychiatry, 128,* 549–559.
Erikson, E. (1950). *Childhood and society.* New York: Norton.
Erikson, E. (1958). *Young man Luther,* New York: Norton.
Erikson, E. (1964). *Insight and responsibility.* New York: Norton.
Erikson, E. (1965). Youth: fidelity and diversity. In E. Erikson (Ed.), *The challenge of youth.* New York: Anchor Books/Doubleday.
Erikson, E. (1968). *Identity: Youth and crisis,* New York: Norton.
Freud, S. (1905). Three essays on the theory of sexuality. *Standard Edition, 7,* 125–243. London: Hogarth Press.
Gilligan, C. (1982). *In a different voice: Psychological theory and women's development.* Cambridge, MA: Harvard University Press.
Hirschman, A. (1970). *Exit, voice, and loyalty: Responses to decline in firms, organizations and states.* Cambridge, MA: Harvard University Press.
James, W. (1902/1961). *The varieties of religious experience.* New York: Collier, 1961.
Kingston, M. (1976). *The woman warrior: Memoirs of a girlhood among ghosts.* New York: Knopf.
Kohlberg, L. (1958). The development of modes of thinking and choices in years 10–16. Unpublished doctoral dissertation. University of Chicago.

Kohlberg, L. (1981). *The philosophy of moral development: Moral stages and the idea of justice: Essays on moral development, 1.* San Francisco: Harper & Row.

Kohlberg, L. (1984). *The psychology of moral development, 2.* San Francisco: Harper & Row.

Murdoch, I. (1970). *The sovereignty of good.* Boston: Routledge & Kegan Paul.

Offer, D. (1969). *The psychological world of the teenager. A study of normal adolescent boys.* New York: Basic Books.

Offer, D. & Offer, J. (1975). *From teenager to young manhood.* New York. Basic Books.

Steiner-Adair, C. (1984). The body politic: Normal female adolescent development and the development of eating disorders. Unpublished doctoral dissertation. Harvard Graduate School of Education.

Weil, S. (1977). Human personality. In G. Panichas (Ed.), *The Simone Weil reader.* New York: David McKay.

9

Adolescents' Relatedness and Identity Formation
A Narrative Study

HANOCH FLUM AND MICHAL LAVI-YUDELEVITCH

In Erikson's (1950, 1968) psychosocial approach, identity formation comprises complex processes with agentic and communal aspects. Whereas the agentic facet has been more often at the foreground in conceptualizations and empirical studies of identity formation in adolescence, the relational facet has been in the background. Indeed, in the traditional approach, the process of separation–individuation has been viewed as a hallmark of adolescent development (Blos, 1967). This emphasis reflects a conception of mature selfhood that is achieved through separation and marked by autonomy and independence. The relational context of development in adolescence, with a special focus on relationships with parents, serves largely as the backdrop against which separation takes place. Within this approach, connectedness to family members is mostly interpreted as a source of dependency and as an obstacle to autonomy, individuation, and personal identity development.

More recently, some researchers contextualized the formation of identity in a relational context. Feminists and researchers of women's development (Gilligan, 1982; Gilligan, Lyons, & Hammer, 1990; Jordan, Kaplan, Miller, Stiver, & Surrey, 1991; Josselson, 1987; Lyons, 1983) emphasize the role of relatedness in women's identity. Similarly, research that refers to the Eriksonian conception of identity, with attention to relatedness and belongingness as well as to competency and the individuated aspects of identity, leads to a more complex view of development (Blatt & Blass, 1996; Guisinger & Blatt, 1994; Marcia, 1993), and gives an empirical basis to conceptualizations that stress the interplay between connectedness and identity development for both sexes

From: *Journal of Social and Personal Relationships*. Vol. 19(4), 2002, pp. 527–548. Copyright © Sage Press. Reprinted with permission of Sage Press and Hanoch Flum.

(Allen & Hauser, 1996; Allen, Hauser, Bell, & O'Connor, 1994; Grotevant & Cooper, 1985, 1986; Josselson, 1994; Kroger, 1997; Mellor, 1989). Indeed, this interplay echoes complex dynamics of intrapsychic processes and interpersonal experiences in identity formation, of the relationship between internal dialogue and dialogue with others in the context of the formation of the individuals identity.

This latter approach, which assumes complex reciprocity in these processes, is reflected in the present study. Adolescents' relational experiences are brought to the fore, and the departure point of this investigation is a distinction between adolescents who do not shy away from having a dialogue with the self and their peers who tend to avoid such a dialogue. The overall purpose of this research is to explore how qualities of connection with others are related to identity formation in adolescence. Guided by this general purpose, we probe the interpersonal experiences of adolescents who tend to carry out an internal dialogue with the self and those who report less capacity for or interest in such a dialogue.

This distinction follows a finding in an earlier study. In the course of a study of adolescents' development, we identified two distinctive patterns of response by adolescents to a situation in which they are alone. Whereas some tend to use this time mostly for introspection and reflection, to engage in dialogue with the self about the self or about interpersonal issues (e.g., "I used the time to think about myself," "I thought about my friend and felt…"), others respond by doing and planning, focusing on initiative behavior and accomplishment of an objective (e.g., "I planned a project," "I did my homework," "I got bored reading the book"), and typically avoid internal engagement. Of course, these two response patterns are not necessarily mutually exclusive and many young people combine both, but there are clearly those who prefer one set of responses to the other.

Evidence from previous studies indicates that when a positive perception of a being-alone situation is reported, it is associated with exploration and higher developmental level of identity formation (Flum, 1994; Marcoen & Goossens, 1993). This link with identity formation is not surprising in light of findings by Larson and Csikszentmihalyi (1978) that time spent alone can be perceived by the adolescent as "time out" that serves as a vehicle to self-discovery or that the experience of this situation is related to young adolescents' introspection (Hansell, Mechanic, & Brondolo, 1986). Csikszentmihalyi and Larson (1984) conclude that time spent alone enables adolescents to develop autonomous functioning. They discuss the possible impact of solitude on individuation if the adolescent utilizes the situation to learn about the self. Csikszentmihalyi and Larson conclude: "One must learn to give oneself feedback, as well as to use feedback from others" (p. 196). All in all, being alone is a situation that offers a potential developmental benefit if the adolescent is able to turn to the self and explore.

Is the capacity to be alone and carry on a dialogue with the self related to the kind of dialogue that the young person carries out with others? Do adolescents differ in their experience of relational connection and does this difference relate to their experience of themselves? The focus of the present study was not on with whom (e.g., parent, friend, teacher) the adolescent interacts as much as on the relational quality of the interaction. This represents a shift in perspective, because many studies of adolescents' relationships (e.g., Berndt & Ladd, 1989; Kirchler, Palmonari, & Pombeni, 1993; Youniss, 1980; Youniss & Smollar, 1989) tend to examine relationships based on group categories (e.g., peers vs. parents), on the role or the position of the other, rather than focus on different relational qualities.

Moreover, one of the difficulties in some of the relevant literature is the tendency to utilize general terms and overextend a single concept to stand for a variety of forms of relatedness. In the present study, we elected to listen to adolescents' descriptions of relationships that are important to them. The phenomenology of the actual relational experience of the adolescent as it is represented in the narrative, with all the relational complexity that is articulated by the young person, reflects various qualities of connection. In order to address the research questions, our objective is to detect these qualities, differentiate among them on the one hand, and look into the ways they combine on the other hand.

Dimensions of Relatedness

Relational qualities are defined based on The Space Between Us model (Josselson, 1992) in which relational experiences are parsed into components termed "dimensions of relatedness" (i.e., the aforementioned "relational qualities"). The eight relational dimensions are primary ways "in which we reach through the space that separates us to make connections" (p. 5). Most of these modalities are based on descriptions in various psychological conceptualizations and are further explored and clarified by Josselson (1992) and others. Developmentally, the first four dimensions are: holding, attachment, passionate experience, and validation; the next four tend to appear later: identification, mutuality, embeddedness, and tending (care). Each one of the dimensions is distinct, with its own phenomenologically coherent center, metaphor, and expression, though some dimensions overlap more than others.

Holding refers to the primary experience of feeling "arms around," a secure sense of enclosure and groundedness that protects the infant from falling. An adequate "holding environment" promotes growth (Winnicott, 1965). Developmentally, holding becomes more symbolic and emotional than physical, and is experienced as support. Typically, the other person is there to serve as an emotional container, as a person who is protecting and directing, while accepting and lending emotional support. Fear of falling or a sensation of groundedness, the certainty or uncertainty of the adolescent's sense of being held, may have significant consequences for the adolescent's identity formation (Josselson, 1994).

Attachment is an active relational process of keeping proximity with an attachment figure, an expression of the individual's need for closeness and security to reduce anxiety and loneliness (Bowlby, 1982). To review the mounting research evidence of the significance of attachment would be beyond the scope of this article; however, it should be noted that much of the controversy about adolescents' connectedness and individuality (Bengtson & Grotevant, 1999; Grotevant & Cooper, 1986) centers on empirical studies of attachment to parents vis-à-vis the separation-individuation developmental task. In general, the quality of attachment is found to be related to identity formation, with a sense of secure attachment being associated with higher levels of identity formation (see Kroger, 2000, for a recent review). Similarly, evidence shows that the quality of the adolescent's attachment to parents impacts the adolescent's self-esteem more than the quality of peer attachments (Armsden & Greenberg, 1987; Greenberg, Siegel, & Leitch, 1983). All in all, attachment seems to overshadow other relational experiences in the research literature.

Passionate Experience is an intensely emotional experience that tends to appear in the foreground of a relationship, marked by arousal, a search for union, and love. This is a libidinally driven dimension of relatedness that is often accompanied by much fantasy, especially among adolescents. There are significant differences between adolescent boys and girls in the initial experience of their sexuality and its experience as passion (see Josselson, 1992, pp. 85–88), but gradually, as young people mature, they tend to experience passion as being more integrated with other relational qualities.

Eye-to-Eye Validation is a relational experience that refers to the reflection of the self in the eyes of the other. Seeing the self mirrored by the other, through the other's empathic response, is affirming. Friends and peers provide mirrors for the adolescent (Erikson, 1968; Kroger, 2000) that may play a role in the adolescent's exploration and identity formation (Flum & Porton, 1995).

A fifth dimension of relatedness is that of *Idealization and Identification*, another central aspect of identity development. "The adolescent, on the brink of identity, looks to others to provide models for how and what to be" (Josselson, 1994, p. 96). Through idealizing others, the adolescent expands possibilities for growth and gains motivation. The development of interests, values, and even careers is distinguished by processes of identification and idealization, with a variety of people such as parents and teachers or friends and even strangers.

Mutuality and resonance, the sixth relational dimension, involves standing "side by side with someone, moving in harmony, creating a bond that is the product of both people, an emergent 'we' in the space between people" (Josselson, 1994, p. 97). Here, individuals need to share experiences — not to enlarge their concept of self but to intermingle with others and express themselves. The adolescent's growing self needs companionship, with trust and confidence in the other as important components. Mutuality encompasses play and sharing of the most intimate aspects of life. It ranges from time-limited companionship to being soul-mates together. In mutuality is the joyful expression of identity.

The seventh dimension of relatedness, *Embeddedness*, is central to the process of identity formation in adolescence. "Embeddedness involves finding and taking a place with others; it encompasses belonging. This is one of the central questions posed by adolescents. What shall I stand for? How will I fit in? Where might there be a place for me?" (Josselson, 1994, p. 98). Embeddedness is the soil in which identity grows and is continually refined and redefined. To be embedded within a social network is to belong, to feel included, to share characteristics, to be the same as, and to give up some individuality in the service of interconnection.

Finally, *Tending and Care* is a reaching-out mode, a form of relational connection in which one offers to another what one feels to be good in oneself. Josselson (1992, 1994) observes that, on the one hand, this is a dimension that is rarely talked about in relation to identity, especially to the extent that we emphasize the agentic aspect of identity, and view identity in terms of autonomy and individuality. On the other hand, Erikson assigned tending its own developmental stage under the name of generativity, and he equates the individual's identity with what the individual chooses to tend (Erikson, 1964).

Utilizing this taxonomy of dimensions of relatedness, we investigate adolescents' narratives about their important relationships. The narrative approach allows us to work with the story of the relationship as being told by the adolescent, with the relational experience as perceived by the young person. This story captures the complexity, the intricacies, and the context of the relationship. Hence, the narrative provides us with a window to the interplay between the relational experience and the formation of identity.

We aim at discriminating among the relational dimensions represented in the adolescents' narratives. We then compare the dominant relational qualities of adolescents who respond to solitude with a tendency to explore the self with those who tend to be less internal and reflective. In addition, embedded in the adolescents narratives are indications of how they perceive the self and describe their formation of identity. Hence, these will assist us in illuminating the reciprocal developmental meaning of the relational experience and the crystallization of identity.

Method

Participants

Ten adolescents were selected to participate in this study based on their reported preferences in a being alone situation in a previous study (Lavi-Yudelevitch,

1999) of adolescents' development. They were drawn from a sample of 92 adolescents: 49 females and 43 males, 10th and 11th grade students in the academic track of a comprehensive school, who participated in the previous study. All 92 students responded to a series of questions regarding an experience of a time alone situation.

In a Being-Alone Situation Questionnaire, the participant is asked to recall a recent situation when he or she was alone with no other people present. After writing a description of the situation, the participant is asked a series of open-ended questions about this experience. Two patterns of response were identified in a qualitative analysis of the responses (Lavi-Yudelevitch, 1999). Pattern A represents a preference to utilize the solitude to reflect and be engaged internally. Pattern B represents a preference to focus on doing and a tendency to shun internal engagement with the self. The 10 adolescents who were asked to participate in the current study were among those who exhibited a clear preference for either pattern A or pattern B, and accepted an invitation to be interviewed. They were among the most extreme in terms of a preference for either of these patterns of response.

In addition, participants in the earlier study (Lavi-Yudelevitch, 1999) completed the Identity scale from the Erikson Psychosocial Stage Inventory (EPSI) (Rosenthal, Gurney, & Moore, 1981). This is a 5-point Likert-type scale that consists of 12 statements (e.g., "I know what kind of person I am," "I feel mixed up") and served as a crude measure of a general sense of identity. On this measure, pattern A participants showed a tendency to score relatively high (i.e., indicating a clearer idea of who they are), whereas pattern — participants' scores tended to be at the low end of the same scale (i.e., indicating more identity confusion). In each group (pattern A and pattern B), 2 females and 3 males were interviewed.

All 10 participants were Israeli-born, came from intact families, and their families' socio-economic background was varied. There were no significant background differences between the participants of the two groups.

The Interview

In order to encourage the interviewees to narrate their relational experiences, and to describe the qualities of these relationships as they experience them, we employed a version of Josselson's (1992) relational mapping technique. This interview technique was useful in generating the narratives in the Space Between Us study (Josselson, 1992) and was effective when applied in research projects of a variety of social experiences, such as identity construction following cultural transition (Flum, 1998), homosexual behavior (Mintzer, 1997), and mothers who abuse their children (Price, 1998).

In the present study, each participant was asked to draw two relational space maps, a current one and another, retrospective one depicting the self and others in 8th grade. The 8th-grade diagram represents early adolescence, and the current 10th or 11th grade one represents mid-adolescence. For all the interviewees, the earlier diagram is situated in a somewhat different social environment because they all attended a different school in 8th grade. Hence, both relational continuity and changes are likely to be tapped in the narrative that explains the two maps.

In the interview that follows the drawing of the maps, the interviewer asked questions that were aimed at helping the interviewee to describe the relationship and explain how each person that was drawn on the relational map was important for the interviewee. Relationships are compared and changes that are experienced in a relationship with the same person across time (while tracing across maps) are usually included in the narrative that is generated following the questions, along with examples that reflect both behavioral and affective experience. In other words, with this technique the interview is structured around relationships that are most significant to the interviewee. The narrator is asked to illustrate the relationship, and is encouraged to characterize the nature of the relationship and explicate its personal meaning (for a detailed account of the technique and the instructions to interviewees and interviewers, see Josselson, 1992).

Interviews were tape-recorded and transcribed. They ranged between one and four hours, with most interviews lasting about two hours. The length of the interview was not found to be related to either the sex of the adolescent or pattern group.

Analysis

The narratives of each participant were analyzed according to the features of the relational dimensions characterized by Josselson (1992, 1994; see also Josselson, Lieblich, Sharabany, & Wiseman, 1997). The analysis included the following steps:

Step 1: Analysis of Interpersonal Relationships within Individuals.

(a) Identification of relational dimensions: Each interpersonal relationship was defined as an analysis unit, and the relational dimensions that characterize this relationship were assessed. What we had tried to identify in the narrative of a relationship was the core experience that was described by the interviewee, around which the connection evolved. In many relationships, more than one dominant relational dimension could be identified.

(b) Determination of dominant dimensions: After each relationship was analyzed, the dominant dimensions across relationships for each individual were assessed. A dominant relational dimension for an individual was defined by a combination of the times that the dimension was identified repeatedly in various connections and how powerful was the role played by the relationship in the total relational experience of the individual. When a relational dimension was described extensively in the narrative of the most significant relationships for the interviewee, and the experience was intense, the relational dimension was defined as a dominant one.

Step 2: Analysis Across Individuals.

(a) Examination of relational dimensions across individuals: The analysis in this stage was done by relational dimension, and was carried out by following all the references to a dimension across the individual cases. Each relational dimension was examined in its various phenomenological expressions (i.e., the various descriptions of experiences that were classified as a representation of this relational quality) across the individual adolescents.

(b) Identification of patterns of dominant relational dimensions — comparison between groups: In an effort to find out whether there are differences in the relational patterns that characterize each group, the dominant relational dimensions that were listed for all individuals in the pattern A group were compared with the dominant relational dimensions of individuals from the pattern B group.

Step 3: Identification of Themes of Identity Formation

(a) Within individual narratives, and

(b) Indications of identity formation that were apparent across individuals and on a group basis. Eighty-five percent of the total narratives were analyzed by both authors. Narratives were analyzed independently and compared. In the case of conflicting classification, the final decision was made following a discussion. In addition, the reliability of the analysis was assessed by a comparison with a third judge, a graduate student who is familiar with the model and the method of analysis. The comparison was done in three stages: (a) The blind analysis stage in which the judges had gone through all the analysis steps independently. The agreement percentage was calculated by a comparison of the relational dimensions in each analysis unit (i.e., in each relationship reported by the interviewee). When a dimension was identified by one judge only it was counted as a disagreement. The total agreement at this stage was 71 percent. (b) Judges were exposed to the others analysis and could decide to make changes spontaneously. The total agreement after this stage reached 89 percent. (c) At this stage, the judges discussed the differences in analysis and clarified some of their disagreements. At the end of this procedure, the agreement rate was raised to 95 percent.

Findings and Discussion

An Overall Preview

In following the steps of analysis, it became clear that many of the relationships operated on more than a single dimension and sometimes involved a number of relational experiences. However, at the same time, certain relational qualities emerged as more central experiences than others for each individual and when assessed across relationships the dominant relational dimensions became evident.

When the relational narratives of all participants in the study were examined, Mutuality was the relational dimension most frequently reported, and seemed to play a primary relational role in most cases. And, it should be stressed, this was true for participants of both groups. Hence, various features of Mutuality were widely experienced by adolescents across the two groups that represent the two patterns. Because Mutuality was the most widespread relational phenomenon among our participants in general, this relational dimension will be illustrated first. In the coming section, after this preview, we discuss different circumstances of Mutuality in a variety of relational contexts as they appeared in adolescents' relational stories in general, before the discussion turns to differences between the patterns.

Although all adolescents included Mutuality experiences of connection in their narratives, the form of this experience of relatedness differs. A difference in emphasis on divergent forms of Mutuality that appeared in the stories of adolescents relates to whether Mutuality was the sole dominant relational dimension, the most central one, or whether other dominant ways of connection were experienced. The difference seems to relate to the quality of attachment, to a sense of being held, and to a sense of embeddedness in the adolescent's experience, which in turn affects the form of mutuality that is displayed. Indeed, this dissimilarity was detected in two groups of relational patterning. One pattern was manifest among the participants who tended to emphasize Mutuality as a dominant dimension in a largely unidimensional configuration, whereas another pattern was a multidimensional configuration. This disparity in relational patterns coincides with the distinction between the two patterns of response to a time alone situation, and seems to indicate dissimilar modes of identity development.

Thus, after a discussion of Mutuality as a common relational dimension for all our interviewees and an examination of this experience of relatedness, the difference between the patterns and the disparity of relational experience

will be exemplified and discussed. A return to an overall view with a focus on
relatedness and identity formation will follow, before we turn to concluding
thoughts.

Mutuality: A Relational Experience across Patterns

Mutuality appeared as a central adolescent relational experience in general,
and was identified as a dominant dimension for eight of the ten participants.
Mutuality is a primary form of communion in adolescence that is expressed in
a number of ways and is experienced in different levels of relationships, important and deep connections as well as more superficial and transient encounters.
This is represented in the following examples: Miriam, telling about her best
friend:

> [Talking with her] is so much fun. If we didn't have a time limit, we could
> chat for three days, without stopping for a minute. . . . It is very important to
> me. Very, very, very much . . . [Interviewer: What makes you feel so good
> when you chat?] I dont know, the level of conversation that we reach, the top-
> ics that we cover, all the things that we have together, that we share. . . .

Roy, telling about his best friend:

> I tell him everything. . . . he knows everything there is to know about
> me. . . . [Interviewer: When he is not around, what do you miss most?] The
> sharing. There is nobody else to share with. . . . there are things that I wouldn't
> tell anybody but him. Or, just to do things together, to get wild . . . but mostly
> it is to sit together, to chat, to play . . . in the past, to smoke together.

At the same time, Roy described his relationship with another friend:

> This is a relationship of laughing together, a lot of fun. I don't tell him about
> my problems at home, or anything that disturbs me or hurts me.

Hence, Mutuality takes different forms. It is the experience of the *we* via an
activity that is done together, with the shared affect that resonates, the companionship that resides in adolescent's friendships. In another form, Mutuality
involves self-disclosure and the experience of sharing with another person.
Sharing can appear as no more than a superficial exchange or as a profound
experience with a person who may become a special one, a best friend, via the
resonance that takes place in the connection. This is a person with whom the
adolescent can deposit self-knowledge ("he knows everything . . . about me"),
and thus the connection implies mutual recognition and valuation. Most significant developmentally is the adolescent's need to share the new and intense
experiences and to hear the echo of these experiences in another person.

As reflected in the narratives of the adolescents who were interviewed for this study, Mutuality was the most prominent relational experience with peers. This often includes reports of relationships with a focus on conversations that are carried out in the break between classes, after school, and with the characterization of "hanging out with somebody who thinks the same way," who is "on the same wave." They talk about "everything," about other friends, about a person of the other sex, and "problems." Social problems, problems with parents, school related problems and "problems" that they find less easy to label appeared frequently in their reports about these conversations. Spending time with peers, having "fun together" in dyads or larger peer groups, is a very basic adolescent experience of relatedness that is widely reported in the literature in the context of experimentation, as an arena for trying out new identities and various roles (e.g., Brown, Eicher, & Petrie, 1986; Sullivan, 1953; Youniss, 1980).

A major aspect of mutuality that came up in these narratives as a central issue is loyalty. A dividing line between two very different experiences of mutuality is drawn by the answer to the question of whether the friend could be trusted (a form of holding in the dimensional scheme). The experience of resonance with a friend to whom secrets can be disclosed makes for a different quality relationship in comparison with a relationship marked by a feeling of mistrust when holding is absent from the relationship, even when the other person is still regarded as an important friend and a partner in shared experiences.

A sense of near-total resonance is possible in the context of trust. Sometimes, these relational stories approached twinship fantasies (cf. Kohut, 1971). Miriam, for instance, described her relationship with a best friend in 8th grade:

> We were doing everything together. Whether it is to study for exams, or to go out together, to stay the night at each other's place during the weekend, everything...everything was done together, really everything...And it helped so much! [Interviewer: In what way?] In everything. There are so many things to talk about, many things that bother you...When one gets a period it is a secret, then it is our secret, mine and hers, we both had a period...If we trust each other in something like that, then it can develop to more and more secrets...

To make the complex and bewildering experience an "our" experience, rather than something that marks difference and isolation, "helps" the young adolescent "so much." Adolescents tend to feel essentially different, especially earlier in adolescence, and while they struggle with the difference, they search for basic alikeness. This is an often overlooked aspect of identity formation in adolescence. To be sure, adolescents do not just find alikeness, they create alikeness in a number of ways. A sense of twinship like the one expressed by Miriam is one example. In early adolescence, this form of mutuality is usually an emotionally intense experience and relatively short lived, because it is a relationship that tends to screen out differences. But it may later appear in less intense forms and serve the need to be like someone else and as an arena for exploration of the personally unique as well.

Relationships without any mutuality component tended to be described as less close. In these interviews, they often consisted of connections with adults, such as parents or teachers. In such cases, and mostly with parents, the relationship is with an adult who fulfills a function for the adolescent. The adult is depicted as being responsible for fulfilling the adolescent's basic needs and for giving direction. Indeed, quite typically, the adolescent's point is that the relationship is limited to certain necessary functions that the adult is expected to fulfill, albeit with the emphasis that there is no place for resonance in the relationship. Companionship or sharing are kept out. This was again more indicative of the narratives of early adolescence. An example is Raz's description of his relationship with his mother in 8th grade:

> Unlike nowadays, I didn't think much of her then, I guess...We were very distant. Our relationship evolved around my studies..."how did you do on the exam"? on the one hand, and "get me that, or buy me that" on the other hand. And that was it. I had a girlfriend, and I wouldn't even mention her to my mother for a long time....

This is an example of an adolescent who withdraws any connotation of resonance from the relationship with parents, which is suggestive of an effort at emotional separation. The parent was expected to be available, interested, and caring, but sharing was limited by the adolescent to factual information (White, Speisman, & Costos, 1983; Youniss & Ketterlinus, 1987).

In the reports of our interviewees, Mutuality became a more prominent relational dimension with adolescent development, in a variety of relationships. In addition to the developmental changes that were indicated earlier, this trend seems to manifest the growing cognitive capabilities and the increase in ability to contain emotional complexity. Gradually, the self can be entrusted to the *we* and enriched by the experience without a fear of losing the *me*.

Two Patterns of Relatedness

Following the examination of the narratives in which the central qualities of connection in each participant's stories of relatedness were identified, a difference between two patterns of dominant relational dimensions emerged. In one pattern, multiple dominant relational dimensions were apparent, whereas in the other there were fewer divergent relational qualities. It became clear that the two relational patterns largely overlapped with the two response patterns that served as a criterion in the selection of our interviewees. On the one hand, the narratives of participants who appeared to favor self-dialogue when in solitude included an array of various relational dimensions in their stories of relatedness.

On the other hand, the relational narratives of adolescents who tended to shy away from a dialogue with the self when spending time alone tended to center mostly around forms of mutuality, and thus to exhibit fewer dominant relational dimensions.

A Multidimensional Relational Pattern

In the narratives of adolescents who displayed this relational pattern, besides Mutuality that was a dominant relational dimension for most participants, a combination of other prominent relational dimensions was identified: Holding, Attachment, Eye-to-Eye Validation, and Identification. These dimensions were stressed in the relationships of these adolescents in different kinds of connections. Sometimes all these dimensions appeared in one relationship. Mutuality appeared in a variety of forms, but it clearly tended to have more profound and internal expressions than in the narratives of a unidimensional pattern — a *we* that resonates with a different emotional tone.

Roy's narrative demonstrates the expression of different dimensions in various connections. We already cited earlier examples of Roy's Mutuality experience. Let us turn to an excerpt in which he addresses his relationships with his parents:

Mum...helps in everything...she likes to help, to counsel, not only me. She is a warm, accepting, woman for anybody. She likes to learn...When I get home she tells me about her class, what they had learnt.... I like listening to her stories and she likes to listen to mine. She is just as interested, she asks questions...He (dad) doesn't have the same feminine traits as mum, and yet he is very close to me too...He would come and help me too...He gave me the masculine traits and masculine behavior .... I share much more with mum...He is after all a man, and she is good in giving advice...He is interested, would like to know, I tell him and he shares. He loves, helps...what is special about him is his independence. He accomplished so much completely on his own...I highly value him for that. If you give me an evening with each one of them separately, I know that I would spend it with mum in a restaurant and with dad in a pub or a disco. Still, I'm more with mum. I ended up more like an educator than a wild person...I don't get wild so much. Dad can go and drink and forget everything else, something that I can't do. I was brought up to hold myself in my own arms when necessary.

In his account, one can hear the sense of security that his closeness to parents provides. He feels held by and attached to both parents. His admiration of facets of his parents' personality, along with an echo of suspected internal struggle in the process of identification, reverberate here with expressions of sharing and mutuality. A theme of helping and tending was also emphasized, attributed especially to his mother, a source of admiration and identification, as becomes even clearer when Roy talked about his relationship with his younger sister:

> She is eight years younger, and all the caring for her was eventually on my shoulders...She was born immature and she had some difficulties, and I would sit with her...I was very attached to her...[Interviewer: What did it give you?] Mum's traits...It had a strong impact on me, because I know how to educate. The bottom line is that I was like a good mother for her....

Roy's experience of caring for his sister is important for understanding his dyadic relationship with her. However, in addition, this segment of the narrative confirms his identification with his mother's caring and "educating." It sheds more light on his internal wrestling with what he defines as "masculine" and "feminine" identifications. And most significant is the sense of validation that he seems to derive from his experience of tending his sister. This later point is also reflected in his description of his relationship with his girlfriend:

> ...[S]he knows about me a lot, many things. Our bond is very strong...She is the first girl that I have really loved...She smiles all the time, she would help even people that she doesn't know...[Interviewer: What is most important in this relationship for you?] Maturity, I think...One can unload one's emotions, and she stays close, and you can tell her stuff...With her I'm serious, a man...

Roy is held and validated as a growing up young man. Throughout his account, Roy's sense of validation — as a serious, responsible, mature person — operates along with other relational dimensions. He is busy looking at his reflection in the mirrors of others, constructing his identity in the process.

Roy's narrative includes expressions of aspects of more relational dimensions in his connections than any other interviewee. Although Roy's strong emphasis on Care and Tending as a dominant relational dimension is a unique facet of his narrative, the inclusion of expressions of Attachment, Identification, and Eye-to-Eye Validation (along with Mutuality) represents the typical relational pattern of this group of adolescents. These adolescents seemed to display confidence in their relationships. Being anchored by attachments, they are emotionally open to a variety of experiences (Main, Kaplan, & Cassidy, 1985) that reflect multidimensionality in relatedness. Hence, with a "safe base" to securely ground them, they can explore who they are in the eyes of others without getting too intimidated, or without shattering their core self. Eye-to-Eye Validation can involve a painful experience when the image that is reflected is not all flattering. The nature of the validation process can be particularly useful for providing building blocks in the adolescent's construction of identity, when the adolescent can see authentic pieces of the self reflected by the other. Sharon, in her account of her relationship with one of her teachers, depicted some aspects of the process:

> I like a lot talking with this teacher. He is so smart...He used to hold a high opinion of my ability. [Interviewer: How do you know that?] I used to bombard him with questions, he would have looked at me and I saw it in his eyes, very clearly....Once he even told me that I have a high ability and I don't take enough advantage of it. He knows about my life...and sometimes he tells me harsh things....Once, when I had told him about a job that I'll want to get, he told me not to come for a letter of recommendation...He doesn't think that I'm suitable for this job....He said that I could do a lot of other things with my potential....[Interviewer: How did you feel when he told you that?] An explosion in my head. It hurt me, though deep down I knew it. It didn't hurt me because *he* told me that, I was actually glad to hear it from him. Because if he said that, he thinks that I'm mature enough to accept it. At the same time, this is another person that esteems me less...This is not something that is easy to accept.

Sharon's admiration for her teacher is certainly a factor in the effectiveness of the validation process. Indeed, idealization can be empowering, while at the same time an admission that "I'm not quite there yet." Adolescents are quick to erect heroes, templates that they can pattern themselves on. Admiration and idealization may mark what the adolescent wants to be, but is not. Through idealization the adolescent sets possible growth goals, while identification is an attempt to own them. Roy articulated this process clearly in his narrative. At the same time, the complexity of the necessary integration of part-identifications into a coherent whole, into an identity (Erikson, 1968), can also be detected in Roy's narrative.

A link between the experience of relationships and the experience of the self, between an internal dialogue with the self and a multidimensional dialogue with others, seems to have been established. This is indicated by the overlap between the group of interviewees who articulated a preference to reflect in a being alone situation and those who described their relationships in terms of a combination of relational dimensions. How they experience themselves in a situation that facilitates autonomy seems to be related to how they experience their relational landscape.

A Unidimensional Relational Pattern

These adolescents seemed to be invested mostly in one or two relational dimensions, and this investment reflects a limited emotional involvement and minimal self-expression. The same explications of connection are usually repeated in different kinds of relationships. Mutuality was by far the most pronounced dimension in their narratives, and frequently was in a superficial form. The experience is often a "doing together" one, having fun and participating in activities with others in groups or as a pair. Conversation tends to evolve around activities — "what happened" and "what did I do" — and relatively less sharing of emotions and internal experiences.

Iris's case is an example: From Iris's narrative emerges a vulnerable young female, with low self-esteem and expressions of inferiority. Her relationships with her parents were depicted as distant:

> They have always been in my life, but never really part of them...I have never been open with them, especially with my mum...I have never felt that I should share with her, though she gets hurt...I would only share my school work with them.... dad and mum that feed me and give me money.... I have always had stronger connection with my dad. My dad...I loved him more...he allowed me more freedom....

Throughout her narrative, the affect does not get any deeper, and the same emotional tone was evident in relationships with others. Her relationships are measured by their satisfaction of her basic needs and are affected by her deprivation of validation. Her shaky sense of self is dependent on a very basic recognition by others, with an expressed need to possess them in order to fill her void:

> ...I distanced myself from Lori and became friendly with Michelle. Lori is a popular girl that everybody wants to get close to...and I felt like nothing. With Michelle it's different. With Michelle I felt that she is only mine and I don't have to share her with others.

Her self-value is drawn from a connection that is marked by some sense of mutuality, even a superficial one, with no authentic interest in the other person. She is busy with the question "who told whom and how much," and this becomes the yard stick to measure the quality of the relationship. She strives for reciprocity. Iris described Gabriella, for instance, a good friend who is three years younger:

> She is very mature, psychologically...She used to share with my sister, and tell me nothing. She was open with me...No, first I was open with her, then she started to open up to me....

This striving for reciprocity to allow for a "we" to be engendered, and the inability to maintain it, is further illustrated in her account of a relationship with an older friend:

> We dated in 9th grade....for about two weeks, I think.... we still keep a relationship, some sort of friendship....We are very open with each other,

but I don't tell him what's going on with my friends, we are just very open with each other about what we do, just very open.... He tells me, I tell less. He always tells me about his fantasies and asks me for mine, and I tell him I don't know .... For me this is not merely friendship, it is a romance.... When we meet we are all over each other, and we know that we are not the only partners, we agreed that that is how it would be....

Iris, in her attempt to touch and be touched more profoundly in order to validate herself, was trying to convince the listener and presumably herself that there is a deeper form of mutuality here. However, in its absence, the relationship resorts to casual sexuality.

Though Iris's case is somewhat extreme, it does represent the essential pattern of relatedness that was typical of this group of adolescents. Much of these adolescents' search for closeness was facilitated through activities with others and the experience of the *we*. Friendships evolve around doing, spending time together, and sharing daily experiences. Often, stories of companionship and sharing tend to be told as stories of loyalty testing and an effort to cast a basis for an encircled *we* — a *we* that is "only us" marked by confidentiality and that could serve a holding (or attachment) function along with mutuality. Although these adolescents often focused on "who said what to whom," this seemed to be not so much about social intrigue as much as a struggle with the balance in the relationship.

Like Iris, they tended to display some relational deprivation along with a certain amount of emptiness and a tendency to externalize. In Grotevant and Cooper's (1986) terms, their relationships are often characterized by low permeability. As a result of these adolescents' tendency to externalize their relationship experience (and the "low permeability" of their relationships), an internal process of identity construction (a reflexive process that lends to a clarification of one's identity) is not likely to be triggered. Indeed, a streak of diffused quality, in its Eriksonian sense, was manifest in most of these narratives.

Adolescents who prefer to engage in doing at a being alone situation are the same adolescents who emphasize a doing quality in their description of their relationships. Their relational experience evolves mostly around certain aspects of mutuality that are inclined to be compatible with forms of doing together.

Attachment and Embeddedness: Sources of Relational Security

Next, we turn to a closer look at two of the relational dimensions that played very basic roles in the developmental narratives of our participants. The discussion of each one of these dimensions should assist us in further illuminating another facet of the difference between the two patterns, and can be instrumental in addressing the question of a relationship between relatedness and identity formation in adolescence.

Attachment

The role of Attachment in the narratives of adolescents is worth further elaboration because it was a dominant and basic dimension among most of the participants in the multidimensional pattern group (the exception will be discussed in the next section). Conversely, in the narratives of the unidimensional pattern interviewees (and Iris's narrative that was cited earlier is an example) what was mostly apparent is a yearning for Attachment.

When Attachment was specified in the narratives, it usually appeared in both relationships with parents (or at least one of them) and other significant relationships, peers included. Relationships with parents were depicted as close and warm — parents are there for them. Parents were not portrayed as being merely providers, but as the ones available when in different kinds of need and as a source of support, wisdom, and advice. Often, elements of Attachment and Holding were inseparable. Some adolescents maintained that this aspect of the relationship has always been there, whereas others asserted a change from early adolescence to their current relationships with their parents. As noted, sentiments of closeness and emotional responsiveness tended to be extended to other relationships as well.

Although the link between early secure attachment with parents and later development of social skills is widely discussed (e.g., Jacobson & Wille, 1986; Lamb & Nash, 1989; Main, Kaplan, & Cassidy, 1985), the meaning of close relationships with parents in adolescence is a controversial issue. Our evidence supports the observation that securely attached adolescents expand their attachments to include others, while they keep their closeness to parents (cf. Ainsworth, 1989; Bowlby, 1982; Josselson, 1992).

Sharabany (1994) reports that, with development in adolescence and adulthood, some specific qualities are transferred with some modifications from the close relationships with parents to new close friendships, at the expense of some of the original closeness with parents. In the narratives of our interviewees, we noticed a shift from elements of emotional security in early relationships to an emphasis on emotional responsiveness as being highly valued. We did not observe diminished closeness with parents. On the contrary, the trend was towards a description of closer and more friendly relationships (among those who reported attachment). Generally, our observation is consistent with findings that adolescents' relationships with parents undergo transformation and become more equal and balanced in their nature (cf. Grotevant & Cooper, 1986; Ryan & Lynch, 1989; Youniss & Ketterlinus, 1987; Youniss & Smollar, 1985).

For adolescents who showed a largely unidimensional relational pattern, Attachment and Holding existed mostly in their absence. This paradoxical statement is relationally evident. Distant relationships with parents (in some, more in the past than in the present, though) and an apparent sense of mistrust were coupled with a yearning to be held and a wish for Attachment.

Although we cannot interpret insecurity in Attachment when Attachment was not manifest in a relational story, we found that narratives that are marked by indications of anxious Attachment and distant relationships with parents tended to consist of relationships dominated by relatively shallow forms of Mutuality. Friends are there in order to reach closeness, to demonstrate loyalty, and to show care: "We are very close, we do everything together"; "She has to prove to me that she will come when I'll need her"; "I feel that she likes me, she shows that she cares, she asks about me all the time.... we go shopping together, everywhere..." Although their relationships may include experiences that reflect an additional dimension, the overall impression was that the adolescent seeks substitutes that could fill an emotional void and lend a token of relational–emotional security. While the narrative implied in such cases a sense of relational deficit, there was also a wish for connections that could feel strong, close, and lasting.

Embeddedness

We had expected Embeddedness to be one of the most frequently mentioned dominant relational dimensions in the narratives of our adolescents. Indeed, the presence of Embeddedness was recorded in most interviews, but only in two cases did Embeddedness appear as a dominant dimension. For most adolescents, the experience of Embeddedness was not clearly articulated. It had the quality of an experience that is not at the center of their consciousness, a "taken for granted" quality. When Embeddedness appeared as a dominant dimension, it seemed to play an important role in the adolescent's identity formation. Saul's case is a good example:

Saul is a young man who grew up in a poor area, a neighborhood infected by crime. His parents are absent from his 8th grade relational space map. He drew one circle to represent the whole family. Much more significant is his relationship with a group of friends who are older. With them he collaborated: "We would have walked around the neighborhood like little terrorists.... We used to do bad things.... We stole a lot...." Saul recounts the excitement that he experienced with them, the empowerment and the security that he experienced through belonging to this group. He goes on to specify his relationship with one of them:

> It was fun to walk around with him.... He was older and like a big brother to me... [because of this relationship] I felt older too... I felt cool... That's why I did most of the things that he did.

Besides Mutuality, Identification, and Validation, Saul described in vivid detail the sense of Embeddedness in the group. His belonging to the group defined his identity and facilitated his sense of competence and maturity.

In his narrative about his current relational space map, Embeddedness was very much at the center, but the picture had drastically changed. Following a period of exploration, he decided to leave his delinquent self behind, to cut his ties with the group, and he reported an intense interest in his family and his roots. His map was crowded with individuals from his family, among them some who were deceased but played a role in his return to his roots. His newly established relationships included his parents, whom he reported that he is "getting to know." Saul was learning about his deceased grandfathers:

> My grandmother tells me about them. I like to know much more, to get to know them much better... [Interviewer: What does it signify for you?] To know from where I came... I saw some picture... I used to know very little besides the fact that they had come here from Egypt.... I was told very little....

Saul expressed a strong emotional tie with his family and social group. He is busy exploring the past and experiences Embeddedness through newly constructed old relationships. He defined his niche via Embeddedness, by drawing a line from past to present.

Saul indicated in his narrative a clear developmental change. Earlier, his focus was on doing without much reflective attention to his behavior. His parents did not provide closeness or a sense of being held, and the gang served as a substitute. His early adolescence pattern, by his own account, may have been more similar to the pattern of adolescents who were in the less reflective group. But his present developmental position brought him into a multiple relational dimensions pattern. By utilizing the same relational dimension, Embeddedness, which had been salient throughout adolescence, he developed his current sense of belongingness that became a basis from which he can launch further explorations and facilitate his identity formation process. Embeddedness, rather than Attachment, seemed to provide a sense of security. Indeed, the source of Embeddedness changed during his adolescence, but experimentation with various roles and a range of identity issues were apparent in his current narrative.

Relatedness and Identity Formation: An Overall View

The complex interplay between individuality and connectedness, between forms of relatedness and the identity formation process, came to the fore in the narratives of these adolescents. As demonstrated in the analysis and discussion of the narratives, relational experiences and the construction of identity are woven together, feeding (and fed by) each other. Furthermore, when the evidence from an earlier study with the same participants that found a tendency for pattern A participants to hold a clearer picture of who they are than pattern B participants is put together with the narrative indications of identity formation in this study, a developmental trend is suggested. Relational qualities and their configurations seem to correspond with modes of identity development. Two distinctive patterns of relational dimensions were apparent in the stories of relatedness of the young people who participated in this study. These patterns reflect different developmental modes, one mode that shows a tendency for exploration, crystallization, and self-construction, and another mode that tends to reflect a less clear, somewhat diffused quality in fashioning an identity.

The distinction between the two relational patterns in this study and the corresponding modes of identity formation was derived from participants who were initially selected to represent extreme and clear responses to being in a situation with a potential to exercise autonomy. Adolescents who manifest a clear preference to engage internally in personal and interpersonal reflections, to make use of their time alone for exploration, are at one extreme end. At the other extreme end are adolescents who did not report internal engagement and reflexivity in the same situation. The selection of interviewees at these extremes illuminates the different modes of making use of relational configurations in the process of identity formation.

Although Mutuality was experienced in a variety of forms by adolescents in general, it is clearly the relational center of experience of adolescents who display pattern B (i.e., a preference to focus on doing in a being alone situation). These adolescents describe their experience of relationships as being based mostly on Mutuality, with other relational dimensions either minor in importance or serving experiences of Mutuality. In comparison, adolescents who are more internally attuned in a being alone situation manifested a multidimensional relational pattern and reported mutuality within a pattern that includes other dominant dimensions. Their core pattern tended to consist of Attachment, Identification, and Eye-to-Eye Validation, along with Mutuality.

In the multidimensional pattern, we suggest, a basic sense of security (whether derived from Attachment or Embeddedness) fuels identity exploration and the integration of experiences. These young people report exploration within a wide range of relational experiences. They are able to benefit developmentally by extracting identity building blocks from these experiences (mostly Eye-to-Eye Validation and Identification) and integrating them with the security of attachment, by being supported and held, and through a sense of belongingness and embeddedness.

At the same time, the more constricted pattern of those who favor less dialogue with the self represents a yearning to fill an emotional–relational void that affects the forms of relationships that are sought. Their relational deficit echoes insecurity that keeps them from utilizing forms of relatedness that could facilitate the integration of relational experiences toward the construction of identity.

It is still unclear whether these two modes represent developmental stages or characterological styles. In a developmental argument, the "doing" orientation may reflect a less mature stage of identity formation and may be more likely to be found earlier in adolescence rather than later. Conversely, adolescents who actively explore internally and relationally may represent a developmentally more progressive phase of identity formation. Saul's case may illustrate the developmental change from a less mature mode to a self-construction mode of identity formation via exploration.

Alternatively, these two modes can be viewed as two styles of forging personal identity. One pattern represents a "being style" in which the individual is internally tuned, reflective, and dialogical and that utilizes relational experiences in the service of identity formation. Another pattern represents a "doing style," an emphasis on doing both when the individual is alone and with others, a less internal path to fashioning an identity.

Conclusions

The aim of this study was to explore relational qualities and how they are associated with identity formation in adolescence. To approach this research objective, we chose to encompass the intrapersonal and the interpersonal by an examination of the adolescent's tendency for an internal dialogue vis-à-vis qualities of dialogues with others. Two distinctive relational patterns were identified, a multidimensional one and a unidimensional one, and were found to correspond with the preference of adolescents to engage with the self or to shun internal engagement and engage in doing. These two patterns, it is suggested, may reflect two modes of identity formation.

The examples presented demonstrate the way in which adolescent autonomy grows *with* connections. Relatedness and identity formation were found to be woven together and to appear in various patterns. These patterns represent significant developmental and relational implications for the individual adolescent. In addition, it can be concluded that relationships may change and transform, but they are essential to promote the adolescent's construction of identity.

The world of the adolescent comprises relationships with others, at a variety of levels of complexity. In order to investigate the personal meanings of the relational experience, the adolescent has to be asked to describe them. This is best done with a narrative approach. Allowing the adolescent to narrate her or his own experience and to express the nuances of the relationship is important for understanding adolescent phenomenology and the processes that take part. Only with a narrative approach are we able to deconstruct the relational landscape of the individual into its components, to look into their unique contribution, to investigate the links among these specific relational qualities, and to examine their effect in a larger picture of the individual as a whole. It is absolutely paramount, in our view, not to lose sight of the developing adolescent as a whole person, especially when we study the development of identity. Hence, the narratives of the young people who shared their relational world with us enabled us to analyze the elements of their relational experiences as well as to view them in their entirety, to find out what are the intricate contributions of these experiences to their developing sense of identity.

The young people who participated were chosen to represent a specific phenomenon; hence, each group was defined in terms of a reported preference that they displayed relatively clearly. Therefore, the association between the participants' experience in two contexts (while being alone and in a relational context) and its reflection in the process of identity formation is facilitated by the design of the study. At the same time, because the point of departure was individuals who displayed the phenomenon in its extreme form, the findings of the two distinctive patterns may leave the impression of a dichotomy, whereas the reality for most adolescents could be less clear-cut.

In order to study and make sense of observations, we need the language. The Relational Space Model (Josselson, 1992) provided us with discrete enough concepts and their expressions to enable us to identify the various relational experiences and make sense of their relational qualities. The usefulness of this model is evident here and the conceptualization can be applied to a variety of inquiries of relatedness that focus on the personal meaning of relationships and their developmental implications.

However, a variety of questions can be derived from our investigation. Conceptually, for instance, we question the range of relational experiences that are conceptualized as Mutuality in the model and wonder whether further differentiation is in order. In addition, further research should reveal whether relational experiences are the same and carry the same meaning and relevance in the context of different cultures. One of the questions that we ask ourselves in light of our findings is whether Saul's path of relational and identity development has to do with a specific cultural background. From a somewhat different perspective, the question is in what context Embeddedness becomes a central frontstage relational experience, and when does it remain a quiet one. How the sense of belongingness enhances the individual's identity construction and how self-definition as an individual facilitates the sense of belongingness is at the center of human experience.

References

Ainsworth, M. D. S. (1989). Attachments beyond infancy. *American Psychologist, 44*, 709–716.

Allen, J. P. & Hauser, S. T. (1996), Autonomy and relatedness in adolescent–family interactions as predictors of young adults' states of mind regarding attachment. *Development and Psychopathology, 8*, 793–809.

Allen, J. P., Hauser, S. T., Bell, K. L., & O'Connor, T. G. (1994). Longitudinal assessment of autonomy and relatedness in adolescent–family interactions as predictors of adolescent ego development and self-esteem. *Child Development, 65,* 179–194.

Armsden, G. C. & Greenberg, M. T. (1987). The inventory of parent and peer attachment: Individual differences and their relationship to psychological well-being in adolescence. *Journal of Youth and Adolescence, 16,* 427–451.

Bengtson, P. L. & Grotevant, H. D. (1999). The individuality and connectedness Q-sort: A measure for assessing individuality and connectedness in dyadic relationships. *Personal Relationships, 6,* 213–225.

Berndt, T. J. & Ladd, G. W. (Eds.). (1989). *Peer relationships in child development.* New York: Wiley.

Blatt, S. J. & Blass, R. B. (1996). Relatedness and self-definition: A dialectic model of personality development. In G. G. Noam & K. W. Fischer (Eds.), *Development and vulnerability in close relationships* (pp. 309–338). Mahwah, NJ: Erlbaum.

Blos, P. (1967). The second individuation process of adolescence. *The Psychoanalytic Study of the Child, 22,* 162–186.

Bowlby, J. (1982). *Attachment and loss: Vol. 1. Attachment* (rev. ed.). New York: Basic Books.

Brown, B. B., Eicher, S. A., & Petrie, S. (1986). The importance of peer group ("crowd") affiliation in adolescence. *Journal of Adolescence, 9,* 73–96.

Csikszentmihalyi, M., & Larson, R. (1984). *Being adolescent.* New York: Basic Books.

Erikson, E. (1950). *Childhood and society.* New York: Norton.

Erikson, E. (1964). *Insight and responsibility.* New York: Norton.

Erikson, E. (1968). *Identity, youth and crisis.* New York: Norton.

Flum, H. (1994). Styles of identity formation in early and middle adolescence. *Genetic, Social and General Psychology Monographs, 120,* 437–467.

Flum, H. (1998). Embedded identity: The case of young high-achieving Ethiopian Jewish immigrants in Israel. *Journal of Youth Studies, 1,* 143–161.

Flum, H. & Porton, H. (1995). Relational processes and identity formation in adolescence: The example of "A Separate Peace." *Genetic, Social and General Psychology Monographs, 121,* 369–389.

Gilligan, C. (1982). *In a different voice: Psychological theory and women's development.* Cambridge, MA: Harvard University Press.

Gilligan, C., Lyons, N. P., & Hammer, T. J. (Eds.). (1990). *Making connections: The relational worlds of adolescent girls at Emma Willard school.* Cambridge, MA: Harvard University Press.

Greenberg, M. T., Siegel, J. M., & Leitch, C. J. (1983). The nature and importance of attachment relationships to parents and peers during adolescence. *Journal of Youth and Adolescence, 12,* 373–386.

Grotevant, H. D. & Cooper, C. R. (1985). Patterns of interaction in family relationships and the development of identity exploration in adolescence. *Child Development, 56,* 415–428.

Grotevant, H. D. & Cooper, C. R. (1986). Individuation in family relationships: A perspective on individual differences in the development of identity and role-taking skill in adolescence. *Human Development, 29,* 82–100.

Guisinger, S. & Blatt, S. J. (1994). Individuality and relatedness: Evolution of a funda-mental dialectic. *American Psychologist, 49*, 104–111.

Hansell, S., Mechanic, D., & Brondolo, E.(1986). Introspectiveness and adolescent development. *Journal of Youth and Adolescence, 15*, 115–B132.

Jacobson, J. L. & Wille, D. E. (1986), The influence of attachment pattern on devel-opmental changes in peer interaction from the toddler to the preschool period. *Child Development, 57*, 338–347.

Jordan, J. V., Kaplan, A. G., Miller, J. B., Stiver, I. P., & Surrey, J. L. (Eds.). (1991), *Women's growth in connection: Writings from the Stone Center.* New York: Guilford Press.

Josselson, R. L. (1987). *Finding herself: Pathways of identity development in women.* San Francisco, CA: Jossey-Bass.

Josselson, R. L. (1992). *The space between us: Exploring the dimensions of human relationships.* San Francisco, CA: Jossey-Bass.

Josselson, R. L. (1994). Identity and relatedness in the life cycle. In H. A. Bosma, D. J. de Levita, T. L. G. Grastina, & H. D. Grotevant (Eds.), *Identity and develop-ment: An interdisciplinary approach* (pp. 81–102). Thousand Oaks, CA: Sage.

Josselson, R. L., Lieblich, A., Sharabany, R., & Wiseman, H. (1997). *Conversation as method: Analyzing the relational world of people who were raised communally.* Thousand Oaks, CA: Sage.

Kirchler, E., Palmonari, A., & Pombeni, M. L. (1993). Developmental tasks and adole-cents' relationships with their peers and their family. In S. Jackson & H. Rodri-guez-Tomè (Eds.), *Adolescence and its social worlds* (pp. 145–167). Mahwah, UK: Erlbaum.

Kohut, H. (1971). *The analysis of the self.* New York: International Universities Press.

Kroger, J. (1997). Gender and identity: The intersection of structure, content, and con-text. *Sex Roles, 36*, 747–770.

Kroger, J. (2000). *Identity development: Adolescence through adulthood.* Thousand Oaks, CA: Sage.

Lamb, M. E. & Nash, A. (1989). Infant–mother attachment, sociability, and peer com-petence. In T. J. Berndt & G. W. Ladd (Eds.), *Peer relationships in child devel-opment* (pp. 219–245).New York: Wiley.

Larson, R. & Csikszentmihalyi, M. (1978). Experiential correlates of time alone in adolescence. *Journal of Personality, 46*, 677–693.

Lavi-Yudelevitch, M. (1999). Together and alone in the process of identity formation: Different styles of adolescents. Unpublished master's thesis, Ben-Gurion Uni-versity, Israel.

Lyons, N. P. (1983). Two perspectives: On self, relationships and morality. *Harvard Educational Review, 53*, 125–145.

Main, M., Kaplan, N., & Cassidy, J. (1985), Security in infancy, childhood, and adult-hood: A move to the level of representation. In I. Bretherton & E. Waters (Eds.), Growing points of attachment theory and research. *Monographs of the Society for Research in Child Development, 50* (Serial No. 209), 66–104.

Marcia, J. E. (1993), The relational roots of identity. In J. Kroger (Ed.), *Discussions on ego identity* (pp. 101–120). Mahwah, NJ: Erlbaum.

Marcoen, A. & Goossens, L. (1993). Loneliness, attitude towards aloneness, and solitude: Age differences and developmental significance during adolescence. In S.
Jackson & H. Rodriguez-Tomè (Eds.), *Adolescence and its social worlds* (pp.
197–227). Mahwah, NJ: Erlbaum.

Mellor, S. (1989). Gender differences in identity formation as a function of self–other
relationships. *Journal of Youth and Adolescence, 18*, 361–375.

Mintzer, A. (1997). Stability and satisfaction in close relationships and associated factors: Relationship style, homosexual identity and social support in male homosexuals in Israel. Unpublished doctoral dissertation, The Hebrew University of
Jerusalem.

Price, J. (1998). Suffer the little child: Mothers who abuse. Unpublished doctoral dissertation, New York University.

Rosenthal, D. A., Gurney, R. M., & Moore, S. M. (1981). From trust to intimacy: A new
inventory for examining Erikson's stages of psychosocial development. *Journal
of Youth and Adolescence, 10*, 525–537.

Ryan, R. M. & Lynch, J. H. (1989). Emotional autonomy versus detachment: Revisit-
ing the vicissitudes of adolescence and young adulthood. *Child Development,
60*, 340–356.

Sharabany, R. (1994). Continuities in the development of intimate friendships: Object
relation, interpersonal, and attachment perspectives. In R. Erber & R. Gilmour
(Eds.), *Theoretical frameworks for personal relationships* (pp. 157–175). Mahwah, NJ: Erlbaum.

Sullivan, H. S. (1953). The interpersonal theory of psychiatry. New York: Norton.

White, K. M., Speisman, J. C., & Costos, D. (1983). Young adults and their parents. In
H. D. Grotevant & C. R. Cooper (Eds.). *Adolescent development in the family:
New directions in child development* (pp. 61–76). San Francisco, CA: Jossey
Bass.

Winnicott, D. W. (1965). *The maturational process and the facilitating environment.*
Madison, CT: International Universities Press.

Youniss, J. (1980). *Parents and peers in social development.* Chicago: University of
Chicago Press.

Youniss, J. & Ketterlinus, R.(1987). Communication and connectedness in mother—
and father—adolescent relationships. *Journal of Youth and Adolescence, 16*,
265–280.

Youniss, J. & Smollar, J. (1985). *Adolescent relations with mothers, fathers, and
friends.* Chicago: University of Chicago Press.

Youniss, J. & Smollar, J. (1989). Adolescents' interpersonal relationships in social context. In T. J. Berndt & G. W. Ladd (Eds.), *Peer relationships in child development* (pp. 300–316). New York: Wiley.

10

A Relational Perspective on Adolescent Boys' Identity Development

JUDY Y. CHU

> This may sound completely absurd but it's questionable whether it's right to tell people — it's obviously right, but whether it's realistic to tell people that, you know, it doesn't matter the way you are, because really, I mean really, it does. I mean, that's the way things are. (Taylor, age 15)

Much of recent literature on boys has focused on ways in which boys' socialization toward culturally prescribed conventions of masculinity can be detrimental to boys' development. For instance, clinicians propose that pressures for boys to accommodate images of masculinity that emphasize physical toughness, emotional stoicism, and projected self-sufficiency can diminish boys' sensitivities to people's feelings, including their own (Kindlon & Thompson, 1999), and undermine boys' abilities to achieve intimacy in their relationships (Pollack, 1998). Similarly, researchers suggest that boys' gender socialization may result in gender role strain, for instance when their failure to conform to masculine standards leads to feelings of inadequacy, when they are traumatized by pressures to conform to masculine norms, and when they internalize masculine ideals that inherently are not conducive to their overall well-being (Pleck, 1995). Studies have also shown that adolescent boys who internalize conventional norms of masculinity tend to exhibit more problem behaviors (Pleck, Sonenstein, & Ku, 1994) and have lower levels of self-esteem (Chu, Porche, & Tolman, in press). In short, this literature suggests that boys' gender socialization may have negative consequences for boys' psychological health, social behaviors, and relationships, despite social advantages of emulating cultural constructions of masculinity.

While these theories and findings have raised important questions about the course and purpose of boys' development, there has been a tendency in

From: Way, Niobe and Chu, Judy Y. (Eds). (2004). *Adolescent boys: Exploring diverse cultures of boyhood.* (pp. 78–104). New York: New York University Press. Copyright © New York University Press. Reprinted with permission.

this discourse to conceptualize boys' gender socialization as a linear model of cause-and-effect wherein cultural messages about masculinity are introduced and directly impact boys' attitudes and behaviors. In focusing primarily on social aspects, such as the content of the messages boys receive and the sources of pressure in boys' lives to accommodate these messages, this literature tends to objectify boys by depicting them as passive participants in, or even victims of, their gender socialization (e.g., Pollack, 1998). Seldom considered are psychological aspects, such as the ways in which boys experience and make meaning of cultural messages and social pressures to which they are exposed, and how boys are thereby able to mediate the effects of their gender socialization on their developmental outcomes.

With regard to boys' identity development in particular, recent discourse is further limited in its tendency to focus on the extent to which a boy fits a particular construction of masculinity and on the consequences of aligning oneself too closely or deviating too much. As active participants in their identity development, boys are responsive in the sense that they have the capacity to internalize and resist masculine norms and ideals that manifest, for instance, through other people's expectations for and assumptions about them. However, boys are also creative in the sense that they construct their identities, or senses of self, in ways that reflect their individual experiences as well as their cognitive abilities. Therefore, in order to arrive at a more comprehensive understanding of adolescent boys' identity development, it is important to consider how boys are influenced by cultural messages and social pressures but also how boys draw on their continually evolving self-knowledge and conceptions of reality as they develop an understanding of who they are and what they are like.

Examining Boys' Development Through a Relational Framework

In this chapter, I present two cases from a larger qualitative study that examined boys' development through a relational framework (Chu, 1998, 1999). Focusing on boys as active participants in their gender socialization my study investigated how boys negotiate their senses of self, behaviors, and styles of relating in light of cultural constructions of masculinity that they encounter in their interpersonal relationships. Against a back-drop of literature suggesting that boys' gender socialization causes them to become disconnected from themselves (e.g., unable to recognize or articulate their own thoughts and feelings) and disconnected from others (e.g., unable to develop close, mutual relationships), I was interested to learn from boys how their experiences of gender socialization might undermine or lead them to shield their connection to self, connection to others and genuine self-expression. I was also interested in how boys may preserve their relational ways of being by resisting and/or challenging pressures associated with their gender socialization (Chu, 2000).

While the importance of relationships is widely acknowledged in developmental and psychological theory (Erikson, 1968; Piaget, 1954; Vygotsky, 1978), what distinguishes a relational framework is that it starts from the premise that all humans have a fundamental capacity and desire for close, mutual relationships (Trevarthan, 1979; Tronick,1989; Tronick & Gianino 1986; Weinberg & Tronick, 1996), and that our senses of self (e.g., how we see and understand ourselves to be) are inextricably embedded in our interpersonal relationships as well as our sociocultural environments (Gilligan, Brown, & Rogers. 1990). In highlighting the centrality of relationships in people's lives (Gilligan, 1996; Jordan, Kaplan, Miller, Stiver, & Surrey, 1991; Miller. 1994), a relational framework emphasizes the fact that human development occurs not in isolation with the option of having relationships but primarily through and within our relationships with other people (Gilligan, 1982; Miller 1976). Thus, a relational framework calls into question models of development that focus on individuation and separation to determine maturity and health.

With the goal to learn about boys' experiences from boys own perspectives, I adopted a relational approach to psychological inquiry (Brown & Gilligan 1992), which conceptualizes the study of people's experiences as a practice of relationships and emphasizes the fact that the nature of data collected depends in part on qualities of the researcher-participant relationship (Brown et al., 1988; Brown & Gilligan, 1990). Given that the boys' willingness to share their experiences with me would be determined by the dynamics of our interactions and also by their perceptions of me, I centered my research methods on developing comfortable and trusting relationships between the boys and myself, and noted how I engaged and responded to these boys as well as how they engaged and responded to me within these relationships. In my study, I also started from a position of not knowing and explained to the boys that, because I am female and therefore do not know what it is like to be a boy, I would be looking to them as my teachers and relying on them to help me understand their experiences.

A School for Boys

The participants in my study were 58 adolescent boys (ages 12–18) attending a private boys' secondary school (grades 7–12) in New England. Of these boys, 82.8 percent were White, 12.1 percent African American, and 5.2 percent Asian American. Most of these boys came from middle- and upper-middle-class families and planned to attend colleges and universities after graduating. Although this population of boys (i.e., predominantly White, middle-class) has been the focus of recent discourse on boys and past psychological and developmental studies, few researchers have investigated boys' experiences from boys' own perspectives among this group (much less other populations of boys). Thus, the complexities and nuances of their lives are seldom represented in the literature.

Over the course of one academic year, I collected data with these boys using qualitative observation and interview methods. I began in the fall by engaging in weekly ethnographic observations that enabled me to establish rapport with potential interviewees through informal contact and casual interactions. In other words, I spent time "hanging out" with these boys so they could inquire about my intentions and get to know me, and so I could get to know them as individuals. Most of my observations took place in common areas at the school during "free periods." However, at the boys' suggestion, I also observed classes in session and attended after-school activities, including sports practices and play rehearsals, in order to develop a fuller sense of these boys' various contexts and relationships at school. In short, I told the boys that I was interested in learning about their lives and experiences and they generously took me under their wing, so to speak, and let me know what I should be sure to see. By the end of the fall semester, the boys had become familiar with me and were accustomed to having me around. For instance, at a sports event when a parent noticed me and asked one of the boys who I was, he casually replied, "Oh, that's just Judy. She's here to study us." As the boys pointed out, my taking the time to develop this sense of comfort and trust with them turned out to be crucial to eliciting their honest thoughts and opinions when it came time for my interviews.

During the spring, I conducted semi-structured, one-on-one interviews while continuing my observations. Interviewees were recruited on a volunteer basis and written consent was obtained from each boy's parent or guardian. Each interview began with a brief explanation of my research interests (e.g., "I'm interested in learning about how ideas about masculinity, like what it means to be a man — being strong, being tough, whatever — how that affects the way you think about yourself and your identity, the way you act, if it affects the way you act, and your relationships") and a question about whether, as males, they have ever felt that they were expected to act or be a certain way. For the most part, I then allowed the boys to introduce topics and issues that they felt were central and/or significant in their lives. As I followed the boys' leads, my questions served primarily to encourage the boys to elaborate on their experiences so that I might better understand their meaning. Given this open-ended format, the boys typically talked about their relationships with peers, friends, family, and other adults (e.g., school faculty and staff), as well as their personal interests and aspirations. Occasionally, if a boy was shy or hesitant, I tried more actively to initiate conversation by asking questions based on topics that other boys had raised, for instance about their relationships and interests in and out of school.

Observational and interview data were analyzed using conceptually clustered matrices (Miles & Huberman, 1994) and also a voice-centered method

(Brown et al., 1988; Brown & Gilligan, 1990, 1991; Gilligan Spencer, Weinberg, & Bertsch, in press). Whereas the conceptually clustered matrices were used to identify distinct, recurring, and organizing principles or ideas in the data, the voice-centered method was used to focus this analysis on themes pertaining to the boys' developing senses of self, and to note patterns and shifts in the boys' self-expression around these themes. The creation of conceptually clustered matrices involved organizing excerpts from the boys' interview narratives by boy (columns) and according to themes (rows) to enable comparisons across individuals. The application of a voice-centered method involved multiple readings of the text to highlight the content of what was said (e.g., issues and topics that were addressed) and also ways in which the boys represented themselves and other people in describing their experiences.

Specifically, the first reading of the voice-centered method served to determine the plot (i.e., who, what, when, where, why) of each episode or excerpt and to document the "reader's response," and thereby account for my presence, influence, and reactions as I observed the boys' interactions, engaged them during interviews, and interpreted their narratives. Thus, considerations of how my own identity, biases, and relationships with these boys affected the interpersonal dynamics of my observations and interviews were also integral to this analysis. The second reading involved tracking the boys' modes of self-expression. For instance, when referring to themselves, the boys' use of the first person pronoun "I" was compared with their use of "you," which could extend to people in general (e.g., "You always have to keep up your guard"), and with their use of "we," which indicated a partnership or group of which they felt a part (e.g., "We helped each other a lot"). The boys' use of "they" to refer to a nonspecific group of others (e.g., "Kids just attack...if they think you're vulnerable") was also examined. The third and fourth readings focused on the boys' perceptions of how other people see them (e.g., adults' expectations and assumptions regarding boys in general and them in particular) and how they see themselves (e.g., the boys' notions of who they are and what they are like) to examine how these perceptions intertwined with and influenced each other, as evidenced in the boys' descriptions.

Selves in Relationship

Contrary to popular discourse that tends to portray adolescent boys as emotionally deficient and relationally impaired, analyses of these data, particularly the boys' interview narratives, revealed these boys to be clearly capable of thoughtful self-reflection and deep interpersonal understanding. These analyses also revealed ways in which the boys' senses of self are embedded in cultural constructions of masculinity, as typically encountered through other people's expectations and assumptions. Consistent with relational theories of development, the boys' senses of self obviously are not self-generated, as though the boys exist in a vacuum. Rather, the boys negotiate their senses of self in light of their experiences in relationships with specific individuals (e.g., friends and family) and with their broader social contexts (e.g., school community).

A pervasive theme in the boys' interview narratives concerned discrepancies that the boys perceived between how other people see them and how they see themselves. The boys were familiar with the masculine norms and stereotypes that influence people's views of boys in general and of them in particular. The boys therefore understood why people might expect them to be rugged and athletic or assume that they are rebellious, disinterested, and oblivious to interpersonal cues. Nevertheless, the boys struggled with the inaccuracies and limitations of these depictions, which seemed to constrain their possibilities of being recognized and valued for the full range of their qualities and abilities. Moreover, the boys' descriptions suggest that the ways in which they reconcile these discrepancies may ultimately shape their senses of self.

An examination of ways in which the boys reconciled discrepancies between other people's views of them and their own views revealed two dominant patterns of response. Both patterns could be seen to some extent in most of the boys in this sample but varied in their prominence across individual boys. One pattern involves internalizing or yielding to other people's views, particularly expectations that reflect cultural norms and ideals, sometimes to the effect of changing how one sees oneself. The other pattern involves resisting or overcoming other people's views, particularly assumptions based on stereotypes and misconceptions, sometimes to the effect of changing how one is seen by others.

These patterns call to mind Piaget's (1954) concepts of assimilation and accommodation, which he used to describe how young children interact with their environmental contexts. Through assimilation, individuals modify environmental input to fit with their existing schemas and conceptions (and thereby resist the imposition of social and cultural constructions). Taken to an extreme, assimilation can result in egocentrism and possibly disconnections from one's relationships and social realities. Through accommodation, individuals modify their existing schemas and conceptions in light of new experiences of their environments (e.g., by internalizing social and cultural constructions). Taken to an extreme, accommodation can result in social conformity and possibly psychological dissociation, or a decreased awareness of one's own thoughts, feelings, and desires. Just as Piaget suggests that healthy development arises through the balanced interplay of assimilation and accommodation, one could define a boy's healthy sense of self in terms of his ability to consider without necessarily succumbing to other people's views of him.

An exploration of differences between boys who were inclined to yield to other people's expectations and boys who managed to resist other people's assumptions indicated that relationships may be key to boys' resilience as they strive to develop a sense of self that feels true to themselves and also grounded in reality. Recent studies have shown that having access to a confiding relationship is the single best protector against psychological and social risks for adolescents (Masten, 1994; Masten & Coatsworth, 1998; Resnick et al., 1997; Rutter, 1990; Wang, Haertel, & Walberg, 1994; Werner & Smith, 1982). Findings from this analysis further suggest that, beyond having access to relationships, the ways in which boys experience themselves in their relationships (e.g., as being understood and valued by others) are also crucial to their psychological adjustment and social well-being. For instance, boys who felt misunderstood or misrepresented in their relationships seemed more susceptible to internalizing other people's expectations, even at the cost of discounting their own perspective. In contrast, boys who felt known and validated in their relationships seemed better supported to resist other people's assumptions, perhaps to the effect of preserving their integrity.

In the following sections, I present an example of each of these two patterns (i.e., of internalization and resistance) to offer insight into ways in which adolescent boys' experiences in relationships can support or undermine their resistance and subsequently influence their senses of self. The boys described in these examples are similar in a number of ways. Both come from White middle-class families living in suburban neighborhoods. Both have access to relationships, particularly friendships, in which they feel supported. Both feel that they are regarded within their school community as not fitting conventional norms of masculinity. However, their experiences of self-in relationships differ such that one struggles despite his friendships to fit in within the school community while the other manages through the support of his friendships to create a niche within the school community where he can fit in and be how he wants to be. Of course, these examples are not intended to represent or be easily generalized to the experiences of all boys everywhere. Rather, they were selected because they point to issues and concerns that were commonly mentioned by the boys in this study and yet seem under-represented in the literature on boys.

Taylor

For Taylor, a 15-year-old sophomore, the process of negotiating his sense of self centers on his efforts to counterbalance his image as an outsider within the school community with his conviction that he is not as deviant as people believe him to be. In terms of his physical appearance, Taylor is lanky without being awkward or clumsy and has straggly blond hair that hits just below his ears. Although his attire conforms to the school's dress code — which requires students to wear a jacket and tie, a button-down shirt (tucked in), and pants (no jeans are allowed) — his appearance departs from its prim and proper image. As we meet at the end of the school day, Taylor arrives with his jacket and tie in hand, the collar of his shirt loosened, and his shirttail hanging loosely outside his pants. His style is effortless; rather than trying to project an image of nonchalance, he seems genuinely comfortable and relaxed.

During our interview, Taylor is articulate and speaks easily and openly about his experiences. While his passionate and persuasive tone indicates that this topic evokes strong feelings for him and that he has given this a lot of thought, his readiness to share his perspective and his responsiveness to my interest suggest that opportunities to express these sentiments beyond his circle of friends (or with an adult) may be rare. With Taylor, my question about whether he has ever felt as though he is expected to act or be a certain way prompts a discussion about expectations that he perceives within his school environment and how not meeting these expectations has affected his status and relationships and also his sense of self in this context. As Taylor replies:

> Yeah, there's obviously an expectation for people to act a certain way, especially at an all-boys school, I think. And problems arise when you don't necessarily fall into that category. Like problems have come up, especially with me 'cause I don't necessarily fit into that category very well.

When I ask Taylor about these expectations, he suggests that they involve displaying certain behaviors and attitudes:

> Just in general, things that you would equate with masculinity.... It was kind [of an] expectation for kids to, I dunno, pick on each other and have a lack of interest in anything besides, you know, athletics and stuff like that. And I don't know, 'cause it's weird, I used to be a lot like that and I used to be kind of, you know, the all-around normal kind of kid up until 4th and 5th grade and then suddenly I completely changed. And I don't know what it was. I became a lot more intellectual, I guess. And there were problems at [this school] for me, in 7th and 8th grade especially, because I'd kind of look around and I'd see how kids were treating each other and I couldn't, like, relate to it at all because I didn't, you know, I couldn't fit into that.

Consistent with cultural stereotypes, Taylor perceives expectations for boys to be boisterous, indifferent to everything but sports, anti-intellectual, and insensitive. Taylor further suggests that this stereotyped image of boys is perpetuated not only among his peers but within the wider school community as well. As Taylor explains, "It was almost as if the school condoned the way kids treated each other because it was their expectation. Their attitude was, you know, 'That's the way boys act.'" It seems these expectations are not so much ideals for boys to strive toward but assumptions about how boys are and how boys act. All the same, so long as they are a part of the dominant culture of this school and in society at large, there are consequences to not meeting these expectations such that Taylor experiences problems when, as a result of becoming "more intellectual," he finds he can no longer "relate to" and "fit into" that image of being an "all-around normal kind of kid."

Being Marginalized

For Taylor, perhaps the most significant consequence of not meeting his school's expectations for boys is that it becomes difficult for him to be acknowledged within the school community for who he thinks he is. Based on his experience, Taylor suggests that people are often unable or unwilling to see beyond the fact that he does not embody the stereotyped image of boys that pervades the school's culture. As Taylor continues to describe what this image entails, he suggests:

> So much of it has to do with sports. That's almost what it is, but it's more than that. It's the, I don't know, "Boys will be boys" attitude, I guess. You know, like fooling around and, you know, doing stupid things and I feel like so many kids acted, you know — and I could never, I couldn't really act that way.... And one of my problems was that from early on I'd try — I was always trying to let people know who I was through doing things like, I dunno, speaking contests and poetry contests and so I kind of got a reputation as like this annoying poetry kid. And so I've had that reputation ever since 7th grade. But I guess that's the price I have to pay for not conforming.

Taylor also finds that people's views tend to be limited by dichotomous conceptions of what a boy can be. As he explains:

> Everything is either black or white. You can't be a good athlete and an actor — 'cause I mean, before I came to [this school], I considered myself as much an athlete as I did in theater, but they don't let you. It's a little as though they can't accept that idea and you either have to be, you know, the jock or you have to be, you know, the fringe, kind of. And I have problems because I'm often seen as being like the fringe of the [school] community. I don't consider myself that. I guess that's life and it's not a big deal for me.

As Taylor cannot bring himself to engage in the rambunctious behaviors and macho posturing that might help secure his masculinity and establish his worth within his school community, and while his athletic abilities are negated by his artistic interests, Taylor becomes marginalized. Moreover, in this context where not fitting "that category" overshadows other aspects of his character, the discrepancy between how others see him and how he sees himself seems inevitable and opportunities to correct other people's misconceptions seem rare. While Taylor portends his resignation to this reality ("I guess that's life") and claims that being seen as "the fringe" is "not a big deal," there is some evidence of his resistance as he continues, at least for now, to hold a different view of himself ("I don't consider myself that").

Interestingly, in Taylor's case, being marginalized does not imply being isolated. He knows that there are others who also do not meet the school's expectations for boys and who are similarly regarded as outsiders within the school community. In fact, his friends are mostly these boys. However, while Taylor may feel connected to his friends, these relationships do not seem to be sufficient; he nevertheless longs to be accepted and valued within the wider school community. He even makes a point to distinguish himself from those, including his friends, who may feel resentment toward the culture and community that discount their differences. As Taylor explains:

> Unlike a lot of people who are in my situation, I think I have less animosity toward [this school] than a lot of them do because — I mean, I like [this school] a lot more than a lot of my friends do, 'cause most of my friends don't fit that category either, but I respect [this school] because it — you know, for different reasons.

Whereas his friends may shun or rebel against expectations according to which they are deemed deviant and deficient, Taylor harbors a hope of being recognized and validated within this community. Thus, while he is not isolated, he may still feel alone.

Being Excluded

In addition to having implications for Taylor's status, not meeting his school's expectations for boys also affects how other people relate to him and how he is able (or allowed) to relate to others in this context. As he describes:

> There's a certain feeling of identity between the kids who you call, you know, masculine, you know, like "the guys," I guess. And there's a certain identity that they have that I don't think that I'll ever really have, but I may. I have it with some of my friends, but I can never have it at [this school] 'cause I'm not seen, I guess, as fitting into that category. There's a certain closeness that they have. Although I have closeness with a lot of my friends, I can never be seen with [the guys] in that situation, you know, talking about the Red Sox, even though I would with a lot of my friends.

Again, Taylor's marginalized status does not hinder his ability to have any relationships. In fact, Taylor suggests that the feelings of identity and closeness that he shares with his friends are comparable to what he observes among "the guys," or boys who are valued within the school community. Rather than constraining his access to relationships or even the quality of his relationships, Taylor's status mainly limits with whom he can identify and feel close (e.g., not with "the guys" or the school community as a whole). As Taylor explains,

> For instance, I had a speech a few weeks ago. I was talking about sports and stuff like that. And it was almost as if ["the guys"] rejected it, not because they rejected the ideas but they rejected the fact that I was giving it and they saw me as this kid who didn't have the right to talk about the Bruins because, "What does he know? He doesn't play hockey. He's not one of us." And that hurts because that's not really who I am. But I accept the fact and I understand why I've been, you know, put into that category [of not being one of "the guys"] and I guess I don't have any regrets.

What is remarkable about this passage is not Taylor's exclusion by "the guys," which is undoubtedly harsh, but his apparent acceptance and understanding of their rejection. Taylor's hesitation ("I *guess* I don't have any regrets") suggests that he does not fully accept his lot. However, the way in which he soon shifts from expressing his feelings and perspective ("And that hurts because that's not really who I am") to justifying his exclusion by "the guys" ("I accept the fact and I understand why...") suggests that his resistance against other people's views of him has begun to waiver.

Furthermore, as Taylor is excluded not only from relationships with "the guys" but from the masculine identity that "the guys" collectively embody, his sense of masculinity is also called into question. Continuing to comment on ways in which he is distanced from "the guys," Taylor describes:

> I guess it's the fact that they are able to be, you know, "guys." It's almost as if just they are able to be that and anyone [else] isn't really allowed to.... It's the fact that they have that male identity and they have it with, like, themselves and with the faculty members. It all comes down to, really, athletics 'cause so much of the faculty and the students, that's how they identify themselves and it's hard for someone like me to relate.

As Taylor sees it, involvement in sports not only plays a pivotal role in determining one's masculinity, popularity, and worth, but also serves as a primary means by which "the guys" bond with each other and with the school, including faculty members. Given that only a select few get to be "guys" in this context, Taylor and others like him who are not hearty athletes and thus do not "have that male identity" are left to establish themselves, at best, in opposition or as deficient in comparison to this elite and exclusive group. Likewise, with "the guys" occupying the highest or central positions of status within the school community, Taylor and his friends are relegated to subordinate positions and end up participating from the periphery. To the extent that not fitting "that category" determines who he can be (e.g., not one of "the guys"), with whom he can have relationships (e.g., not with "the guys"), and even how he can act in this context (e.g., not talking publicly about sports), Taylor's exclusion is ensured.

Wishing to be Truly Seen and Known

Taylor seems to understand why "the guys" see him as "not one of us," even though he disagrees with their view ("that's not really who I am"). He also acquiesces to the probability that, while he experiences something similar with his friends, he will never be seen as sharing common interests and goals ("a certain feeling of identity") or having an intimate connection ("a certain closeness") with "the guys" and with the school community. However, he struggles with how his alleged deviance stifles his every-day interactions. As Taylor observes:

It's hard for certain teachers and certain kids to relate to someone like me who doesn't necessarily embody that sort of identity. Although they may respect me, they could never be, like, truly on the same level — they'll never put themselves on the same level because they can't relate to the fact that I don't have this kind of male, generic, you know, idea. Like, for instance, my history teacher I think is a great guy and I like him a lot but he — there's always something about him that's reserved towards me because I'm not a sports hero or whatever. But that's the way it is.

When I ask Taylor how the closeness that "the guys" have with each other compares with the closeness that he has with his friends, he suggests that the main differences between "the guys" and himself are not in their experiences of relationships but in the parameters of their relationships (e.g., with whom they are permitted to be close) and in the value given to their perspectives. As Taylor explains excitedly:

See there's no difference, but what the difference is — this is so hard to explain — they're allowed to have that closeness in the [school community]. Like I said, they're allowed to be guys in the [school] community and it's just they that are able to do that. No one else is allowed to kind of fit, like, the guy identity, although they may outside of school and with their friends.... And it's funny. I always remember, you know, since the earliest days, I'd always say to myself, you know, "I wish they could see me with my friends so they could know that I act just like they do with their friends."

Although Taylor claims complacency ("I guess I don't have any regrets") and acceptance ("that's the way it is"), his desire to be truly seen and known within his school community remains evident throughout his narrative ("I wish they could see"). For now, Taylor remains convinced that his marginalized status and exclusion in this context are based on other people's narrow views of what he is like. Thus, despite feeling oppressed by the cliques within his school's culture, Taylor remains hopeful that, if only people could see him for who he really is, they would see that he is also sociable, worthy of respect, and not as different from "the guys" as they may think.

At the same time, there is some evidence that Taylor is beginning to question his convictions. For instance, when I ask Taylor what it would take for people to be able to see him for who he is, he replies:

I think that it would take a more, wide acceptance, I guess. But I'm not sure either if it's necessarily — I never really liked questioning, you know, the course of society. I often think the way people are — the way like boys are and men are — is, you know, let it happen. That's why I don't have a lot of dislike about [this school]. I mean, I think that a lot of the reason they are the way they are is, you know, that's the way it is. And I think that I respect [people] for being the way they are, although I wish they would sometimes, you know, at some time see me for who I think I am. I also understand that I may not be who I think I am. I may be a lot more, you know, whatever. I may be what they think I am instead of what I think I am. And so, I dunno.

What makes you say that?

I dunno. Well, maybe the fact that I seem to be so universally put into one category, so maybe it may be true.

Taylor's response suggests that he has internalized the notion that there exists a natural state of male being ("the way boys are and men are") and course of male development ("let it happen"). While he recognizes that he deviates from these, he accepts and respects their predominance nonetheless. Perhaps as a result, Taylor's wish to be seen for "who I think I am" becomes linked with doubts that he knows who he is ("I may be what they think I am").

Taylor's confusion is particularly evident when one follows the progression of his thinking by extracting and tracking his "I" statements in this passage:

I think, I guess, I'm not sure,
I never really liked questioning,
I often think,
That's why I don't have a lot of dislike,
I mean, I think,
That's the way it is,
I think, I respect, I wish,
Who I think I am,
I also understand, I may not be,
Who I think I am,
I may be, I may be,
What they think I am,
What I think I am,
I dunno,
I dunno, I seem to be,
Maybe it may be true.

In focusing on how Taylor frames his self-expression, one can see his discomfort ("I think," "I guess," "I'm not sure") when my question leads him to critique society ("I never really liked questioning"). As he deliberates his reality ("the way people are," "who I think I am"), one can also see how he begins with his thoughts and feelings ("I think," "I respect," "I wish") and tries to acknowledge other people's views ("I also understand," "I may not be," "I may be") but becomes increasingly uncertain ("I dunno") and ends up questioning his own perspective ("Maybe it may be true"). Although Taylor tries to consider other people's views ("what they think I am") and also sustain his sense of self ("who I think I am"), his experiences of being "so universally put into one category" seem to undermine his conviction that he is not the misfit that people suppose him to be.

It seems that Taylor could potentially draw strength to resist this process from the sense of belonging and acceptance that he experiences with his friends. However, the fact that his friends are also marginalized within the school community may ironically lead Taylor to disregard their views. Thus, despite having relationships, Taylor struggles on his own to establish himself in this context. And by cutting himself off from the support of his relationships, Taylor may be especially susceptible to internalizing other people's conceptions of him, including those he previously resisted as misconceptions, to the detriment of his self-concept.

Ethan

For Ethan, an 18-year-old senior, the process of negotiating his sense of self centers on his efforts to be true to himself and to ascertain what that entails as he engages in relationships and social interactions at school and beyond. Like Taylor, Ethan also describes himself as someone who does not fit conventional images of masculinity. However, whereas Taylor's deviance is inadvertent, Ethan's deviance seems more deliberate. One area where this difference is apparent is in how the boys look and dress. Whereas Taylor seems to pay little attention to his appearance, Ethan's style reflects his desire to be different. For instance, Ethan has sideburns at a time when they are not a part of mainstream fashion. And instead of wearing the standard navy blazer with an Oxford shirt and khaki pants, Ethan might wear a tan jacket with a plaid flannel shirt and corduroy pants. While Ethan's style may be considered "alternative," wearing plaid flannel shirts and corduroy pants is not uncommon and there are students who are more outrageous in their dress (e.g., wearing bright green pants or multi-colored checkered jackets). Moreover, Ethan always looks well groomed, not sloppy or grungy, and tends to be soft-spoken and mild-mannered. Thus, Ethan is somewhere in the middle; he manages to distinguish himself but the distinction is subtle and he can easily blend in at this school.

During our interview, Ethan's calm and quiet disposition is evident. He is thoughtful in responding to my questions and occasionally asks for clarification to make sure he understands what I am asking. He becomes slightly timid during pauses in the conversation. However, for the most part, he expresses himself confidently yet modestly and gives the impression of being self-assured but not self-righteous.

Drawing Strength from Relationships

In contrast to Taylor's experience, Ethan emphasizes ways in which his relationships, especially his closest friendship, have helped him to be true to himself and supported his efforts to show others what he is really like. When I ask Ethan whether, as a male. he has ever felt expected to be or act a certain way,

he begins by describing how he has fallen short of his dad s notions of how a
boy should be:

> I think that I feel pressure to be more masculine, like I feel like my dad
> sometimes-like when I do things, just the fact that I was never good at regu-
> lar sports when I was younger, like baseball or whatever. I was never good
> at that and I could tell, I felt like he was pretty disappointed in me. Or when
> I didn't want to do work, like yard work or something, he'd always be disap-
> pointed. And I felt like, like he's trying to get me to be more like a little boy
> or like a young boy or something. And I think lately, not really, I think my
> parents have come to realize that I'm not really like a gung-ho masculine
> type of guy.

Ethan also describes feeling coerced by his mom's efforts to shape him
according to her own ideals:

> I think I reached a breaking point when I was about, like, 12 or 13 when
> — because my mom, especially my mom, really tried to get me to be like, I
> don't know what she tried to get me to be but it was just, I felt like I wasn't
> being myself at all.... It just felt like she was forcing me to try to impress
> other people and just have me dress the way she wanted me to dress and — I
> mean, I assume all kids are like that but I just felt like she was really trying
> to make me be the person that she really wanted me to be. And, um, I sup-
> pose I rebelled.

While his dad's disappointment may have undermined Ethan's sense of being
sufficiently masculine in the past, Ethan indicates that he has come to accept
the discrepancy between his dad's expectations and the reality of who he is,
even if his parents have not ("not really"). Likewise, although Ethan may
have resented his mom's attempts to foster behaviors that felt contrived and/or
uncomfortable to him ("I felt like I wasn't being myself at all"), he has found
ways to make his own decisions about who he wants to be and how he wants
to act.

Namely, Ethan explains that his relationship with his closest friend has
enabled him to resist pressures to accommodate himself, or at least his behaviors, to his parents' expectations and ideals. As Ethan explains:

> When I was 13, I met my closest friend right now and he really helped me to
> become who I want to become. I felt like we both kind of helped each other
> grow into, like, who we want to be right now. Up until that time, I'd kind
> of been thinking, "Well, I don't really like this, so why am I doing it?" but
> continued to do it, like just dressing all neat and trying to impress everyone I
> met and trying to be like the perfect kid. But in meeting my friend, he really
> helped — we both helped each other a lot to become who we are right now.
> And we both like who we are right now, to some extent.... But before that,
> I felt my mom was really pressuring me to be the perfect kid. And I think

that's probably why I hate that so much now. Because it really got me mad
and it gets me mad now.

When I ask how he and his friend helped each other, Ethan elaborates:

Like, he pointed out all the stuff that my mom was doing to me that I realized, but I never realized that it was there. Like I knew it was happening, but
I didn't really. And then he pointed it out to me and I was like, "Hey yeah,
that's wrong." And so, we both were like, "Hey, why don't we just be who
we want to be."

As Ethan indicates, it is not that his feelings necessarily changed as a result of
his relationship with his closest friend. Ethan had disagreed with his mother's
expectations ("I don't really like this") and questioned his compliance ("So
why am I doing it?"), even before meeting his friend. Rather, talking with his
friend has brought to light underlying feelings that Ethan sensed but did not
fully realize ("I knew... but I didn't really"), and feeling joined by his friend
has made the options of resistance and choice seem more viable. Ethan's closest friendship has not negated his parents' influence. Rather, by raising his
awareness of how his sense of self is influenced by his parents' expectations,
this relationship has enhanced Ethan's ability to consider his parents' wishes
without necessarily relinquishing his own goals and desires.

Feeling Seen and Known

In addition to helping him resist pressures to accommodate other people's
expectations, Ethan's closest friendship fosters a sense of validation and support by providing a space in which he feels truly seen and known. For instance,
Ethan describes an intimacy he feels with his closest friend that enhances and
is enhanced by their ability each to be themselves in the relationship. As Ethan
explains:

I really feel like he's the person I'm closest with and he really helped me
— we helped each other a lot through our conversations.... It's just like he's
the person he wants to be and I'm the person I want to be and they're completely different but we're both happy because we both know that we want
to be that.. .. We're, like, very different. But at the same time, I have a very
strong bond with him. Every time I see him, it's just the greatest time ever.
It's just, he's the best.

Ethan seems especially proud of the fact that he and his friend have "helped
each other" not to the effect of becoming more alike but of enabling each
other to attain their individual goals ("He's the person he wants to be and I'm
the person I want to be"). Likewise, Ethan seems empowered by the fact that

he and his friend have "a very strong bond" despite being "very different." In other words, the strength of their bond does not depend on their being similar to each other or having the same goals, aside from their shared desire to be true to themselves. Instead, their appreciation and respect for one another has grown from their ability to acknowledge their differences and to accept and support each other nonetheless. Thus, Ethan learns through experience that relationships can withstand and even cultivate differences.

In turn, Ethan's experience of being truly seen and known in relationships seems to shield him from pressures to conform to societal expectations for boys and inspire his confidence to assert himself, especially when people assume him to be less than he is. As Ethan describes:

> I really feel like I can be who I want to be at [this school] and that there's not that much pressure. I mean, I try to be different from other people, in general. I think maybe that's why I don't feel enormous pressure. But I feel like there's not much pressure around the [school] community to be that masculine.

Ethan's perception that there is little pressure within his school community to project a certain image of masculinity is obviously different from what Taylor described. However, it is not that Ethan perceives his school culture and community to be free of expectations; Ethan's very efforts to differentiate himself ("I try to be different from other people") in this context imply the existence of standards and norms. Rather, there is something that protects Ethan from their potentially negative influence that Taylor apparently lacked. It appears that what protects Ethan is the experience of being supported by his teachers and friends to be different and thus true to himself. For instance, when I ask what enables him to be different, Ethan explains:

> It really irritates me when people try to conform and just be who people want them to be. And so that kind of drives me to try to be different, 'cause I hate to see people try to conform and just like give up their own qualities and ideals to be like other people. And all my teachers have always fostered the sense of independence and stuff. And all my friends are pretty supportive of that and all my closest friends are like me and they try to be different themselves and just do what they want to do as opposed to what other people want them to do.

Through nurturing his self-acceptance and self-assurance, Ethan's relationships with teachers and friends make it possible for him to "be who I want to be" despite pressures he may encounter within this context and elsewhere. While Ethan's irritation may motivate his resistance, it is mainly through the support of his relationships that Ethan feels able to act on his feelings.

Overcoming Assumptions and Misconceptions

Although Ethan associates his efforts to be different with his desire to be true to himself (e.g., by not conforming or otherwise compromising his integrity), these efforts often lead him to feel underestimated and unduly dismissed. For instance, when I ask about difficulties he has encountered, Ethan replies:

> I feel like that's — people look on as just like, "He's being a teenager. He's trying to be different. He's trying to be like the generic teenager. He's trying to just get adults angry or whatever and make adults think he's being weird and stuff." Especially during the whole college process when I see other kids trying to really be all perfect and preppy and everything. I feel like I'm really out of place trying to just be myself and stuff.... Um, primarily with adults, when I'm with a group of adults and I'm the only teenager or whatever. I feel out of place and like I'm frowned upon and stuff. And I feel like once people get to know me, they realize that I'm not really like a freak or whatever.

Rather than being defensive or becoming discouraged by these views, Ethan seeks to show people what he is really like ("not really like a freak"), namely through relationships ("once people get to know me"). As Ethan explains further:

> I think a lot of people, when they see my physical appearance, they're like, "Oh, he must be a bad kid," or whatever. And I feel like I have to overcome that through speaking or whatever or talking to them and then, through getting to know them. I feel that, if I get to know a person, I feel like they respect me more. But I think that, automatically, people assume that I'm just weird or whatever. I think that, especially with adults, not so much with my peers, but adults, when they initially see me, just assume that I'm not the person I actually am and stuff like that.

> *What do you think that they expect of you?*

> Um, just to be really disrespectful and to be the typical teenager who doesn't care about anything, just stuff like that, to be stupid and to be, like, just really like, the generic teenager that adults dislike. And I feel like I try to overcome that when I get to know them.

Ethan's optimism that he can change people's views of him by getting to know them and by letting them get to know him is worth noting. For one thing, Ethan's desire to be seen for who he really is challenges stereotypes that depict adolescent boys as indifferent to what other people, particularly adults, think of them. Likewise, Ethan's belief that he can overcome adults' misunderstandings — a belief that may be linked to his experiences of having worked through different viewpoints in his existing relationships — raises questions about how relationships may indirectly shape boys' attitudes and outlooks. Just as Ethan develops his sense of self in light of his parents' expectations, he also comes to understand who he is ("the person I actually am") through reconciling other people's assumptions about him with his own views. Even if he does not always succeed in correcting their misconceptions (e.g., that he is "a bad kid," "just weird," "really disrespectful," "the typical teenager who doesn't care about anything," "stupid," "the generic teenager that adults dislike") the process of trying to counter their views with his own helps him to clarify in his own mind who he thinks he is and how he wants to be.

Discussion

Through framing boys' identity development as a relational process and using a relational approach to learn about boys' experiences from their perspectives, this study highlights ways in which adolescent boys negotiate their senses of self in relationships with specific others (e.g., friends and family) and with their broader social contexts (e.g., peers and adults in their school community). Contrary to popular discourse that tends to depict adolescent boys as disconnected from their emotions (Kindlon & Thompson, 1999) and from their relationships with others (Pollack, 1998), these boys' interview narratives indicate that their relational ways of being, which are detectable in infancy (Trevarthan, 1979; Tronick, 1989; Tronick & Gianino, 1986; Weinberg & Tronick, 1996) and early childhood (Chu, 2000), carry forth into adolescence. Namely, these adolescent boys showed themselves to be (1) keenly aware of their own thoughts, feelings, and desires; (2) sensitive and responsive to the dynamics of their interpersonal relationships; and (3) attuned to the realities of their social and cultural contexts. The boys also indicated ways in which they are able to resist as well as internalize cultural constructions of masculinity that they encounter, for instance, through other people's expectations and assumptions regarding what boys are like and how boys should act. Thus, while boys' gender socialization may influence their senses of self, and also their attitudes and behaviors, boys are able to mediate these effects through the importance they place on adhering to conventions of masculinity and with the support of their relationships to challenge our culture's current portrayal of boys.

The examples presented in this chapter were selected because they underscore discrepancies between how other people see boys and how boys see themselves, as described by the adolescent boys in this study. These examples also highlight ways in which boys may reconcile these discrepancies as they develop an understanding of who they are, of their relationships to others, and of their realities or "the way things are." In particular, these examples illustrate two predominant patterns of response that emerged in the boys' narratives. The first pattern, as exemplified by Taylor's case, emphasizes one's internalization of other people's views, possibly to the detriment of one's own sense of self. The second pattern, as exemplified by Ethan's case, emphasizes one's potential to resist other people's views and thereby sustain, or even strengthen, one's own sense of self. These two patterns also correspond to some extent to Piaget's (1954) conceptualizations of accommodation and assimilation wherein one's accommodation to society involves the internalization of its expectations, one's assimilation implies a degree of self-preservation and thus resistance to prevalent stereotypes and assumptions, and one's self-concept reflects the ability to balance these two processes.

A comparison of boys exhibiting each of these two patterns suggests that relationships can crucially influence whether a boy internalizes or resists societal expectations and assumptions. While most boys are exposed to cultural constructions of masculinity that manifest in other people's views of boys in general and of them in particular, there are differences in how, as individuals, they struggle to define themselves and choose to incorporate other people's views into their self-concept. Although boys' different patterns of response may be partly explained by individual difference (e.g., in age, temperament, attitudes, values, beliefs), what stood out in the boys' narratives were relational differences, particularly in their experiences of self-in-relationship. For instance, while Taylor and Ethan both have friends and they both suggest how their relationships have shaped their senses of self, they do not make meaning of and draw upon their friendships in the same ways. For Taylor, the fact that his friends consider him to be an outsider like them may provide him with a sense of belonging. However, as he feels unjustly marginalized within the school community because he does not see himself as being that different from the boys who are valued in this context, Taylor's friendships seem an unlikely source of support. Without the validation he seeks from his friends as well as his school community, Taylor's doubts begin to undermine his conviction that he is not as deviant or misfit as people think he is. Conversely, Ethan's sense of being truly seen and known in his closest friendship enables him to assert himself (e.g., by choosing to be different and trying to show people who he thinks he is) and to feel supported as he resists pressures to conform. That is, beyond having access to relationships, boys' experiences of being validated and valued in relationships appear to be key to boys' resistance and resilience.

Whether boys internalize or resist other people's views as they negotiate their senses of self, they are diligent in striving to understand who they are and conscientious in seeking ways to participate socially while remaining true to themselves. In illustrating how societal expectations and assumptions can infiltrate boys' senses of self, the examples presented in this chapter suggest a complexity to boys' experiences and a breadth and depth to their relational abilities (e.g., skills and strategies for expressing themselves and engaging in their relationships), which are seldom represented in popular depictions of boys. However, this is only a beginning. As these findings are based on a specific group of boys, it will be important for future studies to explore how other populations of boys negotiate their senses of self and reconcile discrepancies between how they are said to be and how they see themselves to be. Given that human development is embedded in interpersonal relationships as well as in society and culture, there are likely to be group differences (e.g., by age, race, ethnicity, socioeconomic status, sexual orientation, and religious faith) as well as individual differences in how boys navigate through these processes. Further research is also needed to examine more specifically how boys' experiences of gender socialization — in conjunction with their experiences in relationships — can hinder and enhance their psychological and social growth. If our goal is to support boys' development in ways that account for their experiences and are relevant to their lives, we must start with their own stories. For it is only by considering boys' perspectives on where they are coming from and what they feel they are up against that we can learn how best to foster their consciousness, awareness, and critical reflection and thus help them to make more informed decisions about who they want to be and how they want to act.

References

Brown, L. M., Argyris, D., Attanucci, J., Bardige, B., Gilligan, C., Johnston, K., Miller, B., Osborne, D., Ward, J., Wiggins, G., & Wilcox, D. (1988). *A guide to reading narratives of conflict and choice for self and moral voice. (Monograph No. 1).* Cambridge, MA: Harvard Graduate School of Education, Center for the Study of Gender, Education, and Human Development.

Brown, L. M. & Gilligan, C. (1990). Listening for self and relational voice: A responsive/resisting reader's guide. Paper presented at the American Psychological Association, Boston, August.

Brown, L. M. & Gilligan, C. (1991). Listening for voice in narratives of relationship. In M. B. Tappan, & M. J. Packer (Eds.), *Narrative and storytelling: Implications for understanding moral development* (pp. 43–62). San Francisco: Jossey-Bass.

Brown, L. M. & Gilligan, C. (1992). *Meeting at the crossroads: Women's psychology and girls' development.* Cambridge, MA: Harvard University Press.

Chu, J. Y. (1998). Relational strengths in adolescent boys. Paper presented to American Psychological Association, San Francisco.

Chu, J. Y. (1999). Reconsidering adolescent boys' behaviors using qualitative methods. Paper presented to American Educational Research Association, Montreal, Canada.

Chu, J. Y. (2000). Learning what boys know: An observational and interview study with six four-year-old boys. Unpublished dissertation. Harvard University.

Chu, J. Y., Porche, M. V., & Tolman, D. L. (in press). *The adolescent masculinity ideology in relationships scale: Development and validation of a new measure for boys. Men and Masculinities.*

Erikson, E. (1968). *Identity, Youth, and Crisis.* New York: Norton.

Gilligan, C. (1982). *In a different voice: Psychological theory and women's development.* Cambridge, MA: Harvard University Press.

Gilligan, C. (1996). The centrality of relationship in human development. In G. Noam & K. Fischer (Eds.), *Development and vulnerability in close relationships* (pp. 237–261). Mahwah, NJ: Erlbaum.

Gilligan, C., Brown, L. M., & Rogers, A. G. (1990). Psyche embedded: A place for body, relationships, and culture in personality theory. In A. I. Rabin, R. A. Zucker, R. A. Emmons, & S. Frank (Eds.), *Studying persons and lives* (pp. 86–147). New York: Springer.

Gilligan, C., Spencer, R., Weinberg, M. K., & Bertsch, T. (in press). On the listening guide: A voice-centered relational method. In L. Yardley (Ed.), *Qualitative research in psychology: Expanding perspectives in methodology and design.* Washington, DC: American Psychological Association Press.

Jordan, J. V., Kaplan, A. G., Miller, J. B., Stiver, I. P. & Surrey, J. L. (1991). *Women's growth in connection*. New York: Guilford Press.

Kindlon, D. & Thompson, M. (1999). *Raising Cain: Protecting the emotional life of boys*. New York: Ballantine Books.

Masten, A. S. (1994). Resilience in individual development: Successful adaptation despite risk and adversity. In M. C. Wang & E. W. Gordon (Eds.), *Educational resilience in inner-city America: Challenges and prospects* (pp. 3–25). Hillsdale, NJ: Erlbaum.

Masten, A. S. & Coatsworth, J. D. (1998). The development of competence in favorable and unfavorable environments: Lessons from research on successful children. *American Psychologist, 53*(2), 205–220.

Miles, M. B., & Huberman, A. M. (1994). *Qualitative data analysis: An expanded sourcebook* (2nd ed.). Thousand Oaks, CA: Sage.

Miller, J. B. (1976). *Toward a new psychology of women*. Boston: Beacon Press.

Miller, J. B. (1994). Women's psychological development: Connections, disconnections, and violations. In M. M. Berger (Ed.), *Women beyond Freud: New concepts of feminine psychology* (pp. 79–97). New York: Brunner/Mazel.

Piaget, J. (1954). *The construction of reality in the child*. New York: Basic Books.

Pleck, J. H. (1995). Gender role strain paradigm: An update. In R. F. Levant & W.S. Pollack (Eds.), *A new psychology of men* (pp. 11–32). New York: Basic Books.

Pleck, L. H., Sonenstein, F. L., & Ku, L. C. (1994). Problem behaviors and masculinity ideology in adolescent males. In R. D. Ketterlinus & M. E. Lamb (Eds.), *Adolescent problem behaviors: Issues and research* (pp. 165–186). Hillsdale, NJ: Erlbaum.

Pollack, W. S. (1998). *Real boys: Rescuing our sons from the myths of boyhood*. New York: Random House..

Resnick, M. D, Bearman, P. S., Blum, R. W, Bauman, K. E., Harris, K. M., Jones, J.,Tabor, J., Beuhring, T., Sieving, R. E., Shew, M., Ireland, M., Bearinger, L. H., & Udry, R. (1997). Protecting adolescents from harm: Findings from the national longitudinal study on adolescent health. *Journal of the American Medical Association, 278*, 823–832.

Rutter, M. (1990). Psychosocial resilience and protective mechanisms. In S. Weintraub (Ed.), *Risk and protective factors in the development of psychopathology* (pp. 181–214). New York: Cambridge University Press.

Trevarthan C. B. (1979). Communication and cooperation in early infancy: A description of primary intersubjectivity. In M. Bullowa (Ed.), *Before speech: The beginnings of communication*. Cambridge, UK: Cambridge University Press.

Tronick, E. (1989). Emotions and emotional communication in infants. *American Psychologist, 44*(2), 112–119.

Tronick, E. & Gianino, A. (1986). Interactive mismatch and repair: Challenges in the coping infant. *Zero to Three, 6*(3), 1–6.

Vygotsky L. S. (1978). *Mind in society.* Cambridge, MA: Harvard University Press.

Wang M. C., Haertel, G. D., & Walberg, H. J. (1994). Educational resilience in inner cities. In M. C. Wang, & E. W. Gordon (Eds.), *Educational resilience in inner-city America: Challenges and prospects* (pp. 45–72). Hillsdale, NJ: Erlbaum.

Weinberg, K. M. & Tronick, E. Z. (1996). Infant affective reactions to the resumption of maternal interaction after the still-face. *Child Development, 67*(3), 905–914.

Werner, E. E. & Smith, R. S. (1982). *Vulnerable but invincible: A longitudinal study of resilient children and youth.* New York: McGraw-Hill.

11
Adolescent Thinking

BÄRBEL INHELDER AND JEAN PIAGET

It is surprising that in spite of the large number of excellent works which have been published on the affective and social life of the adolescent — we hardly need remind the reader of the studies of Stanley Hall, Comparyé, Mendousse, Spranger, Charlotte Bühler, Landis, Wayne Dennis, Brooks, Fleming, or Debesse, or those by psychoanalysts such as Anna Freud and Helene Deutsch, and by sociologists and anthropologists such as Malinowski and Margaret Mead, not to mention others — so little work has appeared on the adolescent's *thinking*.

The few detailed studies of adolescent thinking which do exist are all the more valuable because of their scarcity. But, until now, there have not been enough to approximate a coherent outline of the whole. On the one hand, intelligence tests such as Terman's, Burt's, and especially Ballard's nonsense phrases have furnished information on the hypothetico-deductive nature of formal thought. With a different emphasis a number of works on adolescent mathematical and physical thought — Johannot, Michaud, etc. — have brought out the residues of infantile thinking found throughout adolescence; they result from a sort of overflow of concrete level problems onto a more abstract plane.

In the light of this deficit, in this final chapter, we should like to see whether the results of the earlier chapters — on the experimental thinking of adolescents in situations which impel them toward both action and thought at the same time — enable us to set down the broad lines of this picture which neither tests nor the study of verbal (or even mathematical) thought have outlined before.

From the standpoint of logical structures, this work seems to imply that the thinking of the adolescent differs radically from that of the child. The

From: Inhelder, Bärbel, & Piaget, Jean. (1955). *The growth of logical thinking from childhood to adolescence; an essay on the construction of formal operational structures* (pp. 334–350). Translated by Anne Parsons and Stanley Milgram. New York: Basic Books, 1958. Copyright © Perseus Books Group. Reprinted with permission.

child develops concrete operations and carries them out on classes, relations, or numbers. But their structure never goes beyond the level of elementary logical "groupings" or additive and multiplicative numerical groups. During the concrete stage, he comes to utilize both of the complementary forms of reversibility (inversion for classes and numbers and reciprocity for relations), but he never integrates them into the single total system found in formal logic. In contrast, the adolescent superimposes propositional logic on the logic of classes and relations. Thus, he gradually structures a formal mechanism (reaching an equilibrium point at about 14–15 years) which is based on both the lattice structure and the group of four transformations. This new integration allows him to bring inversion and reciprocity together into a single whole. As a result, he comes to control not only hypothetico-deductive reasoning and experimental proof based on the variation of a single factor with the others held constant (all other things being equal) but also a number of operational schemata which he will use repeatedly in experimental and logico-mathematical thinking.

But there is more to thinking than logic. Our problem now is to see whether logical transformations fit the general modifications of thinking which are generally agreed — sometimes explicitly but often implicitly — to typify adolescence. We should like to show briefly not only that they do but also that the structural transformation is like a center from which radiate the various more visible modifications of thinking which take place in adolescence.

However, we must begin by eliminating a possible source of ambiguity. We take as the fundamental problem of adolescence the fact that the individual begins to take up adult roles. From such a standpoint, puberty cannot be considered the distinctive feature of adolescence. On the average, puberty appears at about the same ages in all races and in all societies, although there is widespread opinion to the contrary. (In fact, a short delay has been verified in Canada and in Scandinavia, but not the wide gap between north and south, etc., that legend would have us believe.) But the age at which adult roles are taken up varies considerably among societies and even among social milieus. For our purposes, however, the essential fact is this fundamental social transition (and not physiological growth alone).

Thus we will not attempt to relate formal thinking to puberty. There are, of course, a number of links between the rise of formal structures and transformations of affective life which we shall consider in greater detail presently. But these relations are complex and are not one-way affairs. Even at this point, our thinking would be muddled before we started if we wished to reduce adolescence to the manifestations of puberty. For example, one would then have to say that love appears only in adolescence; but there are children who fall in love; and, in our societies, what distinguishes an adolescent in love from a child in love is that the former generally complicates his feelings by constructing a romance or by referring to social or even literary ideals of all sorts. But the fabrication of a romance or the appeal to various collective role models is neither the direct product of the neurophysiological transformations of puberty nor the exclusive product of affectivity. Both are also indirect and specific reflections of the general tendency of adolescents to construct theories and make use of the ideologies that surround them. This general tendency can only be explained by taking into account the two factors which we will find in association over and over again — the transformations of thought and the assumption of adult roles. The latter involves a total restructuring of the personality in which the intellectual transformations are parallel or complementary to the affective transformations.

However, even though the appearance of formal thought is not a direct consequence of puberty, could we not say that it is a manifestation of cerebral transformations due to the maturation of the nervous system and that these changes do have a relation, direct or indirect, with puberty? Given that in our society the 7–8-year-old child (with very rare exceptions) cannot handle the structures which the 14–15-year-old adolescent can handle easily, the reason must be that the child does not possess a certain number of coordinations whose dates of development are determined by stages of maturation. In a slightly different perspective, the lattice and group structures are probably isomorphic with neurological structures[1] and are certainly isomorphic with the structures of the mechanical models devised by cybernetics in imitation of the brain.[2] For these reasons, it seems clear that the development of formal structures in adolescence is linked to maturation of cerebral structures. However, the exact form of linkage is far from simple, since the organization of formal structures must depend on the social milieu as well. The age of about 11–12 years, which in our society we found to mark the beginning of formal thinking, must be extremely relative, since the logic of the so-called primitive societies appears to be without such structures. Moreover, the history of formal structures is linked to the evolution of culture and collective representations as well as their ontogenetic history. Since Greek adults became aware of some of these structures only in their logical and mathematical reflection, it is probable that the Greek children were behind our own. Thus the age of 11–12 years may be, beyond the neurological factors, a product of a progressive acceleration of individual development under the influence of education, and perhaps nothing stands in the way of a further reduction of the average age in a more or less distant future.

In sum, far from being a source of fully elaborated "innate ideas," the maturation of the nervous system can do no more than determine the totality of possibilities and impossibilities at a given stage. A particular social environment remains indispensable for the realization of these possibilities. It follows that their realization can be accelerated or retarded as a function of cultural and educational conditions. This is why the growth of formal thinking as well as the age at which adolescence itself occurs — i.e., the age at which the individual starts to assume adult roles — remain dependent on social as much as and more than on neurological factors.

As far as formal structures are concerned, we have often taken special note of the convergence between some of our subjects' responses and certain aspects of instruction in school. The convergence is so striking that we wonder whether the individual manifestations of formal thinking are not simply imposed by the social groups as a result of home and school education. But the psychological facts allow us to reject this hypothesis of complete social determinism. Society does not act on growing individuals simply by external pressure, and the individual is not, in relation to the social any more than to the physical environment, a simple *tabula rasa* on which social constraint imprints ready-made knowledge. For, if the social milieu is really to influence individual brains, they have to be in a state of readiness to assimilate its contributions. So we come back to the need for some degree of maturation of individual cerebral mechanisms.

Two observations arise out of this circular process which characterizes all exchanges between the nervous system and society. The first is that the formal structures are neither innate *a priori* forms of intelligence which are inscribed in advance in the nervous system, nor are they collective representations which exist ready-made outside and above the individual. Instead, they are forms of equilibrium which gradually settle on the system of exchanges between individuals and the physical milieu and on the system of exchanges between individuals themselves.

Moreover, in the final analysis the two systems can be reduced to a single system seen from two different perspectives. And this comes back to what we have said many times before.

The second observation is that between the nervous system and society there is individual activity — i.e., the sum of the experience of an individual in learning to adapt to both physical and social worlds. If formal structures are laws of equilibrium and if there is really a functional activity specific to the individual, we would expect adolescent thinking to show a series of spontaneous manifestations expressing the organization of formal structures as it is actually experienced — if adolescence is really the age at which growing individuals enter adult society. In other words, formal development should take place in a way that furthers the growth of the adolescent in his daily life as he learns to fill adult roles.

But first we must ask what it means to fill adult roles? As opposed to the child who feels inferior and subordinate to the adult, the adolescent is an individual who begins to consider himself as the equal of adults and to judge them, with complete reciprocity, on the same plane as himself. But to this first trait, two others are indissolubly related. The adolescent is an individual who is still growing, but one who begins to think of the future — i.e., of his present or future work in society. Thus, to his current activities he adds a life program for later "adult" activities. Further, in most cases in our societies, the adolescent is the individual who in attempting to plan his present or future work in adult society also has the idea (from his point of view, it is directly related to his plans) of changing this society, whether in some limited area or completely. Thus it is impossible to fill an adult role without conflicts, and whereas the child looks for resolution of his conflicts in present-day compensations (real or imaginary), the adolescent adds to these limited compensations the more general compensation of a motivation for change, or even specific planning for change.

Furthermore, seen in the light of these three interrelated features, the adolescent's adoption of adult roles certainly presupposes those affective and intellectual tools whose spontaneous development is exactly what distinguishes adolescence from childhood. If we take these new tools as a starting point, we have to ask: what is their nature and how do they relate to formal thinking?

On a naive global level, without trying to distinguish between the student, the apprentice, the young worker, or the young peasant in terms of how their social attitudes may vary, the adolescent differs from the child above all in that he thinks beyond the present. The adolescent is the individual who commits himself to possibilities — although we certainly do not mean to deny that his commitment begins in real-life situations. In other words, the adolescent is the individual who begins to build "systems" or "theories," in the largest sense of the term.

The child does not build systems. His spontaneous thinking may be more or less systematic (at first only to a small degree, later, much more so); but it is the observer who sees the system from outside, while the child is not aware of it since he never thinks about his own thought. For example, in an earlier work on the child's representation of the world, we were able to report on a number of systematic responses. Later we were able to construct the systems characterizing various genetic stages. But *we* constructed the system; the *child* does not try to systematize his ideas, although he may often spontaneously return to the same preoccupations and unconsciously give analogous answers.[3] In other words, the child has no powers of reflection — i.e., no second-order thoughts which deal critically with his own thinking. No theory can be built without such reflection.

In contrast, the adolescent is able to analyze his own thinking and construct theories. The fact that these theories are oversimplified, awkward, and usually contain very little originality is beside the point. From the functional standpoint, his systems are significant in that they furnish the cognitive and evaluative bases for the assumption of adult roles, without mentioning a life program and projects for change. They are vital in the assimilation of the values which delineate societies or social classes as entities in contrast to simple interindividual relations.

Consider a group of students between 14–15 years and the baccalaureat.[4] Most of them have political or social theories and want to reform the world; they have their own ways of explaining all of the present-day turmoil in collective life. Others have literary or aesthetic theories and place their reading or their experiences of beauty on a scale of values which is projected into a system. Some go through religious crises and reflect on the problem of faith, thus moving toward a universal system — a system valid for all. Philosophical speculation carries away a minority, and for any true intellectual, adolescence is the metaphysical age *par excellence*, an age whose dangerous seduction is forgotten only with difficulty at the adult level. A still smaller minority turns from the start toward scientific or pseudo-scientific theories. But whatever the variation in content, each one has his theory or theories, although they may be more or less explicit and verbalized or even implicit. Some write down their ideas, and it is extremely interesting to see the outlines which are taken up and filled in later life. Others are limited to talking and ruminating, but each one has his own ideas (and usually he believes they are his own) which liberate him from childhood and allow him to place himself as the equal of adults.[5]

If we now step outside the student range and the intellectual classes to look at the reactions of the adolescent worker, apprentice, or peasant, we can recognize the same phenomenon in other forms. Instead of working out personal "theories," we would find him subscribing to ideas passed on by comrades, developed in meetings, or provoked by reading. We would find fewer family and still fewer religious crises, and especially a lower degree of abstraction. But under different and varied exteriors the same core process can easily be discerned — the adolescent is no longer content to live the interindividual relations offered by his immediate surroundings or to use his intelligence to solve the problems of the moment. Rather, he is motivated also to take his place in the adult social framework, and with this aim he tends to participate in the ideas, ideals, and ideologies of a wider group through the medium of a number of verbal symbols to which he was indifferent as a child.

But how can we explain the adolescent's new capacity to orient himself toward what is abstract and not immediately present (seen from the outside by the observer comparing him to the child), but which (seen from within) is an indispensable instrument in his adaptation to the adult social framework, and as a result his most immediate and most deeply experienced concern? There is no doubt that this is the most direct and, moreover, the simplest manifestation of formal thinking. Formal thinking is both thinking about thought (propositional logic is a second-order operational system which operates on propositions whose truth, in turn, depend on class, relational, and numerical operations) and a reversal of relations between what is real and what is possible (the empirically given comes to be inserted as a particular sector of the total set of possible combinations). These are the two characteristics — which up to this point we have tried to describe in the abstract language appropriate to the analysis of reasoning — which are the source of the living responses, always so full of emotion, which the adolescent uses to build his ideals in adapting to society. The adolescent's theory construction shows both that he has become capable of reflective thinking and that his thought makes it possible for him to escape the concrete present toward the realm of the abstract and the possible. Obviously, this does not mean that formal structures are first organized by themselves and are later applied as adaptive instruments where they prove individually or socially useful. The two processes — structural development and everyday application — both belong to the same reality, and it is *because* formal thinking plays a fundamental role from the functional standpoint that it can attain its general and logical structure. Once more, logic is not isolated from life; it is no more than the expression of operational coordinations essential to action.

But this does not mean that the adolescent takes his place in adult society merely in terms of general theories and without personal involvement. Two other aspects of his entrance into adult society have to be considered — his life program, and his plans for changing the society he sees. The adolescent not only builds new theories or rehabilitates old ones; he also feels he has to work out a conception of life which gives him an opportunity to assert himself and to create something new (thus the close relationship between his system and his life program). Secondly, he wants a guarantee that he will be more successful than his predecessors (thus the need for change in which altruistic concern and youthful ambitions are inseparably blended).

In other words, the process which we have followed through the different stages of the child's development is recapitulated on the planes of thought and reality new to formal operations. An initial failure to distinguish between objects or the actions of others and one's own actions gives way to an enlargement of perspective toward objectivity and reciprocity. Even at the sensorimotor level, the infant does not at first know how to separate the effects of his own actions from the qualities of external objects or persons. At first he lives in a world without permanent objects and without awareness of the self or of any internal subjective life. Later he differentiates his own ego and situates his body in a spatially and causally organized field composed of permanent objects and other persons similar to himself. This is the first decentering process; its result is the gradual coordination of sensori-motor behavior. But when symbolic functioning appears, language, representation, and communication with others expand this field to unheard-of proportions and a new type of structure is required. For a second time egocentrism appears, but this time on another plane. It still takes the form of an initial relative lack of differentiation both between ego's and alter's points of view, between subjective and objective, but this time the lack of differentiation is representational rather than sensori-motor. When the child reaches the stage of concrete operations (7–8 years), the decentering process has gone far enough for him to be able to structure relationships between classes, relations, and numbers objectively. At the same stage, he acquires skill in interindividual relations in a cooperative framework. Furthermore, the acquisition of social cooperation and the structuring of cognitive operations can be seen as two aspects of the same developmental process. But when the cognitive field is again enlarged by the structuring of formal thought, a third form of egocentrism comes into view. This egocentrism is one of the most enduring features of adolescence; it persists until the new and later decentering which makes possible the true beginnings of adult work.

Moreover, the adolescent manifestation of egocentrism stems directly from the adoption of adult roles, since (as Charlotte Bühler has so well stated) the adolescent not only tries to adapt his ego to the social environment but, just as emphatically, tries to adjust the environment to his ego. In other words, when he begins to think about the society in which he is looking for a place, he has to think about his own future activity and about how he himself might transform this society. The result is a relative failure to distinguish between his own point of view as an individual called upon to organize a life program and the point of view of the group which he hopes to reform.

In more concrete terms, the adolescent's egocentrism comes out in a sort of Messianic form such that the theories used to represent the world center on the role of reformer that the adolescent feels himself called upon to play in the future. To fully understand the adolescent's feelings, we have to go beyond simple observation and look at intimate documents such as essays not written for immediate public consumption, diaries, or simply the disclosures some adolescents may make of their personal fantasies. For example, in the recitations obtained by G. Dumas from a high-school class on their evening reveries, the most normal students — the most retiring, the most amiable — calmly confessed to fantasies and fabulations which several years later would have appeared in their own eyes as signs of pathological megalomania. Without going into the details of this group, we see that the universal aspect of the phenomenon must be sought in the relationship between the adolescent's apparently abstract theories and the life program which he sets up for himself. Then we see that behind impersonal and general exteriors these systems conceal programs of action whose ambitiousness and näiveté are usually immoderate. We could also consider the following sample taken from the dozen or so ex-pupils of a small-town school in Rumansch, Switzerland. One of them, who has since become a shopkeeper, astonished his friends with his literary doctrines and wrote a novel in secret. Another, who has since become the director of an insurance company, was interested among other things in the future of the theater and showed some close friends the first scene of the first act of a tragedy — and got no further. A third, taken up with philosophy, dedicated himself to no less a task than the reconciliation of science and religion. We do not even have to enumerate the social and political reformers found on both right and left. There were only two members of the class who did not reveal any astounding life plans. Both were more or less crushed under strong "super-egos" of parental origin, and we do not know what their secret daydreams might have been.

Sometimes this sort of life program has a real influence on the individual's later growth, and it may even happen that a person rediscovers in his adolescent jottings an outline of some ideas which he has really fulfilled since. But in the large majority of cases, adolescent projects are more like a sort of sophisticated game of compensation functions whose goals are self-assertion, imitation of adult models, participation in circles which are actually closed, etc. Thus the adolescent takes up paths which satisfy him for a time but are soon abandoned. M. Debesse has discussed this subject of egotism and the crisis of juvenile originality. But we believe that, in the egocentrism found in the adolescent, there is more than a simple desire to deviate; rather, it is a manifestation of the phenomenon of lack of differentiation which is worth a further brief discussion.

Essentially, the process, which at any one of the developmental stages moves from egocentrism toward decentering, constantly subjects increases in knowledge to a refocusing of perspective. Everyone has observed that the child mixes up subjective and objective facts, but if the hypothesis of egocentrism did nothing more than restate this truism it would be worth next to nothing.[6] Actually, it means that learning is not a purely additive process and that to pile one new learned piece of behavior or information on top of another is not in itself adequate to structure an objective attitude. In fact, objectivity presupposes a decentering — i.e., a continual refocusing of perspective. Egocentrism, on the other hand, is the undifferentiated state prior to multiple perspectives, whereas objectivity implies both differentiation and coordination of the points of view which have been differentiated.

But the process found in adolescence on the more sophisticated plane of formal structures is analogous. The indefinite extension of powers of thought made possible by the new instruments of propositional logic at first is conducive to a failure to distinguish between the ego's new and unpredicted capacities and the social or cosmic universe to which they are applied. In other words, the adolescent goes through a phase in which he attributes an unlimited power to his own thoughts so that the dream of a glorious future or of transforming the world through Ideas (even if this idealism takes a materialistic form) seems to be not only fantasy but also an effective action which in itself modifies the empirical world. This is obviously a form of cognitive egocentrism. Although it differs sharply from the child's egocentrism (which is either sensori-motor or simply representational without introspective "reflection"), it results, nevertheless, from the same mechanism and appears as a function of the new conditions created by the structuring of formal thought.

There is a way of verifying this view; namely, to study the decentering process which later makes it possible for the adolescent to get beyond the early relative lack of differentiation and to cure himself of his idealistic crisis — in other words, the return to reality which is the path from adolescence to the true beginnings of adulthood. But, as at the level of concrete operations, we find that decentering takes place simultaneously in thought processes and in social relationships.

From the standpoint of social relationships, the tendency of adolescents to congregate in peer groups has been well documented — discussion or action groups, political groups, youth movements, summer camps, etc. Charlotte Bühler defines an expansive phase followed by a withdrawal phase, although the two do not always seem clearly distinguishable. Certainly this type of social life is not merely the effect of pressures towards conformity but also a source of intellectual decentering. It is most often in discussions between friends, when the promoter of a theory has to test it against the theories of the others, that he discovers its fragility.

But the focal point of the decentering process is the entrance into the occupational world or the beginning of serious professional training. The adolescent becomes an adult when he undertakes a real job. It is then that he is transformed from an idealistic reformer into an achiever. In other words, the job leads thinking away from the dangers of formalism back into reality. Yet observation shows how laborious and slow this reconciliation of thought and experience can be. One has only to look at the behavior of beginning students in an experimental discipline to see how long the adolescent's belief in the power of thinking endures and how little inclined is the mind to subjugate its ideas to the analysis of facts. (This does not mean that facts are accessible without theory, but rather that a theoretical construction has value only in relation to empirical verification.)

From this standpoint, the results of chapters 1–15 of this work (Inhelder & Piaget, 1955) raise a problem of general significance. The subjects' reactions to a wide range of experimental situations demonstrate that after a phase of development (11–12 to 13–14 years) the preadolescent comes to handle certain formal operations (implication, exclusion, etc.) successfully, but he is not able to set up an exhaustive method of proof. But the 14–15-year-old adolescent does succeed in setting up proofs (moreover, spontaneously, for it is in this area that academic verbalism is least evident). He systematically uses methods of control which require the combinatorial system — i.e., he varies a single factor at a time and excludes the others ("all other things being equal"), etc. But, as we have often seen, this structuring of the tools of experimental verification is a direct consequence of the development of formal thought and propositional logic. Since the adolescent acquires the capacity to use both deduction and experimental induction at the same time, why does he use the first so effectively, and why is he so late in making use of the second in a productive and continuous task (for it is one thing to react experimentally to an apparatus prepared in advance and another to organize a research project by oneself)? Furthermore, the problem is not only ontogenetic but also historical. The same question can be asked in trying to understand why the Greeks were limited (with some exceptions) to pure deductive thought[7] and why modern science, centered on physics, has taken so many centuries to put itself together.

We have seen that the principal intellectual characteristics of adolescence stem directly or indirectly from the development of formal structures. Thus, the latter is the most important event in the thinking found in this period. As for the affective innovations found at the same age, there are two which merit consideration; as usual, we find that they are parallel to intellectual transformations, since affectivity can be considered as the energetic force of behavior whereas its structure defines cognitive functions. (This does not mean either that affectivity is determined by intellect or the contrary, but that both are indissociably united in the functioning of the personality.)

If adolescence is really the age at which growing individuals take their place in adult society (whether or not the role change always coincides with puberty), this crucial social adjustment must involve, in correlation with the development of the propositional or formal operations which assure intellectual structuring, two fundamental transformations that adult affective socialization requires. First, feelings relative to ideals are added to interindividual feelings. Secondly, personalities develop in relation to social roles and scales of values derived from social interaction (and no longer only by the coordination of exchanges which they maintain with the physical environment and other individuals).[8]

Naturally, this is not the place for an essay on the psychology of affects; still, it is important to see how closely these two essential affective aspects of adolescence are interwoven with the transformations of behavior brought on by the development of formal structures.

First, we are struck by the fact that feelings about ideals are practically nonexistent in the child. A study of the concept of nationality and the associated social attitudes[9] has shown us that the child is sensitive to his family, to his place of residence, to his native language, to certain customs, etc., but that he preserves both an astonishing degree of ignorance and a striking insensitivity not only to his own designation or that of his associates as Swiss, French, etc., but toward his own country as a collective reality. This is to be expected, since, in the 7–11-year-old child, logic is applied only to concrete or manipulable objects. There is no operation available at this level which would make it possible for the child to elaborate an ideal which goes beyond the empirically given. This is only one among many examples. The notions of humanity, social justice (in contrast to interindividual justice which is deeply experienced at the concrete level), freedom of conscience, civic or intellectual courage, and so forth, like the idea of nationality, are ideals which profoundly influence the adolescent's affective life; but with the child's mentality, except for certain individual glimpses, they can neither be understood nor felt.

In other words, the child does not experience as social feelings anything more than interindividual affects. Even moral sentiments are felt only as a function of unilateral respect (authority) or mutual respect. But, beginning at 13–15 years, feelings about *ideals* or *ideas* are added to the earlier ones, although, of course, they too subsist in the adolescent as well as the adult. Of course, an ideal always exists in a person and it does not stop being an important interindividual element in the new class of feelings. The problem is to find out whether the idea is an object of affectivity because of the person or the person because of the idea. But, whereas the child never gets out of this circle because his only ideals are people who are actually part of his surroundings, during adolescence the circle is broken because ideals become autonomous. No commentary is needed to bring out the close kinship of this affective mechanism with formal thought.

As for personality, there is no more vaguely defined notion in psychological vocabulary, already so difficult to handle. The reason for this is that personality operates in a way opposite to that of the ego. Whereas the ego is naturally egocentric, personality is the decentered ego. The ego is detestable, even more so when it is strong, whereas a strong personality is the one which manages to discipline the ego. In other words, the personality is the submission of the ego to an ideal which it embodies but which goes beyond it and subordinates it; it is the adherence to a scale of values, not in the abstract but relative to a given task;[10] thus it is the eventual adoption of a social role, not ready-made in the sense of an administrative function but a role which the individual will create in filling it.

Thus, to say that adolescence is the age at which adolescents take their place in adult society is by definition to maintain that it is the age of formation of the personality, for the adoption of adult roles is from another and necessarily complementary standpoint the construction of a personality. Furthermore, the life program and the plans for change which we have just seen as one of the essential features of the adolescent's behavior are at the same time the changing emotional force in the formation of the personality. A life plan is above all a scale of values which puts some ideals above others and subordinates the middle-range values to goals thought of as permanent. But this scale of values is the affective organization corresponding to the cognitive organization of his work which the new member in the social body says he will undertake. A life plan is also an affirmation of autonomy, and the moral autonomy finally achieved by the adolescent who judges himself the equal of adults is another essential affective feature of the young personality preparing himself to plunge into life.

In conclusion, the fundamental affective acquisitions of adolescence parallel the intellectual acquisitions. To understand the role of formal structures of thought in the life of the adolescent, we found that in the last analysis we had to place them in his total personality. But, in return, we found that we could not completely understand the growth of his personality without including the transformations of his thinking; thus we had to come back to the development of formal structures.

Notes

1. We know that W. McCulloch and W. Pitts (*Bull. Math. Biophys, 4,* 115–133, 1943), have applied the schemata of propositional logic to neuronal connections.
2. See J. Piaget, Structures opérationnelles et cybernétique, *Année Psychologique,* 33, 379–388, 1953.
3. For an example, see J. Piaget, (1952) *Play, dreams and imitation in childhood,* chapter IX, New York: Norton.
4. Translators' *note: baccalaureat* — a French examination taken at the end of secondary school or about 18–19 years of age. Although, in its details, the analysis of the adolescent presented fits the European better than the American pattern, one might suggest that even if metaphysical and political theories are less prominent, the American dating pattern and other phenomena typical of youth culture are a comparable "theoretical" or "as if" working out of types of interpersonal relations which become serious at a later point; thus the difference is one of content but not of structure.
5. Of course, the girls are more interested in marriage, but the husband they dream of is most often "theoretical," and their thoughts about married life as well often take on the characteristics of "theories."
6. *Translators' note:* This passage refers to an opinion more prevalent in Europe than in America, namely that the authors' work simply demonstrates a normative view of the child as an irrational creature. In the United States, where problems of motivation are more often given precedence over purely intellectual functions both from the normative standpoint and in psychological research, another but parallel misinterpretation has sometimes been made; namely, that in maintaining that the child is egocentric, the authors have neglected the fact that he is capable of love. It should be made clear in this section that egocentrism, best understood from its root meaning — that the child's perception is cognitively "centered on his own ego" and thus lacks a certain type of fluidity and ability to handle a variety of perspectives — is not to be confused with "selfish" or "egoistic."
7. No one has yet given a serious explanation of this fact from the sociological standpoint. To attribute the formal structures made explicit by the Greeks to the contemplative nature of one social class or another does not explain why this contemplation was not confined to metaphysical ideologies and was able to create a mathematical system.
8. *Translators' note:* "Interindividual" and "social" are used as oppositional terms to a greater extent in French than in English. The first refers to face-to-face relationships between individuals with the implication of familiarity, and the second to the relationship of the individual to society as a whole, to formal institutional

structures, to values, etc. Here the meaning is that the child relates only to small groups and specific individuals while the adolescent relates to institutional structures and to values as such.

9. J. Piaget, & A. M. Weil (1951). Le développement chez l'enfant de l'idée de patrie et des relations avec l'etranger, *Bulletin International des Sciences Sociales* (UNESCO), Vol. III, pp. 605–621.

10. For the relationship between personality and the task, see I. Myerson, *Les fonctions psychologiques et les oeuvres (Vrin)*.

Part IV

Erik Erikson and Psychosocial Identity

12

The Problem of Ego Identity

ERIK ERIKSON

In a number of writings (Erikson, 1946, 1950a, 1950b, 1951) I have been using the term *ego identity* to denote certain comprehensive gains which the individual, at the end of adolescence, must have derived from all of his pre-adult experience in order to be ready for the tasks of adulthood. My use of this term reflected the dilemma of a psychoanalyst who was led to a new concept not by theoretical preoccupation but rather through the expansion of his clinical awareness to other fields (social anthropology and comparative education) and through the expectation that such expansion would, in turn, profit clinical work. Recent clinical observations have, I feel, begun to bear out this expectation. I have, therefore, gratefully accepted two opportunities offered me to restate and review the problem of identity. The present paper combines both of these presentations. The question before us is whether the concept of identity is essentially a psychosocial one, or deserves to be considered as a legitimate part of the psychoanalytic theory of the ego.

First a word about the term identity. As far as I know Freud used it only once in a more than incidental way, and then with a psychosocial connotation. It was when he tried to formulate his link to Judaism that he spoke of an "inner identity"[1] which was not based on race or religion, but on a common readiness to live in opposition, and on a common freedom from prejudices which narrow the use of the intellect. Here, the term identity points to an individual's link with the unique values, fostered by a unique history, of his people. Yet, it also relates to the cornerstone of this individual's unique development: for the importance of the theme of "incorruptible observation at the price of professional isolation" played a central role in Freud's life (Erikson, 1954). It is this identity of something in the individual's core with an essential aspect of a group's inner coherence which is under consideration here: for the

From: *Journal of the American Psychoanalytic Association*, Vol. 4, 1956, 56–121 (Selections: pp. 56–57; 65–74; 77–81; 83–88). Copyright © American Psychoanalytic Association. Reprinted with permission of the American Psychoanalytic Association and Kai Erikson.

young individual must learn to be most himself where he means most to others — those others, to be sure, who have come to mean most to him. The term identity expresses such a mutual relation in that it connotes both a persistent sameness within oneself (selfsameness) and a persistent sharing of some kind of essential character with others.

I can attempt to make the subject matter of identity more explicit only by approaching it from a variety of angles — biographic, pathographic, and theoretical; and by letting the term identity speak for itself in a number of connotations. At one time, then, it will appear to refer to a conscious *sense of individual identity;* at another to an unconscious striving for a *continuity of personal character;* at a third, as a criterion for the silent doings of *ego synthesis;* and, finally, as a maintenance of an inner *solidarity* with a group's ideals and identity. In some respects the term will appear to be colloquial and naïve; in another, vaguely related to existing concepts in psychoanalysis and sociology. If, after an attempt at clarifying this relation, the term itself still retains some ambiguity, it will, so I hope, nevertheless have helped to delineate a significant problem, and a necessary point of view....

Genetic: Identification and Identity

1. The autobiographies of extraordinary (and extraordinarily self-perceptive) individuals are a suggestive source of insight into the development of identity. In order to find an anchor point for the discussion of the universal genetics of identity, however, it would be well to trace its development through the life histories or through significant life episodes of "ordinary" individuals — individuals whose lives have neither become professional autobiographies (as did [George Bernard] Shaw's) nor case histories, such as will be discussed in the next chapter. I will not be able to present such material here; I must, instead, rely on impressions from daily life, from participation in one of the rare "longitudinal" studies of the personality development of children, and from guidance work with mildly disturbed young people.

Adolescence is the last and the concluding stage of childhood. The adolescent process, however, is conclusively complete only when the individual has subordinated his childhood identifications to a new kind of identification, achieved in absorbing sociability and in competitive apprenticeship with and among his age-mates. These new identifications are no longer characterized by the playfulness of childhood and the experimental zest of youth: with dire urgency they force the young individual into choices and decisions which will, with increasing immediacy, lead to a more final self-definition, to irreversible role pattern, and thus to commitments "for life." The task to be performed here by the young person and by his society is formidable; it necessitates, in different individuals and in different societies, great variations in the duration, in the intensity, and in the ritualization of adolescence. Societies offer, as individuals require, more or less sanctioned intermediary periods between childhood and adulthood, institutionalized *psychosocial moratoria*, during which a lasting pattern of "inner identity" is scheduled for relative completion.

In postulating a "latency period" which precedes puberty, psychoanalysis has given recognition to some kind of *psychosexual moratorium* in human development — a period of delay which permits the future mate and parent first to "go to school" (i.e., to undergo whatever schooling is provided for in his technology) and to learn the technical and social rudiments of a work situation. It is not within the confines of the libido theory, however, to give an adequate account of a second period of delay, namely, adolescence. Here the sexually matured individual is more or less retarded in his psychosexual capacity for intimacy and in the psychosocial readiness for parenthood. The period can be viewed as a *psychosocial moratorium* during which the individual through free role experimentation may find a niche in some section of his society, a niche which is firmly defined and yet seems to be uniquely made for him. In finding it the young adult gains an assured sense of inner continuity and social sameness which will bridge what he was as a child and what he is *about to become*, and will reconcile his *conception of himself* and his *community's recognition* of him.

If, in the following, we speak of the community's response to the young individual's need to be "recognized" by those around him, we mean something beyond a mere recognition of achievement; for it is of great relevance to the young individual's identity formation that he be responded to, and be given function and status as a person whose gradual growth and transformation make sense to those who begin to make sense to him. It has not been sufficiently recognized in psychoanalysis that such recognition provides an entirely indispensable support to the ego in the specific tasks of adolescing, which are: to maintain the most important ego defenses against the vastly growing intensity of impulses (now invested in a matured genital apparatus and a powerful muscle system); to learn to consolidate the most important "conflict-free" achievements in line with work opportunities; and to resynthesize all childhood identifications in some unique way, and yet in concordance with the roles offered by some wider section of society — be that section the neighborhood block, an anticipated occupational field, an association of kindred minds, or, perhaps (as in Shaw's case) the "mighty dead."

Linguistically as well as psychologically, identity and identification have common roots. Is identity, then, the mere sum of earlier identifications, or is it merely an additional set of identifications?

2. The limited usefulness of the *mechanism of identification* becomes at once obvious if we consider the fact that none of the identifications of childhood (which in our patients stand out in such morbid elaboration and mutual contradiction) could, if merely added up, result in a functioning personality. True, we usually believe that the task of psychotherapy is the replacement of

morbid and excessive identifications by more desirable ones. But as every cure attests, "more desirable" identifications, at the same time, tend to be quietly subordinated to a new, a unique Gestalt which is more than the sum of its parts. The fact is that identification as a mechanism is of limited usefulness. Children, at different stages of their development, identify with those *part aspects* of people by which they themselves are most immediately affected, whether in reality or fantasy. Their identifications with parents, for example, center in certain overvalued and ill-understood body parts, capacities, and role appearances. These part aspects, furthermore, are favored not because of their social acceptability (they often are everything but the parents' most adjusted attributes) but by the nature of infantile fantasy which only gradually gives way to a more realistic anticipation of social reality. The final identity, then, as fixed at the end of adolescence is superordinated to any single identification with individuals of the past: it includes all significant identifications, but it also alters them in order to make a unique and a reasonably coherent whole of them.

If we, roughly speaking, consider introjection-projection, identification, and identity formation to be the steps by which the ego grows in ever more mature interplay with the identities of the childs models, the following psychosocial schedule suggests itself:

The mechanisms of *introjection and projection,* which prepare the basis for later identifications, depend for their relative integration on the satisfactory mutuality (Erikson, 1950a) between the *mothering adult(s) and the mothered child.* Only the experience of such mutuality provides a safe pole of self-feeling from which the child can reach out for the other pole: his first love "objects."

The fate of *childhood identifications,* in turn, depends on the child's satisfactory interaction with a trustworthy and meaningful hierarchy of roles as provided by the generations living together in some form of *family.*

Identity formation, finally, begins where the usefulness of identification ends. It arises from the selective repudiation and mutual assimilation of childhood identifications, and their absorption in a new configuration, which in turn, is dependent on the process by which a *society* (often through subsocieties) *identifies the young individual,* recognizing him as somebody who had to become the way he is, and who, being the way he is, is taken for granted. The community, often not without some initial mistrust, gives such recognition with a (more or less institutionalized) display of surprise and pleasure in making the acquaintance of a newly emerging individual. For the community, in turn, feels "recognized" by the individual who cares to ask for recognition; it can, by the same token, feel deeply — and vengefully — rejected by the individual who does not seem to care.

3. While the end of adolescence thus is the stage of an overt identity *crisis,* identity *formation* neither begins nor ends with adolescence: it is a lifelong development largely unconscious to the individual and to his society. Its roots go back all the way to the first self-recognition: in the baby's earliest

exchange of smiles there is something of a *self-realization coupled with a mutual recognition.*

All through childhood tentative crystallizations take place which make the individual feel and believe (to begin with the most conscious aspect of the matter) as if he approximately knew who he was — only to find that such self-certainty ever again falls prey to the *discontinuities of psychosocial development* (Benedict, 1938). An example would be the discontinuity between the demands made in a given milieu on a little boy and those made on a "big boy" who, in turn, may well wonder why he was first made to believe that to be little is admirable, only to be forced to exchange this effortless status for the special obligations of one who is "big now." Such discontinuities can amount to a crisis and demand a decisive and strategic repatterning of action, and with it, *compromises* which can be compensated for only by a consistently accruing sense of the social value of such increasing commitment. The cute or ferocious, or good small boy, who becomes a studious, or gentlemanly, or tough big boy must be able — and must be enabled — to combine both sets of values in a recognized identity which permits him, in work and play, and in official and in intimate behavior to be (and to let others be) a big boy *and* a little boy.

The community supports such development to the extent to which it permits the child, at each step, to orient himself toward a complete *"life plan"* with a hierarchical order of roles as represented by individuals of different age grades. Family, neighborhood, and school provide contact and experimental identification with younger and older children and with young and old adults. A child, in the multiplicity of successive and tentative identifications, thus begins early to build up expectations of what it will be like to be older and what it will feel like to have been younger — expectations which become part of an identity as they are, step by step, verified in decisive experiences of psychosocial "fittedness."

4. The *critical phases* of life have been described in psychoanalysis primarily in terms of instincts and defenses, i.e., as "typical danger situations" (Hartmann, 1939). Psychoanalysis has concerned itself more with the encroachment of psychosexual crises on psychosocial (and other) functions than with the specific crisis created by the maturation of each function. Take for example a child who is learning to *speak:* he is acquiring one of the prime functions supporting a sense of individual autonomy and one of the prime techniques for expanding the radius of give-and-take. The mere indication of an ability to give intentional sound-signs immediately obligates the child to *"say* what he wants." It may force him to *achieve* by proper verbalization the attention which was afforded him previously in response to mere gestures of needfulness. Speech not only commits him to the kind of voice he has and to the mode of speech he develops; it also *defines him* as one responded to by those around him with changed diction and attention. They, in turn, expect henceforth to be understood by him with fewer explanations or gestures. Furthermore, a spoken

word is a *pact:* there is an irrevocably committing aspect to an utterance remembered by others, although the child may have to learn early that certain commitments (adult ones to a child) are subject to change without notice, while others (his) are not. This intrinsic relationship of speech, not only to the world of communicable facts, but also to the social value of verbal commitment and uttered truth is strategic among the experiences which support (or fail to support) a sound ego development. It is this psychosocial aspect of the matter which we must learn to relate to the by-now-better-known psychosexual aspects represented, for example, in the autoerotic enjoyment of speech; the use of speech as an erotic "contact"; or in such organ-mode emphases as eliminative or intrusive sounds or uses of speech. Thus the child may come to develop, in the use of voice and word, a particular combination of whining or singing, judging or arguing, as part of a new element of the future identity, namely, the element "one who speaks and is spoken to in such-and-such-a-way." This element, in turn, will be related to other elements of the child's developing identity (he is clever and/or good looking and/or tough) and will be compared with other people, alive or dead, judged ideal or evil.

It is the ego's function to integrate the psychosexual and psychosocial aspects on a given level of development, and, at the same time, to integrate the relation of newly added identity elements with those already in existence. For earlier crystallization of identity can become subject to renewed conflict, when changes in the quality and quantity of drive, expansions in mental equipment, and new and often conflicting social demands all make previous adjustments appear insufficient, and, in fact, make previous opportunities and rewards suspect. Yet, such developmental and normative crises differ from imposed, traumatic, and neurotic crises in that the process of growth provides new energy as society offers new and specific opportunities (according to its dominant conception and institutionalization of the phases of life). From a genetic point of view, then, the process of identity formation emerges as an evolving *configuration* — a configuration which is gradually established by successive ego syntheses and resyntheses throughout childhood; it is a configuration gradually integrating *constitutional givens, idiosyncratic libidinal needs, favored capacities, significant identifications, effective defenses, successful sublimations, and consistent roles.*

5. The final assembly of all the converging identity elements at the end of childhood (and the abandonment of the divergent ones)[2] appears to be a formidable task: how can a stage as "abnormal" as adolescence be trusted to accomplish it? Here it is not unnecessary to call to mind again that in spite of the similarity of adolescent "symptoms" and episodes to neurotic and psychotic symptoms and episodes, adolescence is not an affliction but a *normative crisis,* i.e., a normal phase of increased conflict characterized by a seeming fluctuation in ego strength, and yet also by a high growth potential. Neurotic and psychotic crises are defined by a certain self-perpetuating propensity, by

an increasing waste of defensive energy, and by a deepened psychosocial isolation; while normative crises are relatively more reversible, or, better, traversable, and are characterized by an abundance of available energy which, to be sure, revives dormant anxiety and arouses new conflict, but also supports new and expanded ego functions in the searching and playful engagement of new opportunities and associations. What under prejudiced scrutiny may appear to be the onset of a neurosis, often is but an aggravated crisis which might prove to be self-liquidating and, in fact, contributive to the process of identity formation.

It is true, of course, that the adolescent, during the final stage of his identity formation, is apt to suffer more deeply than he ever did before (or ever will again) from a diffusion of roles; and it is also true that such diffusion renders many an adolescent defenseless against the sudden impact of previously latent malignant disturbances. In the meantime, it is important to emphasize that the diffused and vulnerable, aloof and uncommitted, and yet demanding and opinionated personality of the not-too-neurotic adolescent contains many necessary elements of a semideliberate role experimentation of the "I dare you" and "I dare myself" variety. Much of this apparent diffusion thus must be considered *social play* and thus the true genetic successor of childhood play. Similarly, the adolescent's ego development demands and permits playful, if daring, experimentation in fantasy and *introspection*. We are apt to be alarmed by the "closeness to consciousness" in the adolescent's perception of dangerous id contents (such as the Oedipus complex, and this primarily because of the obvious hazards created in psychotherapy, if and when we, in zealous pursuit of our task of "making conscious," push somebody over the precipice of the unconscious who is already leaning out a little too far. The adolescent's leaning out over any number of precipices is normally an experimentation with experiences which are thus becoming more amenable to ego control, provided they can be somehow communicated to other adolescents in one of those strange codes established for just such experiences — and provided they are not prematurely responded to with fatal seriousness by overeager or neurotic adults. The same must be said of the adolescent's "fluidity of defenses," which so often causes raised eyebrows on the part of the worried clinician. Much of this fluidity is anything but pathological; for adolescence is a crisis in which only fluid defense can overcome a sense of victimization by inner and outer demands, and in which only trial and error can lead to the most felicitous avenues of action and self-expression.

In general, one may say that in regard to the social play of adolescents' prejudices similar to those which once concerned the nature of childhood play are not easily overcome. We alternately consider such behavior irrelevant, unnecessary, or irrational, and ascribe to it purely regressive and neurotic meanings. As in the past the study of children's spontaneous games was neglected in favor of that of solitary play,[3] so now the mutual "joinedness" of adolescent clique behavior fails to be properly assessed in our concern for the individual adolescent. Children and adolescents in their pre-societies provide for one another a sanctioned moratorium and joint support for free experimentation with inner and outer dangers (including those emanating from the adult world). Whether or not a given adolescent's newly acquired capacities are drawn back into infantile conflict depends to a significant extent on the quality of the opportunities and rewards available to him in his peer clique, as well as on the more formal ways in which society at large invites a transition from social play to work experimentation, and from rituals of transit to final commitments: all of which must be based on an implicit mutual contract between the individual and society.

6. Is the sense of identity conscious? At times, of course, it seems only too conscious. For between the double prongs of vital inner need and inexorable outer demand, the as-yet experimenting individual may become the victim of a transitory extreme *identity consciousness* which is the common core of many forms of self-consciousness typical for youth. Where the processes of identity formation are prolonged (a factor which can bring creative gain) such preoccupation with the "self-image" also prevails. We are thus most aware of our identity when we are just about to gain it and when we (with what motion pictures call "a double take" are somewhat surprised to make its acquaintance; or, again, when we are just about to enter a crisis and feel the encroachment of identity diffusion — a syndrome to be described presently.

An increasing sense of identity, on the other hand, is experienced preconsciously as a sense of psychosocial well-being. Its most obvious concomitants are a feeling of being at home in one's body, a sense of "knowing where one is going," and an inner assuredness of anticipated recognition from those who count. Such a sense of identity, however, is never gained nor maintained once and for all. Like a "good conscience," it is constantly lost and regained, although more lasting and more economical methods of maintenance and restoration are evolved and fortified in late adolescence.

Like any aspect of well-being or for that matter, of ego synthesis, a sense of identity has a preconscious aspect which is available to awareness; it expresses itself in behavior which is observable with the naked eye; and it has unconscious concomitants which can be fathomed only by psychological tests and by the psychoanalytic procedure. I regret that, at this point, I can bring forward only a general claim which awaits detailed demonstration. The claim advanced here concerns a whole series of criteria of psychosocial health which find their specific elaboration and relative completion in stages of development preceding and following the identity crisis....

Pathographic: The Clinical Picture of Identity Diffusion

Pathography remains the traditional source of psychoanalytic insight. In the following, I shall sketch a syndrome of disturbances in young people who can neither make use of the institutionalized moratorium provided in their society, nor create and maintain for themselves (as Shaw did) a unique moratorium all of their own. They come, instead, to psychiatrists, priests, judges, and (we must add) recruitment officers in order to be given an authorized if ever so uncomfortable place in which to wait things out.

The sources at my disposal are the case histories of a number of young patients who sought treatment following an acutely disturbed period between the ages of sixteen and twenty-four. A few were seen, and fewer treated, by me personally; a larger number were reported in supervisory interviews or seminars at the Austen Riggs Center in Stockbridge and at the Western Psychiatric Institute in Pittsburgh; the largest number are former patients now on record in the files of the Austen Riggs Center. My *composite sketch* of these case histories will remind the reader immediately of the diagnostic and technical problems encountered in adolescents in general (Blos, 1953) and especially in any number of those young borderline cases (Knight, 1953) who are customarily diagnosed as preschizophrenias, or severe character disorders with paranoid, depressive, psychopathic, or other trends. Such well-established diagnostic signposts will not be questioned here. An attempt will be made, however, to concentrate on certain common features representative of the common life crisis shared by this whole group of patients as a result of a (temporary or final) inability of their egos to establish an identity: for they all suffer from *acute identity diffusion.* Obviously, only quite detailed case presentations could convey the full necessity or advisability of such a "phase-specific" approach which emphasizes the life task shared by a group of patients as much as the diagnostic criteria which differentiate them. In the meantime, I hope that my composite sketch will convey at least a kind of impressionistic plausibility. The fact that the cases known to me were seen in a private institution in the Berkshires, and at a public clinic in industrial Pittsburgh, suggests that at least the two extremes of socioeconomic status in the United States (and thus two extreme forms of identity problems) are represented here. This could mean that the families in question, because of their extreme locations on the scale of class mobility and of Americanization, may have conveyed to these particular children a certain hopelessness regarding their chances of participating in (or of successfully defying) the dominant American manners and symbols of success. Whether, and in what way, disturbances such as are outlined here also characterize those more comfortably placed somewhere near the middle of the socioeconomic ladder, remains, at this time, an open question.

Time of Breakdown

A state of acute identity diffusion usually becomes manifest at a time when the young individual finds himself exposed to a combination of experiences which demand his simultaneous commitment to *physical intimacy* (not by any means always overtly sexual), to decisive *occupational choice,* to energetic *competition,* and to *psychosocial self-definition.* A young college girl, previously overprotected by a conservative mother who is trying to live down a not-so-conservative past, may, on entering college, meet young people of radically different backgrounds, among whom she must choose her friends and her enemies; radically different mores especially in the relationship of the sexes which she must play along with or repudiate; and a commitment to make decisions and choices which will necessitate irreversible competitive involvement or even leadership. Often she finds among very different young people a comfortable display of values, manners, and symbols for which one or the other of her parents or grandparents is covertly nostalgic, while overtly despising them. Decisions and choices and, most of all, successes in any direction bring to the fore conflicting identifications and immediately threaten to narrow down the inventory of further tentative choices; and, at the very moment when time is of the essence, every move may establish a binding precedent in psychosocial self-definition, i.e., in the type one comes to represent in the types of the age-mates (who seem so terribly eager to type). On the other hand, any marked *avoidance of choices* (i.e., a moratorium by default) leads to a sense of outer *isolation* and to an *inner vacuum* which is wide open for old libidinal objects and with this for bewilderingly conscious incestuous feelings; for more primitive forms of identification; and (in some) for a renewed struggle with archaic introjects. This regressive pull often receives the greatest attention from workers in our field, partially because we are on more familiar ground wherever we can discern signs of regression to infantile psychosexuality. Yet the disturbances under discussion here cannot be comprehended without some insight into the specific nature of transitory adolescent regression as an attempt to postpone and to avoid, as it were, a psychosocial foreclosure. A state of paralysis may ensue, the mechanisms of which appear to be devised to maintain a state of minimal actual choice and commitment with a maximum inner conviction of still being the chooser. Of the complicated presenting pathology only a few aspects can be discussed here.

The Problem of Intimacy

The chart [omitted] which accompanied the preceding section shows "Intimacy vs. Isolation" as the core conflict which follows that of "Identity vs. Identity Diffusion." That many of our patients break down at an age which is properly considered more pre-adult than postadolescent is explained by the fact that often only an attempt to engage in intimate fellowship and competition or in sexual intimacy fully reveals the latent weakness of identity.

True "engagement" with others is the result and the test of firm self-delineation. As the young individual seeks at least tentative forms of playful intimacy in friendship and competition, in sex play and love, in argument and gossip, he is apt to experience a peculiar strain, as if such tentative engagement might turn into an interpersonal fusion amounting to a loss of identity, and requiring, therefore, a tense inner reservation, a caution in commitment. Where a youth does not resolve such strain he may isolate himself and enter, at best, only stereotyped and formalized interpersonal relations; or he may, in repeated hectic attempts and repeated dismal failures, seek intimacy with the most improbable partners. For where an assured sense of identity is missing even friendships and affairs become desperate attempts at delineating the fuzzy outlines of identity by mutual narcissistic mirroring: to fall in love then often means to fall into one's mirror image, hurting oneself and damaging the mirror. During lovemaking or in sexual fantasies, a loosening of sexual identity threatens: it even becomes unclear whether sexual excitement is experienced by the individual or by his partner, and this in either heterosexual or homosexual encounters. The ego thus loses its flexible capacity for abandoning itself to sexual and affectual sensations, in a fusion with another individual who is both partner to the sensation and guarantor of one's continuing identity: fusion with another becomes identity loss. A sudden collapse of all capacity for mutuality threatens, and a desperate wish ensues to start all over again, with a (quasi-deliberate) regression to a stage of basic bewilderment and rage such as only the very small child knew.

It must be remembered that the counterpart of intimacy is *distantiation*, i.e., the readiness to repudiate, to ignore, or to destroy those forces and people whose essence seems dangerous to one's own. Intimacy with one set of people and ideas would not be really intimate without an efficient repudiation of another set. Thus, weakness or excess in repudiation is an intrinsic aspect of the inability to gain intimacy because of an incomplete identity: whoever is not sure of his "point of view" cannot repudiate judiciously.

Young persons often indicate in rather pathetic ways a feeling that only a merging with a "leader" can save them — an adult who is able and willing to offer himself as a safe object for experimental surrender and as a guide in the relearning of the very first steps toward an intimate mutuality, and a legitimate repudiation. To such a person the late adolescent wants to be an apprentice or a disciple, a follower, sex mate or patient. Where this fails, as it often must from its very intensity and absoluteness, the young individual recoils to a position of strenuous introspection and self-testing which, given particularly aggravating circumstances or a history of relatively strong autistic trends, can lead him into a paralyzing borderline state. Symptomatically, this state consists of a painfully heightened sense of isolation; a disintegration of the sense of inner continuity and sameness; a sense of over-all ashamedness; an inability to derive a sense of accomplishment from any kind of activity; a feeling that life is happening to the individual rather than being lived by his initiative; a radically shortened time perspective; and finally, a basic mistrust, which leaves it to the world, to society, and indeed to psychiatry to prove that the patient does exist in a psychosocial sense, i.e., can count on an invitation to become himself.

Diffusion of Time Perspective

In extreme instances of delayed and prolonged adolescence an extreme form of a disturbance in the experience of time appears which, in its milder form, belongs to the psychopathology of everyday adolescence. It consists of a sense of great urgency and yet also of a loss of consideration for time as a dimension of living. The young person may feel simultaneously very young, and in fact baby-like, and old beyond rejuvenation. Protests of missed greatness and of a premature and fatal loss of useful potentials are common among our patients as they are among adolescents in cultures which consider such protestations romantic; the implied malignancy, however, consists of a decided disbelief in the possibility that time may bring change, and yet also of a violent fear that it might. This contradiction often is expressed in a general slowing up which makes the patient behave, within the routine of activities (and also of therapy) as if he were moving in molasses. It is hard for him to go to bed and to face the transition into a state of sleep, and it is equally hard for him to get up and face the necessary restitution of wakefulness; it is hard to come to the hour, and hard to leave it. Such complaints as, "I don't know," "I give up," "I quit," are by no means mere habitual statements reflecting a mild depression: they are often expressions of the kind of despair which Edward Bibring (1953) has recently discussed as a wish on the part of the ego "to let itself die." The assumption that life could actually be made to end with the end of adolescence (or at tentatively planned later "dates of expiration") is by no means entirely unwelcome, and, in fact, can become the only pillar of hope on which a new beginning can be based. Some of our patients even require the feeling that the therapist does not intend to commit them to a continuation of life if (successful) treatment should fail to prove it really worth while; without such a conviction the moratorium would not be a real one. In the meantime, the "wish to die" is only in those rare cases a really suicidal wish, where "to be a suicide" becomes an inescapable identity choice in itself. I am thinking here of a pretty young girl, the oldest of a number of daughters of a mill worker. Her mother had repeatedly expressed the thought that she would rather see her daughters dead than become prostitutes; at the same time she suspected "prostitution" in their every move toward companionship with boys. The daughters were finally forced into a kind of conspiratorial sorority of their own, obviously designed to elude the mother, to experiment with ambiguous situations, and yet probably also to give one another protection from men. They were finally caught in compromising circumstances. The authorities, too, took it for granted that they intended to prostitute themselves, and they were sent to a variety of institutions where they were forcefully impressed with the kind of "recognition" society had in store for them. No appeal was possible to a mother who, they felt, had left them no choice; and much good will and understanding of social workers was sabotaged by circumstances. At least for the oldest girl (and this, because of a number of reasons) no other future was available except that of another chance in another world. She killed herself by hanging after having dressed herself up nicely, and having written a note which ended with the cryptic words "Why I achieve honor only to discard it..."

Less spectacular but not less malignant forms and origins of such "negative identities" will be taken up later.

Diffusion of Industry

Cases of severe identity diffusion regularly also suffer from an acute upset in the sense of workmanship, and this either in the form of an inability to concentrate on required or suggested tasks, or in a self-destructive preoccupation with some one-sided activities, i.e., excessive reading. The way in which such patients sometimes, under treatment, find the one activity in which they can re-employ their once lost sense of workmanship is a chapter in itself. Here, it is well to keep in mind the stage of development which precedes puberty and adolescence, namely, the elementary-school age, when the child is taught the prerequisites for participation in the particular technology of his culture and is given the opportunity and the life task of developing a sense of workmanship and work participation. The school age significantly follows the Oedipal stage: the accomplishment of real (and not only playful) steps toward a place in the economic structure of society permits the child to re-identify with parents as workers and tradition bearers rather than as sexual and familial beings, thus nurturing at least one concrete and more neutral possibility of becoming like them. The tangible goals of elementary practice are shared by and with age-mates in places of instruction (sweathouse, prayer house, fishing hole, workshop, kitchen, schoolhouse) most of which, in turn, are geographically separated from the home, from the mother, and from infantile memories: here, however, wide differences in the treatment of the sexes exist. Work goals, then, by no means only support or exploit the suppression of infantile instinctual aims; they also enhance the functioning of the ego, in that they offer a constructive activity with actual tools and materials in a communal reality. The ego's tendency to turn passivity into activity here thus acquires a new field of manifestation, in many ways superior to the mere turning of passive into active in infantile fantasy and play; for now the inner need for activity, practice, and work completion is ready to meet the corresponding demands and opportunities in social reality (Hendrick, 1943; Ginsburg, 1954).

Because of the immediate oedipal antecedents of the beginnings of a work identity, the diffusion of identity in our young patients reverses their gears toward oedipal competitiveness and sibling rivalry. Thus identity diffusion is accompanied not only by an inability to concentrate, but also by an excessive awareness as well as an abhorrence of competitiveness. Although the patients in question usually are intelligent and able and often have shown themselves successful in office work, in scholastic studies and in sports, they now lose the capacity for work, exercise, and sociability, and thus the most important vehicle of social play, and the most significant refuge from formless fantasy and vague anxiety. Instead infantile goals and fantasies are dangerously endowed with the energy emanating from matured sexual equipment and increased aggressive power. One parent, again, becomes the goal, the other, again, the hindrance. Yet this revived oedipal struggle is not and must not be interpreted as exclusively or even primarily a sexual one: it is a turn toward the earliest origins, an attempt to resolve a diffusion of early introjects and to rebuild shaky childhood identifications — in other words, a wish to be born again, to learn once more the very first steps toward reality and mutuality, and to acquire the renewed permission to develop again the functions of contact, activity, and competition.

A young patient, who had found himself blocked in college, during the initial phase of his treatment in a private hospital nearly read himself blind, apparently in a destructive overidentification with father and therapist both of whom were professors. Guided by a resourceful "painter in residence" he came upon the fact that he had an original and forceful talent to paint, an activity which was prevented by advancing treatment from becoming self-destructive overactivity. As painting proved a help in the patient's gradual acquisition of a sense of identity of his own, he dreamed one night a different version of a dream which previously had always ended in panicky awakening. Now he fled, from fire and persecution, into a forest which he had sketched himself; and as he fled into it, the charcoal drawing turned into live woods, with an infinite perspective.

The Choice of the Negative Identity

The loss of a sense of identity often is expressed in a scornful and snobbish hostility toward the roles offered as proper and desirable in one's family or immediate community. Any part aspect of the required role, or all parts, be it masculinity or femininity, nationality or class membership, can become the main focus of the young person's acid disdain. Such excessive contempt for their backgrounds occurs among the oldest Anglo-Saxon and the newest Latin or Jewish families; it easily becomes a general dislike for everything American, and an irrational overestimation of everything foreign. Life and strength seem to exist only where one is not, while decay and danger threaten wherever one happens to be. This typical case fragment illustrates the superego's triumph of depreciation over a young man's faltering identity: A voice within him which was disparaging him began to increase at about this time. It went to the point of intruding into everything he did. He said, "If I smoke a cigarette, if I tell a girl I like her, if I make a gesture, if I listen to music, if I try to read a book — this third voice is at me all the time 'You're doing this for effect; you're a phony.'" This disparaging voice in the last year has been rather relentless. The other day on the way from home to college, getting into New York on the train, he went through some of the New Jersey swamplands and the poorer sections of the cities, and he felt that he was more congenial with people who lived there than he was with people on the campus or at home. He felt that life really existed in those places and that the campus was a sheltered, effeminate place.

In this example it is important to recognize not only an overweening superego, overclearly perceived as an inner voice, but also the acute identity diffusion, as projected on segments of society. An analogous case is that of a French-American girl from a rather prosperous mining town, who felt panicky to the point of paralysis when alone with a boy. It appeared that numerous superego injunctions and identity conflicts had, as it were, short-circuited in the obsessive idea that every boy had a right to expect from her a yielding to sexual practices popularly designated as "French."

Such estrangement from national and ethnic origins rarely leads to a complete denial of *personal identity* (Piers & Singer, 1953), although the angry insistence on being called by a particular given name or nickname is not uncommon among young people who try to find a refuge from diffusion in a new name label. Yet confabulatory reconstructions of one's origin do occur: a high-school girl of Middle-European descent secretly kept company with Scottish immigrants, carefully studying and easily assimilating their dialect and their social habits. With the help of history books and travel guides she reconstructed for herself a childhood in a given milieu in an actual township in Scotland, apparently convincing enough to some descendants of that country. Prevailed upon to discuss her future with me, she spoke of her (American-born) parents as "the people who brought me over here," and told me of her childhood "over there" in impressive detail. I went along with the story, implying that it had more inner truth than reality to it. The bit of reality was, as I surmised, the girl's attachment, in early childhood, to a woman neighbor who had come from the British Isles; the force behind the near-delusional "truth" was the paranoid form of a powerful death wish (latent in all severe identity crises) against her parents. The semideliberateness of the delusion was indicated when I finally asked the girl how she had managed to marshal all the details of life in Scotland. "Bless you, sir," she said in pleading Scottish brogue, "I needed a past."

On the whole, however, our patients' conflicts find expression in a more subtle way than the abrogation of personal identity: they rather choose a *negative identity,* i.e., an identity perversely based on all those identifications and roles which, at critical stages of development, had been presented to the individual as most undesirable or dangerous, and yet also as most real. For example, a mother whose first-born son died and who (because of complicated guilt feelings) has never been able to attach to her later surviving children the same amount of religious devotion that she bestows on the memory of her dead child may well arouse in one of her sons the conviction that to be sick or dead is a better assurance of being "recognized" than to be healthy and about. A mother who is filled with unconscious ambivalence toward a brother who disintegrated into alcoholism may again and again respond selectively only to those traits in her son which seem to point to a repetition of her brother's fate, in which case this "negative" identity may take on more reality for the son than all his natural attempts at being good: he may work hard on becoming a drunkard and, lacking the necessary ingredients, may end up in a state of stubborn paralysis of choice. In other cases the negative identity is dictated by the necessity of finding and defending a niche of one's own against the excessive ideals either demanded by morbidly ambitious parents or seemingly already realized by actually superior ones: in both cases the parents' weaknesses and unexpressed wishes are recognized by the child with catastrophic clarity. The daughter of a man of brilliant showmanship ran away from college and was arrested as a prostitute in the Negro quarter of a Southern city; while the daughter of an influential Southern Negro preacher was found among narcotic addicts in Chicago. In such cases it is of utmost importance to recognize the mockery and the vindictive pretense in such role playing; for the white girl had not really prostituted herself, and the colored girl had not really become an addict — yet. Needless to say, however, each of them had put herself into a marginal social area, leaving it to law-enforcement officers and to psychiatric agencies to decide what stamp to put on such behavior. A corresponding case is that of a boy presented to a psychiatric clinic as "the village homosexual" of a small town. On investigation, it appeared that the boy had succeeded in assuming this fame without any actual acts of homosexuality except one, much earlier in his life, when he had been raped by some older boys.

Such vindictive choices of a negative identity represent, of course, a desperate attempt at regaining some mastery in a situation in which the available positive identity elements cancel each other out. The history of such a choice reveals a set of conditions in which it is easier to derive a sense of identity out of a *total* identification with that which one is *least* supposed to be than to struggle for a feeling of reality in acceptable roles which are unattainable with the patient's inner means. The statement of a young man, "I would rather be quite insecure than a little secure," and that of a young woman, "At least in the gutter I'm a genius," circumscribe the relief following the total choice of a negative identity. Such relief is, of course, often sought collectively in cliques and gangs of young homosexuals, addicts, and social cynics.

A relevant job ahead of us is the analysis of snobbism which, in its upperclass form, permits some people to deny their identity diffusion through a recourse to something they did not earn themselves, namely, their parents' wealth, background, or fame. But there is a "lower lower" snobbism too, which is based on the pride of having achieved a semblance of nothingness. At any rate, many a late adolescent, if faced with continuing diffusion, would rather be *nobody or somebody bad, or indeed, dead — and this totally, and by free choice — than be not-quite-somebody.* The word "total" is not accidental in this connection, for I have endeavored to describe in another connection (Erikson, 1953) a human proclivity to a "totalistic" reorientation when, at critical stages of development, reintegration into a relative "wholeness" seems impossible....

Notes

1. "...die klare Bewusstheit der inneren Identität" (Freud, 1926).
2. William James (1896) speaks of an abandonment of "the old alternative ego," and even of "the murdered self."
3. For a new approach see Anna Freud's and Sophie Dann's (1951) report on displaced children.

References

Ackerman, N. (1951). "Social role" and total personality. *American Journal of Orthopsychiatry, 21,* 1–17.

Benedict, R. (1938). Continuities and discontinuities in cultural conditioning. *Psychiatry, 1,* 161–167.

Bibring, E. (1953). The mechanism of depression. In P. Greenacre (Ed.), *Affective disorders* (13–48). New York: International Universities Press.

Blos, P. (1953). The contribution of psychoanalysis to the treatment of adolescents. In M. Heiman (Ed.), *Psychoanalysis and social work.* New York: International Universities Press.

Erikson, E. (1946). Ego development and historical change. *The Psychoanalytic Study of the Child, 2,* 359–396. New York: International Universities Press.

Erikson, E. (1950a). *Childhood and society.* New York: Norton.

Erikson, E. (1950b). Growth and crises of the "Healthy Personality." In M. Senn (Ed.), *Symposium on the healthy personality, supplement II; Problems of infancy and childhood.* New York: Josiah Macy, Jr. Foundation.

Erikson, E. (1951). On the sense of inner identity. In *Health and human relations.* Report of a Conference on Health and Human Relations held at Hiddesen near Detmold, Germany, August 2–7, 1951. Sponsored by the Josiah Macy, Jr. Foundation. New York: Blakiston, 1953.

Erikson, E. (1953). Wholeness and totality. In C. Friedrich (Ed.), *Totalitarianism.* Proceedings of a conference held at the American Academy of Arts and Sciences, March. Cambridge, MA: Harvard University Press, 1954.

Erikson, E. (1954). The dream specimen of psychoanalysis. *Journal of the American Psychoanalytic Association, 2,* 5–56.

Freud, A. & Dann, S. (1951). An experiment in group upbringing. *The Psychoanalytic Study of the Child, 1,* 127–149. International Universities Press.

Freud, S. (1926). Ansprache an die Mitglieder des Vereins B'nai B'rith. *Gesammelte Werke, 17,* 49–53. London: *Imago,* 1941.

Ginsburg, S. (1954). The role of work. *Samiksa, 8,* 1–13.

Hartmann, H. (1939). Ego psychology and the problem of adaptation. In D. Rapaport (Ed.), *Organization and pathology of thought.* New York: Columbia University Press, 1951.

Hendrick, I. (1943). Work and the pleasure principle. *Psychoanalytic Quarterly, 12,* 311–329.

James, W. (1896). The will to believe. *New World, 5.*

Knight, R. (1953). Management and psychotherapy of the borderline schizophrenic patient. *Bulletin of the Menninger Clinic, 17,* 139–150.

Mead, G. (1934). *Mind, self and society.* Chicago: University of Chicago Press.

Piers, G., & Singer, M. (1953). *Shame and guilt.* Springfield, IL: Thomas.

13
Ego and Actuality [On Dora]

ERIK ERIKSON

Among the stories of Freud's (1904) preanalytic years which assume a mythological quality in our training is the report of one of Charcot's evening receptions when the master, during a bit of shop talk about hysteria in women, "suddenly broke out with great animation: *'Mais, dans des cas pareils c'est toujours la chose génitale, toujours.... toujours.... toujours'....* I know that for a moment I was almost paralysed with amazement and said to myself: 'Well, but if he knows that, why does he never say so?' But the impression was soon forgotten; brain anatomy.... absorbed all my interest" (p. 14).

Since then psychoanalytic enlightenment has come full cycle and it is not sexuality that remains unmentioned at evening receptions. Heirs of radical innovation, however, carry a double burden: they must do together what the founder did in lonely years and also strive to keep ahead of the habituations which result from success. They may well, at intervals, ask themselves what they have come to know and what they on occasion say with "great animation," without pursuing it with the momentum of discovery.

One such item, I submit, is our knowledge of human strength. We have all heard psychoanalysts (including ourselves) in private conversations or in unguarded moments of clinical discussion, describe with wonder the evidence for some patient's regained health. Such evidence often seems hard to classify because it appears to have resulted from unexpected encounters "in the outside world" and from opportunities beyond our theoretical anticipations.

During a recent discussion in a small circle, Anna Freud made the observation that children who come to feel loved become more beautiful. Does libido, then, so the discussants wondered half-humorously, "jump" from one person to another? At any rate, our theory of inner psychic economy does not tell us what energy transforms the whole appearance of a person and heightens, as

From: Erikson, Erik (1964). *Insight and responsibility; lectures on the ethical implications of psychoanalytic insight*, (pp. 161–177). New York: W. W. Norton. Copyright © Kai Erikson. Reprinted with permission of Norton and Kai Erikson.

it were, his tonus of living. A similar dilemma was circumscribed by W. H. Auden in a book review (1960) in which he pointed out how difficult it is for the psychoanalyst to conceptualize deeds in contrast to behavior, that is (to paraphrase him), to differentiate action which makes memorable difference in the shared lives of many from such stereotyped private behavior as can be studied in clinical isolation. Is this an essential limitation of psychoanalysis? Can we conceptualize man only if he is fragmented in acute inner conflict, that is to say, retreating from or preparing for those moments when "his virtues.... go forth of him?"

I frankly do not know whether I will confirm such limitations or point beyond them as I discuss, from a number of angles, my impression that our often half-hearted and ambiguous conceptualization of reality has resulted in a failure to account for important features of adaptive and productive action and their relation to the major phenomena of ego strength.

What do we mean when we speak of the recognition of and the adjustment to reality? Hartmann (1956) has formulated the reality principle as the "tendency to take into account in an adaptive way.... whatever we consider the *real features* of an object or situation" (p. 33) and the psychoanalytic usage of the term reality was quite recently stated again by Loewald (1951) as "the world of things *really existing in the outer world*." Freud's criteria of reality are (as Hartmann, 1956, has not uncritically pointed out) "the criteria of science, or more correctly, those that find their clearest expression in science.... which accepts as 'objective' what is *verifiable by certain methods*" (p. 257). The emphases are mine, but the statements clearly say that the psychoanalytic method by its very design attempts to further man's adjustment by helping him to perceive facts and motives "as they are," that is, as they appear to the rational eye. Yet, Hartmann has also clarified the limited applicability of such rationalism to human adaptation: "there is no simple correlation between the degree of objective insight and the degree of adaptiveness of the corresponding action" (p. 40). And, indeed, radical rationalism could lead to a preoccupation so strenuous that it would expose man to the dilemma of that centipede which found itself completely immobilized because it had been asked to watch carefully which of its feet it was going to put forward next. If Hartmann's approach to these matters develops from the consideration of thought, attention, and judgment to that of action, he follows faithfully, although he expands it firmly, the course of psychoanalytic preoccupation with reality. But this thinking harbors such terms as "acting *in regard*" to reality (p. 40), "action *vis-à vis* reality" (p. 41), and acting *in the "outer world"* (p. 47; italics added). Maybe our habitual reference to man's environment as an "outer world" attests, more than any other single item, to the fact that the world of that intuitive and active participation which constitutes most of our waking life is still foreign territory to our theory. This term, more than any other, represents the Cartesian strait jacket we have imposed on our model of man, who in some of our writings seems to be most himself when reflecting horizontally — like a supine baby or a reclining patient, or like Descartes himself, taking to his bed to cogitate on the extensive world.

I believe that we can undo this strait jacket only by separating from our concept of *reality* one of its more obscure implications, namely, *actuality,* the world verified in immediate immersion and interaction. The German word *Wirklichkeit,* often implied in Freud's use of the word *Realität,* does combine *Wirkung,* that is, activity and efficacy, with reality. There is in fact, in Freud's papers on metapsychology [specifically, 1917] a mysterious footnote promising a "later passage on the distinction between testing with regard to reality and testing *with regard to immediacy"* (italics added; p. 233, footnote 2). Freud's original term for what is translated as "immediacy" was *Actualitaet.* The editor of the *Standard Edition* adds that no reference to this seems to occur anywhere else; and that the footnote may be "one more reference to a missing paper."

I will not attempt to surmise what kind of differentiation Freud had in mind so long ago. I can only state the problem as I see it in our day. The term "actuality" may strike us with different connotations depending upon whether we are devotees of small or big dictionaries. The shorter the annotation, the more does "actual" mean the same as "real." "Actuality," thus, can be just another word for phenomenal reality, and yet its linguistic origin vouches for a reality due to a state of being actual, present, current, immediate. It is in the verbs "to activate" and "to actuate" that this meaning has most strongly survived, for what actuates "communicates motion," "inspires with active properties."

I intend here to make the most of this linguistic difference and claim that we must put into their proper relations — sometimes close to identical, sometimes directly antagonistic — that *phenomenal reality* which by psychoanalytic means is to be freed from distortions and delusions, and the meaning of reality as *actuality* — which is participation free (or to be freed) from defensive or offensive "acting out." *Reality,* then (to repeat this), is the world of phenomenal experience, perceived with a minimum of distortion and with a maximum of customary validation agreed upon in a given state of technology and culture; while *actuality* is the world of participation, shared with other participants with a minimum of defensive maneuvering and a maximum of mutual activation.

Mutual activation is the crux of the matter; for human ego strength, while employing all means of testing reality, depends from stage to stage upon a network of mutual influences within which the person actuates others even as he is actuated, and within which the person is "inspired with active properties," even as he so inspires others. This is *ego actuality;* largely preconscious and unconscious, it must be studied in the individual by psychoanalytic means. Yet actualities are shared, as are realities. Members of the same age group share analogous combinations of capacities and opportunities, and members of different age groups depend on each other for the mutual activation of their complementary ego strengths. Here, then, studies of "outer" conditions and of inner states meet in one focus. One can speak of actualities as co-determined by an individual's *stage of development,* by his *personal circumstances,* and by *historical and political processes* — and I will, in fact, speak of all of these.

The concept of activation is intimately related to one of the last dominant interests of the late David Rapaport (1953/1967), who left a paper in which he frees from the tangle of conflicting formulation the various meanings of the terms "activity" and "passivity," in order to formulate the ego's active and passive states. The ego's active state leads to integrated action while the ego's passive state is characterized by "helplessness in the face of drive demand" and by the "paralysis.... of [ego] control" (p. 555). I wonder whether it would not be better to leave the term passivity to other phenomena and to speak of the ego's *inactivation* rather than of its passivity as the state essential to all dangers to the ego. For passivity can be an active adaptation, while only inactivation results in paralysis. At any rate, it is the ego's very essence to maintain an active state not merely by way of making compromises with reality but by a selective involvement in actualities.

Here, it seems, an issue which first arose with the psychoanalysis of children awaits systematic clarification. I mean the assessment of variations of therapeutic technique not only from the point of view of the patient's "analyzability" but also from that of his adaptability, i.e., his chances of re-establishing active ego tension in his actuality. For it is clear that each stage of development has its own acuteness and immediacy, because a stage is a new configuration of past and future, a new combination of drive and defense, a new set of capacities fit for a new setting of tasks and opportunities, a new and wider radius of significant encounters. The truly recovering patient of any age must turn his powers of recognition toward fellows by whom he in turn will be recognized, and must direct his needs for activation toward those who in turn will be activated by him. As Shakespeare says (in *Troilus and Cressida),* man

> ....feels not what he owns, but by reflection
> As when his virtues shining upon others
> Heat them, and they retort that heat again
> to the first giver.

But before attempting to define *developmental actuality,* let me illustrate its clinical relevance by discussing a question which we have all asked ourselves at one time: what *was* it Dora (Freud, 1905) wanted from Freud?

When we use Freud's cases and dreams for the elucidation of what we are groping to say, it is for one very practical reason: all of us know the material by heart. Beyond this, we always find in Freud's writings parenthetical data worthy of the attention of generations to come. We must assume, of course, that Freud selected and disguised the clinical data he published, thus rendering reinterpretations hazardous. Yet, the repeated study of Freud's case reports strengthens the impression that we are dealing with creations of a high degree of psychological relevance and equivalence even in matters of peripheral concern to him. And Freud always made explicit where he stood and how far he had come. Thus, he concludes his report on the treatment of Dora with an admission as frank as it is rare in professional publications: "I do not know what kind of help she wanted from me" (p. 122).

Dora, you will remember, had returned to him a year after she had interrupted a treatment that had lasted only three months. She was 20 years old then and had come back "to finish her story and to ask for help once more" (p. 120). But what she told him then did not please Freud. She had in the interval confronted her family with certain shady events denied by all (I will come back to their nature), and she had forced them to admit their pretenses and their secrets. Freud considered this forced confrontation an act of revenge not compatible with the kind of insight which he had tried to convey to the patient. If she now knew that those events had caused her to fall ill, it was her responsibility to gain health, not revenge, from her insight. The interview convinced him that "she was not in earnest over her request" (p. 121) for more help, and he assured her that he was willing "to forgive her for having deprived [him] of the satisfaction of affording her a far more radical cure" (p. 122). Since Dora was intelligent, however, the judgment that she was "not in earnest" suggested insincerity on her part. And, indeed, Dr. Felix Deutsch (1957), who later — in her middle age and far from the scene of her first treatment — was consulted by Dora, gives an unfavorable picture of her fully developed character — as unfavorable as any that may be seen in clinical annals. What must interest us is that in Freud's original description of the girl, Dora appeared "in the first bloom of youth — a girl of intelligent and engaging looks" (p. 23). If "an alteration in her character" indeed became one of the permanent features of her illness, it seems possible that Dora may have been confirmed in such change by the discontinuance of her treatment.

The description of Freud's fragmentary work with Dora has become the classical analysis of the structure and the genesis of a hysteria. It is clear from his description that Freud's original way of working and reporting was determined by his first professional identity as a physiological investigator: his clinical method was conceived as an analogy to clean and exact laboratory work. It focused on the "intimate structure of a neurotic disorder" — a structure which was really a reconstruction of its origins and a search for the energies, the "quantities of excitation," which had been "transmuted" into symptoms, according to the dominant physicalistic configurations of his era. As to the unbearable excitations "transmuted" into Dora's symptoms, it will suffice to mention the two traumatic sexual approaches made to the girl by a Mr. K., a married man who kissed her once when she was 14 under circumstances indicating that he had set the scene for a more thorough seduction; and who propositioned her quite unequivocally at an outing by an Alpine lake when she was 16. She had rebuked the man on both occasions, but her arousal and repugnance had been so violent that they led to hysterical symptoms which then were traced back by Freud to the sensations, affects, and ideas experienced in those events. This was his method; but how clinically alive and concrete is his question as to what more, or what else, Dora had a right to expect of him. He could not see, Freud relates, how it could have helped her if he "had acted a part. . . . and shown a warm personal interest in her" (p. 109). He did perceive, then, an interpersonal distance in his method; but no patient's demands were to make him dissimulate his integrity as an investigator and his commitment to the truth: they were *his* criteria of the respect due to a patient.

If in the patient's inability to live up to his kind of truth Freud primarily saw repressed instinctual strivings at work, he certainly also noted that Dora, too, was in search of some kind of truth. He registered the fact that the patient was "almost beside herself at the idea of its being supposed that she had merely fancied the conditions which had made her sick" (p. 118) and that she kept "anxiously trying to make sure whether I was being quite straightforward with her." And, indeed, the girl had every reason to suspect the whole older generation of having conspired against her; had not her father asked Freud "to bring her to reason"? Freud was to make his daughter drop the subject of her attempted seduction by Mr. K. The father had good reason for this wish, for — and here we come to the suspicion of an erotic barter with which she subsequently confronted her family — Mr. K.'s wife was his own mistress, and he seemed willing to ignore Mr. K.'s advances to his daughter if he could remain unchallenged in his own affair.

Dora, no doubt, was in love with Mr. K. whom Freud found to be quite a presentable man. But I wonder how many of us can follow without protest today Freud's assertion that a healthy young girl would, under such circumstances, have considered Mr. K.'s advances "neither tactless nor offensive." The nature and severity of Doras pathological reaction make her, of course, the classical hysteric of her day; but her motivation for falling ill, and her lack of motivation for getting well, today seem to call for developmental considerations which go beyond (although they include) the sexual conflicts then in the focus of Freud's studies.

As pointed out, Freud's report indicates that Dora was concerned not only with the recognition but also with the joint acknowledgment of the historical truth, while her doctor insisted on the psychic reality behind the historical truth: for, according to his view, only her own conflict between love and repugnance could explain the nature of her symptoms. At the same time she wanted her doctor to be "truthful" in the therapeutic relation, that is, to keep faith with her on her terms rather than on those of her father or seducer. That her doctor did keep faith with her in terms of his investigative ethos she probably appreciated up to a point; after all, she did come back. But why then surprise him with the fact that she had confronted her parents with the historical truth?

This insistence on action may impress some of us even today as "acting out." With Freud, we may predict that the patient would gain a permanent relief from her symptoms only by an ever better understanding of her own unconscious, an understanding which would eventually permit her to adjust to the "reality" both of the events and of her reaction to them, for neither could now be helped. And it is sometimes too easy to flee from psychic reality into historical proof of one's victimization. Strictly speaking, however, we could expect a full utilization of such insight only from a "mature ego," and Dora's neurosis was rooted in the developmental crisis of adolescence. The question arises whether today we would consider the patient's active emphasis on the historical truth a mere matter of resistance to the inner truth; or whether we would discern in it also an adaptive pattern specific for her stage of life, challenged by her special conditions, and therefore subject to consideration in her treatment. For we may suspect that at each stage of life, what appears to us as "acting out" may contain an adaptive if immature reaching out for the mutual verification by which the ego lives; and that, between adolescence and young adulthood, the pursuit of "the truth" may be of acute relevance to the ego's adaptive strength.

There are, of course, many ways in which a young person may express a sudden preoccupation with truth — at first perverse and obsessive, changeable and pretentious, and altogether defensive in Anna Freud's sense, but gradually taking hold of relevant issues and productive commitments. He may come to have a personal stake in the accuracy, veracity, and authenticity, in the fairness, genuineness, and reliability of persons, of methods, and of ideas. I have elsewhere postulated the quality of *fidelity* as the essence of all these preoccupations. As in adolescence, powerful new drives must find sanctioned expression or be kept in abeyance, and as wild regressive pulls must be resisted, it is a prime necessity for the ego that the capacity to pledge and receive fidelity emerge and mature during this period — even as societies, for the sake of their rejuvenation, must receive from their youth, by way of all manner of "confirmations," the pledge of particular fidelities in the form of ideological commitment.

Inhelder and Piaget (1955/1958), who have studied the thought processes of adolescents by confronting them with certain experimental tasks, have recognized in adolescence the ripening of a mode of thinking both "hypothetical" and "deductive." That is: the adolescent, before beginning to manipulate the material at hand, as the pre-adolescent would do with little hesitation, waits and hypothesizes on the possible results, even as he lingers after the experiment and tries to fathom the truth behind the known results. This capacity forms,

I think, a basis for the development, in later adolescence, of the *historical perspective* which makes room not only for imaginative speculation about all that could have happened in the past, but also a deepening concern with the narrowing down of vast possibilities to a few alternatives, often resolved only by a "totalistic" search for single causes. Youth is, at the same time, preoccupied with the danger of hopeless determination, be it by irreversible childhood identifications, by ineradicable secret sins or socially "stacked" conditions, and with the question of freedom in many urgent forms. Where a sense of fatal predetermination prevails, the quest for its causes becomes an ideological one, defying a merely intellectual approach. Thus, what we would consider an interpretation to youth easily becomes a statement of doom. Patients such as Dora, therefore, may insist that the inner meaning of their sickness find recognition within an assessment of the historical truth, which separates that which has become irreversible from the freedom of opportunities yet undetermined.

The employment of the particular cognitive gains of any stage of life is thus not just a matter of exercising intelligence, for these gains are part of a new pattern of verification which pervades a person's whole being. We know in pathology that certain forms of psychopathic evasion and of truly psychotic denial must wait for the full establishment of historical perspective in adolescence. Only he who comprehends the nature of irreversible historical truth can attempt to circumvent or to withdraw from it.

If fidelity, then, is a central concern of youth, Dora's case appears to be a classic example of fatefully perverted fidelity. A glance back at her history will remind us that her family had exposed her to multiple sexual *infidelity* and *perfidy*; while those concerned — father and mother, Mr. K. and Mrs. K. — tried to compensate for it all by making Dora their *confidante,* each burdening her (not without her perverse provocation, to be sure) with truths and half-truths which were clearly unmanageable for an adolescent. It is interesting to note that the middle-aged Dora, according to Felix Deutsch's (1957) report, was still obsessed with infidelities — her fathers, her husband's, and her son's; and she still turned everybody against everybody else. But lest it appear that I agree with those of Freud's social critics to whom Dora seemed only a case illustrating typical Viennese and bourgeois infidelity, I must add that other and equally malignant forms of fidelity-perversion can characterize late adolescent case histories in other societies and periods. The specific social and cultural conditions of her place and time, however, determined her milieu's confusing role demands. As a woman, Dora did not have a chance. A vital identity fragment in her young life was that of the *woman intellectual* which had been encouraged by her father's delight in her precocious intelligence, but discouraged by her brother's superior example as favored by the times. When Freud last saw her, she was absorbed in such evening education as was then accessible to a young woman of her class. The negative identity of the *déclassée* woman (so prominent in her era) she obviously tried to ward off with her sickness. Mr.

K., at the lake, had tried to seduce her with the selfsame pleading, namely, that his wife left him unsatisfied, which had previously been successfully used with a domestic (who also had confided in Dora). She may well have sought in Mrs. K., whom Freud recognized primarily as an object of Dora's ambivalent homosexual love, that *mentor* who helps the young to overcome unusable identifications with the parent of the same sex: Dora read books with Mrs. K. and took care of her children. But, alas, there was no escape from her mother's all-pervasive "housewife's psychosis." I would, in fact, conclude that it was this identity fragment which Dora blended with her own *patient identity*. For we know today that if patienthood is permitted to become a young patient's most meaningful circumstance, his identity formation may seize on it as a central and lasting theme. And, indeed, Felix Deutsch reports that the middle-aged Dora, "chatting in a flirtatious manner. . . . forgot about her sickness. . . . displaying great pride in having been written up as a famous case" (p. 162). To be a famous, if uncured, patient had become for this woman one lasting positive identity element; in this she kept faith with Freud.

This brings us, finally, to the therapeutic relationship itself. At the time, Freud was becoming aware of the singular power of transference and he pursued this in his evidence. Today we would go beyond it. We know that this most elemental tie is always complemented by the patient's relation to the analyst as a "new person." This has been most forthrightly formulated by Loewald (1960) in a paper which anticipates much of my argument about the role of reality-testing within the actuality of the therapeutic relationship. Young patients in particular appoint and invest the therapist with the role of mentor, although he may strenuously resist expressing clinically what he believes and stands for. His patient's demands do not obligate him, of course, to "play a part," as Freud so firmly refused to do. True mentorship, far from being a showy form of emotional sympathy, is always part of a discipline of outlook and method. No good therapist or teacher need protest "human" respect, personal friendship or parental love. But the psychotherapist must recognize what his role is in what we are here trying to circumscribe as the actuality of a young person.

We have used the question as to what Dora wanted from Freud to come closer to essential aspects of a young patient's actuality. To establish and share the historical truth may have been a need surpassing childish revenge; to call the older generation's infidelities by their name may have been a necessity before she might have been able to commit herself to her own kind of fidelity; to establish some of the co-ordinates of her own identity as a young woman of her class and time may have been a necessary prelude for the utilization of more insight into psychic reality; while the conviction of mutual trustworthiness may have been a condition for the toleration of the transference, whether she saw in her persistent doctor another seducer or another critical authority.

Beyond all this, however, we face here a problem of general therapeutic urgency. Some mixture of *"acting out"* and of *age-specific action* is to be expected of any patient of whatever age, and all patients reach a point in treatment when the recovering ego may need to test its untrained or long-inhibited wings of action. In the analysis of children, we honor this to some extent, but in some excessively prolonged treatments of patients of all ages, we sometimes miss that critical moment while remaining adamant in our pursuit of totally cleansing the patient of all "resistance to reality." Is it not possible that such habitual persistence obscures from us much of the ego's actuality, and this under the very conditions which would make observation possible on clinical homeground?

I have spoken earlier of fidelity and indicated that I consider it a pervading quality which matures during the stage of youth. On another occasion I have called this quality a basic virtue, and I would like to share with you briefly the kind of thinking which may motivate a psychoanalyst to use such a word.

"Virtue" has served different value systems for their various purposes. The Romans meant by it what made a man a man, and Christianity, what added spirit to men and soulfulness to women. It has lent itself to qualities of sternness and fortitude, of meekness, compassion, and self-denial. But it has always meant *pervading strength,* and *strength of efficacy* — not only shining, then, but "heating and retorting heat." I therefore put the word to our use to underscore the fact that only basic strength can guarantee potency to any value; that ego strength develops from an interplay of personal and social structure; and that it emerges, as do all human capacities, in stages of development and, that is to say, stages of changing actualities.

Fidelity, therefore, cannot be integrated before the stage of youth, and this for all manner of maturational reasons (physiological, cognitive, psychosexual, and psychosocial) which I shall not repeat here. For the same reasons, however, it must mature in youth lest the individual ego suffer an unduly aggravated crisis or lasting damage. Such a virtue, then, is built into the schedule of individual development as well as into the basic structure of any social order, for they have evolved together. It may be brash to imply by the use of the very word virtue that a tendency toward *optimum mutual activation* exists in the ego and in society. But the concept of reality, or so it seems to me, already implies an optimum correspondence between mind and the structure of the environment. A patient, we say, is impaired in his testing of reality. But, we may now add, he is also inactivated in actuality; and we can help him grasp reality only to the extent to which we, within our chosen method, become actual to him. This, at any rate, I want to offer for our consideration.

I cannot discuss here my nominations for the corresponding criteria of ego vitality at other stages of the life cycle. To become plausible, each would have to be anchored in the psychosexual, psychosocial, and cognitive components of its stage of emergence and each given a specific place in the hierarchy of all the stages. But I assume that the anchorage of the first of these criteria, hope, in the experiences of the oral stage is clinically apparent, and that the role of a lack or loss of hope in all the disturbances related to that stage is familiar to us. In passing, however, I would like to raise a question which is fundamental to the assumption of the stage by stage development of man's central strength. If the newborn infant brings with him to this life the pervasive quality that insures what is waiting for him (and relying *on* him) in the needs and drives of individual women, in the tradition of generations of mothers, and in universal institutions of motherhood, does it really make sense to speak of an infant's rudimentary ego as being "weak" and to liken it to what is weak in an isolated adult's neurotic dependence? Why burden infancy with the prototype of a weak ego and adulthood with the utopia of a strong one? It is here that our traditional concept of reality fails to account for the fundamental fact that the infant, while not yet able to grasp and to test what we call our reality, is competent in his actuality. True, all beginnings are characterized by vulnerability, but as long as vulnerability is accompanied by an active adaptation to protective conditions, it is not a state of weakness. Actuality at all stages rests on the complement of inner and outer structure. Ego strength at any level is relative to a number of necessities: previous stages must not have left a paralyzing deficit; the stage itself must unfold under conditions favorable to its potentials; and maturing capacities must evoke cooperative responses in the *Umwelt* backed up by conditions necessary for joint survival. This, then, is *developmental actuality*. It depends at every stage on active, selective principles being in charge, and enabled to be in charge by an *Umwelt* which grants each stage the conditions it needs.

I cannot conclude these developmental remarks without expressing the belief that considerations of this kind will clarify what clinical and genetic observation can contribute to a future ethics — ethics not based on the moral injunction of avoiding affront to the ideal but on the ethical capacity to provide strength in the actual.

References

Auden, W. (1960, June). Greatness finding itself. *Mid-Century, 13.*

Deutsch, F. (1957). A footnote to Freud's "Fragment of an analysis of a case of hysteria," *Psychoanalytic Quarterly, 26,* 159–167.

Freud, S. (1904). On the history of the psycho-analytic movement. *Standard Edition, 14,* 3–66. London: Hogarth Press.

Freud, S. (1905). Fragment of an analysis of a case of hysteria, *Standard Edition, 7,* 3–122. London: Hogarth Press.

Freud, S. (1917). A metapsychological supplement to the theory of dreams. *Standard edition, 14,* 217–235. London: Hogarth Press.

Inhelder, B. & Piaget, J. (1955). *The growth of logical thinking from childhood to adolescence.* New York: Basic Books, 1958.

Hartmann, H. (1947). On rational and irrational actions. *Psychoanalysis and the social sciences, Vol. 1.* New York: International Universities Press.

Hartman, H. (1956). Notes of the reality principle. *The Psychoanalytic Study of the Child,* Vol. 1. New York: International Universities Press.

Loewald, H. (1951). Ego and reality. *International Journal of Psycho-analysis, 32,* 10–18.

Loewald, H. (1960). On the therapeutic action of psycho-analysis. *International Journal of Psycho-analysis, 41,* 16–33.

Rapaport, D. (1953). Some metapsychological considerations concerning activity and passivity. In M. Gill (Ed.), *The collected papers of David Rapaport* (pp. 530–569). New York: Basic Books, 1967.

Part V

Adolescent Identity Formation and the Internal World

14

Personality Changes in Female Adolescents

KAREN HORNEY

In analyzing adult women with neurotic troubles or character disturbances one frequently finds these two conditions: (1) Although in all cases the determining conflicts have arisen in early childhood the first personality changes have taken place in adolescence. At this time they often have not been alarming to the environment and have not given the impression of being pathological manifestations endangering future development or requiring treatment, but have been regarded as transient troubles natural for this period of life, or even as desirable and promising signs. (2) The onset of these changes coincides approximately with the beginning of menstruation. This connection has not been apparent either because the patients have not been aware of the coincidence, or, even if they have observed a temporal coincidence, they have not attributed any significance to it, because they have not noticed or have "forgotten" the psychic implications menstruation has had for them. Personality changes, in contrast to neurotic symptoms, develop gradually and this also helps to disguise and obscure the real connection. Usually it is only after the patients have gained insight into the emotional effect that menstruation has had on them that they spontaneously see the connection. Tentatively, I am inclined to distinguish these four types of changes:

(1) girl becomes absorbed in sublimated activities — develops aversion against erotic sphere;
(2) girl becomes absorbed in erotic sphere (boy-crazy) — loses interest in and capacity for work;
(3) girl becomes emotionally "detached," acquires "don't care" attitude — cannot put energy into anything;
(4) girl develops homosexual tendencies.

This classification is incomplete and certainly does not cover the entire range of existing possibilities (for instance, the development of the prostitute and

From: *The American Journal of Orthopsychiatry, 5,* 1935, pp. 19–26. Copyright © American Psychological Association. Reprinted with permission.

criminal) but refers only to those changes which I had the opportunity of observing, directly or by inference, among the patients who incidentally came in for treatment. Besides, the division is arbitrary, as divisions of behavior types necessarily are, involving the fiction that clear-cut types always appear, while in reality all sorts of transitions and mixtures are frequently present.

The first group consists of girls who have shown a natural curiosity regarding questions of anatomical and functional differences in the two sexes and the riddles of propagation and who have felt attracted to boys and have liked to play with them. Around the time of puberty they suddenly become absorbed in mental problems, in religious, ethical, artistic, or scientific pursuits, while at the same time they lose interest in the erotic sphere. Usually the girl who undergoes this change does not come for treatment at this time because the family is pleased at her seriousness and her lack of flirtatious tendency. Difficulties are not apparent. They will appear only later in life, particularly after marriage. It is easy to overlook the pathological nature of this change for these two reasons: (1) to develop intense interest in some mental activity is expected during these years; (2) the girl herself is for the most part not conscious that she really has an aversion against sexuality. She only feels that she loses interest in boys and more or less dislikes dances, dates and flirtations and gradually withdraws from them.

The second group presents the reverse picture. Very gifted, promising girls at this time lose interest in everything except boys, cannot concentrate, and drop all mental activities a short time after undertaking them. They become completely absorbed in the erotic sphere. This transformation, just as the reverse one, is regarded as "natural" and defended as such with the similar rationalization that it is "normal" for a girl at this age to turn her attention to boys, dances and flirtations. Surely that is so, but what about the following trends? The girl compulsively falls in love with one boy after the other, without really caring for any of them, and after she is sure of having conquered them she either drops them or provokes them to drop her. She feels utterly unattractive in spite of evidence to the contrary and usually she shrinks from having actual sexual relations, rationalizing this attitude on the basis of social demands, although the real reason is that she is frigid, as is shown when she eventually hazards this step. She becomes depressed or apprehensive as soon as there is no man around to admire her. On the other hand, her attitude toward work is not, as the defense would imply, the "natural" outcome of the fact that her other interests have been forced into the background because of her preoccupation with boys, but the girl is in reality very ambitious and suffers intensely from a feeling of inability to accomplish anything.

The third type becomes inhibited in the spheres of both work and love. Again this is not necessarily apparent on the surface. Superficially observed, she may give the impression of being well adjusted. She has no difficulties in making social contacts, has girl and boy friends, is sophisticated, talks frankly about everything sexual, pretends to have no inhibition at all, and sometimes also enters into one or the other kind of sexual relations without becoming emotionally involved in any of them. She is detached, remote, an observer of herself and of others, a spectator of life. She may deceive herself about the existing aloofness, but at times, at least, she is keenly aware that there is no deep positive emotional tie to anyone or anything. Nothing matters much. There is a marked inconsistency between her vitality and gifts, and her lack of expansiveness. Usually she feels her life to be hollow and boring.

The fourth group is the easiest to characterize and best known. Here the girl turns away from boys altogether and develops crushes and intense friendships with girls, the sexual character of which may or may not be conscious. If she becomes aware of the sexual character of these tendencies such a girl may suffer from intense feelings of guilt as though she were a criminal. Her attitude toward work may vary. Ambitious and at times very capable, she often has difficulty in asserting herself or has "nervous breakdowns" in between times of efficiency.

These are four very different types, yet even a surface observation, if accurate only enough, shows that they nevertheless have trends in common: insecurity regarding their female self-confidence, conflictual or antagonistic attitude toward men and incapacity to "love" — whatever this term may mean. If they do not dodge the female role altogether they rebel against it or exaggerate it in a distorted manner. In all these cases much more guilt is connected with sexuality than they admit. "Not all are free who ridicule their chains."[1]

Psychoanalytic observation shows a still more striking similarity, so much so that for a while one is apt to forget about the differences shown in their attitudes toward life: All of them feel a general antagonism against everyone, men and women, yet there is a difference in their attitude to men and women. While the antagonism toward men varies in intensity and motivation and is elicited comparatively easily, toward women there is an absolutely destructive hostility and consequently it is deeply hidden. They may be vaguely aware of its existence but never realize its real scope, its violence and ruthlessness and its further implications.

All of them have a strongly defensive attitude toward masturbation. At most they may remember having masturbated as small children or they even deny its ever having played a role. They are quite honest about it on a conscious level. They really do not practice it or do so only in a very disguised form, and they feel no conscious desire to do so. As is shown later, powerful impulses of this sort exist but are completely dissociated from the rest of their personality and are concealed in this way because they are mixed up with enormous feelings of guilt and fear.

What accounts for the extreme hostility against women? Only part of it is understandable from their life history. Certain reproaches against the mother come up: lack of warmth, protection, understanding, preference for a brother, over-strict demands as to sexual purity. All of this is more or less supported by facts but they feel themselves that the hostility is out of proportion to the amount of existing suspicion, defiance and hatred.

The real implications become apparent, however, in their attitudes toward a woman analyst. Omitting technical details and omitting not only individual differences but also the differences in the defenses, characteristic for the types under discussion, the following picture gradually develops: They are convinced of being disliked by the analyst; they suspect that the analyst is really malevolent toward them, that she resents their being happy and successful, particularly that she condemns their sexual life, interferes with it or wants to do so.

While this is being disclosed as a reaction to feelings of guilt, and as an expression of fears, one gradually sees that they have some reason to be apprehensive because their actual behavior toward the analyst in the analytic situation is dictated by an enormous defiance and by the tendency to defeat the analyst no matter if they defeat their own ends at the same time.

The actual behavior, however, still is only an expression of the existing hostility on the reality level. Its entire scope is revealed only if one descends into the fantasy life as it appears in dreams and daydreams. Here the hostility is lived out in the most cruel, archaic forms.

These crude, primitive impulses, lived out in fantasies, allow an understanding of the depth of the guilt feelings toward the mother and mother images. Furthermore they eventually allow an understanding of why masturbation has been entirely repressed and is still, at the present time, tinged with horror. The fantasies have accompanied masturbation and therefore have aroused guilt feelings about it. Guilt feelings, in other words, have not concerned the physical process of masturbation but the fantasies. Yet only the physical process and the desire for it could be repressed. The fantasies have kept on living in the depths and, having been repressed at an early age, have kept their infantile character. The individual, though not aware of their existence, keeps on responding with guilt feelings.

Yet the physical part of masturbation is not unimportant either. Intense fears have issued from it, the essence of which is the fear of being damaged, of being injured beyond repair. The content of this fear has not been conscious but it has found numerous disguised expressions in all sorts of hypochondriac fears concerning all organs from the brain down to the feet — fears that something is wrong with them as women — fears that they will never be able to marry and have children — and finally, common to all cases, fears of being unattractive. Though these fears go back directly to the physical masturbation, they, too, are understandable only from the psychic implications of masturbation.

The fear really implies: "Because I have cruel, destructive fantasies toward my mother and other women I ought to be afraid that they want to destroy me in the same way. 'An eye for an eye and a tooth for a tooth'."

The very same fear of retaliation is responsible for their not feeling at ease with the analyst. In spite of the consciously existing confidence in her fairness and dependability, they cannot help feeling deeply concerned that the sword hanging over them is bound to fall. They cannot help feeling that the analyst, maliciously and intentionally, wants to torment them. They have to choose a narrow path between the danger of displeasing her and the fear of revealing their hostile impulses.

Since they are constantly in fear of a fatal attack it is easy enough to understand why they feel the vital necessity to defend themselves. And they do it by being evasive and trying to defeat the analyst. Their hostility, therefore, in an upper layer, has the connotation of defense. Similarly most of their hatred toward the mother has the same connotation of feeling guilty in reference to her and of warding off the fear connected with this guilt by turning against her.

When this has been worked through, the primary sources of the antagonism toward the mother are emotionally accessible. Their traces have been visible from the beginning in this fact: that with the exception of Group 2, who goes in for competition with other girls though with an enormous apprehensiveness, all of them carefully avoid competition with other girls. Wherever another woman is in the field, they retreat immediately. Being convinced of their own lack of attractiveness they feel inferior to any other girls who are around. In this fight, they may be observed to carry out with the analyst the same tendencies to avoid a competitive appearance. The actually existing competitive struggle is hidden behind their feeling hopelessly inferior to her. Even if eventually they cannot but admit their competitive intentions, they do so only with reference to intelligence and capability in work, while they shun comparisons which would indicate competition on the female level. For instance, they consistently repress disparaging thoughts about the analyst's appearance and dress and are in deadly embarrassment if thoughts of this kind come to the surface.

Competition has to be avoided because there has been a particularly strong rivalry with the mother or with an older sister in childhood. Usually one or the other of the following factors has greatly intensified the natural competition of the daughter with the mother or an older sister: being prematurely aroused sexually and thereby becoming prematurely sex conscious; early intimidations which prevented them from feeling self-confident; marital conflicts between the parents, which forced them to side with one or the other parent; open or disguised rejection on the part of the mother; demonstrations of an over-affectionate attitude on the part of the father to the little girl, which may range from singling her out with attentions to overt sexual approaches. Schematically summarizing the facts, we find that this vicious circle has been set up: jealousy and rivalry toward mother or sister — hostile impulses lived out in fantasies — guilt and fear of being attacked and punished — defensive hostility — reinforced fear and guilt.

The guilt and fear from these sources is, as I said, most firmly anchored in the masturbatory fantasies. They do not, however, remain restricted to these fantasies but spread in a major or minor degree to all sexual desires and sexual relations. They are carried over to sexual relations with men and surround them with a guilty and apprehensive atmosphere. They are responsible, to a great extent, for the fact that relations with men remain unsatisfactory.

There are other reasons, too, accounting for this result which have to do more directly with their attitude toward men themselves. I mention them only briefly because they have little bearing on the points I want to stress in this paper. They may have an old resentment against men, issuing from old disappointments and resulting in a secret desire for revenge. Moreover on the basis of feeling unlikable they anticipate rejection from men and react antagonistically toward them. Insofar as they have turned away from their female role, because of its being too conflictual, they often develop masculine strivings and carry over their competitive tendencies into their relations with men; competing now with men in masculine fields instead of with women. If this masculine role appeals to them as being highly desirable, they may develop strong envy toward men with the tendency to disparage their faculties.

What happens when a girl of about this structure enters puberty? At the time of puberty there is an increase of libidinal tension; sexual desires become more demanding and necessarily encounter the barrier of guilt and fear reactions. These are reinforced by the possibility of actual sexual experiences. The onset of menstruation at this time, for the girl who has a fear of being damaged by masturbation, emotionally means a definite proof that this damage has in fact occurred. Intellectual knowledge about menstruation does not make any difference, because the understanding is on a superficial level and the fears are deep and so they do not reach each other. The situation is getting acute. Desires and temptations are strong, and fears are strong.

It seems that we cannot long bear to live under the stress of conscious anxiety; "I would rather die than have a real attack of anxiety," patients say. Therefore, in situations like these, vital necessity compels us to search for means of protection; i.e., we try automatically to change our attitude toward life in such a way that we either avoid anxiety or establish safeguards against it.

Regarding the basic conflicts present in all of the four types under discussion, they represent various ways of warding off anxiety. The fact that various ways are chosen accounts for the differences in the types. They develop opposite characteristics and opposite trends although they have the common aim of warding off the same sort of anxiety. The girl in Group 1 protects herself against fears by avoiding competition with women altogether and dodging the female role in a rather complete way. Her competitive urge becomes uprooted from its original soil and transplanted to some mental field. Competing for having the best character, the highest ideals, or for being the best student is so far removed from the competition for a man that her fears also are greatly attenuated. Her striving for perfection, at the same time helps her to overcome guilt feelings.

The solution, being quite radical, has great temporary advantages. For years she may feel quite content. The reverse side only appears if eventually she comes in contact with men, particularly if she marries. One may then observe that her contentment and self-assurance break down rather suddenly and the contented, gay, capable, independent girl changes into a discontented woman greatly troubled with inferiority feelings, easily depressed and refraining from taking an active share in the responsibilities of marriage. She is frigid sexually, and, instead of a loving attitude toward her husband, a competitive attitude toward him prevails.

The girl in Group 2 does not resign her competitive attitude toward other women. Her wide-awake protest against other females drives her to beat them whenever an opportunity arises, with the result that she has, in contrast to the girl of Group 1, a rather free-floating anxiety. Her way of warding off this anxiety is by clinging to men. While the first-mentioned girls retreat from the battlefield, these latter seek allies. Their insatiable thirst for the admiration of men is no indication whatever of their being constitutionally in greater need of sexual gratification. In fact, they, too, prove to be frigid if they enter into actual sexual relations. The fact that men have for them the function of serving as a reassurance becomes apparent as soon as they fail to have one or several boy friends: their anxiety then comes near the surface and they feel desolate, insecure and lost. Winning the admiration of men also serves as a reassurance for them in reference to their fear of not being "normal," which as I have indicated is an outcome of the fear of being damaged by masturbation. There is far too much guilt and fear connected with sexuality to allow them to have a satisfactory relation with men. Therefore only the ever-renewed conquest of men may serve the purpose of reassurance.[2]

The fourth group, the potential homosexuals, try to solve the problem by overcompensation for their destructive hostility toward women. "I don't hate you, I love you." One might describe the change as a complete, blind denial of the hatred. How far they succeed with it depends on individual factors. Their dreams usually show an extreme degree of violence and cruelty toward the girl to whom they feel consciously attracted. A failure in their relations with girls throws them into spasms of despair and often brings them near to suicide, which indicates a turning of the aggression against themselves.

Like Group 1, they dodge their own female role completely with the one difference that they more definitely develop the fiction of being a man. On a non-sexual level their relation to men often is devoid of conflicts. Furthermore while Group 1 resigns sexuality altogether these girls resign their heterosexual interests only.

The solution toward which Group 3 is driven is fundamentally different from the others. While all the others aim at reassurance by emotionally clinging to something: to accomplishment, to men, to women, their main way is that of stunting their emotional life and thereby diminishing their fears. "Don't become emotionally involved, then you wont get hurt." This principle of detachment is perhaps the most effective, lasting protection against anxiety, but the price paid for it seems to be very high too, in so far as it usually means attenuation of vitality and spontaneity and a considerable deterioration in the amount of available energy.

No one familiar with the intricate complexity of psychic dynamics which leads to a *seemingly* simple result will mistake these statements about the four types of personality changes for a complete revelation of their dynamics. The intention was not to give an "explanation" of the phenomenon of homosexuality or of detachments, for instance, but to regard them from one point of view only, as representing different solutions or pseudo-solutions for similar underlying conflicts. Which solution is chosen does not depend on the free volition of the girls, as the term "chosen" might imply, but is strictly determined by the concatenation of events in childhood and the girls' reactions to them. The effect of circumstances may be so compelling that only one solution is possible. Then one will encounter the type in its pure, clearly delineated form. Others are driven by their experiences during or after adolescence to abandon one way and to try another. The girl who is a female Don-Juan type for a period, for instance, may develop ascetic tendencies later on. Furthermore one may find different attempts at solution tried simultaneously, as for instance the boy-crazy girl may show trends of detachment, though never in the pronounced way of Group 3. Or there may be imperceptible transitions between Group 1 and 4. The changes in the picture and the mixture of typical trends do not offer any particular difficulty to our understanding, provided we have understood the basic function of the various attitudes as presented in the clear-cut types.

Still a few remarks about prophylaxis and treatment: It is evident I hope, even from this rough outline, that any prophylactic effort made at puberty, such as a sensible enlightenment about menstruation comes too late. Enlightenment is received on the intellectual level and does not reach the deeply barricaded infantile fears. The prophylaxis can only be effective if it starts from the first days of life. I think one may be justified in formulating its aim in this way: to educate children in courage and endurance instead of filling them with fears. All such general formulae however may be more misleading than helpful because their value depends entirely on the special and exact implications one derives from them, which should be discussed in detail.

Concerning treatment: Difficulties of minor nature may be cured by favorable life circumstances. I doubt whether clear-cut personality changes of this kind are accessible to any psychotherapy working with a less delicate instrument than psychoanalysis, for, in contrast to any single neurotic symptom, these disturbances indicate an insecure foundation in the whole personality. We must not forget however that, even so, life may be the better therapist.

Notes

1. "Es sind nicht alle frei die ihrer Ketten spotten," (Schiller).
2. A more exact description of the mechanisms at work in this type is given in ... [Horney, 1934].

Reference

Horney, K. (1934). The overvaluation of love: A study of a common present-day feminine type. *Psychoanalytic Quarterly, 3*, 605–638.

15
On Adolescence

JEANNE LAMPL-DE GROOT

Adolescence is often regarded as a "stepchild" in psychoanalysis, in a theoretical as well as in a practical sense. A number of analysts consider the treatment of adolescent boys and girls to be very difficult, sometimes even impossible, though in some cases good results have been achieved, especially with inhibited, depressive, and compulsive-neurotic patients.

Many authors stress that our theoretical knowledge of adolescence is incomplete. I shall not review the literature in detail, but refer to the surveys of this subject by Leo Spiegel in 1951 and by Anna Freud in 1958.

Out of the many problems of adolescence, my paper will focus on two points: (1) a practical experience; and (2) some theoretical considerations, especially in connection with the formation of superego and ego ideal.

I

Anna Freud has reminded us of the fact that "our knowledge of the mental processes of infancy has been derived from reconstructions in the analyses of adults and was merely confirmed and enlarged later on by analyses or observations carried out in childhood" (1958, p. 259n). It is Anna Freud's opinion that in the treatment of adult cases one seldom succeeds in reviving their adolescent experiences in full force.

I think most authors will agree with this statement, and I have done so myself. However, a number of years ago two adult patients came to me for analytic treatment, a man and a woman, both in their early thirties, in whose analyses a wealth of adolescent experiences, real events as well as fantasies and impulses, came to the fore with remarkable liveliness and were accompanied by strong emotions and impulses. I hasten to add that this re-experiencing only emerged in the later phases of the analyses. In the beginning of treatment the

From: *The Psychoanalytic Study of the Child, 15,* 1960, 95–103. New York: International Universities Press. Copyright © International Universities Press. Reprinted with permission.

adolescent material was brought forward merely as an account of the patient's life history in the way described by Anna Freud. The most interesting point was that the reliving of affects connected with this material did not become possible until the patient's childhood had been uncovered and reconstructed. Confronted with these observations, I recalled a statement which Freud made to me some thirty years ago. Freud told me about a young woman who had cooperated well in her analysis and whose childhood development had been fairly well reconstructed — however without a therapeutic result. Most of the patient's symptoms had persisted until she suddenly and vividly recollected a traumatic experience that had occurred in her fifteenth year of life. After this traumatic situation and all the emotions involved had been worked through, the patient was cured.

My own observations led me to review a number of other cases, and I gained the impression that in some of them the failure or incompleteness of success might have been due to the lack of revival of the adolescent experiences. Of course, I now had to ask myself what causes might have been responsible for the fact that in these cases childhood development could be reconstructed without difficulty and re-experienced with full emotional force, whereas the adolescent period remained deprived of a full affective conviction.

From the direct study of adolescent cases we are all familiar with the charged atmosphere in which the adolescent lives, with the intensity and depth of his feelings, the sudden and unexpected mood swings, the strength of his impulses, and the force of anxiety and despair. However, are we really entitled to assume that in small children feelings, impulses, demands, unforeseen swings from complete happiness toward deepest sorrow and desperation are less intense than similar phenomena in adolescence?

There is indeed a difference in the demands of the instinctual drives in childhood and in adolescence, because infantile sexuality is different from genitality, which has to become the leading factor in the adolescent and adult love life.

I have the impression, however, that it is not merely the intensity of feelings, impulses, and mood swings, but other factors which are more responsible for the difficulties of reviving the adolescent mental processes. These factors seem to lie in ego and superego development.

The little child's ego, undeveloped as it is, has to rely upon the auxiliary ego borrowed from the mother in order to master outer and inner conflicts. The superego is not yet established as an independent mental agency in infancy. Norms and restrictions are imposed upon the child by the parents. Only in the oedipal phase a structuration of the personality takes place. In latency the child develops into a more or less individual personality, though he is still dependent upon the parents. A wealth of ego capacities is established and mature during this period. In the sphere which is relatively free from conflict, intelligence, knowledge, special talents, and abilities are developed, whereas in the conflictual sphere, adaptations, reaction formations, and defense mechanisms gradually become character traits. The superego as an inner institution supervises the latency child's behavior to a large extent.

This brief outline of a child's development is very sketchy and incomplete, but it may suffice as a prelude to our considerations about adolescence.

When in puberty the instinctual drives make their new and intensified demands upon the youngster, they meet with a different personality than they did in childhood. The adolescent ego has many more ways and means of coping with the drives; in a certain sense, we could call this ego stronger. However, on the other hand, it lacks the support of the parents' auxiliary ego because the adolescent turns away from the parents. The loosening of the ties with the parents is a difficult and protracted process, often accompanied by genuine mourning, as Root (1957) and Anna Freud (1958) have pointed out. In this respect the adolescent ego presents itself as much weaker than the child's ego. A similar process is going on in the superego. On the one hand, the adolescent superego is now established as an inner conscience; on the other hand it is shaken in its foundation by the very process of turning away from the parents and the parental norms and morals. The adolescent has to rely upon his own superego. The adult, looking back upon his life history, feels more responsible for his adolescent than for his infantile behavior; he feels more guilty and more ashamed about his adolescent conflicts, disharmonies, and oddities. As he usually remembers the factual events of adolescence, he tries to escape the revival of the accompanying guilt- and shame-burdened emotions, either by suppressing and denying every emotion of that period or by retreating to infantile experiences.

This is precisely what we often observe in analytic treatment. The patient brings us a wealth of infantile material, more and more, in different forms and associations, even when the childhood history has already been fairly well reconstructed and re-experienced. He clings tenaciously to infantile material; yet when we look at this material closely we realize that adolescent features have entered into the picture. The patient has used the infantile material in order to ward off adolescent experiences. The analyst must then analyze the defensive character of, and the underlying anxiety in regard to, this material and confront the patient with his adolescent feelings of shame, guilt, hurt pride, etc. In a number of cases the result will be a real revival of the patient's adolescence in full force.

In trying to accomplish this task we meet with difficulties, not exclusively due to the patient's reluctance to face his own adolescent problems, his unbalanced behavior, his extreme feelings, his extravagant emotions, and his oddities. We also have to cope with the analyst's reactions to it. The analyst is prepared to encounter the patient's acting out in the transference. When the patient transfers impulses upon the analyst from his childhood period and in an infantile form, it is much easier for the latter to keep to his attitude of friendly understanding and neutrality. The adolescent has made use of all of his intelligence, capacities, and special gifts to ward off his intolerable impulses, his disappointments, and his conflicts. This is especially true in connection with his hostility toward parents and toward adults in general. Hence, in encouraging an adult patient to relive his adolescent experiences, the analyst must cope with a refined form of the patient's aggression.

One can smile at a little child's direct form of aggressive behavior, but an adolescent's aggression is clothed in a much more irritating, tormenting, and sometimes nearly intolerable shape. It may happen that the analyst, being a human creature himself, is (unconsciously) inclined to follow the patient in his flight toward infancy in order to escape the patient's refined criticisms, reproaches, and hostile demands. In every adult, traits not only from the little child but also from the adolescent persist. This is especially true for our patients. They tend to excuse themselves for their accusations and tormenting attacks in taking for granted that the analyst is an omnipotent and therefore invulnerable person. The interplay between the patient's desire to relive his adolescent emotions and conflicts and the analyst's unconscious shyness to bear the adolescent forms of aggression might be one of the causes of the difficulties we encounter in analyzing and working through an adult patient's adolescence.

II

I now come to my second point: some theoretical considerations, which, I hope, will contribute to our understanding of the practical difficulties just mentioned as well as of adolescent psychic life in general. In the scope of this presentation I can only throw light upon a few points. My assumptions are based partly on material gained in the treatment of adolescents, mainly, however, on reconstruction of adolescent experiences in adult cases.

A youngster's ego can react in an infinite variety of ways to the newly flourishing demands of his instinctual drives and to the newly arising social demands which are so different from those made upon the little child. The adolescent has on the one hand the ardent wish to be grown up because he usually imagines adults to be free, independent, and self-supporting, and he tries to use all his faculties in order to equal or even to better them. On the other hand, however, he wants to remain a little child in order not to have to relinquish his infantile ties with the parental objects. It is very well known how difficult a task this is. Having lost a beloved person or even having renounced the love of a still existing object is followed by a certain amount of "work of mourning" ("Trauerarbeit"; see Anna Freud, 1958). Whether the outcome of the mourning process will be a relatively normal or a pathological one depends on a wealth of factors, among them upon the amount of aggression originally directed toward the parents. We know that the little child holds his parents responsible for his distress and losses, and he responds to all sorts of pain with hatred and death wishes toward his parents. When in puberty the infantile object relationships are revived, the adolescent begins to react in a similar way. The more intense his archaic hostility was, the more difficulties he will have in dealing with his death wishes. The mourning processes are colored by the aggression turned inward. The result may be a depressive neurotic disorder, psychotic reactions, acting out or antisocial behavior, or a combination of these various disturbances. Many authors have described several outcomes in clinical and theoretical papers.

I shall now turn to another problem of adolescence which is very different from childhood processes and nevertheless very closely dependent upon them. I mean the superego problems. I have already mentioned that in adolescence the superego has become an inner agency, whereas in early childhood behavior was directed by the parents' demands, prohibitions, and morals. The little child cooperates with them mainly in order to avoid loss of love or punishment. Only gradually does he internalize the parental norms, which subsequently become the content of the superego. Now in adolescence he must give up his old incestuous ties to the parents — a process partly equivalent to losing the love object. But in addition he must also give up a fundamental part of his superego content — that part of the restrictions, norms, and ideals which, though internalized, are still closely linked to the incestuous object. The very fact that these superego contents are internalized implies that the adolescent must give up something that is essentially a part of his self. To turn away from a love object is a hard and painful process; to disengage oneself from a part of one's own personality is still more difficult to achieve.

In order to examine these events more closely I propose once more to distinguish between the superego in a narrower sense as the restricting and prohibiting instance and the ego ideal as comprising norms, ethics, ideals. I have made this distinction in previous papers and it has, in my opinion, some advantages. The compliance with parental restrictions and prohibitions requires renunciation of direct pleasure, but this compliance is rewarded with love and approval from the side of the parents. The formation of ideals, however, has an additional function and has already been on the way long before parental restrictions have become internal demands. The little child idealizes the parents and conceives of them as perfect, omnipotent creatures. He clings tenaciously to these ideas because he feels himself so extremely powerless. The introjection of the almighty and faultless parental images is a compensation for the feeling of helplessness; it begins in very early childhood and is a narcissistic satisfaction *par excellence*. These introjected images give rise to fantasies of grandeur and omnipotence, which in the magic phase of development are among the fundamentals of the child's self-esteem and self-maintenance. It is well known that part of the feelings of grandeur continue to exist, though unconsciously, throughout life.

The adolescent must bear not only the pain of losing love objects, of coping with the attending mourning, and of revising old patterns of restriction and prohibition. In addition to all these hard tasks, he must endure the narcissistic injuries caused by his self-esteem being shaken in its fundamentals and therefore more or less lost. We know too well that a certain amount of narcissistic cathexis of the personality is indispensable for healthy development. When the basis of the ideal formation has gone to pieces, the youngster is utterly helpless. I hasten to add that the loss of love is of course partly felt as a narcissistic injury as well. The finding of a new love object raises the person's self-esteem, too. However, it seems to make a considerable difference when an essential part of the ego (ego ideal) is damaged or lost and has to be newly built up. New love objects are relatively easily found in adolescence in teachers, leaders, companions, etc. New ideals that compensate for the essential helplessness of human beings are more difficult to acquire (at least in our civilization). The youngster very well knows, and feels, that adults are not omnipotent but vulnerable creatures. We find a confirmation of this assumption in studying those adolescents who do not respond to offers of love and guidance from a new object (relative, teacher, therapist, companion, etc.). These youngsters could not overcome the depth of their inner narcissistic injuries; consequently, they are indifferent to supplies of love from the outer world. It is possible that a number of strange reactions, unexpected attitudes, and unpredictable mood swings are due to this basic disturbance in the economy of narcissistic libido and the ego's failure to restore it. Moreover, it is just the narcissistic injuries that are pre-eminently apt to give rise to aggression, and this hostility in turn diminishes a person's susceptibility to another person's loving assistance and to the offer of new ideals and norms.

In the transference during treatment we can observe that a patient's deep and refined hostility, severe criticisms of the analyst, reproaches that the analyst is impotent and worthless go side by side with an unconscious, archaic conviction of the analyst's omnipotence. The ideal image of almighty parents and analyst not only is indispensable for the youngster's maintenance of narcissistic cathexis, but is secondarily used to diminish the guilt feelings aroused by precisely this same hostile and aggressive behavior. It is as if the youngster says to himself: "Parents and analysts are omnipotent, consequently they are invulnerable; so I can scold, torment, and act out every aggression without having to feel guilty or reproach myself."

It would be tempting to illustrate these assumptions with detailed analytic material. However, in this paper, I merely wanted to emphasize the importance of the problems around the ego ideal in adolescence. The adolescent's clinging to the very archaic, idealized parental images makes it so difficult for him to cope with the narcissistic injuries occasioned by the necessity of having to give them up and finding new ideals in a more reality-adapted form. Furthermore, they need to hold on to this idealized picture because it also serves as a defense against guilt and shame engendered by the intense hostility.

When many analysts agree that adolescent patients are often not suitable for analytic treatment, we must, in our attempts to understand adolescent psychology, rely mainly on observations and reconstructions of adolescence in adult cases. But even these reconstructions, as has been pointed out, are extremely difficult to achieve. This paper has endeavored to investigate some of the obstacles in the way of such reconstruction and to indicate means of overcoming them.

I believe that we might be successful in reviving adolescence in a number of cases if we make an effort to overcome our own resistance against the patient's adolescent forms of aggression, if we focus our and the patient's attention upon his hidden ideals and fantasies of omnipotence attributed to his parents and later on internalized, and if we support the patient in enduring his narcissistic hurts and in giving up the defensive character of his archaic ideal. I believe that this effort is worth while.

References

Freud, A. (1958). Adolescence. *The Psychoanalytic Study of the Child, 13,* 255–278.

Root, N. N. (1957). A neurosis in adolescence. *The Psychoanalytic Study of the Child, 12,* 320–334.

Spiegel, L. A. (1951). A review of contributions to a psychoanalytic theory of adolescence: individual aspects. *The Psychoanalytic Study of the Child, 6,* 375–393.

16
Son and Father

PETER BLOS, SR.

As the title of this presentation indicates, I shall limit myself to a narrowly confined aspect of object relations. It is a topic that defies precise circumscription partially due to its vast ramifications and to its still contentious and unsettled place in psychoanalytic theory. The fact that my chosen subject is one of momentous importance in human life requires no persuasion nor testimony. In choosing it I emphasize a current trend in clinical and theoretical psychoanalysis. I shall begin with a brief overview of recent developments as well as the historical ones in the orbit of son and father.

The discovery of the Oedipus complex, its fateful role in life and, particularly, in neurosogenesis has led to an ever-deepening investigation of its complexity. Originally, gender polarity represented a core configuration in oedipal conflict formation; this fact is still discernible today in oedipal terminology when we speak of the positive and the negative Oedipus complex. For brevity's sake I shall refer in this text simply to the "positive complex" or the "negative complex." As far as I propose modifications of their classical definitions, I trust that my presentation as a whole will convey the qualifications in psychoanalytic theory I intend to suggest.

The case of Dora permits us to contrast early and contemporary views of oedipal dynamics. Dora illustrates the pathogenic valence that Freud (1905) attributed to the positive complex and its influence on her life, even though he gave ample evidence of his suspicion or, indeed, his conviction that the negative complex was at the root of her illness. This he stated clearly in the case study itself (pp. 60–61) and in a letter to Fliess (October 14, 1900), even though it played a minor role in the analytic work with the girl — at least, as far as we can glean from the clinical report. The degree as well as the kind of pathogenic valence the clinician assigns to preoedipality and to one or the other of the two complexes in their dynamic interplay, often remain a matter of emphasis

From: *Journal of the American Psychoanalytic Association, 32,* 1984, pp. 301–324. Copyright © American Psychoanalytic Association. Reprinted with permission.

or preconception. In contrast to the treatment of Dora, the pathogenicity of preoedipal object relations is taken for granted in almost any case today, and afforded a prominent place not only in the evolutionary history of a given neurosis, but explicitly and increasingly in the analytic work itself

The polarity of gender — son–mother, daughter–father — has dominated the concept of the oedipal constellation since its inception and has weighed heavily in the etiologic formulation of the neurotic conflict. However, clinical observations have attributed an increasingly persuasive significance to isogender early object relations. Indeed, both constellations, namely those of isogender and allogender partnership, have received slowly, at times reluctantly, the recognition of equal significance in the theoretical formulations of normal and pathological development. This historical reference might sound groundless or overstated at its first hearing, yet we cannot deny that the positive complex and its resolution have received far more attention in the analytic literature than the natural history as well as the resolution of the negative complex ever has.

It was this extreme sparseness of investigations in male isogender object relations from the earliest stages of development onward that prompted me to inquire into these neglected issues. My analytic work had convinced me that early isogender experiences not only dominate and shape the son–father relationship at infancy, but influence critically the boy's creation of his self and object world for a lifetime. This complexity of the son–father relationship has always been known, even if never sufficiently illuminated. Freud has described the contrasting roles played by the father in the son's life.

The Oedipal father is by definition the restraining and punishing father under whose threat of retaliation the little boy abandons his competitive strivings, as well as his patricidal and incestuous animus. There has never been any doubt that this father picture is incomplete and misleading because we know that the typical father also acknowledges and elicits his little son's self-assertion; being emulated by the son fills the father with pride and joy as does the junior toddler's phallic, narcissistic, and exhibitionistic exuberance.

A well-known comment by Freud will remind us that we revisit old and familiar territory: "As regards the prehistory of the Oedipus complex.... We know that that period includes an identification of an affectionate sort with the boy's father...." (Freud, 1925, p. 250). This early experience of being protected by the father and caringly loved by him becomes internalized as a lifelong sense of safety in a Boschian world of horrors and dangers. It seems to me that too exclusive a contribution to the sense of bodily integrity has been attributed to the early mother. We have ample occasion to observe in the analysis of adult men the enduring influence of this father imago, especially when it remains unaltered by reality. The "overidealization of the analyst and analysis" reflects the father's role in the child's life during the first two years (Greenacre, 1966). The resistance aroused whenever the analytic work threatens to deprive the patient of this father-illusion confirms the life-sustaining influence of the early child–father relationship. The patient will not let go of it easily:"...the terrifying impression of helplessness in childhood aroused the need for protection — for protection through love — which was provided by the father" (Freud, 1927, p. 30). The little boy seeks by active and persistent solicitation the father's approval, recognition and confirmation, thus establishing a libidinal bond of a profound and lasting kind. Some questions force themselves upon us: Where do the origins of those affections lie? At which stage of object relations do they flourish? Under what conditions do these hallmark emotions of the negative complex seemingly vanish or what transformations do they undergo? One receives the impression from the literature that the negative complex declines by the ascendancy and subsequent resolution of the positive complex or, in other words, that the fully developed triadic configuration effects by its sheer ascension the resolution or transformation of the negative complex. Of course, every analyst knows that this is not the case. Yet, until recently, very little attention has been paid to the process or the timing of this particular kind of isogender attachment resolution. We are presently justified to say that the qualitative and pathogenic specificity of this closeness derives from an unaltered perpetuity in the son–father relationship, the beginnings of which are to be found in a quasimaternal bonding by substitution.

It is a well-known historical fact that with the establishment and growth of child analysis the frontiers of psychoanalytic practice and, consequently, of theory-building were pushed out farther and deeper into the realms of infancy as well as adolescence, namely, into those two epochs of life during which psychic structure formation, initiated by physical maturation, proceeds on a grand scale. Detailed and direct child observation provided a wealth of new and subtle details with regard to psychic differentiation and developmental moves, thus amending and altering in precision and complexity our previous knowledge of psychic structure formation as derived from reconstruction. These exploratory penetrations into the developmental terrains of both infancy and adolescence delivered findings that enriched the general body of psychoanalysis and, consequently, widened the scope of our science. Instead of relying largely on the reconstruction of infantile trauma and object relations, of internalization processes, of psychosexual and ego development from the analysis of adults, it became possible to observe them in their germinal states and follow their growth. Observing first-hand what had previously been largely inferred, enhanced our knowledge of a more exact schedule — comprising sequences and timing — of infantile and adolescent development.

As a first consequence of psychoanalytic infant research, the preoedipal mother moved prominently to center-stage, eclipsing oedipality to a considerable degree in the etiological determination of mental disturbances as they became manifest later in life. By virtue of distinguishing more clearly the preoedipal determinants in pathogenicity generally, the limits and the criteria of analyzability became more sharply delineated. What I want to call attention to at this point is the importance of the preoedipal father in the life of the male child. Here we find ourselves on territory not yet fully charted, but with sufficiently explored contours of the terrain to know in which directions to advance our search. The findings just alluded to not only have changed our knowledge of timing as to paternal recognition by the infant, but have drawn a sharper outline of the earliest stages of parental imitation, internalization, and identification. The dating of core gender identity to an earlier period relegates many classical psychoanalytic tenets of psychosexual development to the archives of our science.

I have devoted the major portion of my professional life to the investigation of the adolescent process. Adolescence thus became the focus of my clinical observations from which my theoretical constructs radiated backwards and forwards into the proto-adolescent and the meta-adolescent stages of the life cycle. I refer here to my adolescent research because the theme of this paper is launched from these observations and their theoretical inferences. Edging my way into the substance of this presentation, I state now a proposition which I advanced some years ago. I share the well-established opinion that the male child arrives at a resolution of the positive complex prior to his entry into latency, but beyond that, I have postulated that his negative complex, having its origin in the dyadic stage of object relations, survives in a repressed, more or less unaltered, state until adolescence (Blos, 1974). Developmentally speaking, the necessity arises to differentiate between a dyadic and a triadic positive and negative complex.

Whatever course the individual resolution of the positive complex will take, its achievement is always reflected in the formation of a new structure, the superego. Dual parental preoedipal determinants are always recognizable in the final superego structure. What appears, however, to acquire prominence in the male superego is the dominant voice of the father principle which is, at its dyadic origin, not yet instinctually conflicted, but belongs to a precompetitive, idealizing stage of the "good father." Both father and mother complex operate at this level more or less reactively and compensatorily rather than in an antagonistic libidinal entanglement. The prototypical dyadic split into pleasure and unpleasure parental figures precludes by its very nature the formation of an internal conflict. This preconflictual state is further upheld by the attribution of pain to the external world, the "not-me" realm of perception and the attribution of pleasure to the "me" experience, inclusive of the pleasure object; within this dawning affective awareness lies the emergence of the self. Precursors of this process are apparent from early infancy on; they become organized and stabilized in psychic structure with the decline of the oedipal phase. All this is well established psychoanalytic knowledge. It is also well known that positive and negative components of the complex are inseparably intertwined but nevertheless distinguishable by the preponderance or dominance of one or the other in their constant ebb and flow. Alongside these differentiating processes in the male child — so I submit — the negative complex is not sub-jected to as radical a transformation during prelatency as the positive one is. In other words, its definitive transformation into psychic structure is delayed until adolescence.

With the advent of sexual maturation arrives the biological imperative for definitive and irreversible sexual identity; as a coefficient of this impera-tive we can isolate, observe, and define adjunct identities of a social, cogni-tive, and self-representational nature. They form in their synergic evolution the post-latency personality. This process of psychic restructuring affects every facet of the adolescent's life and promotes forcefully the terminal resolution of the negative complex. What had appeared to me earlier in my work as the resuscitation of the positive complex which, by deflection, transformation, and displacement turns in an apparently predetermined fashion to extra-familial heterosexual object-finding, gradually acquired in my clinical judgment the character of a largely defensive operation. Here I have in mind the fact that the boy's dyadic father relationship which fluctuated between submission, self-as-sertion, and sharing the father's grandeur is drawn into the sexual realm with the advent of puberty. The regressive pull is counteracted by sexual gender assertion. I came to see ever so clearly that this defense springs into action in the wake of a resurgence of the boy's negative complex which reaches, at puberty, the apex of its conflictuality.

The defensive state I speak of is transitory in nature and declines with the definitive resolution of the negative complex at the closure of adolescence. I am fully aware that this exposition does not tell the whole story, but I highlight here intentionally what appears to me a neglected stage in the ontogeny of mature male object relations and of the mature self. This particular compre-hension of male sexuality at adolescence gained further clarity and plausibility from the analytic observation that inordinate, compulsive, heterosexual activ-ity or, conversely, anxiety arousal due to heterosexual inaction or passivity, subsided markedly with the resolution of the negative complex. I noticed that the decline of this conflict introduces a kind of heterosexual attachment behav-ior which possesses a different quality; to this we refer as a mature (or more mature) love relationship in which the defensive nature of the attachment has dropped away and recognition as well as appreciation can be extended to the uniqueness of the partner as a whole person. When the defensive quality of the immature bonding between sexually mature partners has gradually dissipated, then the formation of the adult personality is reasonably assured.

The termination of adolescence constitutes a critical and contributory stage in the formation of the adult neurosis. Indeed, it is the persistent inca-pacity of the young man to surmount his negative complex which leads to the consolidation of the manifest and definitive neurosis of his adult life. By infer-ring that the Oedipus complex as a dynamic totality does not yield normally to a postoedipal level of object relations until the closure of adolescence, I simultaneously postulate that the structuralization of the adult neurosis cannot be thought of as completed until adolescence has passed. I shall not elaborate here on the far-reaching consequences of the adolescent process, delivered or aborted, on the ultimate attainment of emotional maturity or psychopathology, but continue on the path that brings us closer to the core of my presentation.

In accordance with the oedipal schema just outlined, I am now ready to say that the resolution of the Oedipus complex in its totality advances in a biphasic fashion: the resolution of the positive component precedes latency — in fact, facilitates its formation — while the resolution of the negative component has its normal timing and takes its normal course in adolescence or, to be more precise, in late adolescence when it facilitates the entry into adulthood. This schema became further complicated by my analytic observation that the flight of the adolescent boy to the father, defensively manifested by rising opposition-alism and aggression, is usually commensurate to the intensity and urgency of the son's need for a protective closeness to him *vis-a-vis* the magnetic and mysterious female to whom he is irresistibly drawn. This drive constellation is too frequently and too readily identified with homosexuality; such a simplis-tic equation demands a vigorous disclaimer. What we observe is the male's defensive struggle against passivity in general, not against homosexuality in particular. I must insert at this point that I am aware of having left aside some well-known and relevant facts about the boy's competitive and antagonistic struggle with the oedipal father. After all, adolescence is the stage in life when the universal polarities of active and passive are in conflict and in final combat on a Promethean scale. In the analysis of the adolescent boy it is imperative that this double-faceted defensive struggle — against submissiveness and pas-sivity as well as against self-assertion and patricide — becomes disentangled. How this dilemma appeared in a treatment and was acted out in the transfe-rence, I shall illustrate with a clinical episode.

A late-adolescent boy had reacted for some time to my interpretations of his violent behavior toward his parents, especially the father, as proof of my taking sides with them and considering his accusatory and demeaning comments about them as amoral and demented. This reaction had reached paranoid proportions. I abstained from interpreting his acting out in the trans-ference because I knew that repeated interpretations too often lose their credi-bility. During a session which I shall now describe, the patient accused me in a highly agitated state of thinking of him as a helpless and weak child, scared to stand up against his father. He was obviously trying to pick a fight with me and stand his ground. When his shouting attack mounted and threatened to get out of hand, I told him firmly and stentorially that he had to stop telling me what is on my mind or leave. His outburst suddenly subsided; he became calm and pensive. After a long silence, he said quietly: "I just remembered a dream I had last night. I am wrestling with my father, not fighting, just wrestling. Suddenly I feel that I'm coming — I cannot control it — I get panicky and I yell: 'No, no — I don't want to make up with you!' I repeat these words again and again, getting more and more desperate. I can't stop the orgasm. I have it." After the recall of this dream neither patient nor analyst had much difficulty in recognizing son and father's sporty playfulness which was a rare event in the boy's early and middle childhood. "I hardly ever played with my father. He was not there — especially when I was afraid of my mother. I saw just enough of him — or perhaps more than enough of my mother — to know how much I missed him." The dream reflects the son's present struggle between a murderous defense against submission and a passionate yearning for paternal acknowledgment of his manhood. The paranoid reverberations of his past, examined in the struggle of his adolescent life, freed the young man from the fixation on the preoedipal father and facilitated his advance toward the oedipal level. Alongside this developmental progression, the compulsive and defensive need for "having sex" gave way to a wish and a budding capacity to form a relationship of a sexual as well as a personal, emotional, and romantic nature.

Returning to the discussion of analytic developmental theory, I must admit that much of what I had attributed to the triadic relationship in my first realization of the adolescent boy's libidinal attachment to the father had to be relegated to the dyadic phase. In other words, the father of the negative complex is intrinsically fused with the father of the preoedipal period. The regressive pull to the father of the dyadic phase becomes apparent when the adolescent boy is viewed in a developmental continuum, as outlined above. Pursuing this course of thinking and developmental allocation in the analytic work with adolescent boys and adult men, it became apparent to me that the loved and loving father of the preoedipal and oedipal period (i.e., the father of the negative complex) ascends to a paramount conflictual position at the terminal stage of adolescence. Once alerted to this phenomenon, I became used to its omnipresence as a normal constituent of the male adolescent process and I gradually desisted from relegating the manifestations of these inordinate passions to the realm of abnormal development or oedipal psychopathology. It is no uncommon observation, especially if derived from the microscopic scrutiny of the tidal currents of emotions as is possible in analytic work, that isogender libidinal drives break through after their relative calm of the latency years has passed. These urges do not represent *prima facie* a homosexual inclination or disposition, but rather confirm that the normal adolescent formation of male sexual identity is on its way. What we observe, then, are the emotional and expressive manifestations of the normal negative complex in transition.

As early as 1951, Loewald made the following comment of a general developmental nature: "Against the threat of the maternal engulfment the paternal position is not another threat of danger, but a support of powerful force" (p. 150). Mahler [and Goslinger, 1955] confirmed this finding by saying that "the stable image of a father or of another substitute of the mother, beyond the eighteen-months mark and even earlier, is beneficial and *perhaps a necessary prerequisite* [italics added] to neutralize and to counteract the ego-- characteristic oversensibility of the toddler to the threat of re-engulfment by the mother" (p. 209). Of course, both statements refer in equal measure to boy and girl infant. A psychoanalytic researcher and clinician who paid particular attention to the development of the early relationship between infant and father during the dyadic period is Abelin (1971, 1975; Panel, 1978). Ross (1977, 1979) has written a comprehensive overview of the literature that deals with the role of the father in the development of the young child from its beginnings through the early formative years; and Herzog (1980) has contributed original research in this field.

Returning to the mainstream of my deliberations, I have so far submitted two theoretical statements which are the outcome of my analytic work with adolescent boys. As the next step, I endeavor to integrate them into the body of psychoanalytic theory, its schema of development, and the dynamics of neurosogenicity. One of the two propositions, as stated above, attributes to adolescence the final resolution of the negative complex, implying that the resolution of the Oedipus complex proceeds in a biphasic progression. The other proposition states that much of what had been generally attributed to the revival of the oedipal father in adolescence is more profitably understood — as to origin and nature — if related to the preoedipal father imago of the dyadic period. Such an adjudication requires some evidence to be persuasive.

At this point a differentiation — even a tentative and incomplete one — between the son–father relationship of the dyadic and of the triadic period should be welcome. The preoedipal father takes over from the early mother some significant portions of the infantile attachment emotions, inclusive of the split in good and bad object. Should the father at this stage serve only as a simple replacement of the mother, then the relationship can be expected to become pathogenic; should the father, however, be perceived and used differently by his son, then a healthy expansion and enrichment of the child's incipient personality becomes discernible. The father assumes for the little boy, early in life, a charismatic quality in his physical presence which is different in its constitutional disposition and bodily responsiveness from that of the mother. The respective quality of the way the father or the mother holds the infant or plays with him demonstrates well the variance or disparity of which I speak. The father of the dyadic period is indeed a facilitator who, in conjunction with the mother, activates the individuation process and finally becomes for his son a savior from the beckoning regression and the threatening reengulfment during the rapprochement subphase (Mahler & Goslinger, 1955). This father, i.e., the dyadic father, has been called "uncontaminated" due to the fact that he has never been a full-fledged symbiotic partner. He belongs to the post-differentiation, preambivalent, idealizing stage of early object relations. Jealousy is indeed noticeable and so is the quest for total object possession. However, the son's turn to the father is not yet affected or burdened by sexual jealousy, patricidal conflict, and retaliatory anxiety these emotional discordances belong to the father of the oedipal era. The idea of a belated resolution of the negative complex at adolescence forced itself on my mind by the eloquent role this emotional conflict plays in the analysis of every male adolescent.

When I once made a comment to an older male adolescent about his complacent, unconflicted and timeless dwelling in analysis, he responded with the recall of a blissful feeling, similar to the one that suddenly had welled up in him when I spoke. He remembered the precious occasions when he was permitted as a little boy to sit quietly in his father's study while the father worked at his desk. He reexperienced in the analytic situation the dyadic bliss of his childhood. In pursuit of this recollection, he came to realize that his life-long thirst for great accomplishments and fame was not only due to the meekly attempted and prematurely abandoned competition with his father, but — more basically — it embodied his passionate quest for his father's love, indeed, for union and oneness with him. When the patient gleaned this insight through the vehicle of transference interpretations he was deeply moved and said: "It feels like being accepted for the first time in my father's arms or to have a life of my own, not just playing at it." I came to realize that what originally had led to the neurotic stalemate was his need for dyadic bonding which, in turn, left only make-believe or inauthentic action open to him in his never-ending effort to transcend his fixation.

The dyadic father attachment and the sharing of father-greatness became arrested in this case on the level of reflection and imitation. It never progressed to the level of identification. He admired the father who could work, while he, the son, could only keep frantically busy, propelled by exalted anticipations. In his despair of ever fulfilling his father's expectations and giving him the pleasure of gratification, the young man finally blamed his father for not using his extraordinary mind to the fullest and doing great things which, in turn, would provide the son with hope and trust in himself by reflection. The awareness of his emotional father involvement was summarized by the patient saying: "If I'll ever be able to let anything or anybody go for good — and what else is growing up all about — I have first to say goodbye to my father." We might paraphrase his words to read: "goodbye to my preoedipal father." The character pathology of this case was one of a pernicious, debilitating pseudo purposefulness and incompleteness of action. The patient's insight into the problems just outlined led to a forward move toward identifications along the father series of which the analyst was one if not, indeed, the first. The fact that the patient could not tolerate the deidealization of the father at adolescence fixated his emotional development at the terminal stage of childhood, thus consolidating his neurosis on the threshold to adulthood. I speak here of the adolescent deidealization of the father as a symbolic patricide which sets the son free by setting into motion the deidealization of the self.

At this point I have to introduce a correction in the portrayal of the dyadic son–father relationship of which — I fear — I have inadvertently given too idyllic a picture. What has to be introduced are the father's ambivalent emotions toward his infant son which throw dark shadows over his infantile exuberance and lust for life. Even when love, pride, and devotion are the father's manifest emotions, negative feelings drift into the relationship. They usually are not acknowledged by the father; they remain unconscious. However, if not neutralized to some degree, they tend to affect adversely the early son–father attachment. The father who harbors feelings of envy, resentment, and death wishes toward his son is dramatically represented in the Greek myth by King Laius who set out to kill his infant son Oedipus by abandoning him in the wilderness to certain death. The inference that the unnatural deed Laius committed was initiated by the voice of the oracle only speaks of the ubiquitous danger of hostile emotions which the birth of an infant son unleashes in the father. Normally they are reduced to insignificance under the onrush of joy and elation evoked by paternity. Ross (1982) has written a persuasive paper on this issue, designating this particular component of the son–father configuration as the Laius complex which every son has to face when the becomes the father of a son.

Two comments are in order here. One refers to a component of the common oppositional and self-assertive stance of the son *vis-à-vis* the father as a defense against passivity. This dynamic explication is convincingly supported by the fact that the analysis of repressed passivity transmutes disorganized and disorganizing oppositionalism into adaptive and organized behavior, solidifying in its course a stable as well as harmonious sense of self. The second comment refers to the theme, which I shall call the search for the loving and loved father. This facet of the father complex assumes in adolescence a libidinal ascendancy that impinges on every facet of the son's emotional life. The quality of this longing as observed in male infants has been called "father hunger" by Herzog (1980) or "father thirst" by Abelin (Panel, 1978). The terminology itself expresses both authors' assumption that the affect of father-yearning is experienced in early childhood within the oral modality.

The resolution of the Oedipus complex finds its ultimate completion in the resolution of the preoedipal father relationship at adolescence. This statement does not alter nor invalidate the overriding importance of the boy's conflict with the oedipal father, but addresses itself to an intrinsic component of the male father complex as a whole. Clinically, the theorem is not restricted to adolescence because it assumes, more often than not, a major role in the analysis of the male adult. The fact of not having surmounted or resolved the father complex, as in the case of an aborted adolescence, lays bare its pathogenic role in the neurotic nexus of any adult male patient. I shall illustrate the theorem just outlined as it emerged in the analysis of a middle-aged man. His emotional bondage to his father was as extreme as his father's unrelatedness to his son

and his uncompromising need that his son submit to his will. Way into manhood, the patient was shaken by the fear that the slightest show of self-assertion
vis-a-vis his father would leave him disinherited, namely, abandoned, starving,
lost. The love for his father — which indeed was "father hunger" — emerged
in the analysis and was acknowledged. In an outburst of tears and sobbing, he
stammered the words: "I love that man." Consciously, the son had resented and
hated the father all his life. Entering analysis, he announced: "I cannot hate my
father for the rest of my life. It kills me." A recent succession of anxiety attacks
and a turn to heavy drinking brought this tortured man to psychoanalytic treatment. In contrast to hating his father, he had always adored his mother about
whom nothing disparaging could ever be said. It was only after the analysis of
the negative complex that he could see her in a new light. He began to express
doubts about her loving nature. Scrutinizing his illusory positive complex he
found a cold, managerial caretaker who had "never hugged or kissed me." The
patient realized that he had cast her in a madonna image when his desire for
emotional closeness to his father had become a lost cause. Now the adult son
could say: "I loved my father too much." He ceased to endear himself to father
figures and concomitantly he ceased to canonize women. With these changes,
his addictiveness faded away and so did his compulsive and superficial and
promiscuous relatedness to women.

As a cogent complement to my analytic experience just cited, I am reminded of Freud's remark about the girl's resolution of her Oedipus complex. In
his work with women patients he was struck by the fact that the positive complex pales into insignificance with the deepening of the analytic work, while
the negative complex moves to the forefront. The analysis of the Oedipus complex — and Freud refers here to its positive component as the one subjected
to analysis — comes to a standstill. Freud (1924) writes: "At this point our
material — for some incomprehensible reason — becomes far more obscure
and full of gaps" (p. 177). In the perplexing pursuit of this problem he came to
realize that the preoedipal period exerts an influence on the emotional development of women that equals or even exceeds the influence of the positive
oedipal position. Freud (1931) states: "... it would seem as though we must
retract the universality of the thesis that the Oedipus complex is the nucleus
of the neuroses." He concludes, that "this correction" is not necessary if we
include in the Oedipus complex the negative component of the girl's exclusive
attachment to the mother and realize that the girl reaches the positive position
only after "she has surmounted a period before it that is governed by the negative complex" (p. 226).

What arouses my attention in this context is the fate of the dyadic father
in the boy's formation of the positive complex or, more specifically, the fate
of the negative complex, its resolution, and its neurosogenic valence. It should
be obvious that this comment of mine refers to a far broader context than that
of homosexuality. In fact, it would be appropriate and clinically supportable

if we made a differentiation between the boy's negative complex of the triadic constellation and the boy's dyadic father complex, which belongs to an earlier stage of object relations, as well as their respective influence on a man's love life and on his sense of self.

I hasten to add that the residues or fixations pertaining to the positive complex are as clearly apparent throughout male adolescence as we have always considered them to be. However, our attention is aroused by the boy's conflictual, i.e., active and passive, father engagement and disengagement, both reflecting a specific quality of emotional exigency and motivational forcefulness.

Contemplating the period of the precompetitive son–father attachment as well as the confidence and security the little boy derives from his father's control and domination, the conjecture presents itself that an indestructible residue of this early father-trust carries over into the tumultuous arena of the triadic struggle. This is to say that the restraining and punishing father is also the rescuer of the son from being taken over by infantile delusions; this so-called rescuer is the early personification of the reality principle who makes growing into manhood an attainable expectancy.

I have traced a roadblock in the path toward this achievement to a father's need for an intense closeness to his isogender infant offspring; in this closeness, the father gratifies vicariously and belatedly his lifelong father hunger. An emotional involvement of this kind always comprises a three-generational network. Under these auspices a potentially liberating infantile attachment turns into an oppressive bondage. One might say that the abandoned seduction theory has reentered here along an unexpected course and in an unexpected guise.

I have observed this kind of interaction between father and son in the analyses of several men who derived excessive pleasure from the caretaking ministrations of their infant son. In one case the child responded to the father's need by becoming a nightly visitor to his bed, always bypassing the mother. No disciplinary interference could keep the now four-year-old child in his room because he kept responding to the father's unrelenting, unconscious wishes for physical and emotional closeness to him. When the patient's deprivation of physical and emotional contact with his early father emerged in the analysis, the little boy began to listen to the request to stay in his room. The nightly commuting to the father's bed faded away with the patient's mounting realization that he gratified vicariously his own preoedipal "father hunger" via his little son's bodily closeness.

In a considerable number of my adult male patients, ranging in age from their twenties way into their late fifties, the negative complex appears often as the rock bottom of their neurotic illness. I remind you here of Freud's 1931 paper on female sexuality which I quoted earlier. There, he calls attention to some of his women patients' all-encompassing fixation on the preoedipal mother lying at the root of their neuroses. One cannot help but wonder why the boy's negative complex, being of equal neurosogenic valence, has never received an equal measure of attention. This neglectfulness persisted despite the fact — as quoted by Mack Brunswick (1940) in her classic paper (written in collaboration with Freud) on the preoedipal phase — that Freud had commented at the time: "on the basis of this new concept of early female sexuality, the preoedipal phase of the boy should be thoroughly investigated" (p. 266). This admonition was never fully heeded.

The residues of the preoedipal attachment experience of son to father lie, to a large extent, buried under a forceful repression once adolescence is passed. This infantile emotional experience, when roused into reanimation during analysis, remains usually inaccessible by sheer verbalization. It finds expression via affectomotor channels, such as uncontrollable weeping and sobbing, while the patient is tormented by overwhelming feelings of love and loss in relation to the dyadic father. One man in his fifties exclaimed at such a moment, choked by tears: "Why did I love my father so much — after all, I had a mother." In contrast to these passionate affects, the manifest and remembered son–father relationship had usually been distant, often hateful, admiring or submissive, governed by fear of rejection and grudgeful with a sense of disappointment.

The foremost structural achievements of both oedipal conflict resolutions at the imminence of latency and, later, of adulthood, are respectively the superego and the adult ego ideal. The male superego preserves for good the circumstances of its origin, namely, the interdiction of incest under the threat of chastisement; it remains an agency of prohibition. The infantile ego ideal, in proximity to object idealization, promotes a forward move in libidinal disengagement, identified in psychoanalytic theory with "the decline of the Oedipus complex." In contrast, the adult ego ideal is an agency of autonomous aspiration; as such it is guarded as a cherished and beloved personality attribute whose archaic origin lies in father attachment, father idealization or, briefly, in the negative complex, i.e., the adult ego ideal is the heir of the negative Oedipus complex. "Genetically," as Bibring (1964) commented, "it [the ego ideal] derives its strength mainly from positive libidinal strivings in contrast to the superego, in which aggressive forces prevail" (p. 517). This view is supported by the clinical fact that the adult ego ideal holds unambivalently to its position, once acquired, with steadfast loyalty. Here Nunberg's (1932) comment comes to mind: "Whereas the ego submits to the superego out of fear of punishment, it submits to the ego ideal out of love" (p. 146). It seems that without the dual challenge of oedipal anxiety and guilt as well as preoedipal father attachment and father hunger, the personality development of the boy is seriously endangered; a disposition in the direction of social and libidinal malfunction might be in store for him. To particularize the inferences I just made, I submit a contribution from the phenomenology of the ego ideal in transition during adolescence.

We are familiar with the adolescent boy's proverbial hero worship and his search for models of emulation, characteristically expressed in his construction of a personal hall of fame. We observe that the personalities on posters and albums, inhabiting the inner sanctum of the adolescent's world, represent his transient but intense idealizations and trial identifications. These imaginary relationships, while highly emotional, are devoid of sexual, i.e., genital constituents and are — due to sublimatory transformations — devoid of infantile attachment emotions. The ego-syntonic affects are exclusively those of admiration, idealization, and devotion to the respective hero's qualities of excellence and perfection, most frequently attached to personalities in the field of sports, music, or stage. The bearers of these qualities are predominantly acclaimed performers and almost exclusively male. We witness here in *statu nascendi* the socialization of the infantile ego ideal alongside the structuring of the adult ego ideal during adolescence.

Adolescence cannot be comprehended by the classical psychoanalytic recapitulation theory because certain emotional experiences and tasks do not find their normal timing until adolescence, when the developmental progression confronts the child with novel, maturationally evoked, conflictual constellations. A major one is singled out for my deliberation in this paper. The event of sexual maturation, i.e., puberty, is the biological signal that the passing of childhood has arrived; any undue prolongation of it becomes an indication of a developmental derailment. The shift in object choice or the adolescent displacement of the primary love object is well understood in the son–mother relationship. What is less understood is the fate of the son's libidinal father attachment. Simple displacement along isogender lines is observed only when a durable fixation prevents libidinal modulation to advance in puberty toward a heterosexual identity. Simple displacement onto object relations of the father series will endanger the son's heterosexual identity or weaken, indeed prevent, its formation and irreversible constancy.

Having discarded the protective envelope of childhood, the safekeeping of purpose and meaning of life passes over into the guardianship of the self. I conceive the dynamics of this personality change as intrinsically related to the resolution of the dyadic father relationship which becomes increasingly divested of infantile dependency needs. In other words, its resolution in the male is not and cannot be effected by object displacement, but only by the formation of a new psychic institution, which is to say, by a structural innovation. I postulated that the object libido which gave life to the negative complex is compelled and propelled by sexual maturation to undergo a transformation into a psychic structure which is sustained by narcissistic libido. In this new structure I recognized the adult ego ideal (Blos, 1974).

The proposition of a biphasic resolution of the Oedipus complex would logically be followed by the conclusion that the definitive organization of the adult neurosis has its timing during the terminal stage of adolescence. It is stating the obvious to say that contributary and essential contributions to the construction of a neurotic illness are identifiable all through the stages of proto-adolescent development. Evoking the image of the arch, it is also obvious that its construction remains incomplete and its ultimate self-support and solid rigidity are not achieved until the keystone is dropped into place. In an analogous fashion, the definitive neurosis, i.e., the adult neurosis, remains incomplete until the closure of adolescence declares that the psychobiological period, called childhood, is passed. Whenever a derailment of the phase-specific differentiation in object relations or an abnormal consolidation of psychic structure occurs during childhood, the developmental injury meets a last chance of spontaneous healing during adolescence. Beyond that, temperamental ingenuity and ego resourcefulness present a myriad of adaptational potentials, one of which is the neurotic compromise, the neurosis. The assertion that the decline of the Oedipus complex proceeds in two stages of preadulthood implies the view that psychological childhood comes to its close at the end of adolescence. To this assertion has to be added that the dyadic isogender attachment experience of the male child contributes a basic determinant in the neurotic formations as they appear later in his life. I would not be surprised if the outcome of my research and its claim for amendments to the classical theory are met both with agreement and incredulity. I do acknowledge that my propositions are not supported by extensive research. All I can ask from the audience is a response of critical attention and a testing by clinical observation.

I mentioned earlier in this presentation that the dyadic state operates in polarities which are reflected in the split into the "good" and "bad" object. The cognitive level of thought, when restricted to the exclusive use of polarities, is of a primitive nature and of limited efficiency because complexities are dealt with in terms of simple dichotomies. The advance to the triadic level lifts the thought process onto a higher level or, rather, it establishes the precondition for this advance. We might say the triadic complexity of object relations and its implicit experience of a higher-level conflict produce an infinite multitude of possible diversity within its realm; of these, a selected few are retained and stabilized in transcending the triadic stage. The oedipal complexity of interpersonal experiences is reflected on the cognitive level in the emergence of the dialectic process. We recognize in this process the triadic nature of thesis, antithesis, and synthesis. The complexity of this thought process permits by the choice of determinations an endless sequence of possible cognitive combinations or permutations, each pressing forward toward a resolution on an ever higher level of thought.

From postulating a biphasic resolution of the Oedipus complex it would follow by implication that the so-called higher levels of thought make their appearance at the time of its terminal resolution, which occurs at the adolescent period. This theoretical assumption finds a validation in the adolescent research by Inhelder and Piaget (1958). To quote: "The adolescent is an individual who begins to build 'systems' or 'theories' in the largest sense of the term.... the adolescent is able to analyze his own thinking and construct theories" (p. 339). The capacity to execute such mental operations declares the readiness of the adolescent mind to deal with the abstractions inherent in ideologies, philosophy, epistemology, and science. The child does not possess a thought faculty of this kind. The researchers claim that these higher thought constructs serve the purpose of furnishing "the cognitive and evaluative bases for the assumption of adult roles. They are vital in the assimilation of the values which delineate societies or social classes as entities in contrast to simple inter-individual relations" (p. 340).

I have commented that the primitivity of thought, anchored in dyadic affectivity, stands in stark contrast to the intricacy of the dialectic thought process. The triadic state is concerned with self, object, and identity, as well as with object-directed emotional and sexual issues; it transcends, so to say, its infantile origin and instinctual involvement by perpetuating its existential nature in the cognitive sphere, namely, in the interminable effort to comprehend the world and the self in ever more complex terms and configurations.

Summary

I have traced in my deliberations the mutual influence of drive and ego development throughout the male child's dyadic and triadic father relatedness as it proceeds within a changing soma and social surround during the first two decades of life. I have made the effort to conceptualize the normal developmental progression in male personality formation with explicit reference to the fate of the boy's dyadic father relationship as well as his negative Oedipus complex in general. These considerations, restricted as they are in scope and gender, assign to the dyadic father complex a nuclear role in neurosogenesis as well as recognize in it an etiological factor in relation to specific forms of psychopathology throughout the male life cycle.

References

Abelin, E. (1971). The role of the father in the separation-individuation process. In J. B. McDevitt & C. F. Settlage (Eds.), *Separation-individuation: Essays in honor of Margaret S. Mahler* (pp. 229–252). New York: International Universities Press.

Abelin, E. (1975). Some further observations and comments on the earliest role of the father. *International Journal of Psycho-Analysis, 56,* 293–302.

Bibring, G. L.(1964). Some considerations regarding the ego ideal in the psychoanalytic process. *Journal of the American Psychoanalytic Association, 12,* 517–521.

Blos, P. (1974). The genealogy of the ego ideal. *The Psychoanalytic Study of the Child, 29,* 43–88.

Freud, S. (1887–1902). *The origins of psychoanalysis: Letters to Wilhelm Fliess, drafts and notes.* New York: Basic Books, 1954.

Freud, S. (1905). Fragment of an analysis of a case of hysteria *Standard Edition, 7,* 7–122.

Freud, S. (1924). The dissolution of the Oedipus complex. *Standard Edition, 19,* 173–179.

Freud, S. (1925). Some psychical consequences of the anatomical distinction between the sexes. *Standard Edition, 19,* 248–258.

Freud, S. (1927). The future of an illusion. *Standard Edition, 21,* 5–56.

Freud, S. (1931). Female sexuality. *Standard Edition, 21,* 225–243.

Greenacre, P. (1966). Problems of overidealization of the analyst and of analysis. *The Psychoanalytic Study of the Child, 21,* 193 –211.

Herzog, J. M. (1980). Sleep disturbance and father hunger in 18- to 28-month-old boys. *The Psychoanalytic Study of the Child, 35,* 219–233.

Inhelder, B., & Piaget, J. (1958). *The growth of logical thinking from childhood to adolescence.* New York: Basic Books. (Originally published, 1955)

Loewald, H. W. (1951). Ego and reality *International Journal of Psycho-Analysis, 32,* 10–18.

Mack Brunswick, R. (1940). The *preoedipal phase of libido development.* In R. Fliess (Ed.), *The psychoanalytic reader* (pp. 261–284). New York: International Universities Press, 1948.

Mahler, M. S., & Goslinger, Bertram. (1955). On symbiotic child psychosis. *The Psychoanalytic Study of the Child, 10,* 195–212.

Nunberg, H. (1932). *Principles of psychoanalysis.* New York: International Universities Press, 1955.

Panel (1978). The role of the father in the preoedipal years. R. C. Prall (Reporter), *Journal of the American Psychoanalytic Association, 26,* 143–161.

Ross, J. M. (1977). Toward fatherhood: The epigenesis of paternal identity during a boy's first decade. *International Journal of Psycho-Analysis, 4,* 327–347.

Ross, J. M. (1979). Fathering: A review of some psychoanalytic contributions on paternity. *International Journal of Psycho-Analysis, 60,* 317–327.

Ross, J. M. (1982). Oedipus revisited: Laius and "the Laius complex." *The Psychoanalytic Study of the Child, 37,* 169–200.

Part VI

Challenges to Identity Coherence and Maintenance

17

From Home to Street
Understanding Young People's
Transitions into Homelessness

JUSTEEN HYDE

A growing body of research conducted with homeless young people has demonstrated that this group is disproportionately vulnerable to a host of negative physical and mental health problems. Early research called attention to the multitude of dangers that homeless young people are confronted with in their daily lives, including a lack of access to basic needs, such as food, clothing, and shelter, sexual exploitation, and violent victimization (Robertson, 1989; Whitbeck & Simons, 1990; Daddis, Braddock, Cuers, Elliot, & Kelly, 1993). In more recent years, attention has turned to the behaviours of homeless young people, such as substance use and sex, and the risks that engagement in these behaviours presents with respect to HIV and Hepatitis B and C infections, sexually transmitted infections, pregnancies, and long-term homelessness (Rotheram-Borus, Koopman, & Ehrhardt, 1991; Farrow, Deisher, Brown, Kulig, & Kipke, 1992; Kipke, O'Connor, Palmer, & MacKenzie, 1995; Kipke, Palmer, LaFrance, & O'Connor, 1997b; Robertson & Toro, 1998; Rew, 2003). Such findings have highlighted not only the social disparities and health risks of this population, but have also been instrumental in efforts to secure funding for programs and services that can provide basic assistance (e.g., food, clothing, health care, temporary shelter) to young people living on the streets.

The development of assistance programs and services for this population has been informed by research that examines why young people become homeless. Traditionally, leaving or running away from home was viewed as a form of delinquency characterized by disobedience and "acting out" (Lipschutz, 1977; Hier, Korboot, & Schweitzer, 1990; Zide & Cherry, 1992; Schaffner, 1999). In the mid- to late-1970s, discourses about homeless youth began to change.

From: *Journal of Adolescence*. Special Issue: Homeless and Runaway Youth. 28(2), 2005, pp. 171–183. Copyright © Elsevier. Reprinted with permission.

Coinciding with an increased recognition of child maltreatment as a major public health and safety issue for children in the United States, a small handful of researchers began demonstrating that young people living on the streets have extensive histories of familial abuse and neglect; leaving home is one of the few options they have to escape from maltreatment (Miller, Hoffman, & Duggan, 1980; Robertson, Richard, & Richard, 1985; Kufeldt & Nimmo, 1987). Unlike normative notions of "the family" which assume that all families are places of nurture and support (Wright, 1997), the families of many homeless young people have been characterized by parent–child conflict, discipline problems, poor communication, poor supervision, physical and sexual abuse, lack of affection and caring, and substance abuse problems (Miller et al., 1980; McCormack, Janus, & Burgess, 1986; Miller, Eggertson-Tacon, & Quigg, 1990; Whitbeck & Simons, 1990; Rotheram-Borus et al., 1991; Kipke et al., 1997). Other issues documented less frequently in the literature include conflicts arising over sexuality and sexual orientation, pregnancy, and youths' own alcohol and drug use (Whitbeck, Hoyt, & Ackley, 1997; Mallon, 1998).

Although there is a growing body of evidence documenting the strained and often violent relationships between homeless young people and their parents or guardians, very little research has examined how young people perceive these relationships and how these perceptions frame their experiences of homelessness. Service providers and child welfare advocates often depict homeless young people as victims, emphasizing complex histories of child abuse and neglect, domestic violence, substance abuse and poverty. Although a politically important strategy for calling public attention to a range of contemporary social problems, the depiction of homeless youth solely in terms of their victimization has a number of unintended consequences. Leaving home is a measure that young people take to protect themselves from further emotional and physical danger. This is a measure that exposes young people to a number of risks, including interpersonal violence, substance use and abuse, poor nutrition, and long-term poverty. When viewed through the lens of victimization, service providers understand young people's movements from home to street as desperate acts that reflect a sense of powerlessness. The question of whether or not young people share this perspective is important to consider; their perceptions of how and why they are homeless directly impact their perceptions of homelessness as well as their ability or willingness to transition into more stable housing.

In this paper, I draw on life history interviews conducted with young homeless people in Los Angeles to suggest that many view themselves as active agents in the events that led them from home to street. Although leaving home and becoming homeless is not an optimal choice, it is one of the few actions available to young people to protect themselves from physical and/or emotional abuse. Regardless of the turbulent and often violent circumstances that underlie young people's decisions to leave home, many recounted these events in a way that allowed them to feel empowered. The problem-oriented perspective that informs social services often does not resonate with young homeless people who have struggled to redefine their experiences in ways that enable them to live in the here and now. This disjuncture may inhibit some young people from utilizing assistance services that can help them meet their daily needs as well as provide support to secure more stable housing.

Methods

The narratives presented here are drawn from a larger ethnographic study conducted between 1999 and 2001 with a group of young people living on the streets in Los Angeles. One of the aims of this study was to understand, from the perspective of participants, the life events and relationships that incited participants' movements from home to street. Life history interviews were employed as a primary methodology because it allows participants to identify and discuss the events and relationships that they believe are significant in these life transitions. Approval for this research was granted by the Institutional Review Board at Childrens Hospital Los Angeles before formal research activities began.

Recruitment

Individuals were eligible to participate in this research if they were between the ages of 18 and 23 and reported that they were both homeless and had injected drugs in the previous 30 days. Fifty young adults were recruited from a range of sites in three areas of Los Angeles: Hollywood, Pasadena, and Santa Monica. Participants were recruited from social service agencies (e.g., drop-in centres, needle exchange programs, and free medical clinic) and outdoor areas (e.g., public parks, lucrative panhandling areas) where young homeless people were known to hang out.

Interview Structure

A total of 74 one-on-one interviews were conducted, 50 of which were designed as life history interviews, and 24 that focused on details of daily life. Life history interviews began with basic demographic questions, such as age, current residential status, and length of time in the area. Participants were then asked to describe the earliest memory they had of their childhood. Initial questions about the circumstances surrounding the memory were asked to help facilitate the conversation. Interviews generally progressed in a sequential manner, with participants describing their primary memories of childhood and adolescence. Most spoke openly about the significant relationships and experiences they had in their lives, including familial interactions, histories of abuse, institutional placements, schooling, drug use, sexual relations, homelessness, and social stigma and isolation. I frequently asked questions for clarification and probed for details about experiences or interactions they discussed, especially with respect to relationships or events underlying a transition in life. Interviews lasted between 1.5 and 3 hours, although some lasted up to 5 hours and were conducted in more than one session. Most interviews were conducted in private or semi-private settings, including parks, fast food restaurants, and social service agencies. All participants received a $20 gift certificate for their time.

Analysis

Interviews were audio-recorded with permission from participants and professionally transcribed. Once transcripts were reviewed for thoroughness, the documents were downloaded into QSR NUD*IST, a qualitative data management program. An initial sample of five transcripts was selected to develop a qualitative codebook. An inductive approach was used to identify categories that described key spheres of influence on the lives of participants (e.g., family conflict, physical, sexual and emotional abuse, education, peer relations) as well as major life events (leaving home, foster care placements, incarceration, death of a loved one). After testing the codebook on an additional sample of five interviews and making necessary adjustments, the codebook was finalized. I worked with the project coordinator to code each of the interviews; together we reviewed all coded transcripts to ensure consistency in the categorization of the data. Transcripts were electronically coded in NUD*IST. Once entered into the program, text segments demarcated by each code were reviewed and analysed. In preparing for this paper, I reviewed data reports on the following codes: (1) reasons for leaving home; (2) family relations; and (3) histories of maltreatment. Analysis of the "reasons for leaving home" report helped identify several themes, most notably familial conflicts, maltreatment, and other transitions in residence (e.g. placement in foster care or with other family members). I reviewed additional reports related to these themes to understand the circumstances surrounding young people's departure from home. These results are presented below. Although themes were evident, a single text segment was inadequate to convey the complex set of circumstances underlying transitions into homelessness. In this paper, I present two edited life stories that represent the major themes identified.

Results

Participants

The sample is comprised of 25 women and 25 men. Nearly three-quarters of participants identified their primary ethnic background as Caucasian/White, while slightly more than one-quarter of the respondents were of mixed ethnicities, including Mexican/Anglo-European, Argentinian/Mexican, Persian, Native American/Anglo-European, and East Indian/Brazilian. The mean age of participants was 20.5 years.

Histories of Homelessness

The histories of homelessness among this sample varied in both length of time and cycles of residential (in)stability. Approximately 73% were living in squats or encampments at the time of recruitment. The remaining 27% had histories of homelessness, but were staying at a motel, shelter or other temporary place. Twelve percent of the sample reported being homeless for less than 1 year, 56% between 1 and 5 years, and 32% for more than 5 years.

The majority of participants (88%) began living on the streets when they were minors (under 18 years of age). Nearly two-thirds of respondents (60%) were living in single parent households at the time of their departure from home, while 16% were living with extended kin. The six respondents (12%) who began living on the streets after they became legal adults (age 18) had transitioned out of foster care placement with no financial or social support systems in place to help them take the first steps into independent living. Those who had been living on the streets for more than 1 year typically had some periods where they were housed and employed for varying lengths of time.

Reasons for Leaving Home

Discussions about leaving home revealed a multifaceted set of circumstances that were not easy to reduce to one factor. Coinciding with previous research, the majority of participants depicted familial relations that were under intense duress while growing up. The majority of participants discussed physical abuse (59%) and intense familial conflict (50%) as primary factors underlying their decisions to leave home. Approximately 75% of participants were raised in a single-parent household for much of their childhood. Nearly all of these participants also described experiences of adapting to changing configurations in the household introduced by a re-marriage or domestic partnership. Most described deeply strained relationships with their parents' new partners. Physical abuse was often perpetrated by mothers in single parent households. However, the most severe experiences of physical and sexual abuse were perpetrated by step-fathers or mothers' domestic partners. Both abuse and family conflict were often attributed to parents' substance abuse (30%), but also to differences with respect to personal style (e.g., clothing, hair colour and cut, body piercing, etc.) (16%), religious beliefs (8%), sexual orientation (6%), and educational performance (12%).

Although the stress and conflict surrounding family relationships has been fairly well documented, participants' narratives also highlight an active sense of agency with respect to decisions to leave home. More than half of participants claimed that they left home because they were "fed up" with the conditions they were living in. Nearly 20% discussed their own personal and emotional troubles, acknowledging that they were responsible for at least some of the conflicts that led to their departure from home. Nearly a quarter (22%) claimed that they left home because they wanted to travel and experience new opportunities. None of these explanations alone adequately explains the participants' trajectories into homelessness.

In the remainder of this paper, I present two edited stories depicting a multifaceted set of circumstances influencing participants' transitions from home to street. As the majority of participants were raised in families split by divorce and reconfigured by new marriages or domestic partnerships, I begin with a story that illustrates some of the conflicts that many participants faced in these transitions and the circumstances leading up to their departure from home. The second story highlights the splintering impact of stressful life events on families and the ensuing downward spiral in familial relations that can occur in the perceived absence of social support. These stories are not representative of all experiences of homeless young people, but do convey the complicated sense of agency and empowerment that young people espouse when discussing reasons for leaving home.

Twig

The nickname "Twig" suits him well. Although a tall and very thin young man, his demeanor is rough, erratic, and easily gives one the impression that he could "snap" at any minute. At the age of 21, Twig had been living on and off the streets for about 6 years. He considers himself a "traveller," which is a distinction that many participants made between themselves and other individuals living on the streets. Like many others, he travels through Los Angeles every year or so, en route to San Francisco, San Diego, or any one of several outdoor music festivals that allow camping at the venue. Despite feeling constantly harassed by the police when he enters a new city, he claims to love his lifestyle and the opportunities for new adventures that it affords him.

I had seen Twig around town for 2 weeks before we conducted the interview. He easily responded to the initial demographic questions, but his tone visibly changed when I asked him to describe an early memory. He described a time when he was trying to help his mother clean the blood off her face after one of his parents' many violent disputes. He had given her his teddy bear to sleep with "so that she wouldn't be afraid." This was not a unique experience during his early childhood; intense, and often violent disputes were common in his house and comprised his primary memories. Although the violence was usually inflicted on one another, Twig and his younger brother were also victims in their parents' disputes. On more than one occasion he remembered being in the emergency room for broken bones. When asked why his parents were violent, Twig told me that both his parents used cocaine and drank heavily at the time. He knew about the drinking, but not about the cocaine use until years later.

One night when Twig was 5 years old, his parents got into serious fight that scared him so badly that he called the police. When he told his parents what he had done, his father picked up a few belongings and left the house. He never returned. With the sudden loss of his father's income Twig and his brother and mother struggled to make ends meet. His mom increased the number of hours she worked each week and occasionally took a second job to support her family. Although he remembered some difficult times after his father left, Twig also recalled the initial years as being among the best in his life.

> I mean, it was hard with my mom working so much, but it was definitely better. She still drank quite a bit, but it was nothing compared to when my dad was there. It's the first time I remember there being peace in the apartment. You know, like we weren't scared to be there.

Twig and his mother and brother lived alone for about 7 years. He thought they were a close family and got along well with one another. Twig also noted that he and his brother were typical boys and often played roughly together. He admitted half jokingly that they "were more than a handful."

One night while out drinking with her friends, his mom met a man that she thought would be good for her boys. He had a well-paying job with a construction company and seemed to really like his mom. However, Twig thought from the beginning that he was not "into being a family man"; although he thought that his new step-father probably cared for his mother, it was obvious to him that he did not want the responsibility of raising two step-children.

> My step-father wasn't that great of a guy, he was a real bad drunk and he would always smack me around or push me when he was drunk. Being beat all my life — first by my real dad and then by my step-dad — I mean, I respected the guy for caring for my mom and making money to support the family. But he was constantly jabbing at me and trying to control my life. If he was in a bad mood, I was his punching bag. You know, I took it for a little while, but it was just too much.

When I asked about how his mother responded to the turbulent relationship that he had with her husband, Twig shrugged his shoulders and told me that he thought she probably did the best she could. He suspected that she was economically dependent on him and feared that he would leave her if she tried to intervene. As Twig entered his adolescent years, he began to stay away for longer periods of time in order to avoid conflicts at home. However, this worried his mother and infuriated his step-father. Their arguments grew progressively worse and were often violent.

> When I turned 13 I got sick of it. I snapped one day and tried to kill him. He came in to where I was working out in the garage and started in on me: "You lazy this, you no-good-for-nothing that." I just snapped. I grabbed a chain from the weight bench and just started hitting him. He gave my mom an ultimatum — either he leaves or I leave. I couldn't deal with it anymore, and I didn't want my mom to have to decide. I just packed my shit up and left.

Twig talked with some degree of pride about his decision to leave the house, noting that he was probably more capable of surviving on his own than his mom. The circumstances leading up to this event are undoubtedly more complicated than recounted. Of importance, is the active sense of agency he communicated in the telling of this event; the decision to leave home was his. When Twig left home, he did not immediately become homeless. His mom helped him get on a bus to St. Louis, where his paternal grandmother lived. He hoped to find his biological father, whom he had not seen in the years since he left the family. Twig recalled feeling confused, but also hopeful that he would have a better relationship with his dad now that he was older. When Twig located his dad a few days later, he discovered that he was remarried and had three children. Although hesitant to have his son move in, he agreed to let him stay on a trial basis.

> It was cool to see him and all, but I had a feeling right away that it wasn't gonna work. His wife was a bitch and they didn't get along at all. Their kids were brats and I just didn't fit in, you know? I was an outsider and — well, that wasn't gonna change.... Me and my dad argued a lot too. We were a lot alike, and that probably scared both of us. I know it did me. But, he acted like he was better than he really was trying to tell me how to live my life and shit. Who was he to tell me what to do and how at act?

Twig began leaving home and staying away for extended periods when he was 14 years old. His father and step-mother "argued constantly" and Twig thought it better if he just tried to make it on his own. He began travelling with other young homeless people that he met on the streets in St. Louis. As a minor on the streets, he was frequently picked up by the police and placed in one of several different types of foster placements. Each of his foster placements were unsuccessful and he ended up leaving all of them within the first 3 months. Although the circumstances of each placement varied, Twig repeatedly described his struggles trying to fit into a foster placement that did not acknowledge his past experiences or address the deep and growing anger that he felt toward his parents.

In the 3 years since he turned 18, Twig had held a number of different jobs and on several occasions tried to maintain an apartment. With limited education, however, he could only find low-wage jobs service jobs that he either despised or did not think were worth the effort. Having bounced back and forth between being housed and not housed for a couple of years, Twig told me he preferred living on the streets and "doing [his] own thing." He felt much happier and capable of surviving on the streets than in the mainstream of a society that had been nothing but a disappointment for him.

Myd

At the young age of 22, Myd, a young woman originally from the southern region of the United States, had been living on and off the streets for about 7 years. Myd was born into a large Irish-Catholic family, the 8th of 9 children. She described herself as a relatively shy person while growing up. As a child, she spent most of her days with her father, a soft-spoken, retired military man. Her fondest and most pronounced memories were of her father, the person she trusted and loved most in the world. Her mother, on the other hand, was a person she feared and resented. She described her as having a violent temper and an emotionally distant personality. Her father was an important buffer in their relationship, mitigating the negative impact of her mother's physical and emotional outbursts.

When Myd was 12, her father died unexpectedly of heart failure. His sudden death was devastating on multiple levels. She had lost not only her father but also one of her closest companions. His absence also meant that there was no longer anyone in the house to protect her from the verbal, and sometimes physical abuse that her mother was prone to inflict. Myd's grief and sadness about her father's death was immense. She withdrew from those around her; although she continued to do well in school, she stopped communicating with most of the people in her life. Unlike her mother and other siblings, Myd had a difficult time "moving on" with her life and resuming daily interactions with people around her.

Six months after her father's death, Myd's mother became worried about her daughter's grieving and sought professional psychiatric help for her. Myd reluctantly agreed to see the psychiatrist, but did so to appease her mom. After her first session, Myd's psychiatrist told her she was depressed and prescribed Prozac for treatment. She did not like the medication because it made her emotionally numb and affected her sleep patterns, for which she received a prescription for sleeping pills. She and her mother fought quite a bit during this period. In retrospect, she believes that her mother was trying to help her. However, she looks back on this time with great frustration. She felt as though her attempts to talk openly about what was actually happening in her life, including her mother's abuse, were often ignored by the psychiatrist who "continually turned every conversation [she] had back to the relationship [she] had with her father."

At the age of 14, Myd made one last attempt to reach out and try to talk with someone about the troubles she was experiencing with her mother. As part of the "domestic violence awareness" week activities at her school, volunteers from a local domestic violence shelter came to speak with her class. After the presentation, Myd stayed to talk with the counselors about some of the problems she was having with her mom. The domestic violence counselors referred her to the school counselor who agreed to take over her case. Shortly after the counselors left to make their next presentation, the school counselor picked up the phone and called her mother to "discuss" the allegations of child abuse reported by her daughter. Her mother quickly came down to the school to talk with the counselor.

> Somehow she convinced the counselor that I was a "troubled" child. She told her that I was on anti-depressants because of my father's death. She also told her that I had been caught drinking alcohol with one of my friends. That was true but, I mean, I never understood why that made a difference. I think it was because my mom is a "pillar of the community." Whatever. You know, she went to church and all that stuff. Well, when we finally got out of there I knew it was coming to me. We didn't even get into the car before she backhanded me and started freaking out. All the way home she was yelling, and then when we got inside she stared throwing dishes. I remember her yelling at me and telling me "don't ever bring other people into our business." Well, after that you can believe that I never did.

Myd became increasingly isolated from those around her. She stopped going to church and began skipping school. She also began hanging around a different circle of friends who were using cocaine and drinking alcohol. Although the drugs were fun, their numbing effects also provided a source of comfort for her. Knowing that her mother would "kill her" if she knew that she was using drugs, she began to spend an increasing amount of time away from home. In retrospect, she imagines that this probably worried her mother. But at the time, Myd only knew that her relationship with her mom was getting worse and there was no reprieve in sight. Their fights would often end with Myd either leaving or getting "kicked out" of the house. She never stayed away for too long, and usually returned to an apologetic mother.

At the age of 15, Myd met some young people near where she was living who called themselves "travellers." She had just been kicked out of her house once again and they invited her to travel to Arizona with them. Deciding she had nothing to lose, she hopped on a train for the first time and headed out of town. She experienced a new-found freedom in her first months of travelling; she no longer dreaded the time just before her mother came home from work. She could come and go anywhere she pleased without being questioned, and her surroundings were no longer filled with painful reminders of her deceased father.

> It was great at first. God, I couldn't even imagine having to go back home again and I just wanted nothing more than to be away. There's nothing like hopping on a train and just going wherever the train takes you. I just remember feeling like I could breathe again.

When I first met Myd in Hollywood, she had been living on and off the streets for 7 years. She is proud of her travels, claiming that she has been in nearly every state in the continental U.S.; although she looked back fondly on her years of travelling, the romance of freedom and independence had worn off. At the time of our interview, she was struggling not only with concerns about daily survival, but also with a heroin habit. Like many young people who have been living on the streets for more than a year, she never imagined her life to turn out the way it did.

> I didn't see myself still being out here at 22. I figured I was gonna travel for a little while, get it out of my system. I still wanted to go to college. This was before I started shooting up. Before then I thought I could stop everything I was doing, go back and get my GED and then start college and everything would be great. Then I got hooked on everything all at once... I thought for sure I wasn't going to live to be 21 years old.

Myd was not alone in thinking that leaving home would be a temporary solution to the conflicts she experienced with her family. Although she did not regret her decision, she struggled with the fact that her temporary solution was quickly becoming a way of life.

Discussion

The reasons why young people leave home and become homeless are multifaceted and often complex. Coinciding with previous research conducted with homeless young people, many participants in my research attributed their decisions to leave home to intense conflicts within the family. Physical and emotional abuse was commonly reported, as were struggles to adapt to changing family structures and relationships. Given the turbulent and often abusive family relationships that are found in the life histories of homeless young people, it is not difficult to understand why much of the literature portrays this population as victims. Many families are not supportive and nurturing, and young homeless people often perceive them as antagonists in their life journeys. However, by focusing only on their victimization, service providers are likely to overlook young people's resiliency in the face of adversity and to acknowledge their efforts to create new life experiences. They are also likely to overlook the sense of agency that young homeless people espouse in their every day lives and the importance of maintaining their independence at any cost.

The stories presented in this paper are likely to be familiar to service providers, researchers and others working with this population. Although many young people leave home as a temporary solution to conflicts they have with parents, many find that a temporary solution has become a way of life.

For some individuals, this way of life is one they are comfortable with and perceive to be better than others they have known in their past. Like Twig, participants with histories of severe physical abuse that occurred across different stages of childhood were least likely to express a desire for transitioning off the street. In order to protect themselves, many have completely severed relationships with family members. Without access to social and financial support traditionally provided by families, these young people learn early on that their survival is dependent on no one but themselves. This belief is important to highlight, particularly since it is likely to influence individuals' perceptions of social assistance services. For example, a number of participants were reluctant to access shelter or transitional housing services because they believed it would jeopardize their independence. In professional discourses, resistance to shelter or other supportive services is often linked to psychological or mental health problems. This individual-deficit perspective, however, ignores the fundamental importance for some young people to maintain control over their lives and protect themselves from further emotional or physical harm.

Not all participants expressed the desire to continue living on the streets. Many left home to escape the chronic conflicts they experienced with their parents. These conflicts were often related to stressful life events, such as the re-marriage of a parent or the death of a family member, or participants' own desires for experimentation with personal styles, drugs, political beliefs, and peer relations. Many turned to drugs and alcohol and/or stayed away from home for extended periods of time to avoid conflicts. These behaviours tended to exacerbate conflicts with primary caregivers, eventually leading to decisions to leave home altogether. In retrospect, many claimed some responsibility for the conflicts they had with their parents. Like Myd, some reflected back on their behaviours while at home and acknowledged that their parents might have been concerned about their safety. However, in the midst of conflicts, most participants felt they had few viable alternatives for resolving familial discord. Myd's unsuccessful attempts to reach out and talk honestly with her therapist and school counselor about the troubled relationship she had with her mother were not unique. One or more such experiences left many participants feeling as though leaving home was one of the few means they had of dealing with a stressful period in their lives.

After living on the streets for several years, many participants had conflicting feelings about their homelessness; although proud of their travelling experiences and abilities to survive on their own, they were tired of living on the streets. The process of transitioning off the streets and into housing was neither easy, nor emotionally uncomplicated. First, most housing assistance programs require participants to abstain from drug and alcohol use. This represented a major life change for many participants who had used substances for a number of years as a means of coping with the stresses of daily life. More importantly, many were conflicted over the prospects of participating in the conventions of mainstream society. Some had grown used to living by their own rules and structure and believed they would have to forfeit much of their independence in order to maintain housing. Others were more skeptical of the benefits of the move, noting that with limited education and employment skills, they would find few satisfactory options to support themselves. Finally, many were afraid to fail. For years they had worked independently to build protective barriers around themselves. Social service providers need to recognize that many young people have not had success in obtaining support and assistance from adults in their lives. Resistance to assistance is less likely symptom of a psychological disorder than a concern over vulnerability and disappointment.

Service providers may be limited in their ability to acknowledge the active sense of agency expressed by homeless young people. Funding for homeless assistance programs are predominately deficit-focused, often requiring clinical diagnoses and other classifications to substantiate a "need" for assistance services. To effectively engage and support homeless young people in making positive transitions in their lives, service providers, public policy makers, and other professionals need to rethink the problem-oriented perspective that currently guides the development of supportive services. Rather than translate their life experiences into indicators of pathology and risk, service providers and other professionals may more effectively engage young people in assistance services if there is a greater understanding of how they perceive their life experiences. From this starting point, we are better able to acknowledge their resiliency and understand the significance of their efforts to live their lives on their own terms.

References

Daddis, M., Braddock, D., Cuers, S., Elliot, A., & Kelly, A. (1993). Personal and family distress in homeless adolescents. *Community Mental Health Journal, 29,* 413–422.

Farrow, J., Deisher, R., Brown, R., Kulig, J., & Kipke, M. (1992). Homeless and runaway youth health and health needs —A position paper of the society for adolescent medicine. *Journal of Adolescent Health, 13,* 717–726.

Hier, S., Korboot, P., & Schweitzer, R. (1990). Social adjustment and symptomology in two types of homeless adolescents: Runaways and throwaways. *Adolescence, 26,* 761–771.

Kipke, M., O'Connor, S., Palmer, R., & MacKenzie, R. (1995). Street youth in Los Angeles: Profile of a group at high risk for human immunodeficiency virus infection. *Archives of Pediatric and Adolescent Medicine, 149*, 513–519.

Kipke, M., Palmer, R., LaFrance, S., & O'Connor, S. (1997). Homeless youths' descriptions of their parents' childrearing practices. *Youth & Society, 28*, 415–431.

Kufeldt, K. & Nimmo, M. (1987). Youth on the street: Abuse and neglect in the eighties. *Child Abuse & Neglect, 11*, 531–543.

Lipschutz, M. (1977). Runaways in history. *Crime and Delinquency*, July, 321–332.

Mallon, G. (1998). *We don't exactly get the welcome wagon: The experiences of gay and lesbian adolescents in child welfare systems.* New York: Columbia University Press.

McCormack, A., Janus, M. D., & Burgess, A. W. (1986). Runaway youths and sexual victimization: Gender differences in an adolescent runaway population. *Child Abuse & Neglect, 10*, 387–395.

Miller, D., Hoffman, F., & Duggan, R. (1980). *Runaways — illegal aliens in their own land.* New York: Praeger.

Miller, A. T., Eggertson-Tacon, C., & Quigg, B. (1990). Patterns of runaway behavior within a larger systems context: The road to empowerment. *Adolescence, 25*, 271–289.

Rew, L. (2003). A theory of taking care of oneself grounded in experiences of homeless youth. *Nursing Research, 52*(4), 234–241.

Robertson, M. (1989). *Homeless youth in Hollywood: Patterns of alcohol use: a report to the national institute on alcohol abuse and alcoholism.* Berkeley, CA: Alcohol Research Group.

Robertson, M. & Toro, P., (1998). Homeless youth: research, intervention, and policy. The 1998 National Symposium on Homelessness Research, http://www.aspe.hhs.gov/progsys/homeless/symposium/3- youth.htm.

Robertson, M., Richard, R., & Richard, B. (1985). *The homeless of Los Angeles county: An empirical evaluation. Document No. 4, Los Angeles: Basic shelter research project.* Los Angeles: School of Public Health, University of California.

Rotheram-Borus, M. J., Koopman, C., & Ehrhardt, A. A. (1991). Homeless youth and HIV infection. *American Psychologist, 46*, 1188–1197.

Schaffner, L. (1999). *Teenage runaways: Broken hearts and "bad attitude."* New York: Haworth Press.

Whitbeck, L., Hoyt, D., & Ackley, K. (1997). Families of homeless and runaway adolescentsl a comparison of parent/caretaker and adolescent perspectives on parenting, family violence, and adolescent conduct. *Child Abuse and Neglect, 21*, 517–528.

Whitbeck, L. & Simons, R. (1990). Life on the streets: The victimization of runaway and homeless adolescents. *Youth & Society, 22*, 108–125.

Wright, T. (1997). *Out of place: Homeless mobilizations, subcities, and contested landscapes.* Albany: State University of New York Press.

Zide, M. & Cherry, A. (1992). A typology of runaway youths: An empirically based definition. *Child & Adolescent Social Work Journal, 9*, 155–168.

18

Self-Destructiveness in Adolescence

JOSEPH NOSHPITZ

Idealization

One of the key psychological emergents in the formation of early human attachment is idealization. During infancy, it is likely that this is the normal way the infant perceives its caretaker, and the caretaker the infant. When the relationship between infant and caretaker is positive, the infant regards the mothering figure as all-knowing, all-powerful, and all-rewarding. The mere proximity of mother, the sound of her voice, the smell of her body, the touch of her hand, the image of her face, the experience of her breast, all give rise to a sense of elation. There is a quality of elevated uplift, of heightened responsiveness, of joy in engagement. In particular, there is an awareness of joining with something supernal, something larger than the self. What they are describing in fact is the early experience of idyllic unity.

Nor is mother's perception of her infant far removed in quality from this sense of glow. Baby is adorable, infinitely huggable, good enough to eat. By the same token, for baby, this preverbal kind of emotional surge can have an equally powerful sweep in a negative direction. The experience of rejection, rough handling, abandonment, neglect, abuse — these in turn can produce equally vivid and equally intense feelings of loss, injury, fear, despair, a sense of worthlessness, and an overall sonority of profound dismay. These painful feelings are as total and as exaggerated as the elated ones noted above, albeit in the opposite direction.

The value of such early idealization is self-evident. The positive version would underlie the attachment behavior of both mother and baby. To the extent that mother perceives baby as wonderful, beautiful, ultimately cute, and totally fascinating, she will be drawn to care for it and keep it close, warm, well fed, and safe. To the extent that baby continues to regard mother in these ideal

From: *American Journal of Psychotherapy*, 48, 1994, 330–346. Copyright © Association for the Advancement of Psychotherapy. Reprinted with permission.

terms, it will need her, seek her out, feel drawn to her, and keep close to her. Phylogenetically, this would have had enormous survival value.[1]

As development proceeds, the tendency to idealize develops as well. This process is fundamental to the further elaboration of both negative and positive inner images; with continuing growth, the cluster of ideal formations becomes ever more complex and multifaceted. There is a sense of self and other with negative valences, and a different cluster with positive attributes. The power of these positively or negatively idealized presences continues to wax, for, in time, they take their place among the central regulating agencies in the formation and functioning of personality.

In particular, they are of critical importance as the structures within the psyche that set the goals for personality functioning. To be sure, as they take form, these ideal structures will have a variety of functions. Before exploring them however, it should be recognized that they persist as relatively distinct islands within the dynamic and fluid structural configuration of personality. As adults, we know them best as a sense of ideal presence, e.g., our vision of what is noble, uplifting, and awe inspiring in our ethical and spiritual lives on the one hand, and our awareness of the wicked, the demonic, and the ultimately evil in the dark side of humanity, on the other. As such, their power to lead us, motivate us, and to drive behavior is of considerable proportions. As we experience ourselves drawing near to the one set of ideals or to the other, our moods, affects, and the overall emotional toning of our lives will be radically affected. We must always keep in mind that as structural components, these ideals are the products of preverbal experience initiated during the early months of life. Although they do develop alongside the other functions and aspects of personality, to a considerable extent they never lose their preverbal character. One way or another, they function as part of the motivating and regulating agencies that drive and modulate human behavior. Myron Hofer is quoted as comparing the attachment experience of young infants to the state of addiction. In his view, infants are addicted to their mothers and go through something akin to physiologic withdrawal when they are separated from them for any length of time. "When they are parted the infant does not just miss its mother; it experiences a physical and psychological withdrawal from a host of her sensory stimuli, not unlike the plight of a heroin addict who goes cold turkey" (Gallagher, 1992, p. 13).[2] A parallel view would translate this kind of attachment into the psychological experience of symbiosis (Mahler, Pine, & Bergman, 1975). The infant is linked to mother as the (idealized) source of all that is safe, rewarding, and good. To be with her, to feel at one with her, is ecstasy. By the same token, to lose her is panic and despair.

It is one of the great paradoxes of development that by the second half of the first year of life, the pressures of their own growth processes are driving the infants to renounce some of this closeness, to give up their addiction, to break away from the symbiotic state of psychological fusion, and to begin to seek a measure of autonomy. The infants begin to be interested in toys, to be able to sit up unsupported, to pull themselves erect, to crawl, and, presently, to walk. They become ever more aware of mother as a real person with an inner world like their own rather than as a supernal presence with whom they associate global and overwhelming sensations of elevation — or of terror and despair.

Much of what becomes structured in during this interval is the outcome of temperament, fit, and interaction (Chess & Thomas, 1986). Some infants are more resilient and can make do with minimal supportive input; for them, even a troubled or somewhat depriving mother will suffice; despite her deficiencies such a baby will grow well. Other infants are more vulnerable. Even with average good mothering, they will not be comforted or feel supported and at peace; despite a reasonably wholesome caretaking environment, so great are these infants' needs and sensitivities that they nonetheless feel deprived and upset. In essence it is a matter of fit; an unusually sensitive and giving mother may successfully carry such a special baby through the early critical months. Alternatively, even an unusually resilient baby can be overwhelmed by sufficiently disastrous rearing circumstances. As far as their innate vulnerabilities go, most infants of course fall in between these extremes of excessive neediness and unusual competence. Accordingly, they will do well with the reasonably adequate caretaking most mothers provide. But the "luck of the draw" can make a critical difference.

Where, then, the fit is a good one, the children will have far more gratifying and intensely positive experiences than negative and destructive ones. The ideal structures that presently crystallize out within personality will take their cast from this early interactive sequence. The emotionally charged reward events will overshadow the painful and negative experiences both in number and in intensity, and the positive traces thus laid down will presently differentiate and elaborate into a series of equally positive emergents — a sense of self-confidence and self-esteem, along with an outlook of trust and beneficence toward the surrounding world. One feels loved by one's inner valuator, and anticipates good in others. To be sure, the negative ideal will be present, but it will not be dominant. It will make its presence felt as a conscience that is more or less critical, or more or less severe; or it may find expression in some minor neurotic inhibition or phobia.

Alternatively, however, if there are more negative than positive elements present during the early months, e.g., if mother is immature, depressed, preoccupied, malicious, interested primarily in her drug or alcohol experience, or simply does not like the baby for whatever reason (e.g., he reminds her of her abusive father or abandoning husband), then the ideal structures which are laid down will have a predominantly negative cast.[3] There will be extended intervals of inattention during which the child will cry and feel mounting unbearable tension with no relief; there will be unpredictable responses where the child's efforts at engagement will be thwarted or overreacted to; there will be moments of painful and abusive management during which the child may be screamed at, roughed up, slapped, pinched, thrown about, burnt, or otherwise badly hurt. Mother may be capricious, unpredictable and moody; she may be alternately sexually invasive, hostile, intensely fondling, or dangerously neglectful. The dominant ideal that forms under such circumstances will be essentially negative. It may vary from a mildly unpleasant inner presence that is endlessly carping and devaluing, with accompanying inner feelings of badness, low self-esteem, and a sense of living in a critical and hostile world, to a sure knowledge of a malevolent inner voice that is relentlessly devoted to the destruction both of oneself and of one's world. Many authors (e.g., Jacobson, 1954; Kernberg, 1991) speak of the profound sense of betrayal these infants can experience. More to the point, such configurations take form precociously early. They become stubborn persistent presences that are not easily tempered by subsequent experiences, however wholesome (Kernberg, 1991).

The theme of idealization is all important here; it is the key to understanding what makes these youngsters behave as they do. There are two great epochs for ideal formation in the human life cycle. One is during the first year of life as the new cognitive apparatuses are coming into being, and the other is adolescence.[4] In the nature of things, the idealization is in effect a misperception. In infancy, it is like a great coining machine; it places a stamp on the matrix from which personality will presently form. This impress takes place under the influence of powerful surges of emotion at a time when one lacks the capacity to rein in these affective tides. Borne on waves of emotion, the ensuing images are pushed beyond all reason to the ecstatic or demonic proportions noted above. Like crystals dropped into a supersaturated solution, they become the armatures around which subsequent ideal formations will presently form. Then, as the long slow maturation and differentiation of these functions evolve, and the defensive and constructive mechanisms of the ego take form around them, an evermore and moderate regulatory presence should emerge. The early experience has given the ideal structures their initial profile, and the new experiences will have to overlay and refine them, but these accretions will tend to take their outline from the original configurations. Where the impact of the early experience has not been excessive, the initial structures are more malleable and capable of further growth and refinement. Where, however, the early stresses have been severe, then the initial images "set" precociously and tend to persist in infantile form thereafter.[5]

Hence, where the amount of early caretaker deviance has not been excessive, one may trust that the lessons learned by the infant subsequent to the initial stresses will serve to overcome the potential for a negative outcome (Parker et al., 1992). It is very much a matter of degree. A child whose negative ideal had originally been enhanced by the vicissitudes of his or her rearing pattern, may still recoup. Where enough positive ideal formation is attained later, it can more or less overcome the worst effects of the earlier negative ideal formation. Werner and Smith (1989) give this a quantitative expression in their toting up of early childhood traumata and aligning them with the outcomes observed at late adolescence.

It is important to note that ideal structures of the sort we describe here are the residue of the earliest experiences of interaction, the traces laid down at a time of greatest need and maximum vulnerability, and they will persist in their pristine forms throughout life. As is true of most early formations, they will be largely unconscious. If one desires to study them, to some extent they will be discernible as the elements of conscience. The negative ideal becomes the warning, reproving, shaming, punishing part of conscience; the positive component is what we commonly call the ego ideal. It leads, guides, and rewards the ego and the self. Between them, the two ideals, which never really fuse or unite, form a system that serves as one of the basic regulatory apparatuses of personality. There is no way to be rid of such a negative ideal; there are only different ways of responding to it.

To illustrate the point, we can start with a worst-case scenario. Let us assume that during early development, a child has been subjected to largely negative influences, with almost no leavening of restorative, loving experience to build in a strengthened positive presence. Depending on whether he or she is an internalizer or an externalizer, such a child is likely to grow up to be a predator capable of murder, a suicidal depressive, or some alternating picture of both. In most childrearing sequences, so totally negative a state of affairs seldom exists. There is usually some alternation of good and bad experiences, or some episodic encounter with a caring and responsive other that allows for the formation and enhancement of positive ideal components. Accordingly, the resulting clinical pictures, as we see them later on, are complex and full of paradoxes and inconsistencies. The youngster is alternately hostile, hateful, and destructive, and apologetic, guilty, and regretful. Sometimes the two regulating presences are discernible at once as the youth struggles to make choices. Often the negative ideal is dominant but covert; the youngster behaves well superficially, but ultimately makes the antisocial choices. Fulfilling as it must the mandate of such a negative ideal, the goal of the youngster's behavior becomes the destruction of the self. The paths to achieving this goal can be subtle, devious, covert and complex; not infrequently there will be a considerable involvement of one's surrounding world in the service of bringing down the lighting on one's own head.

As we have noted, the two regulating ideals are never really united; they always remain separate function-clusters.[6] They do, however, interact with one another. The effects of this interaction can be diverse. Where the strength of the positive ideal far outweighs its negative counterpart, the subjective sense of self will include a state of heightened self-esteem. One is approved of by one's inner voice — and one maintains a benign outlook on the world. Most people are perceived as trying to be good, and one reacts to that component of one's social surround. Under such conditions, the negative ideal will seldom find expression, and then only when a specific contextual configuration excites some deeply buried memory. Where the two regulating ideals are more or less equally powerful and maintain a fluctuating but stable balance, then the individual has good moments and bad ones depending on environmental feedback. There are periods of vulnerability and failure, and moments of success accompanied by a feeling of competence. Usually a person learns early to style his or her life so as to maximize the good experiences (those that support the positive ideal); this in turn serves to keep the bad feelings at bay. Indeed, many forms of treatment are designed primarily to address the positive ideal. Such therapists seek to maximize successes, to instill feelings of competence, and to devise ways and means to increase self-esteem. For less serious levels of disturbance, such approaches often work with reasonable degrees of effectiveness. The reason they are effective is because of this inner dynamic — in effect, the existence of two regulating principles that are both grasping for the levers of behavioral control. They are exquisitely sensitive to environmental influences, and the one or the other will be enhanced by the nature of any given context. A criticism or a temptation can stimulate the negative ideal and incline the individual in one direction; a word of praise or an empathic response to an expressed feeling can do just the opposite.

In any case, whichever regulating principle is stronger will dominate both the individual's subjective self-feeling and the objective pattern of conduct he or she displays. Thus, relieving the intensity of the negative ideal by therapy, or increasing the strength of the positive ideal by praise, support, encouragement, and the enhancement of competence, will have different effects but comparable outcomes. The end result is the ascendancy of the one dimension of regulation and the eclipsing of the other. To the extent that the positive is elevated by whatever means, the amelioration of inner pain and outer deviance will follow in proportion. Where, however, the negative ideal far outweighs the positive, we have youngsters whose lives are dominated by a driven need to destroy.[7] In the more extreme cases still, the need is to destroy everything, the self, the significant others, the world (Hauser & Smith, 1991).

Subjective/Dynamic Aspects

Clinically, such youngsters present a number of characteristic findings. To begin with, they feel bad inside. This is not exactly sadness; it is not so much that they are blue or depressed. They feel rather as though they were tainted, soiled, awry; often they speak of hurting inside, a kind of protracted inner ache, like a continuing morbid tone, that underlies their very sense of being.

In itself, this is a most unpleasant aspect of their experience, and they seek to ease this inner pain in a variety of ways. Sometimes they are restless, driven, hyperactive, constantly intruding on others, frantic for external attention, trying always to get out of themselves. It may well be that this hunger for attention is in part a direct consequence of the first-year-of-life experience of neglect. The deprivational stress of that early time results in a chronic nagging hunger for interaction that can overshadow many of the healthier aspects of object relationship strategies. This in turn will be exploited by the negative ideal as another means of bringing failure and rejection into the child's life. A common explanation offered for quite serious forms of deviance such as suicidal gestures or fire-setting is stated in precisely these terms: "I just did it for attention." In fact it seems that this craving for attention must be the product of a rather complex series of developmental events. It reflects both the unmet needs of the infant, and the attempts on the part of the child or teenager to escape from the pain of inner experience by engaging in outer interaction.

The best means of assuring the growth of the positive ideal during early development entails a continuing empathic bond between infant and caretaker. It is the failure of empathy as much as anything else that causes the positive ideal to wither on the vine (Gray, 1982). The inability — or the refusal — to respond to an infant's needs, the miscuing of message exchanges, and the angry or sadistic elements in the caretaker's management style will foster the fullest flowering of the negative ideal.

Where the negative elements predominate, the children come away from this early sequence of exchanges possessed, as it were, by the dominating inner presence of a hate-filled critic and punisher. This gives a very special cast to their subsequent subjective experience. One consequence is the bad inner feeling noted above. When we seek to describe this clinically, we cast it in the language of low self-esteem, poor self-image, lack of a sense of personal worth, or some form of depressive experience. But this outlook is not necessarily confined to the self. Since in fact such fostering of the negative ideal has emerged from interaction with significant and powerful others, such children will continue to perceive much of the social world in a similar light. Authorities and caretaking adults in particular will be regarded with mistrust and suspiciousness, and will be reacted to with challenge and defensiveness. More than that, there will be a veritable flight from the opportunity to form positive attachments. These children have been through a state of needy dependency on adults, they know what happened, and they want no more of that.

Alienation

One of the most pervasive feelings that follows on this pattern of development is the experience of the self as alien. The people among whom one lives do not seem to be dominated by such negative feelings; in some unaccountable way one is different. Most people seem able to feel good, to have fun with one another, to feel secure about their relationships, to trust each other to a

reasonable extent, to feel warm and caring and positive — whereas our youngster feels altogether apart from such experiences. He/she does not know how
they do it. Why don't others feel so out of it, why don't they feel this sense of
inner badness, this differentness from others? The dominance of the negative
ideal is like a cloud hanging overhead; where everyone else seems to live in
the sunshine, such a youngster lives always in the shadows. Thus, a 13-year-
old girl commented in the course of her therapy: "All I do is cause pain to
people. I'm so mixed up. I'm a bad person who doesn't deserve to have good
stuff happen."

The usual consequence is that feeling like an outsider, these youngsters
cannot comfortably fit in. They feel bereft and alienated until, presently,
encountering other such outsiders, true congeners, people who live in the same
penumbral world, they join themselves to them. Thus the youth finds "bad
company," and becomes part of the more or less delinquent group. Later, the
bad company may well be blamed for the ensuing troubles, without recognizing that it was not happenstance that caused the youngster to enter this
congeries of outsiders; the affinity was there to begin with. On a deeper level,
the peer group is often converted in the youngster's fantasy into the empathic
understanding family that was originally missing. In their shared misery, the
illusion is created of caring camaraderie. This is reinforced by the mutual
depredations in which they engage, exciting secret activities that bring them
all together and heighten the image of mutuality. All sorts of variants occur.
For example, one youth described frequently breaking into and entering homes
in his town in order to steal a variety of objects that were then used to set up a
clubhouse, a home of his own, which he could share with his friends.

Given this inner sense of badness and feeling of self as pariah, it is not
surprising that these youngsters become remarkably self-centered. There is
such tension and conflict inside, they are trying so hard to keep the thrusts of
the negative ideal both unconscious and at bay, that they tend to be taken up
largely with their own concerns. More than that, they sometimes try to evade
the negative ideal by flying to the opposite extreme — a sort of pseudo-posi-
tive stance. They become grandiose, boastful, and self-aggrandizing, while
underneath the self-hatred seethes.

One of the logical end-points for the social difficulties they encounter is
presently to attach themselves to some coven of witches, to form an association with a demonic cult, or to join a "church" of devil worshipers. For people
who feel the presence of inner evil, who feel prey to, and ruled by, a demonic
internal enemy, such an association makes good sense. Within this context
they can achieve a measure of kinship, of belonging. If anything, it gives them
a sense of validation.

One of the more striking aspects of this condition is the extraordinary
pressure such youngsters feel to confound their own lives. This is always baffling to the external observer. Sometimes the involved youngsters have evident

strengths. They may be intelligent, good-looking, even talented. But the story of their growing up is an account of a crescendo of mishaps, failures, and disasters. In particular, they cannot tolerate success. Every positive experience, every encounter with pleasure, runs full tilt into the inner (usually unconscious) voice which tells them: "You don't deserve this. This is not for the likes of you. You are fooling people, cheating people. You make them think that you are worthwhile, when you know that you are not. Now do something to spoil what you have achieved, go ahead, do it!"

Often such youngsters maintain their inner equilibrium by provoking punishment. This may go on on many levels. If they sit in a working group, they make noises, make faces, poke the kids around them, act in a clowning manner, try to evoke laughter, ask odd questions, throw things, or otherwise act as irritants and foci of disturbance. Inevitably everyone gets mad at them, and they are likely to be expelled from the group. If they are part of a community with rules about dress, appearance, or places where one may or may not be, they will find many ways to tease and challenge and beard the authorities, and so bring down retaliation on their own heads.

One of the most interesting aspects of the adjustment such youngsters attain is the relative absence of guilt that they sometimes express. At best, they often seem untroubled by their miscreance, or they might even seem to take pride in their depredations. In fact, they can maintain such an equilibrium because they are paying off the inner punisher by a different route. They need not feel the bite of conscience; they substitute the chronic struggle with family, associates, school authorities, police, the neighbors, employers, and other persons who play a role in their lives. By alienating these important others, by exposing themselves to denunciation, threats, humiliation, fights, rejection, and repeated arrest, they stay in a state of perpetual punishment, and thus keep the inner voice appeased. Instead of guilt, they have trouble. And where no other source of external difficulty is available, they have the sure and certain knowledge that they are slowly destroying themselves with the drugs and alcohol they take in. When confronted, they may say they take these things strictly for fun. But even a superficial investigation will reveal that they are all too well aware of the implications of what they do; they are aware as well of their pain and their need to drown it by the drug usage. What they are not aware of is how much guilt they are avoiding by maintaining a pattern of self-destruction.

In the milder cases the struggle with authority figures will be confined to home and school. Sometimes it is expressed only in the one context, or only in the other. The parent — or the teacher — is then amazed to hear the account given by the other. Where parents have divorced and live apart, one parent may see this behavior, while it is kept hidden from the other — with the ensuing predictable dissonances. In the more serious instances, the provocative behavior spills over into the community, and problems of a whole new order of magnitude then supervene. These youngsters may resort to vandalism, theft,

breaking and entering, shoplifting, and all sorts of associated miscreance so
that their presence becomes anathema. They are shunned and avoided by the
neighbors, and they sometimes become known to the police at a very young
age indeed. They are frequently caught and arrested; not as frequently by far
as their depredations merit, but often enough to develop a long arrest record
at an early age. This is a sure sign of their pathology; the less self-destructive
type of young criminal will tend to be more sagacious in his antisocial behavior and will be far less likely to be apprehended. The youngsters of whom we
speak tend to fulfill Freud's (1916) dictum: Criminal from a sense of guilt.
They externalize the brooding and condemning inner presence in order to
encounter it in a safer arena. Within themselves, the negative ideal knows all
about them and is quick to denounce and excoriate. If, however, the site of
interaction can be shifted to its original locus in the outside world, one can
now rally a host of adaptive techniques as coping devices: one can deny, one
can be sneaky, one can lie, one can seek to run away, one can misdirect and
blame others for what happened, one can rationalize or justify the behavior,
one can get a lawyer and have an ally in the encounter. In short, there are a
great many devices to which one can resort in the extrapersonal setting that
avail little if one tries to resolve these issues internally. The inner punisher
is too knowledgeable and too powerful. It is far safer to draw over it a veil of
unconsciousness and not to know that it is there. Of course that does not make
it go away; one re-encounters it immediately as a presence in the outside world.
But taken all in all, that may still be the best deal available. By and large, all
one has to cope with, then, are the effects of the miscreant activities, and, as
noted, there are ways of doing that. Conversely, getting the outside world to
function as punisher and destroyer will eventually lead to the same outcome.
Albeit indirectly, ultimately the negative ideal attains its goal.

Many youngsters become partially aware of what is happening. They say
things like: "I don't know why it is, I always have to mess myself up. I'll start
out in a school year, or in a job, or in a relationship, and for a while everything
goes OK. My grades are good, the boss likes my work, people want to have
me around. And then, for some reason, I start to miss classes or to not hand in
my homework. Or I get into a fight with someone and I'm in trouble with the
principal. Or I'll take money from the cash register or talk back to the boss. Or
I'll let my friends down or start to tease — I just seem to have to spoil whatever it is I'm succeeding at. And I don't have any reason for it; it just seems to
happen."

In some forms of this disorder, the hostile internal presence presses the
youngster for more direct forms of self-injury and self-destruction. When circumstances act to strengthen the negative ideal, e.g., by loss of an important
attachment (for which the youngster feels responsible), by criticism from a
significant other, by some real or threatened rejection or frustration, etc., the
youth is likely to turn against himself in a vengeful and violent manner. Some

beat their fists bloody against a wall or a grating; some hit their heads against a post; some slash or scarify their skin; some burn themselves with matches, cigarettes, curling irons and the like; some tattoo themselves with multiple needle pricks; and others go out and have accidents.

Even more direct forms of self injury tell of the basically self destructive outcome toward which they are being herded. These take the form of preoccupation with death, scratched wrists, and minor overdoses. Suicidal gestures abound in this population, and acts that are far more serious than mere gestures and that take on genuinely life-threatening character are by no means rare.

One characteristic consequence of the early noxious experience that is the source of the negative ideal is a failure to establish clear ego boundaries. These youngsters cannot discern where they shade off and the outside world begins. This becomes dramatically evident when there is any sort of trauma to someone who is close to them and to whom they feel a meaningful sense of attachment. Whatever it is that happens, they regard it as their fault.[8] They are so convinced of their own badness, that any misadventure, any accident or illness, the breakup of a marriage, a desertion, or even a bad fight between significant others, all these are the fault of the youngster. He or she finds a way to attribute what happened to him/herself. The mental gymnastics such youths will perform in order to explain how it was all their fault can be quite amazing. In fact, they will often be able to say that they realize it is not logical, but the feeling is overwhelming; they know they are responsible and that is all there is to it. The next step for them is to seek some way, usually in the form of punishment, to atone for and undo what they have effected — and some self-destructive behavior can follow. When he heard of the death of his cousin in a car accident, one youngster wanted to ride his bike on the highway, get in front of a truck, and get killed. A common response takes the form of an antisocial act, or a series of such acts, for which the teenagers then get into serious trouble.

The pressure of this inner hostile presence is unrelenting. In their efforts to allay their inner sense of pain, alienation, and self-hatred, these youngsters get readily involved with substances of abuse. These are orally traumatized individuals, and the commonest nostrum they seek will be some form of oral anodyne. From an early age they turn to tobacco, inhalants, alcohol, or pills. With the passage of time, this can readily progress to intravenous drug use. Addiction is common, and many of these cases then face all the complications of the addicts' way of life superimposed on an already aberrant social pattern. The stories that presently emerge are tragic and appalling. Major criminal activity, prostitution, and dog-eat-dog patterns of degraded street living feature prominently among the accounts of these teenagers, some of whom are not yet out of junior high school. In seeking to understand this picture, it is important to keep in mind that the archetypical young addict is an individual dominated by an inner demon of sorts which guides him or her surely on a path toward ultimate self-destruction.

Contributing to this is the fact that in many instances, these youngsters' homes have been sites for major drug and alcohol abuse, and they will often have memories of initial contact with marijuana or beer during their preschool years. Thus, one girl reported that as a little child, her parents would help her get to sleep by puffing cannabis smoke into her face. Asked for his earliest memory, a thirteen-year-old recalled stealing beer from the refrigerator when he was five. There are of course many milder forms of this condition. We deal always with a dynamic flux between two regulating ideals, and the corresponding behaviors may reflect this balance — or imbalance — in a variety of ways.

Clinical Example

One youngster attending a posh school in an upper class neighborhood had a history of repeatedly losing his various possessions. Everywhere he went, he habitually left jackets, gloves, athletic equipment, books, book bags, wallets, keys, and anything else that was not literally fastened to him. Intellectually, he was above average; as a student, however, he was often on the brink of failure. Either he did not get his work done, or, if completed at home, he would lose it or forget it so that he could not hand it in. He was personable and engaging, and his teachers noted on their reports how well he contributed to oral discussions in class, and how nice it was to have him around (despite his recurrent failure to do his work). Notwithstanding his sociability, however, somehow he had very few friends and was keenly aware that in some way he could not name, he was unable to get close to people. At home, he was in endless trouble with his mother; he would disobey her, quarrel with her, and defy her; he would steal money from her purse, and then deny it with every evidence of sincerity. In discussing this with his therapist, he was unable to explain why things went so badly in their relationship. The saving grace in his life was his relatively good relationship with his father. This preserved him from total despair, it supported enough of the positive ideal to keep him from major social difficulties, but it was not enough to compensate completely for the more powerful negative ideal.

It must be observed in passing that this is another common feature of this syndrome. There is regularly an account of a poor relationship with mother. Sometimes this extends to father as well; more often than not, no father is present in the home, and the trouble with mother is all encompassing. Not infrequently the youngster is attached to a grandparent as the one positive figure out of the past. Accordingly, there may be a major eruption of symptoms when grandma or grandpa falls ill, has an accident, or dies. This can take form as beginning heavy drug use or as an outbreak of antisocial behavior.

One of the commonest sites for the expression of this negative ideal is failure at school. This is complicated by another phenomenon which is closely related to the establishment of such an ideal. The early failures of empathy and attachment which beget this condition can often have a parallel effect of equally disastrous character on the unfolding of the various cognitive functions of the ego. This is apparently a selective process and cannot be systematically predicted. But should development take such a turn, the buds of the basic integrative functions which allow one to learn to assimilate and manipulate symbols will be pinched off by the impact of the early devastating interpersonal stress. As a result, later efforts to learn to read, to calculate, and to abstract will be severely impeded by these traumatic preliminaries.

Consequently, when the child starts his/her academic career, all too often he/she discovers that there is a handicap — one is different from the other children not only in the basic self-feelings, but in one's capacity to do academic tasks as well. Thus, from the very outset, school becomes an arena of discontent, a site of failure, and a realm of struggle. To add to the difficulties, in addition to the strained peer relationships and the learning problems, all the struggles with the caretaking figures at home are readily transferred to the educators. Within the classroom, it is the teachers who are the nurturers, the rewarders and the punishers, and all the remembered stressful feelings come to be attributed to them. As a result, on many fronts, school provides all too many occasions for painful confrontation.

Where the children are not too badly damaged to begin with, where, for example, cognitive functions have been spared, various compensations can emerge. Thus, the rewards of successful school work can reinforce the positive ego ideal and help overcome some of the force of the negative presence. The attachment to a particularly sensitive and supportive teacher can offer an alternative to the inner messages derived from the critical, rejecting, and nonempathic home. Hence, in some instances, given a proper mix of preserved function and good luck, school experiences can offer potentially troubled children a way out of the jungle. We do not know how many children are saved in this way; we know only that far too many are lost.

For those who have early school difficulties, it is most exceptional for them ever to graduate from high school. In particular, if substance abuse enters the scene by 9 or 10 years of age, the children will most likely drop out in junior high school, truancy laws notwithstanding. Thereafter, the course of their lives tends to be a long spiral downward. With the widespread presence of lethal weapons in our society, that course is all too often abruptly abbreviated.

Summary

This study is an attempt to formulate the dynamics of the group of adolescents involved in major drug use and other antisocial behavior. As consultant to a drug rehabilitation center for teenagers, the author has had occasion to interview and evaluate a large number of youths whose lives had taken such a turn. Certain aspects of the life style and behavior patterns of these young people show striking similarities. In particular, their behavior evidences the presence of a central self-destructive moiety which can be likened to a negative ego ideal; this acts to shape and to direct their lives. This element in the character structure of these patients is described in clinical and theoretical (developmental) terms, with special address to: a chronic low-grade sense of inner malaise, a tendency to self-blame for whatever goes wrong for family and close friends, feelings of alienation from the larger society around them, behavioral provocativeness in the service of seeking the relief that punishment brings, recurrent gestures of self-mutilation, frequent involvement with cults of devil worship, a record of multiple antisocial acts punctuated by numerous arrests, and repeated suicidal gestures and attempts. The origins of the negative regulatory superego elements which make for this type of psychopathology are explored.

Notes

1. Emde (1991) describes "... a clear picture of a separately organized, biologically based system for positive emotions..." (p. 12) which he discerns in the early months of life.
2. This comparison of early attachment to addiction, if taken in conjunction with the idealized way the infant regards mother tells us of the close connection between such idealization and addiction. It explains why the 12-step programs of AA, NA, and other such self-help groups require the invoking of a higher power as one of the steps. The prototype experience is that of an infant interacting with an awesome other, and the union of the individual with a group and with a group ideal that is larger than the self, is a critical part of any such treatment. What is involved here is preverbal experience; it is not surprising that ordinary verbal therapies do not really work well with these problems.
3. Emde (1991) reports that Joy Osofsky studied an at-risk population involving offspring of teenage mothers and found "... almost no evidence of positive affect sharing. Instead, most affect sharing was negative..." which was unusual in the parallel studies of normal children (p. 14). Later still, Emde notes that "... a lack of positive emotions may be a more sensitive indicator of problems than an excess of negative emotions" (p. 16).
4. Hauser and Smith (1991) mention the studies of Fischer, Shaver, and Carnochan (1989) which suggest that times of rapid cognitive growth are also periods of great affective vulnerability. Surely the most dramatic periods of cognitive unfolding take place during in the first year of life and again at puberty and early adolescence. They are also the epochs of most intense idealization.
5. For Parens (1991) just as is true for the other affects, there is a developmental sequence for aggression as well. In particular, irritability and rage are present from birth on (with their threshold and intensity strongly influenced by genetic factors). Rage is the organismic ridding reaction to a noxious stimulus. Anger

and hostility emerge in the second half of the first year. And during the second half of the second year, all of these culminate in hate. That is to say, as hostility attaches to a particular internalized interpersonal event and becomes stable and enduring, it takes on the character of hate. Eventually, these affects determine the nature of ambivalence, and the quality of sadism, masochism, envy, prejudice, and revenge. The inevitable power struggle which the child's growing autonomy strivings initiate between nine and sixteen months take form internally as increasing ambivalence. Inhibition, denial, displacement of hostility and splitting begin to appear. Beginning internalization of maternal dictates follows. These early internalizations are superego precursors. The child is concerned not only with mother's disapproval and the loss of her love, but also with the enactment of his own rage toward her, and her destruction. As the child moves into rapprochement and is torn between the siren call of symbiosis and the inviting prospect of autonomy, the internalized feelings of resentment and hostility can now become structured as hate. Such emotion can be displaced from the object onto others in the form of scapegoating, prejudice and sadism, or onto the self as self-hurt and masochism. Eventually, as the rapprochement subphase gives way to the Oedipal phase, a whole new organization of hostility supervenes with primary emphases on curiosity and rivalry.

6. Emde (1991) notes that there is no correlation between positive and negative emotions, that under conditions of low stress, "positive emotions are measurably independent of negative emotions" (p. 17). Negative emotions are more stable over time and show substantial heritability. Emde observes that Gray (1982) regards positive and negative emotionality as separate functional brain systems. "... these two dimensions of personality might best be thought of as separate dynamic predispositions toward negative and positive affects" (p. 18). Indeed, there is evidence for separate anatomical organization of the positive and negative positions ".... the left anterior hemisphere has been implicated in organizing approach behavior and the right anterior hemisphere in organizing withdrawal behavior and negative affect" (p. 26). Contrariwise, left frontal lesions seem to make for depression, whereas damage to the right frontal area leads to indifference or euphoria.

7. Parens (1991) describes manifestations of aggression in infants four to six months of age He classifies these behaviors into two major clusters, namely: as non-affective and non-destructive aggression (e.g., exploratory activity and chewing) and as unpleasure-related and pleasure-related hostile destructiveness (e.g., rage reactions and teasing behavior). In particular, hostile destructiveness is provoked by experiences of excessive unpleasure (what is excessive being determined by the meaning of the experience to the child's self).

8. Lewis (1991) comments that "...there is evidence to indicate that very young children of sick parents are more apt to internalize blame. They feel they are responsible for their parents' illness or, if they misbehave, they are responsible for it getting worse or continuing..." (p. 67). He goes on to observe that young children are more susceptible to internalization than older children and more apt to blame themselves and to experience shame. In particular, they are likely to condemn themselves for their parents' depression.

References

Chess, S. & Thomas, A. (1986). *Temperament in clinical practice*. New York: Guilford Press.

Emde, R. (1991). Positive emotions for psychoanalytic theory: Surprises from infancy research and new directions. *Journal of the American Psychoanalytic Association, 39* (Suppl.), 5–44.

Fischer, K., Shaver, P., & Carnochan, P. (1989). A skill approach to emotional development. In W. Damon (Ed.), *Child development today and tomorrow* (pp. 107–136). San Francisco: Jossey-Bass.

Freud, S. (1916). Some character types met with in the course of psychoanalytic practice. *Standard Edition, 14,* 309–333. London: Hogarth Press.

Gallagher, W. (1992, July/August). Motherless child. *The Sciences,* 12–15.

Gray, J. (1982). *The neuropsychology of anxiety.* New York: Oxford University Press.

Hauser, S. & Smith, H. (1991). The development and experience of affect in adolescence. *Journal of the American Psychoanalytic Association, 39* (Suppl.), 131–165.

Jacobson, E. (1954). The self and the object world: Vicissitudes of their infantile cathexes and their influence on ideational and affective development. *The Psychoanalytic Study of the Child, 9,* 75–127.

Kernberg, O. (1991). The psychopathology of hatred. *Journal of the American Psychoanalytic Association, 39* (Suppl.), 209–238.

Lewis, M. (1991). Self-conscious emotions and the development of the self. *Journal of the American Psychoanalytic Association, 39* (Suppl.), 45–73.

Mahler, M., Pine, F., & Bergman, A. (1975). *The psychological birth of the human infant.* New York: Basic Books.

Parens, H. (1991). A view of the development of hostility in early life. *Journal of the American Psychoanalytic Association, 39* (Suppl.), 75–108.

Parker, G., Barrett, E., & Hickie, I. (1992). From nurture to network: Examining the links between perceptions and parenting received. in childhood and social bonds in adulthood. *American Journal of Psychiatry, 149,* 877–885.

Werner, E. & Smith, R. (1989). *Vulnerable but invincible: A longitudinal study of resilient children and youth.* New York: Adams Bannister Cox.

19
A Changing Female Identity

RICHARD GORDON

The overwhelming majority of people who develop problems with anorexia and bulimia — regardless of nationality or social class — are female. This simple fact, which is acknowledged by virtually all researchers and clinicians, no matter what their particular theoretical persuasion, is of critical importance in a sociocultural understanding of why these problems have become an epidemic in recent times. And despite its virtually universal acknowledgment, its theoretical significance has yet to be fully appreciated.

At the outset, it is important to acknowledge the possibility that such a lopsided sex ratio may have something to do with biological differences between the sexes. There are a number of possibilities that suggest themselves. For one thing, laboratory studies show that female animals are more able to withstand starvation (that is, they survive longer) than males (see Hoyenga & Hoyenga 1979).[1] Such differential tolerance may have evolutionary significance. In times of food scarcity, the female's ability to tolerate starvation may have particular adaptive value in light of the female role in species propagation. This of course does not account for anorexia nervosa, which occurs under conditions of relative affluence, but it makes it more understandable why females are more likely to draw upon self-starvation as a means of coping with stress. A second possible link has to do with the generally higher ratio of fat to lean tissue in females relative to males, a fact that also can be interpreted from the standpoint of evolution. Again, in periods of famine or food scarcity, it would have been advantageous to females to have reserve stores of fat tissue in order to sustain pregnancy and lactation (Beller, 1977).[2] In human cultures that emphasize the importance of thinness in women, females may experience more stress in efforts at dieting, given their greater biological propensity towards adiposity. A third possibility has to do with the relative complexity of female pubertal development, from the standpoint of hormonal functions

From: Gordon, Richard. (1990). *Anorexia and bulimia. Anatomy of a social epidemic* (pp. 50–65). Cambridge, MA: B. Blackwell, Ltd. Copyright © Richard Gordon. Reprinted with permission of Blackwell and Richard Gordon.

and the intricacy of related brain mechanisms. Such differential complexity may make the pubertal process more susceptible to disruption under stress, as in anorexia nervosa (K. Halmi, personal communication). And finally, it is possible that females are more vulnerable to endogenous depression, which may have some bearing on the proposed linkage of some cases of bulimia to depression (Pope & Hudson, 1984).

Despite the possible role of biological factors in predisposing women to developing eating disorders, it seems virtually impossible to account for the specific psychological features of these conditions without taking into account social and cultural influences. For example, anorexic patients have an enormous drive to be thin and an equally intense fear of becoming fat. It is difficult to understand the centrality of these concerns without taking into account the social and cultural pressures on women to achieve thinness, as well as the specific stigma, peculiar to Western societies, attached to fat women. These pressures have increased significantly throughout the twentieth century, and the particular meanings that they have for women are centrally involved in understanding the eating-disorders epidemic. But in addition, there are more subtle features of the psychology of eating disorders that demand an interpretation in social terms. These revolve around the nearly universal concerns of eating-disordered patients with issues of autonomy, self-esteem, achievement, and control. And this spectrum of psychological issues can be broadly understood as relating to the larger problem of the development of psychosocial identity.

The concept of identity is a difficult one, but it is critical in understanding the central problems confronted by women with eating disorders. It has received its most elaborate formulation in the writings of Erik Erikson (1964; 1975). Erikson suggests that the notion of identity relates to the individual's experience of self-cohesion, or, as he puts it, the sense of continuity and sameness in time. The development of a cohesive or "viable" identity depends on many individual and social factors, but among the most important is the individual's ability to "synthesize" or bring together the divergent and conflicting aspects of his or her social experience. The development of identity is a dynamic process, which unfolds throughout a person's life, and is influenced by a host of factors — historical and sociological conditions, the particularities of family experiences, biological predispositions, and the accidents of development. However, the most critical period for the formation of an identity is during adolescence, the period in which the individual must put together the foundations of the self laid down in childhood experience with the new demands and challenges posed by the personal and social experiences of that period. The process of identity formation is particularly susceptible to disruption by radical changes in social roles or cultural expectations. This is one reason why individuals suddenly exposed to a radically different culture — say, in a situation of migration — seem particularly vulnerable to psychological problems. But it also suggests that even within the same culture, a particular group which is exposed to dramatic changes in cultural expectations — say, through a sudden change in social role — will also be highly susceptible to epidemic symptoms of identity confusion (Murphy, 1982).

In this chapter, I wish to apply this latter notion to an understanding of the epidemic increase in eating disorders. More specifically, I want to develop the notion that eating disorders are the extreme expression of radically altered social expectations on women that have emerged on a mass scale since about mid-century, but particularly since the 1960s. Over a relatively short period of time, young women have encountered a new set of pressures, demanding an orientation towards achievement, competitiveness, and independence — a set of values that conflict sharply with traditional Western definitions of the female role. In a period of increased opportunities but also intensified pressures, many have found it difficult to synthesize a "viable" or "workable" identity, and suffer inwardly from a sense of fragmentation, confusion, and self-doubt (see, for example, Komarovsky, 1985). What I am proposing here is that the central psychological problems experienced by patients with eating disorders, that center on issues of self-esteem, autonomy, and achievement, are a magnified reflection of much more pervasive conflicts in the wider culture about the female role. The young woman with an eating disorder therefore is the unwitting carrier of pervasive cultural crisis.

From the standpoint of the theoretical framework of this book, the person who develops an ethnic disorder, as Devereux (1961, 1978, 1980) suggested, suffers from the psychological conflicts that are pervasive in the culture, but are experienced by the patient in a particularly acute form. The resulting anxiety, depression, or confusion are sufficiently severe for the person to develop symptoms, which serve as defenses against underlying psychological distress. The situation for anorexia is parallel to that of hysteria in the late nineteenth century, which also was an expression of confusion and contradictory prescriptions in the female role (Smith-Rosenberg, 1972). The nature of the conflicts experienced by hysterical patients, however, was quite different, and had to do with the specific historical situation of women at that time. They revolved around issues of strict sexual repression, as well as blanket restrictions on female education and participation in public life. Nevertheless, the current epidemic of eating disorders is very much parallel to the wave of conversion hysteria that seemed to sweep over Europe and America in the nineteenth century. Both are expressions, appropriate to their own times, of the dilemmas of female identity, in a cultural climate in which the female role is ambiguously defined and still limited by institutionalized male control.

Female Identity in Anorexia Nervosa

So central are issues of female identity in anorexia nervosa that it is difficult to see why more has not been made of this issue in previous formulations.

Most cultural interpretations of anorexia have stressed the fashion of female slenderness, which is undoubtedly of central importance in understanding the eating disorders (for example, Schwartz, Thompson, & Johnson, 1983). But few have addressed the more complex issue of *why* the emphasis on thinness is so important to contemporary women, and particularly to those who develop eating disorders. More detailed study of the psychological conflicts that lead certain women to develop anorexia lead centrally to the underlying issues of identity and self-worth that lead the single-minded pursuit of thinness to be "chosen" as the principal symptom.

A central feature of anorexic patients emphasized by Hilde Bruch (1973) is that these are girls or women who grow up with a profound sense of ineffectiveness, a sense of deficiency in their ability to influence their environment and determine their own fate.[3] This lacuna in the sense of the self is a consequence of growing up in a family which places intense emphasis on achievement and performance, but simultaneously deprives the child of opportunities for self-initiated behavior or for the development of her own unique possibilities. When such a child becomes an adolescent, therefore, she is not well equipped to cope with the typical developmental demands of that period, which require a greater degree of independent functioning and autonomous choice. The events that typically trigger the onset of anorexic dieting are just those experiences that challenge the adolescent's sense of independence and power: the first heterosexual relationship, the loss of a friendship, an illness or death of a valued family member, or moving away from home (Bruch, 1978). For those whose sense of autonomy is deficient, these "normal" developmental stresses precipitate a crisis in self-confidence. Dieting and weight loss, which not only bring about positive comments from others but also give the individual an experience of power that she has never before known, become quickly reinforced and then entrenched as a source of pride and perhaps even superiority.

This description of the typical developmental course of anorexia nervosa is now widely accepted, and is well borne out by clinical experience. What is usually not stated is the extent to which the characteristic experiences and problems of anorexic patients mirror and magnify common problems of female identity, problems that are typically encountered in especially acute form during adolescence. For the intense sense of ineffectiveness and exclusive focus on external expectations is the extreme version of a common developmental pattern among girls in Western societies. Studies of normal female development, which have a certain degree of cross-cultural consistency, show that despite changes in public ideology about sex roles, girls are still socialized to be pleasers and are given far less encouragement than boys to develop self-initiated and autonomous behaviors (Block, 1985). Bruch's suggestion that the mothers of anorexic patients fail to respond to their daughters' self-initiated activities and signals actually reflects a more general pattern, established by developmental research, of providing girls with significantly less "response-contingent stimulation" than is typically given to boys (Block, 1985). The orientation towards pleasing others and the intense sensitivity and responsiveness to external demands is of course consistent with girls' socialization to be nurturers, a pattern which persists, despite the changes brought about by feminism. Jean Baker Miller (1976), in her pioneering book about female identity, suggests that women's self-worth is still determined by the requirement to help and assist others, a project that requires the subordination of one's own needs to the needs and expectations of another. Such a formulation is directly applicable to the core experiences of those who develop anorexia nervosa, although the latter is an extreme version of the norm.

One consequence of these patterns of socialization is that by the time a girl reaches adolescence, she is often affected by feelings of powerlessness and dependency, feelings that make it very difficult to break away from the family and establish her own life. This is especially true for anorexic patients, and it provides a direct explanation of why the disorder frequently erupts in adolescence. The experiences that typically trigger anorexic dieting, experiences of loss or separation (real or anticipated), are those that present particular challenges to autonomous functioning. To the pre-anorexic teenager, whose self-esteem is highly vulnerable and sense of autonomy very fragile, such experiences can come as a crushing blow. Going on a diet, and ultimately a starvation diet, becomes a way of achieving a sense of power and independence for a person who has been painfully confronted with his or her own powerlessness. In a culture that values dieting and thinness, such a "solution" seems readily understandable in terms of the positive social response that it typically arouses (at least initially). But also, radical dieting is also powerfully reinforcing for a person whose sense of power and self-control has been so compromised.

For anorexics, another factor often comes into play, one that is at once familial and social: the intense pressure to achieve. The families of anorexics typically place an enormous value on achievement and performance. Although they are not necessarily "affluent," virtually all are driven by middle-class values of upward mobility, performance, and the work ethic (Bruch, 1978, p. 25). Many have a history of economic insecurity and have advanced significantly beyond the economic status of their parents. There is often a sense of anxiety in these families about maintaining their hard-won economic and social status, a concern that falls particularly heavily on the shoulders of the daughter who becomes anorexic. In addition, some studies show that in many of the families of anorexics, there has been a history of male failure or inadequacy, something that may only become apparent if one looks at the grandparent generation (Slade, 1984). In any case, there is often a mythical notion in these families that women must be strong in order to compensate for perceived male inadequacies. These anxieties are not explicitly articulated, but the young woman who develops anorexia often feels them very acutely.

It is extremely important to understand that because of their external focus and pleasing orientation, anorexics feel that their achievements in school or in athletics are a performance for them, not a proof to themselves of their own worthiness. In fact, one of the paradoxes of anorexia nervosa is how worthless these young women feel, despite what is often a high degree of success from an external standpoint. This is again not a unique experience, but one that is very characteristic for contemporary women. Jean Baker Miller (1976) suggests that women often get caught in a cycle of pleasing and depletion, of "doing good and feeling bad" (note 16). This is the consequence of an identity that is based on pleasing and supporting others, rather than behaving according to one's own needs and self-chosen goals. The entire complex of externally oriented achievement and pleasing behavior has been idealized in popular culture in the imagery of the "superwoman," the woman who "has it all" and pleases a largely masculine audience with her feminine charm and worldly accomplishments. This modernized version of the traditional notion of the "good girl" has been widely and justifiably attacked by feminists as a perversion of the ideals of female equality. Because of their own developmental experiences, anorexics seem particularly vulnerable to internalizing this distorted ideology. As Bruch (1978) pointed out, many anorexics experience the ideology of liberation as one more external demand for perfection that they feel compelled to live up to: "growing girls can experience this liberation as a demand and feel that they *have* to do something outstanding.... Many of my patients have expressed the feeling...that there were too many choices and they had been afraid of not choosing correctly" (p. ix).

While not always explicit, anorexics sometimes openly articulate their experiences in terms of confusions about gender role and female identity. Many grow up with a secret though powerful fantasy about being a boy — a "tall, long-legged prince," as one patient put it — a dream which, as Bruch (1973) suggests, is typically shattered by the experience of puberty (p. 98). In some cases this fantasy may represent a wish to be the male child that the father either never had or was disappointed with, but in others it may be a yearning for the power that boys are perceived to have and the anorexic feels so acutely that she lacks. For some anorexics, the slenderness and loss of curves that result from dieting represent a triumphant transformation of the female figure into that of preadolescent boy. Casky (1986), in an interesting treatment of these issues, suggests that the anorexic seeks an identification with an ideal of asensual intellectuality, the mythical image of the *puer*, an image projected onto her father, whose own frequent orientation towards and emphasis on intellectual achievement has had a powerful impact on his anorexic daughter. Some anorexics are quite explicit about their resentment of suffering the social disadvantages of being female. One of Bruch's (1988) patients, Fawn, commented that "it wasn't fair as a little girl. There wasn't any way of winning. You were wrong before you started" (p. 108). And in a wry comment on her feelings about being out of step with new standards of female assertiveness, another patient, Annette, suggested that "it would have been worse [if I had been a boy — ed.] because I would have the same ghastly peace-minded temperament and that is unacceptable in boys. At least in girls it used to be acceptable, but now it is a culturally unacceptable way of behavior. But I continue to behave like that" (p. 126). Annette, in fact, felt that her accomplishments in school were strangely alien to her, as if they were really those of a man — and the purpose of which had been to please her father.

This desire to escape womanhood and to achieve a certain type of masculine ideal — one of intellectuality and spiritual purity — can be understood on one level in terms of familial dynamics. Many anorexics feel particularly bound by their father's expectations, and seek to disengage themselves from their own bodily feelings of femaleness — an effort that is frequently reinforced by a disturbance in their emotional connection to their mothers. However, equally important is the wider social context of these feelings. In an age in which women are thrust into a situation in which they must prove their worth through work and intellectual accomplishment, many women feel that they must prove themselves the equal of men, and for some this may mean disengaging oneself from their own femaleness, which has undergone a cultural devaluation. Anorexics carry out this purge of femaleness in a particularly radical and concrete fashion. The cultural ideal of female thinness, to which anorexics aspire to the extreme, may itself have something to do with the aspirations of women to equal power with men, an idea that will be explored further in the next chapter.

Of particular interest is the much-discussed relationship of anorexic patients with their mothers. The mother–daughter bond in these families tends to be unusually intense, and it is often a consequence of the mother's powerful identification with her daughter as a compensation for a disappointment in her relationship with her husband — a disappointment which typically is unarticulated in the service of preserving "family harmony." The mothers of anorexics have been too frequently blamed in the past for their daughter's illness, partly as a result of the long psychiatric (particularly psychoanalytic) tradition of "mother-bashing." While it is true that the mother's intense closeness and control often blocks the daughter's efforts to achieve autonomy, the social context of the mother's situation is typically not taken into account. The mothers of anorexics are, as Bruch (1978) suggested, typically talented women who sacrificed their own ambitions and careers in the service of their families. Many gave up their careers when their first child was born. In effect, these were the social expectations of women from an earlier, "pre-liberated" generation. Their resulting depression and clinging to their daughters can therefore be understood not only as an individual flaw, but rather as a product of their own social circumstances and experience. What makes the whole situation particularly explosive is that in the environment of the 1970s and 1980s, adolescent girls are everywhere surrounded by an ideology of independence, an ideology that can often induce its own feelings of guilt and inadequacy for not being able to "break away." This poses a particularly painful dilemma for the girl who becomes anorexic, who tends to feel a poignant sense of responsibility for her mother's well-being.

While it is not always the central issue, sexuality frequently plays an important role in the development of anorexia nervosa. The issue of sexuality was probably overemphasized in earlier psychoanalytic formulations about anorexia, in which the resistance to food was seen invariably to represent a symbolic fear of oral impregnation. However, for a number of anorexics, unwanted or problematic sexual experiences trigger the crisis in self-confidence that precipitates severely restrictive dieting. In some instances, the first sexual experience, while voluntary, is experienced as "disgusting" or "painful," and further lowers an already vulnerable sense of self-esteem (Beaumont, Abraham, & Simson, 1981). In a certain number of cases, the experience is a more drastic instance of sexual assault or abuse. In one of the most accessible autobiographies of anorexia, Aimee Liu (1979) opens her story with an account of a preadolescent rape by two boys that took place during a holiday family visit. While Liu does not explicitly tie this experience to the development of her anorexia a few years later, it is clear that this experience of violation and bodily vulnerability is implicated in her efforts to rid her body of its emerging signs of femaleness. Liu's experience is not an isolated one, as clinical experience suggests an extraordinarily high rate of sexual abuse among women with eating disorders, a phenomenon whose significance is just beginning to be appreciated.

Theoretically, the role of sexuality in the development of anorexia nervosa has been emphasized by the English psychiatrist Arthur H. Crisp. Crisp (1980) underscores the important links between female pubertal development and the development of body fat. It has been well established that the emergence of the menstrual cycle is critically connected to the development of a certain amount of body fat (the so-called "critical fat threshold," (Frisch & MacArthur, 1974). In addition, experientially and socially, the development of secondary sexual characteristics, in the form of curves, is also dependent on the development of a certain degree of fatness. Thus, biologically, experientially, and socially, fatness in females is critically connected with the emergence of sexuality in adolescence. The widespread preoccupation of female teenagers with curbing bodily shape and appetite is critically connected with the self-regulation of sexual desires, in an environment in which traditional middle-class sexual morality has unraveled. Anorexia, which Crisp suggests commonly emerges from a family background of puritanical sexual morality and anxiety about unrestrained female sexuality, represents, among other things, a fearful regression to a prepubertal state, in which the presence of disturbing sexual feelings has been effectively banished.

From a cultural standpoint, sexuality is an important component of the wider transformation of female identity. The general relaxation of sexual constraints that took shape in the 1960s probably has had a more powerful impact on females than on males, for whom adolescent sexual activity was formerly tolerated and perhaps even acceptable. Studies of adolescent sexual behavior in the late 1970s and early 1980s, while still few, indicate that female adolescents have in general become more active sexually and at an earlier age, and in fact differ little in their sexual experience from males (Curran, 1977). Meanwhile, the cultural climate regarding sexuality has changed radically in the direction of permissiveness — and exploitation — since the 1960s. The commercial exploitation of the new atmosphere of sexual openness, including soap-opera titillations, sexualized preadolescent fashion models, and pornography, has not been pretty. In this atmosphere, it is not surprising that some vulnerable adolescent females have developed a symptom — anorexia — that represents a radical avoidance and withdrawal from the implications of sexuality. It is of considerable interest that during the same period in which eating disorders have increased, teenage pregnancy has become a problem of growing concern in Western societies, particularly in the United States. As Brumberg (1988) has suggested, both anorexia nervosa and teenage pregnancy may represent two sides of the same coin, the problem of control of female sexuality in an environment in which traditional constraints and standards have crumbled. And these two apparently opposite responses to the dilemma of sexual control may be tied in turn to differences in socioeconomic status, with teen pregnancy representing a hyper-affirmation of sexuality by a deprived adolescent who has no other route to a sense of power, while anorexia represents its negation in the service of newly reinforced cultural ideals of female achievement.

Bulima: The Facade of Perfection and the Secret Self

The dynamics of bulimia, too, seem inextricably bound up with sex-role issues. An early attempt to understand bulimics from this standpoint was a 1976 paper by Boskind-Lodahl, which attempted an explicitly feminist interpretation of both anorexia nervosa and bulimia. Her analysis was based on her observations on a large number of bulimic college students whom she had seen at the Cornell University student health center. One of her aims in writing the paper was a critique of the earlier psychoanalytic formulations, which suggested that all women with eating disorders are symbolically "rejecting femininity" or "refusing womanhood." In contrast, Boskind-Lodahl asserted that precisely the opposite is true. Rather than rejecting the female role, bulimics (or bulimarexics, as she called them) excessively conform to feminine stereotypes. She described her subjects as excessively pleasing, unassertive, and particularly sensitive to criticism or rejection by men. Their striving for thinness and preoccupation with their appearance represents an exaggeration, rather than a rejection, of a cultural female norm. While Boskind-Lodahl's descriptions of bulimics ring true to clinical experience, her critique of the traditional psychoanalytic formulations was somewhat misplaced, since these interpretations were about anorexia nervosa, not the bulimic syndrome. With respect to anorexia, the notion of the rejection of femininity has much greater applicability.

It is my experience, as well as that of others, that most bulimics have experienced some form of significant emotional deprivation in their early life (see, for example, Swift & Letven, 1984; Johnson & Conners, 1985). For some, an illness in a parent, or a problem with depression or alcoholism, leads to the temporary (or chronic) absence or unavailability of a parental figure. In other cases, the parents are in open conflict (much more commonly than in the case in anorexia), sometimes eventuating in a separation or divorce.[4] In many instances, the chronic preoccupation of the parents with external or interpersonal problems results in the child's emotional needs being ignored. Whatever the cause, the child typically early on turns to food as a means of solace, of filling the void left by parental inattentiveness or implicit abandonment. On the surface, however, she typically cultivates a positive façade, an appearance that she "can manage." Underneath, though, she feels needy, childlike, and dependent, feelings of which she is deeply ashamed. Under no circumstances does she permit herself to reveal her primitive feelings of abandonment, sadness, and rage. These are discharged in episodes of binging and purging.

When compared with anorexics, bulimics typically maintain a strong conscious identification with the traditional female sex role. Unlike anorexics, a significant number of whom are sexually avoidant and inexperienced, most bulimics have a history of active sexual involvement and are oriented to pleasing males. Bulimics tend to have had an intensely ambivalent relationship with their fathers. Often, the father has been admired as a role model, and has set high standards of intellectual or professional achievement for his daughter (Boskind-White & White, 1983; Steiger, Van der Feen, Goldstein, & Licher, 1989).[5] Typically, though, the father has been extraordinarily critical, and in some instances overtly abusive; in any case, he continues to be for the bulimic a figure of mystery and fascination. She remains enormously sensitive to male criticism and rejection, and her relationships with men are often turbulent as a result. Nevertheless, for the bulimic the father is a powerful identification figure. In contrast with anorexics, who typically are deeply enmeshed with their mothers, bulimics typically attempt to distance themselves from their mothers, whom they typically perceive as weak and powerless. As Wooley and Wooley (1986) point out, in a period of changing sex-roles in which women increasingly identify with ideals of mobility and power, bulimics reject what they see as their mother's traditionalism and ineffectuality; it is their father's power that they admire and idealize. For bulimics, these attitudes are intimately connected with their ideas about thinness and fatness: thinness is associated with masculine power, fatness with feminine weakness.

Like anorexics, bulimics are unable to work out a satisfactory solution to the problem of identity. They are caught in the dilemma of how to integrate ambition and a need to be powerful with an identity based on pleasing, compliance, and unassertiveness. Their resolution of the problem of identity is a deep split within the self, which entails a façade of perfection, pleasing, and competence, on the one hand, and a secret self that both expresses and binds "messy" feelings of neediness, rage, and helplessness. Thinness is for them the ideal which brings together the conflicting strands of a new female identity, one which is on the one hand powerful, competent, and in control, but on the other is nurturing, submissive, and pleasing to men. Bulimics tend to be extraordinarily vulnerable to external influences, and given their intense concern with their appearance, fashion models and media figures typically have a powerful impact on the standards that they feel they must live up to.

As I suggested earlier, bulimia is a common stress symptom among college-age or working woman, a self-destructive method of working out feelings of loneliness, anxiety, depression, or other discomfiting emotions. The contemporary college campus is an environment in which many of the new contradictory pressures confronting females seem to converge.[6] Intense academic pressures, a fluid and unstructured eating environment, the challenges of sexual relationships in an environment in which the possibility of sexual exploitation is increasingly a matter of concern, all contribute to a situation that can be overwhelming for those who are vulnerable. Of particular significance for many women who develop bulimia are their relationships with men. Many contemporary female college students (as well as males) find heterosexual relationships difficult, for a number of interrelated reasons (Komarovsky, 1985). One of the most important of these is male anxiety in response to female ambition and academic or professional competitiveness. Bulimics are particularly vulnerable to these reactions, given their intense needs to be accepted as feminine and their inordinate need to please men. As a result, they will be more likely than most to suppress their own individual needs and ambitions in the service of maintaining acceptance. Associated feelings of anger and resentment tend to be taken out on the self in the form of binging and purging episodes. In my experience, bulimic women are especially sensitive to the subtle (and not-so-subtle) "put-downs" of females by men, particularly in situations associated with competitiveness or assertion. The relatively high prevalence of bulimia in environments that are bastions of male power — such as medical schools, or the higher levels of the corporate world — is probably understandable in terms of the ambiguities confronting women in these situations.[7] The maintenance of thinness, as well as a façade of perfection, competence, and control, serves to establish an external adaptation to the demands of an environment in which one must compete and not show the softer, more vulnerable side of one's femininity. Secret rituals with food become the only avenue of expression of these carefully hidden needs and feelings.

Cultural Confusion About the Female Role

It has been the main point of this chapter to argue that the transition to a new female identity has left many young women vulnerable to developing eating disorders. The shifts in contemporary Western societies to a new emphasis on female achievement and performance represents a sharp reversal from previous role definitions that emphasized compliance, deference, and unassertiveness. A new sexual ethos, in the direction of greater permissiveness and a loosening of traditional controls, has brought new problems along with it, including an increased vulnerability to exploitation and anxieties among those from conservative or traditional backgrounds. It is not my intention to argue that these changes in and of themselves are bad; this is not a conservative polemic for returning women to the kitchen, the nursery, or the "MRS" degree. It is just that in a period of such radical cultural transition, some young women are vulnerable to becoming caught in the uncertainties and ambiguities of a drastically altered set of expectations. Most female college students, even those who are not having difficulties with food or weight control, will quietly assert that they themselves feel vulnerable to the same problems experienced in acute form by those who develop eating disorders.

I would like to conclude this chapter with mention of two additional problems that make the attainment of female identity in the present environment difficult. The first is that the definition of the new ideal social role (and psychological identity) for women is far from clear. Most contemporary women feel that along with the increased expectations for achievement and performance, the pressure to be traditionally feminine — in the sense of being attractive, pleasing, and unassertive — is as powerful as ever before. It is the multiplicity of role demands, many of which seem to conflict with one another, which makes the contemporary situation for women so difficult. Popular culture has mythologized the notion of the women who "has it all" (that is, who performs all of these roles) in the imagery of the "superwoman."[8] The superwoman is both competent, achieving, and ambitious, and yet pleasingly feminine, sexual, and nurturing. In one popular book promoting this imagery of perfection, it is clear that in addition to fulfilling the multiple demands of modern womanhood, the superwoman devotes considerable attention to her appearance, and is meticulous in the area of weight control — she is, above all else perhaps, thin (Brown, 1982). Research by Catherine Steiner-Adair (1986) in a private population in New York State showed that those girls who strongly identified with the ideology of the superwoman were the very ones who showed symptoms of eating disorders, while those who criticized or rejected the stereotype were relatively free of these problems. Similar conclusions were drawn by a group of researchers at Yale, who found that college students with disordered eating aspired to fulfill both stereotypical male and stereotypical female ideals, while at the same time attributing enormous importance to their physical appearance (Timko, Striegel-Moore, Silberstein, & Rodin, 1987). Conflicts between new cultural ideals and traditional identifications were evident in a German study, in which a group of bulimic women were shown to have relatively large discrepancies between their sex-role attitudes, which were relatively progressive, and their actual behavior, which tended to be more traditional. For example, a bulimic woman might agree with an "attitude" statement such as "In a partnership, both partners should have equal rights," but also might simultaneously endorse a "behavioral" item such as "If I like someone, I give in in cases of disagreement, even if I know I am right" (Rost, Neuhaus, & Florin, 1982).

A second issue is that of persisting devaluation of femininity, despite (perhaps because of?) the gains resulting from feminism and the women's movement. These cultural biases take on a number of forms. One is that despite lip-service to the contrary, female intelligence is still not respected, or alternatively perceived as threatening to male power and dominance. Female college students are often acutely aware of this in the classroom, particularly in the hostile or dismissive reactions of male peers (and sometimes professors) to their efforts to express their opinions. In the corporation, women have experienced the phenomenon of tokenism, whereby even though they have been able to acquire a position, but have had difficulty in advancing to higher levels of management or power (Kanter, 1977). Thus, either female intellect and ambition are discounted, or they are perceived as too aggressive and unfeminine. This problem reinforces the dilemmas of anorexics, who have difficulty in reconciling their own intellectual aspirations with their own femaleness (Lawrence, 1984). Their own solution to the dilemma — diminishing the female characteristics of the body — can be seen on one level as an internalization of cultural misogyny.

The other side of this issue is that contemporary industrial cultures also devalue the traditional female role, that of nurturance. The world outside the family places low value on nurturing activities. Consider the professions in which nurturing is a primary activity — nursing, teaching, child care. These are not high-status occupations in contemporary society, and they are low on the ladder of remuneration. Ambitious women experience particular conflicts along these lines, as it becomes very difficult to balance the demands of a career in the extra-familial world and simultaneously to raise children. Some women have also responded to this cultural devaluation of nurturance by identifying with traditional male values of power, toughness, and control — but often only by repressing their own nurturing side. A suppression of the nurturing side of the self is a central problem for anorexic and bulimic women, who are most obviously unable to nurture (i.e., nourish) themselves.[9]

Males with Eating Disorders: A Neglected Population?

In this chapter, I have argued that women who develop eating disorders are caught in the conflicting expectations and pressures of a period characterized by a dramatic change in the female role. But what about male anorexics and bulimics? Where do they fit into the picture?

Some have asserted that the number of male anorexics (and particularly bulimics) may also have been increasing. There is, however, very little documentation for this (see Andersen & Mickalide, 1983).[10] Most of the evidence that we do have on this question suggests that the increase in eating disorders is particularly prominent among women, with the number of male anorexics remaining relatively constant (see Jones, Fox, Babigan , & Hutton, 1980).[11] If this is in fact the case, it would be consistent with the notion presented in this chapter that the psychological issues in the eating disorders are largely those that affect females, not males.

Interestingly, a significant percentage of those male anorexics who have been studied tend to have explicit conflicts in their *sexual* identity (as opposed to the conflicts in social gender role that we have described for females with eating disorders) — that is, many have explicit homosexual conflicts (Yager, Kurtzman, Landsverk, & Wiesmeier, 1988).[12] In addition, there is some evidence to suggest a relatively higher prevalence of male anorexia and bulimia in the gay community than among heterosexual males (Silberstein, Mishkind, Striegel-Moore, Timko, & Rodin, 1989). This latter could be attributable to a presumably greater preoccupation among gay males, particularly those who play the "female" role, with their physical appearance.[13] It is possible that if males in general become more preoccupied with appearance and thinness, as does seem to be happening to some extent, they too may experience an increase in eating disorders. To me, however, such a development seems unlikely, since it is the broader issue of identity as well as that of appearance that seem to give rise to the eating disorders. And the types of issues that are involved — conflicts about achievement and autonomy, feelings of external determination and low self-esteem — seem peculiarly characteristic of the contemporary female experience.

Notes

1. The greater female tolerance for starvation was known as early as the twelfth century, where Heloise argued that "nature herself has protected our sex with a greater power of sobriety. It is indeed known that women can be sustained with less nourishment, and at much less expense, than men" (Bynum, 1987, p. 387).

2. This book contains a great deal of information about fatness, particularly from an evolutionary and anthropological perspective.

3. This is one of the three core deficiencies in anorexia nervosa cited by Bruch, the others being a disturbance in body image of delusional proportions and an inability to accurately perceive internal need states.

4. These authors characterize the family environment of bulimics as typically "disengaged, chaotic, highly conflicted and neglectful. Family members use indirect and contradictory patterns of communication, are deficient in problem-solving skills, are non-supportive of independent behavior, and are less intellectually and recreationally oriented than the families of normal controls, despite their higher achievement orientations. These family characteristics generally result in children feeling disorganized, disconnected, insecure, and anxious" (p. 137). In line with the theme I am elaborating in this chapter, Johnson and Conners remark that "Despite the high risk loading of both biological and familial factors, if the child were able to lean on a consistent and stable structure within the sociocultural milieu she might be able to compensate for the lack of structure within her immediate family. Unfortunately, particularly for young women, the broader sociocultural context simultaneously exacerbates feelings of instability and, ultimately, suggests a pathological adaptation to that instability" (p. 138).

5. Steiger et al. (1989) found the father–daughter bond to be disturbed for all types of eating disordered women.

6. For an interesting discussion of the particular vulnerabilities to bulimia created by campus life, see Dickstein (1988–1989).

7. See, for example, Deutsch (1986) for a discussion of the after-hours addictions of a number of high-flying corporate women. Interesting anecdotal descriptions of bulimic professionals are contained in Squire (1983). The prevalence of bulimic syndromes among medical students is documented in Herzog, Pepose, Norman, and Rigotti (1985). For an interesting discussion of the issues and a case history, see Barnett (1986). Barnett suggests that "bulimarexia may represent the ambivalence toward filling the sociocultural stereotype of femininity and asserting her personal power in a world that rewards hypermasculinity." As she points out, the most devastating insult that male colleagues or teachers can deliver to a female medical student is that she is "behaving like a nurse."

8. The notion of the "superwoman" was introduced by the journalist Ellen Goodman (1979). A "manifesto" of this ideology is contained in a book by *Cosmopolitan* editor, Helen Gurley Brown (1982).

9. The conception of anorexia as a problem in nurturance has been sensitively discussed by Levenkron (1985). See also Lehman & Rodin (1989).

10. It is, however, likely that some male anorexics and bulimics go unrecognized, both because health professionals are reluctant to diagnose eating disorders and because eating disordered males may be reluctant to come forth with "female" problems.

11. It should be pointed out, though, that some observers who specialize in the treatment of males with eating disorders have expressed skepticism about the generality of homosexual conflicts in this population (see, for example, Andersen, 1988).

12. In this study, which surveyed students attending homosexual rap groups at UCLA, gay students scored much higher than comparable heterosexual males on the Eating Disorder Inventory, a measure of self-reported attitudes and behaviors characteristic of eating disordered patients. However, the actual presence of an eating disorder through direct interview was not determined.

13. Some tendency of male college students to be preoccupied with losing weight was found in Drewnowski and Yee (1987). However, in contrast with females, the men in this sample were equally divided into those who wanted to lose weight and those who wanted to gain it. See also Mishkind, Rodin, Silberstein, and Striegel-Moore (1986).

References

Andersen, A. (1988). Anorexia nervosa and bulimia nervosa in males. In D. Garner & P. Garfinkel (Eds.), *Diagnostic issues in anorexia nervosa and bulimia nervosa* (pp. 166–208). New York: Brunner Mazel.

Andersen, A. & Mickalide, A, (1983). Anoerxia nervosa in the male: An underdiagnosed disorder. *Psychosomatics, 24*, 1066–1075.

Bardwick, J. (1979). *In transition.* New York: Holt, Rhinehart, & Winston.

Barnett, L. (1986). Bulimia as a symptom of sex-role strain in professional women. *Psychotherapy, 23*, 311–315.

Beaumont, P., Abraham, S., & Simson, K. (1981). The psychosexual histories of adolescent girls and young women with anorexia nervosa. *Psychological Medicine, 2*, 131–140.

Beller, A. (1977). *Fat and thin: A natural history of obesity.* New York: McGraw Hill.

Block, J. (1985). *Sex roles and ego development.* San Francisco: Jossey Bass.

Boskind-Lodahl, M. (1976). Cinderella's stepsisters: a feminist analysis of anorexia nervosa and bulimia. *Signs: A Journal of Women, Culture and Society, 2*, 342–356.

Boskind-White, M. & White, W. (1983). *Bulimarexia.* New York: Norton.

Brown, H. G. (1982). *Having it all.* New York: Pocket Books.

Bruch, H. (1973). *Eating disorders: Obesity, anorexia and the person within* (pp. 254–255). New York: Basic Books.

Bruch, H. (1978). *The golden cage.* New York: Vintage Books.

Bruch, H. (1988). *Conversations with anorexics.* New York: Basic Books.

Brumberg, J. (1988). *Fasting girls: The emergence of Anorexia Nervosa as a modern disease.* Cambridge, MA: Harvard University Press.

Bynum, C. (1987). *Holy feast and holy fast: The religious significance of food to medieval women.* Berkeley: University of California Press.

Casky, N. (1986). Interpreting anorexia nervosa. In S. Suleiman (Ed.), *The female body in western culture.* Cambridge MA: Harvard University Press.

Crisp, A. (1980). *Anorexia Nervosa: Let me be.* London: Academic Press.

Crisp, A. (1984). The psychopathology of anorexia nervosa: Getting the "heat" out of the system. In A. Stunkard & E. Stellar (Eds.), *Eating and its disorders* (pp. 209–234). New York: Raven Press.

Curran, J. (1977). Convergence toward a single sexual standard? In D. Byrne & L. Byrne (Eds.), *Exploring human sexuality*. New York: Harper & Row.

Deutsch, C. (1986, Sept. 10). The dark side of success. *New York Times*, p. C1.

Devereux, G. (1961). *Mohave psychiatry and suicide: The psychiatric disturbances of an Indian tribe*. Washington, DC: Smithsonian Institution Press.

Devereux, G. (1978). *Ethnopsychoanalysis: Psychoanalysis and anthropology: Complementary frames of reference*. Berkeley: University of California Press.

Devereux, G. (1980). *Basic problems of ethnopsychiatry*. Chicago: University of Chicago Press.

Dickstein, L. (1988–1989). Current college environments: do these communities facilitate and foster bulimia in vulnerable students? *Journal of College Student Psychotherapy* (Special Edition: The Bulimic College Student: Evaluation, Treatment, and Prevention), *3*, 107–134.

Drewnowski, A. & Yee, D. (1987). Men and body image: Are males satisfied with their body weight? *Psychosomatic Medicine, 49*, 626–634.

Erikson, E. (1964). *Identity, youth and crisis*. New York: Norton.

Erikson, E. (1975). *Life history and the historical moment*. New York: Norton.

Frisch, R. & MacArthur, J. (1974). Menstrual cycles: Fatness as a determinant of minimum weight for height necessary for their maintenance and onset. *Science, 185*, 949–951.

Goodman. E. (1979). *Close to home*. New York: Fawcett.

Herzog, D., Norman, D., Gordon, C., & Pepose, M. (1984). Sexual conflict and eating disorders in 27 males. *American Journal of Psychiatry, 141*, 989–990.

Herzog, D., Pepose, M., Norman, D., & Rigotti, N. (1985). Eating disorders and maladjustment in female medical students. *Journal of Nervous and Mental Disease, 173*, 734–737.

Hoyenga, K. & Hoyenga, K. T. (1979). *The question of sex differences: Psychological, cultural and biological issues*. Boston: Little Brown.

Johnson, C., & Conners, M. (1985). *The etiology and treatment of bulimia nervosa*. New York: Guilford Press.

Jones, D., Fox, M., Babigan, H., & Hutton, H. (1980). Epidemiology of anorexia nervosa in Monroe County, New York: 1960–1976. *Psychological Medicine, 42*, 551–558.

Kanter, R. (1977). *Men and women of the corporation*. New York: Basic Books.

Komarovsky, L. (1985). *Women in college*. New York: Basic Books.

Lawrence, M., (1984). Education and identity: Thoughts on the social origins of anorexia. *Women's Studies International Forum, 7*(4), 201–209.

Lehman, A. & Rodin, J. (1989). Styles of self-nurturance and disordered eating. *Journal of Consulting and Clinical Psychology, 57*, 117–122.

Levenkron, S. (1985). Structuring a nurturant/authoritative psycho-therapeutic relationship with the anorexic patient. In S. Emmet (Ed.), *Theory and treatment of anorexia nervosa and bulimia: Biomedical, sociocultural and biological perspectives*. New York: Brunner Mazel.

Liu, A. (1979). *Solitaire*. New York: Harper & Row.

Malzberg, B. (1969). Are immigrants psychologically disturbed? In S. Plog & R. Edgarton (Eds.), *Changing perspective in mental illness* (pp. 395–421). New York: Holt, Rhinehart, & Winston.

Miller, J. (1976). *Towards a new psychology of women*. Boston: Beacon Press.

Mishkind, M., Rodin, J., Silberstein, L., & Striegel-Moore, (1986). The embodiment of masculinity: Cultural, psychological and behavioral dimensions. *American Behavioral Scientist, 29*, 545–562.

Murphy, H. (1982). Culture and schizophrenia. In I. Al-Issha (Ed.), *Culture and psychopatholog.* Baltimore: University Park Press.

Pope, H. & Hudson, J. (1984). *New hope for binge eaters.* New York: Harper & Row.

Rost, W., Neuhaus, M., & Florin, I. (1982). Bulimia nervosa: sex role attitude, sex role behavior and sex role related locus of control in bulimarexic women. *Journal of Psychosomatic Research, 26*, 403–408.

Schwartz, D., Thompson, M., & Johnson, C. (1983). Eating disorders and the culture. In P. Darby, P. Garfinkel, D. Garner, & D. Coscina. (Eds.), *Anorexia nervosa: Recent developments in research* (pp. 83–95). New York: Alan R. Liss.

Silberstein, L., Mishkind, M., Striegel-Moore, R., Timko, C., & Rodin, J. (1989). Men and their bodies: A comparison of homosexual and heterosexual men. *Psychosomatic Medicine, 51*, 337–346.

Slade, R. (1984). *The anorexia nervosa reference book.* New York: Harper & Row.

Smith-Rosenberg, C. (1972). The hysterical woman. *Social Research, 39*, 652–675.

Squire, S. (1983). *The slender balance.* New York: Pinnacle Books.

Steiger, H., Van der Feen, J., Goldstein, C., & Leicher, P. (1989), Defense styles and parental bonding in eating-disordered women. *International Journal of Eating Disorders, 8*, 131–141.

Steiner-Adair, C. (1986). The body politic: Normal female adolescent development and the development of eating disorders. *Journal of the American Academy of Psychoanalysis, 14*, 95–114.

Swift, W. & Letven, R. (1984), Bulimia and the basic fault: a psychoanalytic interpretation of the binging-vomiting syndrome. *Journal of the American Academy of Child Psychiatry, 23*, 489–497.

Timko, C., Striegel-Moore, R., Silberstein, L., & Rodin, J. (1987). Femininity/masculinity and disordered eating in women: How are they related? *International Journal of Eating Disorders, 6*, 701–712.

Waller, J., Kaufman, R., & Deutsch, F. (1940). Anorexia nervosa: a psychosomatic entity. *Journal of Psychosomatic Medicine, 2*, 3–16.

Wooley, S. & Wooley, O. (1986, Oct.), Ambitious bulimics: Thinness mania. *American Health*, 68–74.

Yager, J., Kurtzman, F., Landsverk, J., & Wiesmeier, E. (1988). Behaviors and attitudes related to eating disorders in homosexual male college students. *American Journal of Psychiatry, 145*, 495–497.

20

Psychodynamic Approaches to Youth Suicide

ROBERT KING

The psychodynamic perspective seeks to understand the meaning of suicidal behavior in terms of feelings, motives, and their conflicts, in the context of past and present interpersonal relationships. For example, in looking at the immediate experiential antecedents of suicidal action, we may ask, what are the intolerable affects from which suicide is a perceived means of escape? What kinds of internal or external events serve to trigger suicidal feelings and behavior and what is their significance in the broader context of the suicidal youngster's life? The psychodynamic approach is also a developmental one that attempts to understand the origins of the vulnerability to suicide and depression in the related developmental vicissitudes of the capacity for self-care and comfort; the ability to develop, sustain and make use of protective affiliations; and the regulation of self-esteem (King & Apter, 1996). Finally, the psychodynamic perspective seeks clues as to how the challenges of a given developmental epoch, such as adolescence, may confer a particular vulnerability to suicidal behavior. The psychodynamic approach to suicide is thus intended not to supplant but to complement the biological, sociological, and nosological approaches to suicide.

The earliest psychoanalytic attempts to understand suicide came early in the twentieth century against the background of a perceived epidemic of youth suicide in Germany and Austria (Neubauer, 1992). Much as in our own day, lay writers sought to blame the schools and the decline of family and social values, while medical writers looked for hormonal defects or "hereditary taints." In 1910, the Vienna Psychoanalytic Society held a symposium "On Suicide with Particular Reference to Suicide among Young Students" (Friedman, 1967) to examine the problem from a psychoanalytic perspective. No comprehensive theory emerged, but several vivid insights emphasized the distinctive themes of guilt, aggression turned against the self, and thwarted love which were to characterize much of later psychoanalytic thinking on suicide. For example, Stekel emphasized the aggressive and self-punitive aspects of the talion principle: "No one kills himself who has never wanted to kill another, or at least wished the death of another" (Friedman, 1967, p. 87). In contrast, Sadger emphasized the libidinal element: "[T]he only person who puts an end to his life is one who has been compelled to give up all hope of love" (Friedman, 1967, p. 76).

In his own later writings on suicide, Freud attempted to move beyond motives such as a refusal to accept loss of libidinal gratification or guilt over death wishes towards others. In trying to understand how the self became the target of its own hatred and destructiveness, Freud (1917) concluded "The analysis of melancholia now shows that the ego can kill itself only if, ... it can treat itself as an object — if it is able to direct against itself the hostility which relates to an object and which represents the ego's original reaction to objects in the external world" (p. 252). As Freud (1923) put it later, "[T]he ego gives itself up because it feels itself hated and persecuted by the super-ego, instead of loved. To the ego, therefore, living means the same as being loved — loved by the superego, which ... fulfills the same function of protecting and saving that was fulfilled in earlier days by the father and later by Providence or Destiny" (p. 58). Freud's formulation thus combined both the aggressive and libidinal strands in the notion that the attack on the self is prompted by the experienced or threatened loss of an intensely needed, but ambivalently loved, object whose own attitude towards the subject is felt to be potentially hateful, critical, or rejecting.

Freud's evocative insights about suicide have proven fertile for theory building and clinical practice (King & Apter, 1996). The challenge for contemporary psychodynamic research, however, is to relate our understanding of suicide to the broader context of developmental psychopathology. To do so, it is essential to operationalize psychodynamic constructs in such a way as to permit their empirical study and to move beyond the consulting room to the study of larger clinical and community populations. The purpose of this paper is to present some of the recent advances in meeting this challenge.

Escape from Unbearable Affects

Most commonly, suicidal behavior occurs as a desperate attempt to escape from an intolerable affect, such as rage, intense isolation, or self-loathing (Hendin, 1991; Shneidman, 1989). Less frequently in adolescence, unbearable anxiety, a sense of inner deadness, or fear of fragmentation may also play a role. Self-awareness becomes unbearable and self-destruction beckons as means of surcease (Baumeister, 1990; Dean & Range, 1999; Dean, Range, & Goggin, 1996).

In a study of adolescent self-poisoners, Hawton, Cole, O'Grady, and Osborn (1982) found, using a card sort procedure, that the commonest reported affective state prior to the ingestions were "angry with someone" (54%), "lonely or unwanted" (54%), and "worried about the future" (40%). Only 54% of these adolescents, however, reported that they clearly wanted to die at the time of their ingestion. Among the other reasons given for their ingestions were: "to get relief from a terrible state of mind" (42%) or "to escape for a while from an impossible situation" (42%).

Negron, Piacentini, Graae, Davies, and Shaffer (1997) found that two-thirds of adolescent suicide ideators or attempters seen in the emergency room reported intense anger, hopelessness, depression, or crying while contemplating suicide.

Kienhorst, DeWilde, Diekstra, and Wolters (1995) studied the reasons endorsed by adolescent suicide attempters and found the most frequently endorsed factor consisted of items related to stopping of consciousness, specifically "I wanted to get relief from a terrible state of mind," "I wanted to stop feeling pain," and "I wanted to die" (endorsed respectively by 58%, 75%, and 73% of attempters).

Although the card sort procedure used by Hawton and others forces the choice of a specific response, in clinical practice it is striking how many adolescents are unable to give a reason for their impulsive suicide attempts or parasuicidal gestures; responses such as "I don't know why I did it; I just felt like it" or "I was upset" are common. Indeed, White (1974) found over half of adolescent self-poisoners unwilling or unable to provide an explanation or motive for their act and Beautrais, Joyce, and Mulder (1997) found that one-third of adolescents making serious suicide attempts were unable to describe any precipitating factor. In the study of Kienhorst et al. (1995), 39% of subjects endorsed "I seemed to lose my self-control and I don't know why I did it then." Further research is warranted to evaluate to what extent this inability represents an acute cognitive disorganization in the face of sudden upset or, alternatively, a more enduring alexithymic cognitive-affectual style that, linked to a paucity of emotional problem-solving skills, renders youngsters vulnerable to feeling unable to cope. Along these lines, Rourke, Young, and Leenaars (1989) speculate that nonverbal learning disabilities, which they believe to be associated with impaired social perception, judgment, and skills, constitute an important risk factor for social isolation, depression, and suicidality.

Understanding the meaning and intensity of the unbearable affects which trigger self-destructive acts requires examining not only their immediate precipitants, but also their longer-standing origins from a developmental, interpersonal context.

Although completed suicides and suicide attempts are sometimes precipitated by extraordinary stresses, such as assault or abuse, in most cases the identifiable precipitants are the commonplace travails of adolescence such as a disciplinary crisis, argument with a parent or romantic partner, teasing, or some form of perceived failure (Apter, Bleich, King, Kron, Fluch, Kotler, et al., 1993; Beautrais, 2001; Shaffer, Garland, Gould, Fisher, & Trautman, 1988). The catastrophic reverberation these events evoke in the suicidal adolescent can be viewed from several perspectives. Emphasizing the reactive element, we might ask what special significance these events hold for the vulnerable youngster.

Alternatively, emphasizing personality and temperamental factors, we may ask, what are the impairments in the youngster's capacity for self-comfort, affect regulation, or problem-solving skills (including the ability to elicit support or comfort from others) that render him or her vulnerable to feeling so desperately overwhelmed? Often, the interpersonal upset that serves as the proximate trigger of a suicidal episode stands against the background of a life-long propensity to form insecure or ambivalent relationships.

Clinicians sometimes infer an underlying interpersonal motive for suicide attempts, such as retaliation against an ambivalently regarded other, an attempt to restore a tie to a vital attachment figure, or an effort to coerce change in what is perceived as an intolerable interpersonal or family situation (e.g., Cohen-Sandler, Berman, & King, 1982a, 1982b; Orbach, 1988; Orbach, Mikulincer, Blumenson, Mester, &, Stein 1999). It is interesting to note, however, that adolescent suicide attempters are less likely than their clinicians to perceive an instrumental interpersonal motive in their attempts (Hawton et al., 1982). In Kienhorst et al. (1995)'s study only 18% to 27% of adolescent attempters endorsed a revenge motive ("to frighten," "get back," or "to make people sorry") and less than half endorsed an appeal motive ("to show how much I loved someone" (23%), "to get help from someone" (27%), "to find out whether someone really loved me" (30%), or "to make people understand how desperate I was feeling" (46%)). Only 11% endorsed "I wanted to try and get someone to change their mind," but a full 80% endorsed "the situation was so unbearable that I had to do something and I didn't know what else to do."

The Role of Loss and Interpersonal Vulnerability

Loss plays a particularly important role, both as an immediate precipitant of adolescent suicide and as a potential antecedent to the vulnerability to depression and suicide (Adams, 1990). As noted, the breakup or disruption of a significant relationship is among the commonest precipitants of attempted or completed adolescent suicides (Adams, 1990; Apter et al., 1993; Shaffer et al., 1988). Although an acute loss may serve as an important proximate precipitant, cumulative losses also appear to confer particular vulnerability. For example, in a sample of preadolescent psychiatric inpatients, we found that, compared to nonsuicidal depressed subjects and other psychiatric subjects, suicidal subjects had significantly higher levels of stressful life events, especially losses, both in the year preceding admission and over their entire life-span (Cohen-Sandler et al., 1982a, 1982b). (The other distinguishing feature of these suicidal young-sters was their high level of aggression directed both towards self and others.)

The term "loss" has been used to cover a variety of disparate stresses, ranging from death or permanent separation from an important other (e.g., by parental divorce) through estrangement or loss of the other's emotional availability or positive regard. Such losses often co-occur and may accompany other forms of family disruption and pathology (which may reflect partially heritable factors); in the untidiness of real life, disentangling the impact of these different elements can be difficult.

Following the loss of one parent, the remaining parent's or surrogate's parenting style and degree of affectionate involvement with the child appear to affect the extent of the child's vulnerability to later depression (Adams, 1990; Brown, Harris, and Bifuico, 1986; Tennant, 1988). Weller, Weller, Fristad, and Bowes (1991) found that 37% of recently bereaved prepubertal children met criteria for major depression; 37% were self-deprecating; and 61% had morbid or suicidal ideation. Those with a prior psychiatric history and a family history of depression were most troubled.

The Role of Attachment

Drawing on studies of experimental and naturally occurring separations and losses, the work of Bowlby (1973, 1980) and colleagues (Ainsworth, Blehar, Waters, & Wall, 1978; Carlson & Sroufe, 1995) provides clues as to the mecha-nisms by which early, ongoing losses or deprivations may confer vulnerability. Further, they also provide a possible empirical paradigm for classifying indi-viduals' characteristic styles of response to interpersonal loss or frustration and the corresponding risk for depression or suicide these styles may convey.

Bowlby (1973, 1980) proposed that the young child's actual experience of the caretaker's physical and emotional availability shaped the child's develop-ment of persisting expectations ("working models of attachment") concern-ing the availability of significant others. Reflecting these working models of attachment, the child also developed enduring styles of interaction or response to disruptions (Carlson & Sroufe, 1995).

As empirically operationalized for infants by Ainsworth et al. (1978), these attachment styles can be classified as: (a) *secure* — characterized by the ability to accept comfort and reestablish positive relations after separation; (b) *insecure-ambivalent* — characterized by helplessness and, despite open expression of distress, trouble being comforted; and (c) *insecure-avoidant* — characterized by failure to initiate interaction and unresponsiveness to and avoidance of the caretaker following reunion.

Although the relative role of experience vs. constitutional factors remains unclear, these attachment styles appear to persist into later childhood, adolescence, and even adulthood, and exert an ongoing influence on the quality of perceived reciprocity, support, and closeness with others (Priel, Mitrany, & Shahar, 1998). For example, empirical studies find that secure attachment persists as a strong but flexible emphasis on relationships. Children with a history of secure attachment as infants are able to express distress directly, to use the caretaker for reassurance when threatened or upset, and to remain confident in the availability of the other and their own ability to effectively elicit care (see review by Carlson and Sroufe, 1995). Such children report having at least one good friend whom they consider reliable and more often report relationship-oriented solutions to stressful situations. As adults, studied using the Adult Attachment Interview (Main & Goldwyn, 1989), they value relationships and, while able to describe freely difficult early relationships, do so from a realistic and flexible perspective. In contrast, insecure-ambivalent attachment endures as an overvaluation of dependent relationships, colored by persistent and intense struggles with attachment figures. Children with such histories are often easily frustrated, overtly anxious, socially inept, and dependently helpless. As adults, they recall earlier dependency issues easily, but remain preoccupied with difficulties with parents and unable to resolve attachment-related issues (Main & Goldwyn, 1989). *Insecure-avoidant* attachment perpetuates itself in discounting and avoidance of relationships; children with such histories fail to initiate interaction or to seek contact in response to perceived threats. Their fantasy play and problem solving are impoverished and lack interpersonal themes. As adults, they are dismissive of attachments and have difficulty recalling attachment-related events (Main & Goldwyn, 1989). Idealized views of parents may persist unintegrated with anecdotes of rejecting or unempathic caretaking (Carlson & Sroufe, 1995).

In addition to the Adult Attachment Interview, a variety of scales, such as Revised Adult Attachment Scale and the Inventory of Parent and Peer Attachment, are suitable for assessing the attachment style or cognitions of adolescents. In longitudinal studies of adolescents, secure attachment style predicts higher levels of perceived and enacted social support (Herzberg, Hammen, Burge, Daley, Davila, & Lindsberg, 1999). When followed into college, female high-school seniors with secure attachment style experienced less chronic strain and fewer stressful events, with less performance anxiety and greater school satisfaction than peers with insecure attachment styles (Burge, Hammen, Davila, & Daley, 1997; Burge, Hammen, Davila, Daley, et al. 1997b).

These studies and others utilizing attachment style and related concepts suggest that the life stresses associated with depression or externalizing disorders are, at least in part, often self-generated and that individuals' interpersonal expectations actively shape their social experiences (Daley et al., 1997; Hammen, 2000; Priel et al., 1998; Rudolph et al., 2000).

This schema of attachment styles suggests a typology which may also be useful in understanding distinctive forms of vulnerability to depression and even suicidality in reaction to frustration. Individuals differ in the forms of self-blame and self-reproach to which they are prone at different ages (A. Freud, 1965). Bibring (1953) proposed further that individuals also differ from each other in their vital aspirations which, when frustrated, lead to depression — a condition which he defined as a state of real or imagined helplessness to preserve cherished aspects of the self or to maintain crucial relationships. For different individuals, Bibring suggested, the vital aspirations, without which life felt unbearable, might be: (a) the wish to be appreciated or lovable, not unworthy; (b) the wish to be strong, superior, and secure, not weak; or (c) the wish to be good and loving, not hateful or destructive. One important research goal is to understand better how developmental, family, and cultural factors determine which aspirations become most problematic for a given youngster, render him or her most vulnerable to depression, and color the affective tone that self-reproach takes.

Drawing on these perspectives, two subtypes of vulnerability to depression have been proposed — the *dependent* and the *self-critical* — each having its own distinctive antecedents, characteristic preoccupation, and specific type of dysphoria (Arieti & Bemporad, 1980; Beck, 1983; Blatt, 1995). As summarized by Blatt (1995; Blatt, Schaffer, Bers, & Quinlan, 1992; Blatt, Hart, Quinlan, Leadbeater, & Auerbach, 1993; Blatt & Homann, 1992), individuals of the *dependent* subtype have a pattern of insecure-ambivalent attachment. As described above, they are characterized by an overvaluation of dependent relationships and a propensity for intense struggles with attachment figures; they are correspondingly preoccupied with dependency and the threat of abandonment and feel helpless in the face of perceived loss. In contrast, individuals of the *self-critical* type are characterized by compulsive self-reliance (Bowlby, 1980) and dismiss the importance of intimate relationships; instead, they are anxiously preoccupied with issues of self-worth and autonomy, with perceived failure triggering humiliating feelings of unworthiness, guilt, and loss of control.

These authors further speculate that these contrasting vulnerability profiles stem in part from distinctive early developmental experiences, with anxiously insecure attachment reflecting neglectful or overindulgent parenting and avoidantly insecure attachment resulting from excessively controlling, rejecting, judgmental, or punitive rearing (Ainsworth et al., 1978; Blatt, 1995; Blatt & Homann, 1992; Carlson & Sroufe, 1995).

This typology of depressive vulnerabilities has been operationalized in an assessment instrument, the Depressive Experiences Questionnaire (DEQ) (and a corresponding Depressive Experiences Questionnaire for Adolescents (DEQ-A)), which characterizes subjects' self-perceptions in a psychometrically reliable fashion along the dimensions of dependency (concerns about rejection or interpersonal loss); self criticism (feeling guilty, self-critical, or falling short of standards); and efficacy (feelings of personal goal-oriented accomplishment) (Blatt et al., 1992). The instrument has proven useful in studying the relationship of these depressive traits to a variety of adolescent problem behaviors (Blatt et al., 1993; Kuperminc, Blatt, & Leadbeater, 1997; Leadbeater, Blatt, & Quninlan, 1995; Luthar & Blatt, 1995).

Hewitt and Flett (1991, 1993; Hewitt, Flett, & Turnbull-Donovan, 1992; Hewitt, Flett, & Weber, 1994, Hewitt, Newton, Flett, & Callender, 1997) have developed a Multidimensional Perfectionism Scale to assess self-oriented, other-oriented, and socially-prescribed forms of perfectionism and have studied the empirical relationship of these measures to suicidality. They found both socially prescribed and self-oriented perfectionism associated with suicidal ideation, with life stress playing a role in the association with self-oriented perfectionism (Hewitt et al., 1994).

Among our adolescent psychiatric inpatients, levels of self-critical or dependent concerns (as measured on the DEQ-A) correlated strongly with the presence of suicidal ideation and attempts (King et al., unpublished data). Other studies using this typology find that dependent individuals are prone to impulsive, manipulative, nonlethal suicide attempts, while self-critical individuals are prone to more planful and serious suicide attempts (Blatt, 1995; Faazia, 2001).

These empirically measurable subtypes may also predict the types of stress likely to precipitate depression or suicidality in different individuals. Studies show that, in dependent individuals, distress or depression is more likely to be precipitated by negative interpersonal events (e.g., rejections or losses) (e.g., Priel & Shahar, 2000). In contrast, self-critical individuals are more likely to become depressed in response to perceived failures in achievement (Brown, Hammen, Craske, & Wickens, 1995; Hammen, Ellicott, Gitlin, & Jamison., 1989; Hewitt & Flett, 1991, 1993).

This body of research and other studies drawn from Action Theory (Shahar, 2001) examine how individuals create the conditions that contribute to their depression and distress by generating contextual risk factors (such as negative life events) and fail to generate contextual protective factors (such as supportive social relations and positive life events) (Shahar, 2002, poster presentation). For example, adolescents high on the self-critical scale of the DEQ-A were less likely to initiate behavior that is intrinsically rewarding (autonomous motivation) and were more likely to initiate behavior to appease, impress or influence people (controlled motivation). As a result, self-critical youngsters experienced more negative achievement-related and interpersonal-related life events and fewer interpersonal- or achievement-related positive events (Shahar & Priel, 2003; Shahar, Blatt, Zuroff, Krupnick, & Sotsky, 2003).

These personality traits may also have implications for response to treatment (Blatt, Zuroff, Bondi, Sanislaw, & Pilkonis, 1998). Depressed self-critical individuals may also have difficulty using psychotherapy (including Interpersonal Therapy and Cognitive-Behavioral Therapy), because of their difficulty forming a therapeutic alliance and deriving satisfaction with social relations (Shahar & Priel, 2002; Zuroff, Blatt, Sotsky, Krupnick, Martin, Sanislow, et al., 2000).

Self-criticism and Suicide

For some highly self-critical youngsters, the proximate cause of suicide may be a narcissistic blow or disappointment, such as a perceived or threatened humiliation or failure to meet an impossibly high, self-imposed standard of achievement. For other, more dependent, youngsters a romantic disappointment or other interpersonal upset may be more likely to precipitate suicidal action.

The perfectionistic or self-critical type of suicide has a special tragic salience for certain high-performing, self-demanding youngsters. A systematic postmortem study of Israeli adolescent suicides occurring in the context of compulsory military service found a substantial proportion of recruits, many serving in prestigious front-line units, who committed suicide despite having received, at the time of their rigorous preinduction screening, outstanding ratings of psychological, intellectual, and physical fitness for combat duty (Apter et al., 1993; King & Apter, 1996). The immediate precipitants of these unanticipated suicides were frequently seemingly unremarkable frustrations. Only as viewed with the clarity of hindsight through the psychological autopsy did it become clear that these young men's high self-expectations, often combined with isolative traits, magnified their distress and left them unable to cope when they encountered external setbacks which they perceived as failures. In some cases, a recent, reactive, and undetected depression appeared to have exacerbated this lethal downward spiral, but help was not sought, apparently out of feelings of intense privacy or shame. In other cases, even on extensive postmortem inquiry, no evidence of depression could be found; however, these young suicides' need to maintain a self-presentation of high achievement and to suppress acknowledgement of personal limitations or dysphoric feelings make this absence of reported symptoms hard to assess.

In contrast to young suicides in the U.S. and Western Europe, substance abuse was absent and antisocial personality rare among Israeli late-adolescent suicides at the time of our original report, while seemingly high-functioning youngsters with high combat fitness scores appeared over-represented (Apter et al., 1993). This pattern may be changing over time, however, as reflected in a progressive decline in the proportion of suicides by recruits with high preinduction fitness scores (Dycian, 1995).

In many respects, these late-adolescent Israeli suicides resemble those of elite students (Thernstrom, 1996), young athletes (Berkow, 1995), and military officers (Lewis, 1996) reported over the past few years in the U.S. press, as well as those of academics and politicians described by Blatt (1995) and Trillin (1993). Similarly, in a review of completed suicides at Oxford over a period of 15 years, Hawton, Simkin, Fagg, and Hawkins (1995) noted that two-thirds were worried about their academic work. "[S]ome students, often despite considerable achievements in various spheres of university life, were tormented by low self-esteem... [that] appeared to lead some to set themselves impossibly high standards" (p. 49). In his pioneering postmortem study of child and early adolescent suicides, Shaffer (1974) noted a subgroup of anxiously perfectionistic subjects.

Although these case studies are intriguing, the need for controlled studies is underlined by the finding of Shaffer et al. (1996) in their large New York area postmortem study that perfectionism (as defined by items drawn from the symptom interview) was equally common in adolescent suicides and controls. Similarly, in their analysis of the Methods for the Epidemiology of Child and Adolescent Mental Disorders (MECA) Study data, Gould et al. (1998) examined the influence of perfectionism, as defined by four items from the Anxiety Disorders module of the structured diagnostic interview: worrying about school- work/job performance; worrying about athletic performance; worrying about making a mistake; or worrying about "making a fool of themselves." Once psychiatric diagnoses were adjusted for, perfectionism was not a significant risk factor of suicidality (These items related primarily to Hewitt and Flett (1991)'s construct of self-oriented perfectionism, whereas it is socially prescribed perfectionism that Hewitt et al. (1997) found to have the strongest association with suicide.)

The interactive dangers of perfectionism combined with social isolation are tragically illustrated by the widely publicized story of Sinedu Tadesse, an Ethiopian student at Harvard who, with much premeditation, hanged herself after murdering her roommate, against whom she turned when the latter announced her intention not to room together again the next semester. As profiled in contemporary newspaper accounts and by Thernstrom (1996), Sinedu was from childhood an academically driven, but deeply isolated young woman, for whom achievement became not only a promised escape ticket from her war-ravaged country, but a substitute for social intimacy. Acknowledging her lack of social skills, she exhorted herself to study social conversation as though it were a required academic course. Caught in a downward spiral of depression, further withdrawal, and deteriorating academic performance, she received word that she was unlikely to be accepted at the elite medical school on which she had set her sights. Far from home, she also withdrew from relatives living nearby. Viewed in retrospect, her diary records a profound inability to use or experience others, past or present, as sustaining presences. As quoted by Thernstrom (1996), Sinedu wrote,

> I don't understand what people mean by the warmth of a family, the love of their mother and the security of their home. I grew up feeling lonely & cold

amidst two parents & four siblings... it took me all my life to figure out what [others] had & what I did not have.... My parents did not beat me or abuse me. They fed me, bought me clothes, sent me to good schools and wished the best for me. As a result I was unable to point at any tangible cause ....
(p. 70)

Returning our attention to the Israeli context, suicide also took a high toll among the early, intensely idealistic, young Zionist pioneers (*chalutzim*) of the second and third aliyah (1904–1923), who had to struggle against harsh and debilitating physical conditions, hunger, illness, military hostilities, and radical cultural dislocation, which included often permanent separation from their families of origin and intense dependence on the group (Lieblich, 1981; Tzur, 1974, 1979). Faced with the near-impossible demands of their ideals, many young men and women appear to have killed themselves when confronted with the void opened by their inability to sustain these ideals or to expose their perceived shortcomings to the collective's anticipated disapproving scrutiny. By one estimate (Tzur, 1974), suicides accounted for over 10% of the obituaries in the labor movement's newspapers of the period. So common were these demoralized and demoralizing young suicides that some observers echoed the discouraged reports of the spies sent by Moses into Canaan (Numbers, XIII, 32): "The land devours its inhabitants" (Tzur, 1979).

Pathological Narcissism

As these many cases illustrate, certain types of perfectionism confer a malignant vulnerability for suicide (Blatt, 1995; Hamachek, 1978). Perfectionism is adaptive for individuals who have high but attainable goals, derive pleasure from their efforts, and acknowledge reasonable personal limitations. In contrast, neurotically or maladaptively perfectionistic individuals draw little pleasure from their achievements, which they are prone to denigrate, and dread each new task with anxious preoccupation lest they fail (Hamachek, 1978).

Much remains to be learned about the development of these various styles of self-evaluation and self-esteem regulation including the impact of parental style and cultural influences. For example, Shahar (2001) suggests that youth with elevated perfectionism may be especially permeable to contemporary society's emphasis on achievement and individuality.

Although the formulations discussed earlier contrast dependent and self-critical depressive traits, both strands may co-exist in anxiously perfectionistic individuals who perceive their parents' (and others') approval and love as conditional on meeting high standards of achievement. These individuals' often life-long, intensely self-critical attitudes and anxious pursuit of perfection seem to represent a desperate, but unending attempt to win approval and a sense of worth (Koestner, Zuroff, & Powers, 1991).

Adolescent Suicide and the Development of Self-Care

Closely related to the development of attachment and maintenance of self-esteem are other important self-regulatory capacities, such as the capacity for bodily self-care, self-protection, and self-soothing. The child's gradual internalization of the parents' attentiveness to the child's bodily care is an important component of the child's ability to see their body and self as worth protecting and caring for (A. Freud, 1965; Khantzian & Mack, 1983; King & Apter, 1996; Orbach et al., 1996a; b; 1997; Orbach, Stein, Shan-Sela, & Har-Even, 2001). When this process goes well, the child is able to transform early experiences of parents' empathic care into a sense of his or her body as being cherished and pleasurable. In addition, the securely attached child is able to evoke a sustaining image of the caring, comforting, or approving other, even when physically absent (Winnicott, 1958). When this process goes awry — as it may for a variety of reasons including chronic illness; temperamental unsoothability; or parental ambivalence, neglect, or abuse — the child may come to feel alienated from or hostile towards his or her body, which is perceived as the source of troubling, problematic feelings (Ritvo, 1984). This hostility or alienation from the body may constitute a risk factor for suicidality (King & Apter, 1996). Children with a history of physical abuse show elevated rates of self-mutilation and suicidal ideation and attempts (Green, 1978; Wagner, 1997), although a parental propensity for domestic violence and child abuse may also imply genetically transmissible vulnerabilities (e.g., impulsivity, aggressiveness) that influence the child in addition to the early experiential factors.

As part of a larger study of adolescent self-destructiveness and the capacity for self-care, we developed a questionnaire assessing adolescents' perceptions of parental attitudes towards their bodily care during childhood. In a sample of adolescent psychiatric inpatients, self-reported life-time history of suicide attempts, as well as the lethality and severity of intent of current (past-month) suicide attempts correlated significantly with perceived lack of empathic parental attentiveness to the child's physical care and perceived paternal physical punitiveness (King, Quinlan, Gammon, unpublished data).

Orbach and colleagues (Orbach et al., 1996a; Orbach, Stein, Palgi, Asherov, Har-Even, & Elizur, 1996b; Orbach, Mikulincer, King, Cohen, Stein, & Apter, 1997; Orbach, Stein, Shan-Sela, & Har-Even, 2001) employed a psychophysiological paradigm to assess suicidal adolescents' alienation from their bodies. Compared to psychiatric and normal controls or accident victims, suicidal adolescents had significantly elevated pain thresholds and increased tolerance for experimentally inflicted pain (Orbach et al., 1996). In another study, Orbach, Loten-Peleg, and Kedem (1995) found that, compared to nonsuicidal depressed and normal adolescents, suicidal adolescents had more negative feelings towards their body (including greater perceived discrepancy between ideal and actual body features), and greater dissociative tendencies, with the magnitude of these measures correlating with the degree of suicidal tendencies. The authors speculated that these potential risk factors for suicidal behavior reflected early trauma and sado-masochistic relationships (Orbach, 1994). In this connection it is interesting to note that anorexics, who suppress pangs of hunger or discomfort and feel alienated from and wary of the body's needs, also have high rates of suicidal feelings and attempts (Apter et al., 1995).

Adolescence as a Developmental Period of Risk for Suicide

Although the rate of completed suicide rises gradually with age throughout the life span for females in the United States, in males it takes a large jump in adolescence and rises even higher in old age (Conwell, 2001). If there are developmental vulnerabilities to depression and suicide, why do depression or suicidal behavior become manifest at one point in an individual's life rather than another?

Certain developmental epochs appear more vulnerable to the hazards of object or narcissistic loss. In elderly males, infirmity, such as the loss of a spouse, is a major trigger for suicide (Osgood & Thielman, 1990). In the case of illness or infirmity, the objective degree of physical impairment appears to be a less important predictor of suicide than its narcissistic impact on the individual. Based on the "disparity between aspiration and accomplishment," Shneidman (1971) was able to identify correctly four of the five suicides in his blind study of the data from the Terman long-term prospective study of gifted students; these suicides, however, did not occur before the fifth decade of life. Certain narcissistically organized individuals may decompensate in middle age, when they are unable to maintain the same level of accomplishment or attractiveness, when cumulative interpersonal difficulties catch up with them, or when it becomes clear that the fantasied rewards of success will not bring satisfaction (Kernberg, 1975).

As discussed elsewhere in this volume, the increased rates of depression seen in adolescence are certainly one factor in the increased levels of suicidality seen in this developmental epoch. Risk factors such as a developmental propensity for recklessness, impulsivity, aggression, or problem behaviors (Clark, Sommerfelt, Schwarz, et al., 1990; Jessor, 1991; Shaffer et al., 1988, 1996), with all of their potentially deleterious consequences, undoubtedly also play a role in the adolescent vulnerability to self-destructive behavior, including suicide. In addition to these risk factors, however, adolescence also appears to be a period of particular vulnerability to object loss or narcissistic disappointment. The process of separating and individuating from parents leaves adolescents particularly sensitive to loss (King, 1990, 2002; Tabachnik, 1981). Friendships and romantic attachments take on a special intensity as a means of establishing independence from the family (A. Freud, 1958). Adolescents who are ambivalently attached to their families may have a propensity to turn to friends and

romantic partners with particular intensity in order to find a substitute for the
parental tie, but unfortunately frequently re-create the same stormy patterns in
these new relationships. Since these friendships are frequently highly charged,
but unstable, such youngsters are particularly vulnerable to suffer frequent and
intense upsets around their disruption. Similarly, the need to prove one's worth
through achievement takes on a new importance in adolescence as a means
of establishing an identity; perceived failures, although appearing minor to
others, may produce despair in the vulnerable adolescent.

Conclusion

The psychodynamic perspective on youth suicide helps to supplement other
biological, sociological, phenomenological, and nosological approaches. The
challenge ahead is to develop better means of empirically studying these psychodynamic constructs and to harness them in the service of identifying more
effective means of treatment and prevention.

References

Adams, K. S. (1990). Environmental, psychosocial, and psychoanalytic aspects of sui-
    cidal behavior. In S. J. Blumenthal & D. J. Kupfer. (Eds.) *Suicide over the life
    cycle: Risk factors, assessment, and treatment of suicidal patients* (pp. 39–96).
    Washington, DC: American Psychiatric Press.
Ainsworth, M. D. S., Blehar, M. C., Waters, E., & Wall, S. (1978). *Patterns of attach-
    ment: A psychological study of the strange situation.* Hillsdale, NJ: Erlbaum.
Apter, A., Bleich, A., King, R. A., Kron, S., Fluch, A., Kotler, M., & Cohen, D. J.
    (1993). Death without warning? A clinical postmortem study of suicide in 43
    Israeli adolescent males. *Archives of General Psychiatry, 50,* 138–142.
Apter, A., Gothelf, D., Orbach, I., Weizman, R., Ratzoni, G., Har-Even, D, & Tyano,
    S. (1995). Correlation of suicidal and violent behavior in different diagnostic
    categories in hospitalized adolescent patients. *Journal of the American Academy
    of Child and Adolescent Psychiatry, 34,* 912–918.
Arieti, S. & Bemporad, J. R. (1980). The psychological organization of depression.
    American Journal of Psychiatry, 137, 1360–1365.
Baumeister, R. F. (1990). Suicide as escape from Self. *Psychological Review, 97,*
    90–113.
Beautrais, A. L. (2001). Child and young adolescent suicide in New Zealand. *Austra-
    lian and New Zealand Journal of Psychiatry, 35,* 647–653.
Beautrais, A. L., Joyce, P. R., & Mulder, R. T. (1997). Precipitating factors and life
    events in serious suicide attempts among youths aged 13 through 24 years.
    Journal of the American Academy of Child and Adolescent Psychiatry, 36,
    1543–1551.
Beck, A. T. (1983). Cognitive therapy of depression: new perspectives. In P. J. Clay-
    ton, & J. E. Barrett (Eds.), *Treatment of depression: Old controversies and new
    approaches.* New York: Raven Press.

Berkow, I. (1995, Oct. 1). An athlete is dead at 17 and no one can say why. *New York Times.* Sports section, pp. 1, 7.

Bibring, E. (1953). The mechanism of depression. In P. Greenacre (Ed.), *Affective disorders* (pp. 13–48), New York: International Universities Press.

Blatt, S. J. (1995). The destructiveness of perfectionism: implications for the treatment of depression. *American Psychologist, 50,* 1003–1020.

Blatt, S. J. & Homann, E. (1992). Parent-child interaction in the etiology of dependent and self-critical depression. *Clinical Psychology Review, 12,* 47–91.

Blatt, S. J., Schaffer, C. E., Bers, S. A., & Quinlan, D. M. (1992). Psychometric properties of the Depressive Experiences Questionnaire for Adolescents. *Journal of Personality Assessment, 59,* 82–98.

Blatt, S. J., Hart, B., Quinlan, D. M., Leadbeater, B., & Auerbach, J. (1993). Interpersonal and self-critical dysphoria and behavioral problems in adolescents. *Journal of Youth and Adolescence, 22,* 253–269.

Blatt, S. J., Zuroff, D. C., Bondi, C. M., Sanislow, C. A. Ill, & Pilkonis, P. A. (1998). When and how perfectionism impedes the brief treatment of depression: further analyses of the National Institute of Mental Health Treatment of Depression Collaborative Research Program. *Journal of Consulting and Clinical Psychology, 66,* 423–428.

Bowlby, J. (1973). *Attachment and loss. vol. II, Separation.* New York: Basic Books.

Bowlby, J. (1980). *Attachment and loss. vol. III, Loss, sadness and depression.* New York: Basic Books.

Brown, G. P., Hammen, C. L., Craske, M. G., & Wickens, T. D. (1995). Dimensions of dysfunctional attitudes as vulnerabilities to depressive symptoms. *Journal of Abnormal Psychology, 104,* 431–435.

Brown, G. W, Harris, T. O., & Bifuico, A. (1986). Long-term effects of early loss of parent. In M. Rutter, C. E. Izard, & S. B. Read (Eds.), *Depression in young people: Developmental and clinical perspectives* (pp. 251–296). New York: Guilford.

Burge, D., Hammen, C., Davila, J., & Daley, S. E. (1997). The relationship between attachment cognitions and psychological adjustment in late adolescent women. *Development and Psychopathology, 9*(1), 151–167.

Burge, D., Hammen, C., Davila, J., Daley, S. E., et al. (1997). Attachment cognitions and college and work functioning two years later in late adolescent women. *Journal of Youth and Adolescence, 26,* 285–301.

Carlson, E. A. & Sroufe, L. A. (1995). Contributions of attachment theory to developmental psychopathology. In D. Cicchetti, & D. J. Cohen (Eds.) *Developmental psychopathology, vol. 1, theory and methods* (pp. 581–617). New York: Wiley.

Clark, D. C., Sommerfeldt, L., Schwarz, M., et al. (1990). Physical recklessness in adolescence: trait or byproduct of depressive/suicidal states? *The Journal of Nervous and Mental Disease, 178,* 423–433.

Cohen-Sandler, R., Berman, A. L., & King, R. A. (1982a). A Follow-up Study of Hospitalized Suicidal Children. *Journal of the American Academy of Child Psychiatry, 21,* 389–403.

Cohen-Sandler, R., Berman, A. L., & King, R. A. (1982b). Life stress and symptomatology: Determinants of suicidal behavior in children. *Journal of the American Academy of Child Psychiatry, 21,* 178–186.

Conwell, Y. (2001). Suicide in later life: a review and recommendations for prevention. *Suicide and Life-Threatening Behavior, 31*(Suppl.), 32–47.

Daley, S. E., Hammen, C., Burge, D., Davila, J., et al. (1997). Predictors of the generation of episodic stress: a longitudinal study of late adolescent women. *Journal of Abnormal Psychology, 106*, 251–259.

Dean, P. J. & Range, L. M. (1999). Testing the escape theory of suicide in an outpatient clinical population. *Cognitive Therapy and Research, 23*, 561–572.

Dean, P. J., Range, L. M., & Goggin, W. C. (1996). The escape theory of suicide in college students: testing a model that includes perfectionism. *Suicide and Life-Threatening Behavior, 26*, 181–186.

Dycian, A. (1995). Suicide in the Israeli military — trends and changes [Abstract]. Paper presented at the International Conference on Understanding Youth Suicide, Tel Aviv, August 30.

Faazia, N. (2001). Dependency, self-criticism and suicidal behavior. Unpublished Master's Thesis, University of Windsor, Ontario.

Freud, A. (1958). Adolescence. The *Psychoanalytic Study of the Child, 13*, 255–278.

Freud, A. (1965). *Normality and pathology in childhood: Assessments of development.* New York: International Universities Press.

Freud, S. (1917). Mourning and melancholia. *Standard Edition, 14*, 289–300.

Freud, S. (1923). The ego and the id. *Standard Edition, 19*, 12–59.

Friedman, P. (Ed.) (1967). On suicide: With particular reference to suicide among young students. *Discussions of the Vienna Psychoanalytic Society—1910.* New York: International Universities Press.

Gould, M. S., King, R., Greenwald, S., Fisher, P., Schwab-Stone, M., Kramer, R., Flisher, A. J., Goodman, S., Canino, G., & Shaffer, D. (1998). Psychopathology associated with suicidal ideation and attempts among children and adolescents. *Journal of the American Academy of Child and Adolescent Psychiatry, 37*, 915–923.

Green, A. H. (1978). Self-destructive behavior in battered children. *American Journal of Psychiatry, 135*, 579–582.

Hamachek, D. E. (1978). Psychodynamics of normal and neurotic perfectionism. *Psychology, 15*, 27–33.

Hammen, C. (2000). Interpersonal factors in an emerging developmental model of depression. In S. L. Johnson, A. M. Hayes, A. M., et al. (Eds.) *Stress, coping, and depression* (pp. 71–88), Mahwah, NJ: Erlbaum.

Hammen, C., Ellicott, A., Gitlin, M., & Jamison, K. R. (1989). Sociotrophy/autonomy and vulnerability to specific life events in patients with unipolar and bipolar disorder. *Journal of Abnormal Psychology, 98*, 154–160.

Hawton, K., Cole, D., O'Grady, J., & Osborn, M. (1982). Motivational aspects of deliberate self-poisoning in adolescents. *British Journal of Psychiatry, 141*, 286–291.

Hawton, K., Simkin, S., Fagg, J., & Hawkins, M. (1995). Suicide in Oxford University Students, 1976–1990. *British Journal of Psychiatry, 166*, 44–50.

Hendin, H. (1991). Psychodynamics of suicide, with particular reference to the young. *American Journal of Psychiatry, 148*, 1150–1158.

Herzberg, D. S., Hammen, C., Burge, D., Daley, S. E., Davila, J., & Lindberg, N. (1999). Attachment cognitions predict perceived and enacted social support during late adolescence. *Journal of Adolescent Research, 14,* 387–404.

Hewitt, P. L. & Flett, G. L. (1991). Perfectionism in the self and social contexts: conceptualization, assessment, and association with psychopathology. *Journal of Personality and Social Psychology, 60,* 456–470.

Hewitt, P. L. & Flett, G. L. (1993). Dimensions of perfectionism, daily stress, and depression: a test of the specific vulnerability hypothesis. *Journal of Abnormal Psychology, 102,* 58–65.

Hewitt, P. L., Flett, G. L., & Turnbull-Donovan, W. (1992). Perfectionism and suicide potential. *British Journal of Clinical Psychology, 31,* 181–190.

Hewitt, P. L., Flett, G. L., & Weber, C. (1994). Dimensions of perfectionism and suicide ideation. *Cognitive Therapy and Research, 18,* 439–460.

Hewitt, P. L., Newton, J., Flett, G. L., & Callender, L. (1997). Perfectionism and suicide ideation in adolescent psychiatric patients. *Journal of Abnormal Child Psychology, 25,* 95–101.

Jessor, R. (1991). Risk behavior in adolescence: a psychosocial framework for understanding and action. *Journal of Adolescent Health, 12,* 597–605.

Kernberg, O. F. (1975). *Borderline conditions and pathological narcissism.* New York: Aronson.

Khantzian, E .J. & Mack.J. E. (1983). Self-preservation and the care of the Self. *The Psychoanalytic Study of the Child, 38,* 209–232.

Kienhorst, I. C. W. M., DeWilde, E. J., Diekstra, R. F. W., & Wolters, W. H. G. (1995). Adolescents' image of their suicide attempt. *Journal of the American Academy of Child and Adolescent Psychiatry, 34,* 623–628.

King, R. A. (1990). Child and adolescent suicide. In R. Michels (Ed.), *Psychiatry,* vol. 2. Philadelphia: Lippincott.

King, R. A. (2002). Adolescence. In M. Lewis (ed.) *Comprehensive textbook of child and adolescent psychiatry,* 3rd ed. (pp. 332–342). Baltimore: Lippincott Williams & Wilkins.

King, R. A. & Apter, A. (1996). Psychoanalytic perspectives on adolescent suicide. *The Psychoanalytic Study of the Child, 51,* 491–511.

Koestner, R., Zuroff, D. C., & Powers, T. A. (1991). Family origins of adolescent self-criticism and its continuity into adulthood. *Journal of Abnormal Psychology, 100,* 191–197.

Kuperminc, G. P., Blatt, S.J., & Leadbeater, B.J. (1997). Relatedness, self-definition, and early adolescent adjustment. *Cognitive Therapy and Research, 21,* 301–320.

Leadbeater, B.J., Blatt, S.J., & Quinlan, D. M. (1995). Gender-linked vulnerabilities to depressive symptoms, stress, and problem behaviors in adolescents. *Journal of Research on Adolescence, 5,* 1–29.

Lewis, N. A. (1996, May 19). Military strives to reduce a relatively low suicide rate. *New York Times,* p. 18.

Lieblich, A. (1981). *Kibbutz Makom.* New York: Pantheon Books.

Luthar, S. & Blatt, S. J. (1995). Differential vulnerability of dependency and self-criticism among disadvantaged teenagers. *Journal of Research on Adolescence, 5,* 431–449.

Main, M. & Goldwyn, R. (1989). *Adult attachment rating and classification system.* Unpublished scoring manual. Department of Psychology, University of California, Berkeley.

Negron, R., Piacentini, J., Graae, F., Davies, M., & Shaffer, D. (1997). Microanalysis of adolescent suicide attempters and ideators during the acute suicidal episode. *Journal of the American Academy of Child and Adolescent Psychiatry, 36,* 1512–1519.

Neubauer, J. (1992). *The fin-de-siècle culture of adolescence.* New Haven, CT: Yale University Press.

Orbach, I. (1988). *Children who don't want to live.* San Francisco, CA: Jossey-Bass.

Orbach, I. (1994). Dissociation, physical pain, and suicide: A hypothesis. *Suicide and Life-Threatening Behavior, 24,* 68–79.

Orbach, I., Lotem-Peleg, M., & Kedem, P. (1995). Attitudes towards the body in suicidal, depressed, and normal adolescents. *Suicide and Life-Threatening Behavior, 25,* 211–221.

Orbach, I., Mikulincer, M., Blumenson, R., Mester, R., & Stein, D. (1999). The subjective experience of problem irresolvability and suicidal behavior: Dynamics and measurement. *Suicide and Life-Threatening Behavior, 29,* 150–164.

Orbach, I., Palgi, Y, Stein, D., Har-Even, D., Lotem-Peleg, M., Asherov.J., & Elizur, A. (1996a). Tolerance for physical pain in suicidal subjects. *Death Studies, 20,* 327–341.

Orbach, I., Stein, D., Palgi, Y, Asherov, J., Har-Even, D., & Elizur, A. (1996b). Perception of physical pain in accident and suicide attempt patients: Self-preservation vs. self-destruction. *Journal of Psychiatric Research, 30*(4), 307–320.

Orbach, I., Mikulincer, M., King, R., Cohen, D., Stein, D., & Apter, A. (1997). Thresholds and tolerance of physical pain in suicidal and non-suicidal patients. *Journal of Consulting and Clinical Psychology, 65,* 646–652.

Orbach, I., Stein, D., Shan-Sela, M., & Har-Even, D. (2001). Body attitudes and body experiences in suicidal adolescents. *Suicide and Life-Threatening Behavior, 31,* 237–249.

Osgood, N. J. & Thielman, S. (1990). Geriatric suicidal behavior: Assessment and treatment. In Blumenthal, S. J. & Kupfer, D. J. (Eds.), *Suicide over the life cycle: Risk factors, assessment, and treatment of suicidal patients* (pp. 39–96). Washington, DC: American Psychiatric Press.

Priel, B. & Shahar, G. (2000). Dependency, self-criticism, social context and distress: Comparing moderating and mediating models. *Personality and Individual Differences, 28,* 515–525.

Priel, B., Mitrany, D., & Shahar, G. (1998). Closeness, support and reciprocity: A study of attachment styles in adolescence. *Personality and Individual Differences, 25,* 1183–1197.

Ritvo, S. (1984). The image and uses of the body in psychic conflict. *The Psychoanalytic Study of the Child, 39,* 449–469.

Rourke, B. P., Young, G. C., & Leenaars, A. A. (1989). A childhood learning disability that predisposes those afflicted to adolescent and adult depression and suicide risk. *Journal of Learning Disabilities, 22,* 169–174.

Rudolph, K. D., Hammen, C., Burge, D., Lindberg, N., Herzberg, D., & Daley, S. E. (2000). Toward an interpersonal life-stress model of depression: The developmental context of stress generation. *Development and Psychopathology, 12,* 215–234.

Shaffer, D. (1974). Suicide in childhood and early adolescence. *Journal of Child Psychology and Psychiatry, 15,* 275–291.

Shaffer, D., Garland, A., Gould, M., Fisher, P., & Trautman, P. (1988). Preventing teen-age suicide: A critical review. *Journal of the American Academy of Child and Adolescent Psychiatry, 27,* 675–687.

Shaffer, D., Gould, M. S., Pischer, P., Trautman, P., Moreau, D., Kleinman, M., & Flory, M. (1996). Psychiatric diagnosis in child and adolescent suicide. *Archives of General Psychiatry, 53,* 339–348.

Shahar, G. (2001). Personality, shame, and the breakdown of social bonds: The voice of quantitative depression research. *Psychiatry: Interpersonal and Biological Processes, 64,* 228–239.

Shahar, G. & Priel B. (2003). Active vulnerability, adolescent distress, and the mediating/suppressing role of life events. *Personality and Individual Differences, 35,* 199–218.

Shahar, G., Blatt, S. J., Zuroff, D. C., Krupnick, J., & Sotsky, S. M. (2004). Perfectionism impedes social relations and response to brief treatment of depression. *Journal of Social and Clinical Psychology, 23,* 140–154.

Shneidman, E. S. (1971). Perturbation and lethality as precursors of suicide in a gifted group. *Suicide and Life-Threatening Behavior, 1.*

Shneidman, E. S. (1989). Overview: a multidimensional approach to suicide. In Jacobs, D., & Brown, H. N. (Eds.), *Suicide: Understanding and responding* (pp. 1–30). Madison, CT: International Universities Press.

Tabachnik, N. (1981). The interlocking psychologies of suicide and adolescence. *Adolescent Psychiatry, 9,* 399–410.

Tennant, C. (1988). Parental loss in childhood: its effect in adult life. *Archives of General Psychiatry, 45,* 1045–1050.

Thernstrom, M. (1996, June 3). Diary of a murder. *The New Yorker,* pp. 62–71.

Trillin, C. (1993). *Remembering Denny.* New York: Parrar, Straus & Giroux.

Tzur, M. (1974). *Not in a coat of many colors* (Le lo Kutonet Pasim). Tel Aviv: Am Oved.

Tzur, M. (1979). *That which is not yet will build that which is* (Ma she'od eynenu yivne et ma she'yesh). *Shdemot, 71,* 72–76.

Wagner, B. M. (1997). Family risk factors for child and adolescent suicidal behavior. *Psychological Bulletin, 121,* 246–298.

Weller, R. A., Weller, E. B., Fristad, M. A., & Bowes, J. M. (1991). Depression in recently bereaved prepubertal children. *American Journal of Psychiatry, 148,* 1536–1540.

White, H. C. (1974). Self-poisoning in adolescents. *British Journal of Psychiatry, 124,* 24–35.

Winnicott, D. W (1958). The capacity to be alone. In *The maturational process and the facilitating environment* (pp. 29–36). New York: International Universities Press. 1965.

Zuroff, D. C., Blatt, S. J., Sotsky, S. M., Krupnick, J. L., Martin, D. J., Sanislow, C. A. Ill, & Simmens, S. (2000). Relation of therapeutic alliance and perfectionism to outcome in brief outpatient treatment of depression. *Journal of Consulting & Clinical Psychology, 68,* 114–124.

Index

A

Abortion, 120
Abstraction, adolescent thinking, 212
Abuse, homelessness, 294, 297–298, 306
Acculturation
  culture shedding, 12
  first-hand *vs.* virtual reality, 10–11
Acquisition of social cooperation, 214
Acting out, Freud, Sigmund, 246, 247
Actuality
  adaptability, 244
  defined, 243
  Freud, Sigmund, 243
  meaning of reality as, 243
  reality, distinction, 243
Adolescence
  adult neurosis, 286–287
  adults manipulated entrance
    and exit from, 22
  cross-cultural approach, 31–43
  defining parameters, 21
  due to growth of reproductive
    capacity, 31–43
  economic independence, 24
  egocentrism, 213–214, 215
    adoption of adult roles, 214
    Messianic form, 214
  ethnic identity development, 47–63
  exit
    age of exit, 22–23
    thresholds, 22
  generalized from male experience, 28
  idealization, 310–312
    negative ideal, 311–312
    positive ideal, 310–311
  industrial society, adolescence
    as creation of, 31
  instilling adult values, 27
  leisure, youth-created and
    dominated, 25
  as liminal state, 21
  literature review, 19–29
  medieval society, 19–20

mind-body problem, 150–151
  naming, 19–20
  neurosis, negative complex, 277–278
  not affliction but normative
    crisis, 228–229
  pre-industrial societies, 31
  puberty, distinguished, 208
  recapturing adult control over, 26, 27
  rites of passage
    peer-group defined, 25
    struggle between youth and adults
      for control and definition, 22
    time frame, 19
    Western Europe, definition, 20
  as sanctioned intermediary
    period between childhood
    and adulthood, 224–225
  as social universal, 32–33
Adolescent boys
  aggressiveness, 38
  competitiveness, 38
  eating disorders, 336
    homosexuality, 336
    sexual identity, 336
  gender socialization, 183–184
  identity formation
    boys' own perspectives, 183–204
    case studies, 189–198, 202
    concepts of assimilation and
      accommodation, 188
    conceptually clustered
      matrices, 186–187
    data analysis, 186–187
    drawing strength from
      relationships, 196–198
    exclusion, 192–193
    expectations, 190–192, 196–198
    feeling seen and known, 198–199
    interviews, 186
    "I" statements, 195
    marginalization, 191–193
    masculinity, 191, 193
    other people's views of
      them, 188–189